Creatures of the Air

NEW
MATERIAL
HISTORIES
of
MUSIC

A series edited by James Q. Davies and Nicholas Mathew

ALSO PUBLISHED IN THE SERIES

Musical Vitalities: Ventures in a Biotic Aesthetics of Music
Holly Watkins

Sex, Death, and Minuets: Anna Magdalena Bach and Her Musical Notebooks
David Yearsley

The Voice as Something More: Essays toward Materiality
Edited by Martha Feldman and Judith T. Zeitlin

Listening to China: Sound and the Sino-Western Encounter, 1770–1839
Thomas Irvine

*The Search for Medieval Music in Africa and Germany, 1891–1961:
Scholars, Singers, Missionaries*
Anna Maria Busse Berger

An Unnatural Attitude: Phenomenology in Weimar Musical Thought
Benjamin Steege

Mozart and the Mediation of Childhood
Adeline Mueller

Musical Migration and Imperial New York: Early Cold War Scenes
Brigid Cohen

The Haydn Economy: Music, Aesthetics, and Commerce in the Late Eighteenth Century
Nicholas Mathew

*Tuning the World: The Rise of 440 Hertz in Music, Science,
and Politics, 1859–1955*
Fanny Gribenski

Creatures of the Air

MUSIC, ATLANTIC SPIRITS,
BREATH, 1817–1913

J. Q. Davies

The University of Chicago Press   CHICAGO AND LONDON

The University of Chicago Press, Chicago 60637
The University of Chicago Press, Ltd., London
© 2023 by The University of Chicago
All rights reserved. No part of this book may be used or reproduced in any manner whatsoever without written permission, except in the case of brief quotations in critical articles and reviews. For more information, contact the University of Chicago Press, 1427 E. 60th St., Chicago, IL 60637.
Published 2023
Printed in the United States of America

32 31 30 29 28 27 26 25 24 23   1 2 3 4 5

ISBN-13: 978-0-226-82613-4 (cloth)
ISBN-13: 978-0-226-82614-1 (e-book)
DOI: https://doi.org/10.7208/chicago/9780226826141.001.0001

This book has been supported by the General Fund of the American Musicological Society, supported in part by the National Endowment for the Humanities and the Andrew W. Mellon Foundation.

Library of Congress Cataloging-in-Publication Data
Names: Davies, J. Q., 1973– author.
Title: Creatures of the air : music, Atlantic spirits, breath, 1817–1913 / J. Q. Davies.
Other titles: New material histories of music.
Description: Chicago : The University of Chicago Press, 2023. | Series: New material histories of music | Includes bibliographical references and index.
Identifiers: LCCN 2022055968 | ISBN 9780226826134 (cloth) | ISBN 9780226826141 (e-book)
Subjects: LCSH: Music—Environmental aspects—History—19th century. | Ecomusicology. | Air. | Respiration. | Ethnomusicology—Gabon—History—19th century. | Mendelssohn-Bartholdy, Felix, 1809–1847. Elias. | Schweitzer, Albert, 1875–1965—Travel—Gabon. | Singing—History—19th century. | Music and technology—History—19th century. | Black people—Brazil—Belém—Music—19th century—History and criticism. | Brazil—Belém—History—19th century. | Brazil—History—Empire, 1822–1889.
Classification: LCC ML3799.3.D38 2023 | DDC 780/.0577 23/ eng/20221—dc28
LC record available at https://lccn.loc.gov/2022055968

♾ This paper meets the requirements of ANSI/NISO Z39.48-1992 (Permanence of Paper).

for shellb

Measure [Das Maass] *is alien to us, let us admit it; the one stimulus that tickles us is the Infinite, the Immeasurable* [Unendlichen, Ungemessenen]. *We surrender our fates to the Infinite, we moderns, we half-barbarians—and are in the midst of our bliss only when we—are most in danger.... we who are modern and, in every sense, short of breath!*

FRIEDRICH NIETZSCHE, *Beyond Good and Evil* (1894)

Contents

List of Illustrations * ix
Introduction * 1

CHAPTER 1
White "Genius": Ngango, Gabon Estuary, 1817 * 28

CHAPTER 2
A Falcon under Glass: Paris, France, 1838 * 56

CHAPTER 3
Moral Atmospherics in *Elijah*: Black Country, Britain, 1846–1860 * 81

CHAPTER 4
Black "Possession": Santa Maria de Belém do Grão-Pará, Brazil, 1871 * 119

CHAPTER 5
A Spectral Image of Breath: New York, United States, 1901 * 147

CHAPTER 6
Albert Schweitzer's Equatorial Piano: Lambaréné, Gabon, 1913 * 169

Epilogue * 207
Acknowledgments * 215
Notes * 219
Index * 271

Illustrations

Figure 1.1. Map of northwestern Africa showing Naängo, Kaylee, Imbeekee, and Ogooawai 29
Figure 1.2. A drawing of Chester Place by Felix Mendelssohn 31
Figure 1.3. Map detail showing "Georges"/Ngango 37
Figure 1.4. Anthropomorphic harp 40
Figure 1.5. "Notes sung" 42
Figure 1.6. *Ngombi* harp 47
Figure 1.7. Gabriel Fauré holds an Ongom (Kele) *ngombi* harp 53
Figure 1.8. Hornbostel's transcription of a harp-song 54
Figure 2.1. Tabarié's pneumatic chamber 57
Figure 2.2. Chambre aéropiésique 58
Figure 2.3. D'Arcet's system 62
Figure 2.4. Half-breath indications in Rossini, *Guillaume Tell* 72
Figure 2.5. Piano-vocal reduction of "Il va venir" 79
Figure 3.1. *Birmingham Musical Festival* prospectus 82
Figure 3.2. Wyld's model of the Earth 91
Figure 3.3. The Great Music Hall at Birmingham Musical Festival 95
Figure 3.4. The New Orchestra at Exeter Hall, London 100
Figure 3.5. Portrait of Rev. John Cumming 103
Figure 3.6. Blueprint sketch of ship hold 112
Figure 3.7. The Great Orchestra at Crystal Palace, London 114
Figure 3.8. Proof copy of *Elijah* prepared for Ewer's 1847 piano reduction 116
Figure 4.1. Map detail in *Atlas do Império do Brasil* 120

x ILLUSTRATIONS

Figure 4.2. Map detail in Edmundo Compton, *Planta da Cidade de Belém do Gram-Pará*   128
Figure 4.3. Representation of the brig of slave trade vessel   139
Figure 4.4. Alfred Jousset, *Traité de l'acclimatement et de l'acclimatation*   140
Figure 4.5. Pythian Sibyl at Opéra Garnier, Paris   145
Figure 5.1. *New York Herald* comic, "Jean de Reszke waiting for his cue"   148
Figure 5.2. De Reszke Minors cigarettes   155
Figure 5.3. Grail narration in Italian, English, and German from Richard Wagner's *Lohengrin*   157
Figure 5.4. "Source des chanteurs" beneath the central gabled portico under a glass roof at Le Mont-Dore   160
Figure 5.5. "Tracings taken from the Chests of Indian Girls," in Thomas J. Mays, "An Experimental Inquiry into the Chest Movements of the Indian Female"   162
Figure 5.6. Images from Lilli Lehmann, *How to Sing* [*Meine Gesangskunst*]   164
Figure 5.7. The tonograph   166
Figure 5.8. Watts-Hughes's voice-prints   167
Figure 6.1. Black labor/white culture on the Ogooué   170
Figure 6.2. *Piano à pédalier* by Gaveau at the Maison Albert Schweitzer in Gunsbach, Alsace   172
Figure 6.3. "Fang warrior," Robert Hamill Nassau, *My Ogowe*   177
Figure 6.4. Part of the 1864 Statue de l'amiral Bruat at the Champ de Mars in Colmar, Alsace, by Frédéric Auguste Bartholdi, designer of the Statue of Liberty in New York   178
Figure 6.5. Detailed map of the head of Lambaréné   182
Figure 6.6. Gesammtansicht des BACH-Skelettes   190
Figure 6.7. Measures from *Il trovatore*'s torture scene in act 4   192
Figure 6.8. Stump of a mahogany tree   194
Figure 6.9. Johann Sebastian Bach, *Passionsmusik nach dem Evangelisten Johannes*, with Albert Schweitzer's annotations   201
Figure 6.10. The islands at Igendja   205

Introduction

Possessed by an invisible music and gasping for air, Eduard Pechuël-Loesche drifted out of consciousness. It was March 27, 1875—a Saturday—at the end of the rainy season in West Central Africa. The geographer was hallucinating, attacked by what he thought was yellow fever. Pechuël-Loesche had collapsed on the Cabinda coast at a trading factory owned by the Liverpool firm of Hatton & Cookson—precise location: five degrees south of the equator at the mouth of the Chiloango River.[1] The German had taken ill the night before. Earlier that day, he had overdosed on quinine, causing a cold sweat. He complained that the humidity made him black out repeatedly. His eyes flickered uncontrollably. White noise roared in his ears.

Pechuël-Loesche, adventurer and musician, called to mind Franz Schubert's "The Wanderer" (D. 489, 1816), a song "expressive of a vast, unordered, inhospitable ground of being, a world indifferent to civilization."[2] His job was to assist the Loango Expedition (1873–1876), backed by the Berlin-based German Society for Equatorial African Research, mostly in meteorological and geomagnetic measurement. The expedition made scientific studies of an as-yet-uncolonized territory, seventy thousand square miles of it, south of the equator. In subsequent testimony, Pechuël-Loesche wrote that the fever arose from "very annoying air." He cited "pestilent fumes," and "vapors [that] rose from the rotting organic matter in the forests and savannahs, lagoons and pools, the muggy, oppressive air impregnated with miasma."[3] There were "vast quantities of winged insects"—moths, cicadas, mosquitos, and grasshoppers so numerous "that they could be gathered by the handful." The "hostile climate," he contended, made him smell "almost or exactly like the worst black man." As people began to die at Chiloango, "the incantations of the *nganga* [traditional healer] resounded everywhere in the surrounding villages." "The dull thuds of the wooden drums," Pechuël-Loesche complained, "mixed with the drawn-out cries of grieving families, the cracking of flintlocks, and all the noise customary at funerals."[4] The *batuco*—a drum- and marimba-inspired dance observed nearby—sought to offer spiritual defense—bodies described as "violently twitched and convulsed"—as local communities worked day and night to repel the disease.[5]

At the height of the fever and at the edge of death, Pechuël-Loesche heard the strains of music by Johann Sebastian Bach. The E-minor prelude and fugue (BWV 548) broke into perception. Note for note and in utmost purity, he wrote, Bach's great masterwork for organ "stood before me in every detail." Later, in a diary now kept at the Bavarian State Library in Munich, he described his vivid experience of the then 150-year-old musical composition. "From whence comes these miraculous sounds in the midst of sickness?" he mused, as he transcribed BWV 548's fugue subject into his diary. The last time he had played that subject, later dubbed "the wedge" because of the way it expands across ever-widening intervals, was seven years earlier on the massive 1863 Walcker Organ at Boston Music Hall in Massachusetts.[6] Back on the Cabinda coast, five thousand miles across the Atlantic, the polyphonic textures of BWV 548 accumulated as if to ward off feverish air. The auditory hallucination brought resuscitation, assisted him to breathe, and helped him survive what he called Africa's "dark side." And, on Sunday morning, the geographer pronounced himself saved. In retrospect, Pechuël-Loesche's remembered that Bach never sounded more gloriously as when inside his head—while he struggled against the mephitic air.

This book accounts for nineteenth-century music in Atlantic worlds through a history of the art's elemental medium: the air. It is an anthology of stories, or "stories, all the way down."[7] The chapters tell of global sites at approximately twenty-year intervals: the Gabon estuary 1817, Paris 1837, Birmingham/London 1848, the Amazon estuary 1871, New York City 1900, back to Gabon 1913. They thematize air, that element in music at once so irremovable from the classicized Romantic-Modern art object and so threatening to its aesthetic purity. Each one—moving about an equatorial core and roughly counterclockwise around the Atlantic rim—has its own stand-alone narrative. Each one—embroiling three metropolitan "world capitals" to the north with three "peripheries" at zero-degrees latitude— engages very different people and very different places. Yet, though disjunct and multiple, these stories converge on a single account: of music's elemental media system. The idea of invisible music, the whole explains, emerged in relation to a system of power-knowledge that targeted the air as a natural resource and extracted value from it. Raising wind gods, spirit cults, as well as stories about breathing and climate, the book addresses an intangible heritage. It interrogates music as an invisible medium and art of air.

To tell of air, the book overlays two subdisciplines in music studies, while accumulating evidence from archives, libraries, and material sites on four continents. First, the scale of explanation is indebted to so-called global music history.[8] This has less to do with the claim to some impossibly high vantage point than with the magnitude of the historical process being described: the emergence of "the air" as a medium and of music as a thing formed in defiance of that medium. (At this scale, it helps to distinguish a very local bid to narrate large-scale historical change from a scientistic need to represent everything. The globalist view—the view from outer space—is, in any case, a ruse, the globe being a provincial construct: a world picture local to those who know how to breathe in spaces outside of the breathable.)[9] The scale of inquiry—rather than embracing some global, transnational, or even circumatlantic totality—orients to an "equatorialism," which is to say that its concerns are to gravitate toward the equator, confound hemispheres, and "change the subject of music history."[10] That said, no such history can avoid being complicit or, as Nietzsche understood, "modern and, in every sense, short of breath."[11]

One "global" priority for the book is to tie the colonial formation we call "music" to the sensory derangements of colonial modernity—to show how the art evacuated itself from the contingencies of long-distance trade and settlement, the displacement and migration of peoples, as well as industrial and ecological change—and all in a period that the doyen of global history Jürgen Osterhammel calls "the European century."[12] Another is to rise above still-standard narrative assumptions about European autonomy. The most prominent *longue durée* music historians long ago established this: that the institution of music as an independent domain of specialist disciplinary knowledge (in the nineteenth century) acted in service of myths of supremacy; the perceived autonomy of the art supplied the idea of Euro-American exceptionalism with ideological backing.[13] The very idea of music, the wide-angle view suggests, at once betrayed a will to the immeasurable and a faith in music's extractability from the bad weather of geopolitical contingency—indeed, its extractability from air. The art as such, when experienced in full disembodied purity, conjured the ideal by which whiteness, imperiled by the proximity of colonized and colonizer, sought to defend itself spiritually and separate out.

Second, the book engages ecocritical theory and method in narrating the Romantic-Modern *discovery of the environment*. Ecomusicology and global music history intertwine here, though not to understand the environment as some prediscursive a priori in the world.[14] Instead, the concern is to frame environmental knowledge as an after-effect of what Arun Agrawal calls "environmentality" or "environmental governmentality."[15] The corollary of a code of ethics devoted to the care of environments, Agrawal argues, was a coordinated industrial and commercial project to take possession of the total conditions of life. Environmental consciousness carries with it, in other words, a biopolitical logic. A principal ecocritical concern of the book is to describe the practices and processes that engendered a newly thickened sense of being in the world, in ways that go beyond celebratory accounts of the romantic love for aesthetic abstraction, fogginess, or abstract reverie. Specifically, it is to address a rationality of power—allied to fossil fuel industries and steam production in particular—that targeted air. These processes are difficult to describe. Achille Mbembe writes of a proprietization of air, understanding the climate crisis as the consequence of atmospheric modernity. He describes "a great chokehold," as "that which we hold in-common" was identified as a resource for capitalization. (Mbembe brings up the Anthropocene, though the Eurocene is better suited to his argument; cognate words like Capitalocene, Secularocene, Plantationocene, and Chthulucene also suggest that certain CO_2-emitting interests caused the climate crisis more than others.)[16] A concern for the air, a domain now rife with political struggle, implicated the highest of the arts precisely because it was held to elude calculation. No art, after all, so blurred the boundaries between outer and inner, ecology and mind, climate and media, knowledge and doubt.[17] As in the experience of Pechuël-Loesche, air was malevolent, infected with iniquitous human knowhow and action. And it was out of its dark resonance and multiplicity, heard before seen, that music was made and into which music intervened.

A second thread, then, accounts for "the air" as a fact and matter of concern.[18] Invariably, men of means defined autonomy and character, indeed morality itself, by their capacity to resist, possess, and reform the air's resounding life properties. Whiteness, so Cheryl I. Harris argued in the 1990s, is the analogue of property, since possessive investment in it justifies racial systems of ownership and plunder.[19] Freedom and enslavement, autonomy and bondage, music and noise: these categories were frequently defined according to racial claims made about perceived states of air, or at least according to whiteness's perceived autonomy from air. "Modernity ushered in a relationship between ownership and subjectivity," Brenna Bhandar agrees in her work on racial regimes of ownership, "wherein the latter was defined through and on the basis of one's capacity to appropriate."[20] Critical to the definition of the modern legal subject was a psyche "in possession" as much of itself as the framing conditions that surrounded and shaped it. And as skin color marked those subjects apparently incapable of resisting climate, so racial categories acted to predict who would win out in the race for domination. For Bhandar, the will to possess explains the need of the "free masculine subject" to invest in art and autonomy, the colonial imperative being that all of nature might eventually be brought under the yoke of biopower. Take Beethoven, famously hailed by Richard Wagner after E. T. A. Hoffmann (around the time that Bach saved Pechuël-Loesche), for his "höchste Besonnenheit," usually translated in English as "highest self-possession," "composure," or "rational awareness," after the verb *besinnen*, to reflect or think.[21] To be "in possession" implied not merely a claim to *res cogitans*, but a juridical right to claim *res extensa*.

Questions of art and freedom raise issues of biomedicine, humanitarianism, and spirit cults. Though the thickness of the media regime was somewhat a consequence of the nature ideologies of nineteenth-century art, the *discovery of the environment* owed more to the empire of Euro-American science—particularly biomedicine. This is why these chapters expend energy documenting colonial sanitation schemes, projects of environmental engineering, forest clearing, and other humanizing techniques devised to overcome or "cure" climates. It is why the tenets of humanitarian discourse also animate the book. According to an emerging band of so-called humanitarians, on the one hand, humanness was a thing benevolently bestowed; it was a gift given by the fortunate few to distantly suffering creatures purportedly incapable of securing their own self-possession. On the other, acts of charity worked to endow free men of property with still greater humanity, expanding their mastery of circumstance. The book shows how music-makers—from performers of *ngombi* harpsongs in chapter 1 to devotees of J. S. Bach such as Albert Schweitzer in chapter 6—struggled over the form and content of the human. Finally, circulation is a preoccupation, particularly the circulation of superstition and religious ideas about waves, vibrations, magnetism, infectious disease, and radioactivity. Ancestral spirits fill the elemental media regime—thick with affective life and stirred up by an industrial energy regime that Françoise Vergès generalizes as the Racial Capitalocene.[22] To recognize the power of these spirits is somewhat to deprivilege Euro-American cosmologies. But it is also to show how much the regime interacted with, appropriated, and annulled belief systems along the Atlantic seaboard.

This history of music, then, is a history of the problem of air. And an inquiry into the art's elemental poetics will need to account not only for multiplicity but also for oneness—and not just for airs but for *the* air. It makes sense for this invisible history, therefore, to tug at the geopolitical-global narrative thread of the book first. In question are the racial ramifications of the project to rescue music from mediation tout court, never mind from air. "We can never have an understanding of the desire for purity in the name of the aesthetic, morality, and reason," writes Simon Gikandi, "unless we preface the pure works of the philosophers of modernity with the racial discourse that haunted these works."[23] Gikandi's point is that aesthetic knowledge—by which he means art theories derived from the eighteenth-century European sciences of sensory perception and cognition—flourished amidst colonial expansion. In the context of his discussion of the "universal convulsion" attendant to the myth of decolonization and state repression, Frantz Fanon observes in the *Wretched of the Earth* (1961) that colonized subjects "discover that violence is atmospheric." Colonial violence, he writes, "ripples under the skin."[24]

Music historians in the Europe-only tradition have long wrangled over the emergence, "around 1800," of the Romantic music aesthetic. The claim to the aesthetic, in the argument of music philosopher Lydia Goehr, involved both a transcendent move and a formalist one.[25] Thirty years ago, Goehr theorized what she called the separability principle. For Goehr, the insistence on music as an independent art involved the renunciation of factors deemed external to it—indeed any factoring whatsoever. Goehr identified what she called the work concept as the focal point of academic music theory and practice. The conditions of performance, matters of instrument choice, the vicissitudes of political life, tasteful interpretation, local variations in climate: the guardians of the art pronounced that *the outside* had nothing to do with it.

The musical work concept was "regulative" for Goehr because it functioned to organize and distribute normative musical practice. It prescribed an ethic of care directed to score-bound activity and states of aesthetic possession, where, as per the Kantian percept, "the subject feels itself as it is affected by the representation."[26] Philosophies of "truth to the work" dominated the pedagogies of conservatory practice across Europe and the colonial world. For the art object to be a thing objecting, protocols for music practice needed to be institutionalized globally. Standards needed to be universally set to naturalize the ideal, as Fanny Gribenski observes in her writing on *Tuning the World* (2023).[27] The work had to sound the same everywhere, no matter the climate conditions. For music to be music, it needed to be archived under the strictest conditions of humidity control.

Gribenski writes that the institution of norms such as standard pitch to regulate musical practices and instrument building in the nineteenth century "grew hand in hand with the growth of international trade, the regulation of industrial exchanges, and the constitution of international scientific and technological networks."[28] Not only that, but the project to collect musical specimens for storage, though it followed strange national trajectories and failed miserably, resulted in modernity's hardened canons. Gribenski notes an ossified relationship to the musical past. And she links that hardening to failed projects to unify global space by the worldwide distribution of imperial norms. The art of music thus reoriented itself to the industrial reproduction of products. In aestheticized form, it was ranked among the *schöne Künste*.

Exclusive, odorless, white: the will to standardization established music, Austro-German instrumental music in particular, as a remote and intangible thing. In Foucauldian terms, according to Gary Tomlinson, faith in the truth of the *aistheton* provoked a rift in the very order of things.[29] Tomlinson identifies a drive to decontextualization, racial decontamination even, as the impetus for the epistemic shift. A colonial rationality—spurred on by the fetishization of musical writing—set Euro-Americans in search of their own nonconscious and prerational super-natures. "Music lodged itself," Tomlinson explains, "at the heart of a discourse that pried Europe and its histories apart from non-European lives and cultures." The *aistheton* worked, that is, in a process of quarantining—where, as Fanon would put it, "the white man is sealed in his whiteness and the black man in his blackness."[30]

Yet not even the most airless art object could fully hold back the turbulent weather of colonial modernity. "The conveying of the transcendental psyche, in Schubert's character pieces and other similar music," Tomlinson explains, "was emblematic of mystical, non-empirical trends that now pushed in at the edges of Europe's Enlightenment."[31] Despite and perhaps because of the psychic presence of Africa in Europe, the effort to purify was aggressive. History severed from anthropology, literature from orature, and cults of the art insisted on the supremacy of the sensuous experience of writing music over the sensuous experience of performed song. Radically disruptive classificatory distinctions emerged, in Tomlinson's telling, between art and nature, art and craft, civilized and primitive. Fellow philosopher James O. Young calls it a "Great Divide," though he refuses to believe in it: that cleft in music history opened when devotees of the cult brought to the contemplation of musical art objects the same attitude of silent introspection they once reserved for contemplation of the Divine.[32]

All the talk of epistemic shifts and great divides, no doubt, overestimates the power of discourse to shape history. Rather than emphasizing dialectic separation, then, it may be better to ask how embodied practice advanced the cause of the Romantic music aesthetic. Rebecca Dowd Geoffroy-Schwinden supplies better precision to the legal history of Goehr's work concept as the product of a postrevolutionary modern property regime (i.e., emergent after 1789). Quite literally, that regime proprietized music to make money out of thin air. Expanding global markets for music literature, the manufacture of printed music books, and institutional investments in music literacy air-locked the thing. Far from falling out of the sky around 1800, the regulative work concept was the industrial product of nineteenth-century mass production. Any historical materialist would agree. It was less philosophizing philosophers than cash-grubbing publishers who masterminded the thingification of music. They turned music, once an airy business, into property, reifying it as "an objectively existing thing—a tangible, concrete entity that can be placed in one's hands in exchange for money."[33] The ideologues, that is, requisitioned coal-fired water vapor, air pressure, and pollution in the project to vacuum seal and canonize.

Perhaps the greatest canonizer of them all was Franz Liszt. A year after publishing his famous paean to "The Imaginary Museum of Musical Works," which supplied the title of Goehr's influential book, the high priest of atmospheric music extolled the "deeply universal motion" of the steam-powered press. (In the classic definition of the Anthropocene by atmospheric chemist Paul J. Crutzen, glacial ice-core samples evidenced the geological impact of steam-engine technologies.[34]) In his "Popular Editions of Important Works" (1836), Liszt observed that due to the effects of the "magnificent improvement to Gutenberg's wonderful machine" on popular music consumption, the *Weltseele* was on the move. All of this served Liszt's vision of a pantheon built in Paris on the model of Louvre to preserve the art-religious objects of music history.[35] A newly spiritual age was in bloom. (One masterwork set aside for storage was the same BWV 546 that Liszt published in an 1852 piano transcription, which saved Pechuël-Loesche at Cabinda.) "Day after day, and hour after hour," the musician-priest proclaimed of steam-printed music, "this mother of revolution continually imposes upon each of us its great prevailing influence, a widespread, and redeeming power."[36] The billowing smoke and smog of automated power presaged a future where "life and progress permeates all spheres of human activity, and it comes from all directions and penetrates all areas." Routinely, Liszt described his music as a civilizing atmospheric power. In the preface to his 1854 symphonic poem *Orpheus*, for example, he spoke of "the serenely civilizing character of the melodies that radiate from every work of art."[37] Liszt imagined his orchestra as a battery of atmospheric weapons. He imagined melodious waves and vibrant chords spread abroad in service of aesthetic supremacy.

Aestheticism, and the belief in it, Gikandi suggests, makes no sense without an Afrological view of the legacies of curatorial containment.[38] Its *Weltanschauung* emerged from what Achille Mbembe calls "the epicenter of global transformations."[39] In the European century, Equatorial Africa remained a primary wellspring for Euro-American economic prosperity. Comparative ideas about climate's determination of race and universal freedom were not only sourced in these territories, but Gikandi also points to an anxiety of influence—another sign of Black presence at the heart of white circumatlantic experience—that was heavily repressed in European aesthetic theory. He writes of the effort to absorb these "nonsemantic and disordered" worlds of feeling. Its threats were carefully managed in European culture, of course. But among the symptoms of global-capitalist production and what Marx called "primitive accumulation" (*ursprüngliche Akkumulation*) was the Romantic-Modern appropriation of frenzied trance states and fetish making in the most rarefied music-obsessed salons in urban Europe.[40] We will get to these threats again later. But to invoke Equatorial Africa as the ground zero of *scientia cognitionis sensitivae* is to see through such boundary concepts as Fortress Europe. It is to refer to that milieu where the experience of Atlantic modernity was most vivid— and to that targeted energy source where modernity took place most.[41]

If the first thread confounds the incantations of the *nganga* with the sounds of Bach, the book's second priority plunges music into the maelstrom of modern climate history, summoning the grandest master narrative of them all. Following the environmental thread, I join that growing chorus of music scholars who blame "western metaphysics," "the normative disciplinary boundaries of music studies," and the "postulation of the culture/nature divide" for being "intimately linked to the discourses, processes, and values that facilitate the Anthropocene."[42] The charge is that rather than being made within air, the ideal forms of nineteenth-century music were made *from out of* air. They were subject, that is, to the ideology that sought, not merely to dominate, but to transform nature. It is a difficult and even atrocious allegation to make: that the claim to aesthetic separability or any kind of musical activity, however industrial, might be implicated in climate change. Is it not true, to cite Arthur Schopenhauer's dictum, that "alongside world history there goes, guiltless and unstained by blood, the history of philosophy, science and the arts"?[43] How could something so innocent as music be said to be implicated in anything at all—let alone a thing so catastrophic as the global environmental crisis? Isn't music good?

I would like to say that this second thread attempts less. Yet it is perhaps no less atrocious to argue that it was only in the nineteenth century that particularly instrumental music, precisely because of its indeterminacy, became expressive and indeed productive of a thickened consciousness of air. It is certainly true that without such a complicit sense of being in the world, such grandiloquent concepts as the Anthropocene would be inconceivable. The insistence on the separability of music from nature notwithstanding, a belief in the transcendent qualities of music held that those who "breathed in" music immersed themselves in nature as never before. It was just that this Nature (I explain the use of capital N in chapter 3) was a distant, higher, and purer pneumatic essence than that which ordinary humans breathed under industrial modernity.

Earlier, I suggested that music became useful to an expanded biopolitical logic that *discovered the air* as a governmental field convenient to the exercise of political power over life. The older rationality maintaining the Atlantic slave trade lingered deep into the nineteenth century and beyond. But the target of disciplinary power had always been bodily rather than environmental. For more than three hundred years, the Atlantic traffic in enslaved Africans insured the steady expansion of Euro-American capital. Power zeroed in on corporeal forms, specifically the flesh of African bodies, their strength, the work of their hands, reproductive value, and so on. It profited off the vital properties of bound muscle, capital being explicitly sourced in corporeality. The life forces of shackled limbs, traded on markets thousands of miles from their points of extraction, built the Atlantic world as known today: Cadiz, Nantes, Caen, Bristol, São Tomé. These port cities accrued their wealth off forced migration, extractive labor, and racial targeting.

The Foucauldian position would be that a similarly tyrannous and historically overlapping environmental rationality had already emerged by the turn of the European century. No longer invested in the bodies of its subjects, this system of government was remarkable for its invisibility. Difficult to identify, but diffuse and *toujours tendues, toujours en activité*, modern power was everywhere and nowhere. It governed, not so much at the level of law, as at the level of norms and routines, turning its face away from the sadistic spectacle of what Foucault once called the anatomo-politics of the human body.[44] According to the revolutionary logic of biotechnical and extrajudicial control, the subject of this atmospheric power no longer targeted individual bodies, or the capacities of enslavable flesh. Instead, Foucault suggests, new governmental and bureaucratic orders addressed whole cultural demographies, ones that meted out violence according to more holistic rationales. Industrial society invented a humanitarian form of biopolitical reason oriented to arguably even more invasive techniques of enviro-bureaucratic management. The focus of regulatory practice shifted to the apparently endless reproductive capacities of global climates and the arts of environment. This regime of moral understanding—oriented to "producing, breathing life into, and increasing freedom, of introducing additional freedom through additional control and intervention"—invested in institution building and environmentality.[45]

Specifically, in the global system Bruno Latour identifies as the "Climatic Regime," power targeted the air.[46] Industrial modernity cultivated life less as a property of the body than as the product of a total ensemble of ecological conditions. The system looked beyond matters of visibility for the optimization of growth, whether economic, spiritual, or social. Instead, it raised to knowledge nature's most intangible assets. The institutions formed in service of modern power botanicized life, manufacturing such built environments as glass-housed gardens, concert halls, schools, public hospitals, shopping arcades, and other indoor-outdoor worlds.[47] By the logic of no-touch bureaucracies of care, men sought to extend life—by projects of biopolitical enclosure: air-conditioning, projects of acclimatization, atmospheric management, swamp or forest clearing, urbanization, colonial pedagogy, plantation management, and so on. The Climatic Regime aimed to reform bodies by first reforming the conditions of breathing—and by innovating new systems of moral and physical containment.

Instead of targeting human resources, then, the institutions of humanitarian commercial reform targeted environmental ones, making obsessive investments in invisibility. The system preferred the spiritual to the physical, the unseen to the seen, luminiferous ether to darkness. "So it is with air," was Plato's classic view: "there is the brightest variety which we call *aether*, the muddiest which we call mist and darkness, and other kinds for which we have no name."[48] It is often said that great musicians, in the

European century, rejected the definition of art as an imitation of nature. Nineteenth-century theories of art preferred to define music as the *expression* of nature.[49] They configured their object of knowledge as a product drawn out of the world and, in ideological terms, as an art productive of brighter worlds. Music, that is, had the capacity not merely to mimic nature but to discover nature. The environmentalist thread of this book, in sum, establishes relations between the newly aesthetic properties of music and the conversion of air into atmospheres for managing life. It describes music as a working out of that newly discoverable and manipulable realm.

The Thingly Element in Music

Thematizing air, then, this book attends to what Martin Heidegger once called "the thingly element" in art.[50] By this, I mean the "stony" in a work of architecture, the "wooden" in a carving, the "clayishness" in a work of pottery, and the *métier* that in itself is refashioned in the act of making. The stuff of any musical activity may count in multiple and complex ways. The bodies of performers, their arrangement and composition in space, identity configurations, the materialities of instruments, infrastructures of transmission, the acoustic properties of buildings, the patterned cognition of listeners, timbral-sonic grain, the texture of place: all of these may be targeted in matters of sonic practice. Any of these elements may be the going matter of concern. But what would it mean to listen, first, to the thinglyness of air, so little observed, discussed, or noticed? To ask the question historically: What might it mean to attend to music's invisible dependencies—to the subtle matter of air, elusive, sometimes audible, but always in motion? Or to suggest that the famed abstraction of nineteenth-century music owed less to ideas of disembodied transcendence than to an awakened European consciousness of air?

Music and air are two very different things, of course, since music (aesthetically speaking) presents as something else over and above air. That something else constituted its artistic nature, since "the work makes public something other than itself; it manifests something other." "Let Music be naught else than Nature mirrored by and reflected from the human breast," Italian pianist Ferruccio Busoni opined towards the end of our period, "for it is sounding air and floats above and beyond the air."[51] Freedom in art, for Busoni, inhered in that *something else* above and beyond the banal matter that mediated it. For him, the creative process was a biological act by which music was made *out* of the natural universe, as much as *in* it. "One must accord music the advantage of being ideal in its essence," echoed German poet August Wilhelm Schlegel at the beginning of our period, "it purifies the passions, as it were, from the material filth with which they are associated, in that music presents these passions to our inner sense entirely according to their own form, without any reference to objects; and after touching an earthly frame, it allows these passions to breathe in a purer ether."[52] These views—Busoni's as much as Schlegel's—exalted music as a way to evacuate air from bodies, the idea of musical creation understood in terms of an (often violent) process of *expression*. Ideally, culture breathed in the purer ether of a remote *Tonwelt*: autonomous, invisible, and discrete unto itself.

I will say upfront that I am skeptical of projects of demystification.[53] I do not think that music's medial home is in the air; nor do I think that once repatriated to some primitive or democratic state, music might be heard to vibrate in its full acoustic glory there. Nor would I want to propound an ethics or advocate for a nonreductive ecological practice suggestive of some more holistic spiritual-sensory experience of the art. Jonathan Sterne has warned against the pursuit of what he calls "the ever-receding horizon of materiality."[54] That horizon slips away, unfortunately, even as it is recovered as a vibrational field and sensed through "intermaterial vibrational practice."[55] The last thing I want to do is pull back the curtain to reveal air (or "the air") as the God-given medium for music. To be sure, the question of what air is has always been as obscure as the question of what music is. I want to insist that there is no preexisting "out there" that we have failed to see and hear. And I have no desire, as shaman-priest, to make audible that elemental sound system preceding all other media sound systems. Nor am I an ethical spokesperson for the rights of environment. Precisely the opposite, since no single critic could ever have privileged sensory access to the essential materiality of that vanishing mediator *extraordinaire*.[56]

Rather, the project is to narrate the artful construction of music, as distinct from the older aria (which configured music as a species or movement of air), as a way of *working air out*. For this, I attend to embodied techniques, physical materialities, and local practices, as well as to the emergence of music out of a thickened nineteenth-century engagement with, fascination for, and terror of air. That *working out* of air, as much as any a priori conception of air, is the chief narrative concern of the book.

Universal Aestheticism

Books like this, necessarily, begin from a long way out. This one starts when Nzame/Nzambi pungu, worshipped across the Black Atlantic, made the sky and earth by breathing upon it, keeping the sky for Himself. As the first principle of creation, air was a domain of spiritual chaos as much as divine order. In many Atlantic religions, life was long associated with air, air being required for breathing, as the essence of what it meant to be human.

"Air is the realm of the universal mind" in *Bwiti* oral traditions—so says Gabonese philosopher Brice Parfait Ndzigou, gesturing to the first cause and principle.[57] For pre-Socratic Greek mystics, Anaximenes of Miletus among them, the soul itself was a kind of weather system formed of air; Diogenes of Apollonia went so far as to argue that air was the soul of the world. The in-breathing and out-breathing of the *anima mundi*, that is, produced all that was good and worth living for. The total mass of the earth's atmosphere—5.5 quadrillion tons of it—bore down with an indiscriminate absolutism. Air eluded human reason as much as it slipped material grasp. There was nothing to know or be done about it. It was merely the means by which all things lived, breathed, and had their being. And it bestowed the provisions of life upon creatures great and small. One is reminded of the joke about the smart-aleck fish in the fishbowl, who shouted across to his younger brethren, "How's the water today, boys?" Swimming along a little, one fish wondered, "What the hell is water?"

It is a claim of this book that, incrementally, during the onrush of the European century, to adapt the argument of Alfred Gell in his "The Technology of Enchantment and the Enchantment of Technology," the sacredness of the medium of breathing fell into doubt. Certain fish began to know. "It was not until 1774 [when Joseph Priestley discovered oxygen]," Lyon Playfair pointed out in 1876, "that we found air was not an element."[58] Himself a child of empire, Bengal-born Playfair amassed a host of evidence for an epochal change in air, styling himself as a chemical historian of "the progress of our knowledge in regard to air." Playfair named a Saracen, Ḥasan Ibn al-Haytham, as the first to investigate the weight and volume of the media system. The great eleventh-century mystic supplied laws to refraction in air and doubted whether air was scattered infinitely throughout space. Half a millennium later, Robert Boyle, also anticipating the change, pondered "the different fictitious kinds of air." Boyle separated the chemical properties of the atmosphere into myriad chemical gases, including nitrogen, and carbonic acid. By the European century, Playfair lamented, a different kind of aerobiosis was at work, a whole host of "minute little organisms" "born in my own time" that carried disease and decay and putrefaction. The devilish swarm mixed into a vast epidemic atmosphere, including 280 million tons of carbonic acid released because of the burning of coal. By the recent addition of ammonia and ozone, Playford warned, the breathing sphere had been "transformed into a huge sewer into which all the pestilential matter goes."[59] The divine air, he complained, was now a cesspool, man being beset on all sides by industrial pollution, and mephitic terror.

Humanity was, in one way or another, "becoming a self-conscious, active agent in the operation of its own life support system."[60] A sign of growing skepticism and self-consciousness toward air was a new religiosity directed away from the sacred provisions of nature and toward the nineteenth-century institutions and cults of art. "In so far as such modern souls possess a religion," Gell writes, "that religion is the religion of art, the religion whose shrines consist of theatres, libraries and art galleries, whose priests and bishops are painters and poets, whose theologians are critics, and whose dogma is the dogma of universal aestheticism."[61] Universal aestheticism: it is a good phrase. It forces the question of whether aesthetic theory makes sense outside of the air-conditioned shrines of sacred-secular archiving and "primitive accumulation." The great climate-controlled temples of art and all the related emporia of nineteenth-century knowledge bore witness to "mankind's great reconstruction of nature," to borrow the phrase of T. J. Clarke.[62] Latour calls it the Great Enclosure: the conversion of the globe into a giant atmospheric storehouse of capital available to Euro-American asset and resource management.[63] Aestheticism, that is, brought the sacred power of air under human control: domesticated, rationalized, and ushered indoors.

If air occupied a once transcendent domain beyond human knowing, nineteenth-century art-religious institutions imagined themselves as surrogate infrastructures for life. By force of magical thinking, these pantheons substituted ideologically for the life-giving function once accorded to air. This they did by stealing nature's sacred pneuma and by investing those mystic powers in aestheticism, particularly in great works of music—music being the essential atmospheric art. "It took the romantic generation," explains leading theorist of nineteenth-century musical natures Alexander Rehding, "to breathe life into music and to endow it with aesthetic autonomy and vital functions in one fell swoop."[64] Archived and catalogued, these art objects shimmered in the evolutionary and civilizational terms of what Rachel Mundy calls "the biological imagination."[65] Charged with both animacy and animating force, the music itself, at once organized and self-organizing, was thus ideologically conscripted to serve "a biological, or rather *vitalistic*, model of the musical work and music history."[66] The art object, that is, instantiated its own individual life-support system. At base, the project of the institutions of art, and more specifically the institutions of music, was to replace air as the medium of divine provision.

Castles built in the air: the temples that the art-religious elites drew to advance life were hardly weatherproof. But this is not to say that the cultural effort to the bypass the filtering system, since the European century, has not been extraordinary. Opera singers know this, when instructed to expunge breathiness from vocal tone. Airiness is the least desirable trait of orchestrally trained wind-instrument players, and a basic hindrance to the production of aesthetic atmospheres in the concert hall. Performance, sadly for air-breathers, is a compromised thing. Unfortunately for connoisseurs, even silent score readers or underwater opera singers, music still requires air, just to keep the poor performers alive.[67] This is true even when you air lock music in libraries, pass it through so many wires, reify it as so many mp3s, store as digital information on so many hard drives, or transduce it through so many earphone speakers. The desire for sonic purity—indeed, the need for *sound as such*—betrays this will to asphyxiation, the dogmas of aestheticism being nowhere more evident than in the most avant-garde sound art. It is the genealogy of this need to "get out of air" and this preference for the aesthetic over the airy—with music the product of air rather than its effect—that I recount in this book.

None of the master stories I have recounted so far, or the sweeping generalizations I have made, escape blind ideology. Gell is quick to stress that myths—about Euro-Northern medial supremacy as much as master narratives about the rise of secular modernity—were precisely that: myths.[68] The question of what music has to do with air is difficult, for reasons that have to do with the strange modern claim to separability from it. I have recounted these myths because of the imperious reach of such projects and narratives. Proceeding circuitously in the chapters that follow, however, I find myself moving against universal aestheticism and thinking toward the musical foibles and habits of local actions and local actors. Instead of epic narratives about heroic mastery, I tell stories of just a few creatures of the air living and breathing as best they can, in the midst of things.

CREATURES OF THE AIR

The phrase *creatures of the air* is adapted from Johann Gottfried von Herder's proto-Romantic writings on sound and climate—from outside this book's chronological and geographic purview. It occurs in the *Ideen zur Philosophie der Geschichte der Menschheit*, wherein the problem of human variation, indeed humanity itself, was submitted to a "geographical aerology." The Prussian theologian, folksong collector, and father of "the global moment of world-music history" was not one to prevaricate.[69] We are beings "precipitated from the ether," Herder announced in 1784, writing from Riga on the Baltic Sea. In the preacher's conception, humanity itself had originally "passed from the invisible to the visible world." All breathing life was born of the nebula—of "electric matter, and the magnetic fluid, phlogiston, and the acidifying principle; the cold-engendering salts, and, perhaps, the particles of light." Herder described a spheroidal gaseous magazine enveloping the circulating orb. He wrote of a vibrating swirl of moistures and exhalations, lightness and weight, heat and cold. His synoptic study sought to unveil "that great hothouse of Nature operating a thousand changes by the same fundamental laws." Whether Mungal, Patagonian, Californian, or Turk, "complexions run into each other," humanity being subject to the shades of climate, or "shades of the same great picture." Race was anathema to history for him because this clumsy idea failed to explain how the "spirit of climate" continuously shaped and reshaped sensibility. Man, that is, was an airborne creature, and the sounds humans made played into the atmosphere's singularly creative and moving spirit.

"We are ductile clay in the hand of Climate," Herder announced, since "her fingers mold so variously, and the laws that counteract them, are so numerous." Herder hoped to bring to light the laws that explained the diversity that he identified in global anthropological organization. The aim of his world geography and comparative history of man was to show how national character formed in relation to the myriad gases breathed in at the various parts of the earth. It was to discover the laws of elasticity, weight, purity, gravity, and density of each part—in the tradition of Boyle, Boerhave, Hales, Franklin, Priestley, Crawford, Wilson, and other connoisseurs of the different species of air. "We live by the inspiration of the air," Herder observed, "and yet its balsam, our vital ailment, is a mystery to us." Herder's aerology worked to make sense of a resounding mystery.

Climate, barely distinguished from air, explained anthropological difference. Herder's climate theory went beyond the old Montesquieuan thesis that the study of aerial variation was also the study of human variation. The constitution of human bodies, Herder explained, "their way of life, the pleasures and occupations to which they have been accustomed from their infancy, and the whole circle of their ideas are climatic." All of earth's people, from Peruvians to Laplanders, molded their maxims of life, including their folk songs, according to this invisible determinant. Herder cited "various active immaterial powers" including "electric and magnetic streams" flowing around the earth, as well as vapors and exhalations ascending "in this place or that." "All affect the constitution and history of every race of man: for man, like everything else, is a nursling of the air [*Ein*

Zögling der Luft], and in the whole circle of his existence is the brother of all organized beings upon earth."[70] "The history of man, he concluded, "is ultimately a theatre of transformations."[71] Not merely this, but also

> as climate is a compound of powers and influences to which both plants and animals contribute, and which everything that has breath forms as an all-encompassing system, there is no question that man is placed in it as a sovereign of the Earth, to alter it by art. Since he stole fire from Heaven, and rendered steel obedient to his hand; since he has made not only beasts, but his fellow man also, subservient to his will, and trained both them and plant to his purposes; he has contributed to the alteration of climate in various ways. Once Europe was a dank forest; and other regions, at present well cultivated, were the same. They are now exposed to the rays of the Sun; and the inhabitants themselves have changed with the climate.[72]

Not only a creation of air then, this creature created atmospheres, wielding his "genius" and "genetic power" to alter climates by art. Man "contaminates the air he breathes," being both a climate-altered and climate-altering species. "He builds up and destroys, improves and alters forms," Herder wrote, "while he changes the World around."[73] Herder was in fact among the first European thinkers to conceive of climates as anthropogenic creations. He worried about the Age of Humanity, concerned as he was about "how far they are capable of going in this respect futurity will show." Though in thrall to the sky, these *Zöglinge der Luft* used art to remake climates to suit their own needs and comfort. "Every man, every animal, every plant has his own climate," Herder explained, "for every one receives all external impressions in his own manner, and modifies them according to his organs." Man's "genius" inhered in the power not so much to master by force but to modify climates and improve himself by art.

The influence of Herder's theories in Europe ran deep. In his *Stimmen der Völker in Liedern* ("Voices of the Peoples in Songs," 2 vols., 1778–79), Herder famously discovered in *Volkslieder*, a word he coined, lyric precipitations of diverse poetic life-worlds shaped by the global spiritual provisions of air. Philip V. Bohlman writes that it was through Herder's salvage ethnography that "folk song entered the history of world music in the 1770s, and by the beginning of the nineteenth century it was the primary material—sonic, literary, narrative, and political—for understanding the history of music worldwide."[74] Matthew Gelbart, meanwhile, lauds Herder less. Gelbart argues that the folk song only makes sense as a concept in relation to the idea of art song, since the concept of "genius" historically indexed, simply, an exalted type of mystic folk bard.[75] Music, for Herder, was "the first of the fine arts, by which the mind is moved" and "the first germ of superior sense [that is, hearing]." For him, "the music of a nation, in its most imperfect form, and favorite tunes displays the internal character of the people, that is to say, the proper tone of their sensations, much more truly and profoundly, than the most copious description of external continencies." The spirit of what would later be called "culture"— a generalized creative spirit—was audible before it was visible. This was because climate operated rather "on the mass, than on the individual." That is, assumptions about the at once pluralizing and sovereign effects of air, as well as distinctions between folk song and art, constituted fundamental organizing principles. These ideas stirred up thoughts of sound-as-resource, the spirit of the people, world literature, world music, as well as comparative concepts of nature, language, and "culture" (especially in the wake of Edward Tylor's landmark *Primitive Culture* [1871])[76] Music was more than a mere play of sensations, Herder insisted in his *Kalligone* (1800); it was the "Art of Humanity."[77]

What Is a Medium?

Peter Sloterdijk names Herder as the original modern—as the first *Zögling der Luft* to be self-conscious about his own being-in-the-air. Herder, that is, provides the model for Sloterdijk's historical atmospherology, written some two hundred years later in the trilogy *Sphären* (1998, 1999, 2004).[78] The metaphor for the emergence of disciplinary or normalizing liberal-capitalist societies, for Sloterdijk, is not so much the panopticon, after Foucault. Rather, modern control societies are best thought of in terms of the life-support system, as in mechanical ventilators in hospital wards. A good way to tell the story of atmospheric modernity after Herder, Sloterdijk writes, is to narrate it in the terms of "atmosphere-explication." By this, he means processes of apprehending air in order to produce atmospheres.[79] Sloterdijk argues that the new target of governmental power for nineteenth-century political economies in industrial Europe was not so much the bodies of its subjects, as the environments that those subjects occupied.

Artificial life support, after all, was only one of many therapeutic technologies invented in the European century. Here, as shown in chapter 2's description of sopranos in hyperbaric chambers, the political rationale was to advance life by subjecting it to air-conditioned enclosure. Nontherapeutic methods were implicated as well, gas attack being a prime example, since military strategies of environmental assault sought to ensure the safety of home populations by targeting not merely the foreign bodies that infected their space but also the environments in which those foreign bodies breathed. Sloterdijk's argument is that "the active manipulation of breathing air first became a cultural matter" at the invention of environmental warfare. (He incorrectly dates this invention to 1915; "chemical attack" was more likely the invention of the British Royal Navy's Thomas Cochrane in 1812, who—besides inventing improvements to gas lighting, convoy lanterns, tubular boilers, and steam propulsion—proposed the wartime use of "sulphur ships," "stink vessels," and "noxious effluvia."[80]) It would seem, pace Sloterdijk, that modern power, though it certainly aspired to the miraculous invisibility of the air, was never so absolute. True, nineteenth-century thinkers did apply environmental thinking to questions of populational control; but it was equally remarkable how often those atmospheric systems leaked or failed to work.[81]

There is a danger, too, of medium creep, as much in the exemplary thought of John Durham Peters on "elemental media" as in Sloterdijk and German media discourse theory generally.[82] Must everything be media— the air, nature, cities, technology, the body, history itself? Robert Mitchell argues that the very idea of "the medium" underwent a profound transformation "around 1800," since its reconceptualization as a key term of mechanics.[83] He points out that it was only very much later that the fine arts were converted into media. The instrumental take on the medium concept occurred only after the invention of the telegraph, phonograph, and radio—those metallic channels of mass-processed dissemination and mechanical reproduction, which manufacturers themselves claimed to transform aesthetic reality and humanity's sense of the world.

For such premodern empiricists as Francis Bacon and Isaac Newton, Mitchell argues, the medium concept denoted the relatively harmless interval enabling the transmission of sound and light. The ancient philological meaning from the Latin referred simply to the ambient matter between here and there. It named a distance traversed across time and space. The enlightenment concept of the medium as the means of communication— facilitating the transmission of odors, the propagation of sound, the flow of magnetic force—was transformed "around 1800," according to Mitchell, by "a newly vitalized sense of what it meant to be amid-things." The category driving this thickened experience of being, apparently, was *life*, a newly sovereign concept that enriched the nineteenth-century epistemic airscape in extraordinary ways. As Foucault put it in the *Order of Things*: "Up to the end of the eighteenth century, in fact, life does not exist: only living beings."[84] Foucault went on to argue, in his analysis of biopower, that the epistemic triumph of life opened new domains for the exercise of governmental control. Life entered into the concept of the medium, a term now clouded such as to designate a powerfully affective sense of *Vermittlung*—of being in the middle of things.

Amidst this newly confounded Romantic environmentality, according to John Guillory, the medium concept came to "figure for the function or dysfunction of language," and the conditions by which the experience of life, indeed one's biology itself, were continually being dissolved and transformed. For Hegel, Guillory writes, "mediation concerns nothing less than the question of *being*; for Marx, the question of *labor* (the mediation of mankind and nature)."[85] A simple matter of communication became a sacred determinant. Georges Canguilhem, relatedly, excavates "the historical stages of the formation of the concept of the *milieu* as "the experience and existence of living things." A basic category of contemporary thought, that word *milieu*, from the French sense of "being in the middle," Canguilhem argues, was bizarre. He argues that the emergence of the term in Lamarck, Saint-Hilaire, Balzac, and Comte, derived from French mechanist adoptions of the Newtonian concept of ether. "This explains," Canguilhem writes, "the passage from the notion of fluid as a vehicle to its designation as a medium."[86] Where once media existed to carry ideas, they were now saturated with affective vitality. Robert Mitchell, in vague terms, blames "romantic-era authors," who "vivified the earlier sense of the term." These authors, Mitchell claims, presented "media not just as vehicles of transmission but also as conditions of possibility for the life and growth of living beings."[87] If the medium concept used to refer to a neutral matter useful to the propagation of sound, it now referred to a matter thick with thought and feeling.

A host of cognate concepts combined to thicken Romantic-Modern experience further. Take the concept of the "environment." "Although the word *environment* and its variants make occasional appearances in English texts as early as the beginning of the eighteenth century (and are found earlier in French)," observes Etienne S. Benson in *Surroundings: A History of Environments and Environmentalisms* (2020), "they did not come into wide usage in anything like their modern senses until the second half of the nineteenth century." Benson cites Claude Bernard's midcentury concept of the *milieu intérieur* to illustrate the idea that modern organisms carry their own microbiomes around with them. In Bernard's sense, Benson writes, "we *are* environments just as much as we are *in* environments; we both surround and are surrounded."[88] Environments, that is, are modern constructs. Benson notes the extent to which environmentality depended on establishing a relationship between "surrounding things" and "something that is surrounded." The environment concept, that is, required "the invention of a new object of scientific inquiry: the 'organism,' which was defined as a combination of specialized parts ('organs') that worked together to allow a living being to survive and reproduce itself under a certain set of external conditions (its 'environment')."

To explain thickened affective experiences of music as a "phenomenon," Friedlind Riedel, relatedly, reveals "atmosphere" to be another nineteenth-century confabulation. The word originated as a speculative percept in seventeenth-century medico-meteorological discourse. It was in medical practice, Riedel observes, where this auratic emanation—alchemized from the Greek "atmos" for "vapor" and "sphaera" for "orb"—acquired modern meaning. In midcentury German musical parlance, "atmosphere" denoted a variety of different but overlapping ontologies: as emanation, sound mass, force, texture, meteorological relation, ambiance, as embeddedness, and so on.[89] In English, according to the *Oxford English Dictionary*, the earliest use of the word to mean "surrounding moral element" occurred in Samuel Taylor Coleridge's *Biographia Literaria* of 1817, the date of the starting point of this book. The English theologian-poet described a distinctive pathology or modulation of perception that affected the tone of exemplary "forms, incidents, and situations."[90] In general, "atmosphere" described a lyric sense of air, or perhaps as "the living air," to quote Wordsworth's attraction to that "sense sublime" and "something far more deeply interfused."[91]

Riedel evokes that "domain of the infinite," to recall E. T. A. Hoffmann's famous words describing Beethoven's instrumental music, "that surrounds us" and "in which we abandon all feelings."[92] Riedel's tendency is to laud rather than interrogate this atmospheric concept of music, one that understands that "wherever music resounds, feelings are likely to unfold in perhaps vague, but nonetheless intrusive and pervasive, spatially extended atmospheres."[93] I tend to think otherwise. Rather than taking such declarative statements at face value, this book probes the colonial genealogy of such a thickened music-sonic experience. How did this atmospheric feeling for music, now ubiquitous in soundscape studies and affect theory, come to be so naturalized?[94] What are the implications of the assumption that music is world-making? And how might we push back against taken-for-granted ideas about acoustic ecology?

Bound to the efforts of Nietzsche's barbarian moderns and the machines of the carbon industry, music attained its exalted status as the immediate expression and embodiment of the sublime, and as an art of the environment. The chapters that follow frame music as a conditioning activity. They describe music—whether as civilizing process, sacred visitation, moral armor, sanitized atmospheric bubble, inoculation against the effects of climate, or as the pneuma of God—as a means of working air out.

Chapters

The book starts in medias res. Chapter 1 begins amidst the legal abolition of the trade in enslaved Africans (at least in British dominions) though not slavery itself. I begin by writing against white encounter stories, ones that stage primal scenes of contact between civilization and savagery. A description of ideas about equatorial life proves useful to chapter 1's genesis story because it was under these most biodiverse of conditions that the climate was deemed, at least in the imagination of European explorers, to be most inhuman. Humanity itself was under violent geophysical construction here, and not only because of the site's historic associations with the slave trade. The point is to show how music writing worked to legitimate the experience of colonial dispossession by heroizing stories of white exceptionalism. Music is established, here, as a vehicle to defend the human (and cognate ideas about art, aesthetics, and freedom) against the purportedly blackening racial contingencies of air.

Chapter 1 isolates a single case of resource extraction: a musical transcription, in pen on paper, by Sarah Wallis Bowdich, English explorer-naturalist, scientist, and pianist. The song was performed by a *ngombi* harp player—a musician with albinism purportedly enslaved among Mpongwe-speaking peoples. The performance took place, according to colonial reports, in the region of the Gabon Estuary, near modern-day Libreville. The harpist's poetic improvisation, as represented, recounted myths about the birth of the world. Bowdich traveled to the estuary as an agent for the African Committee of the Company of Merchants. The archive records the harpist as "the property" of Rassondji, a client trader with circumatlantic interests in Liverpool, New York, and Caen. Reading along the grain of colonial documents, maps, and letters, I examine the struggle over the resources of this environment by proposing three comparative ways of narrating the place of the musician's performance. The chapter presents three ways of animating an environment in sound, alongside three competing ways of ranking the human in relation to each political ecology.

Chapter 2 sweeps north to describe the earliest steam-powered air-conditioning systems in Paris. It opens with a description of singer Cornélie Falcon singing, in 1839, inside a climate-controlled glass sphere. Having lost her voice, the soprano was induced to recover her instrument by entering into a full-body "compression chamber," controlled at a distance by male operators of a steam pump. The case of the soprano under glass opens into a wider inquiry into how barometric knowledge and medico-therapeutic media systems became useful to the biopolitical control of populations. The social production of voices and the social production of bourgeois interiority appear, here, as a dual process beholden to emerging techniques of atmospheric management. I survey the writings of male devotees of Falcon to define "thermodynamic song," which was opposed in contemporaneous discourse to "laryngeal song." The former refers to a style of vocality, coded French, reliant upon air pressure and breath control; the latter attends to a style of execution, coded Italian, dependent on "mechanical" movements of the throat. To know voices thermodynamically was to eschew mechanics and to attend to the total ensemble of breathing conditions. It was to measure the artist's skill, as much as a virtuosic singer, as a creator of tonal atmospheres. Consulting period images and anecdotes about atmospheric engines, techniques, therapies, and theories that concern air, I identify the case of Falcon as the case of the gendered bourgeois individual.

Two central chapters, sweeping west, address modern crises of air pollution and airborne epidemics, respectively. Chapter 3 examines the 1846 debut of Felix Mendelssohn's *Elijah*, premiered in Birmingham at the birthplace of the steam engine in Britain's West Midlands. The first production of the oratorio was in fact financed by the profits of coal-fired energy systems. More than this, municipal reformers and well-meaning environmentalists commissioned the work as means to mitigate against the effects of industrial pollution. First conceived by friends and associates of the inventors of steam technologies, Mendelssohn's composition was puffed as a vehicle of reform—as a means to bring healing to English working populations. The smoke nuisance, specifically, yielded a problem for which massed choral singing, framed as a public health initiative, supplied a purported solution. In this sense, sacred choral song aligned with the so-called great sanitary awakening. First, it was thought to fortify the lungs of the laboring classes. Second, the music itself was held to be spiritually sanctifying. The men who produced *Elijah* at once celebrated the work as a product of a coal-fired energy system and as a means to mitigate against the negative health effects of fossil-fuel industrialism.

Chapter 4 confronts Nature head on, sweeping across the Atlantic to the "lungs of the earth" at the mouth of the Amazon River. It addresses Black musics, and projects for disinfecting purportedly epidemic air. This is the second of three chapters to be situated exactly on the line of the equator. The reader lands, along with US explorer and song collector Joseph Steere, on Caviana Island in the Marajó archipelago in 1871 Brazil. Beginning in 1867, under pressure from the US State Department and at the insistence of the emperor himself, Brazil's Imperial Parliament legalized the traffic of foreign merchant and war ships on the Amazon, thus opening up the river system to international steam navigation and trade. The market for rubber latex, in particular, focused the attention of foreign investors. At the gateway to the Amazon region (supposedly one of the most resource-rich environments in the world), Santa Maria de Belém do Grão Pará was a strategic port long shaped by turbulent pattens of labor migration, domestic slave exchange, and interracial mixing. Increasingly, after 1867, biomedical discourses about infectious disease control aligned with discourses about policing outbreaks of Black musicking in the city. The "atmospheric" legacy of slavery, a proliferating number of emancipationist associations alleged, adversely affected the moral condition of every class of inhabitant. Thus spirit possession, epidemics of dancing, Afro-Catholic festivity, fetishistic animism, and all-night drumming. Black musics, because of the way they supposedly plagued the environment, threatened foreign investment. Using newspaper reports and contemporaneous medical articles, I document legal and public health prohibitions waged against "unhealthy" music in this period. I conclude by reflecting on the global scale of a multinational and lettered project to quarantine racial essence, counting the cost of the incorporation of Black art into a continuously expanding and omnivorous Euro-American archive.

The New York City chapter zeroes in on techniques of vocal breathing. This penultimate chapter frames the Edison phonograph as a technology useful to atmospheric reproduction. It invokes an apparition: the indistinct sounds heard off two "brown wax" cylinder recordings made by the librarian of the Metropolitan Opera House in New York. These cylinders preserve the atmosphere of a single night in 1901, a mythic age of song purportedly lost at the turn of the twentieth century, and the final public performance of Polish tenor Jean de Reszke in the role of Wagner's Lohengrin. This live record captured the voice of a singer then hailed as the greatest living master of breath control. Many Gilded Age technologies proved similarly useful to environmentalization, effecting new ways to suspend, capture, or commodify air. The imperative was to immortalize vocal sound. It was to imagine new spectrographic ways to make psychic interiors visible, using voice-imaging equipment and the spectra of standing wave patterns, resonance vibrations, radio signals, and harmonics. What does it mean "to create an atmosphere": that is, to sing without air, according to ideologies of total breath control, or using modern theories of standing resonance?

A final chapter returns to equatorial Gabon. Its protagonist is Albert Schweitzer, considered, late in life, the "Greatest Man of the Twentieth Century," and 1952 Nobel Prize laureate.[95] The Bach scholar and organist left Alsace in 1913 to establish a medical mission only a few miles southeast of where Bowdich landed a century earlier. Using colonial and missionary reports, the chapter explores the implications of an airproofed piano "equipped with organ pedals" presented to Schweitzer by the Paris Bach Society on the eve of his departure for Lambaréné. The gift, which allowed him to continue his Bach studies, was presented at a time of aggressive French colonial expansion in equatorial Africa. Schweitzer thought of the dangerously vital world he encountered here—Lambaréné was being forcibly integrated into the Atlantic timber trade—as a potent resource for biomusical renewal. His mission was as much to minister to the bodies and souls of Africans as to reawaken the moral potency of what he called "the Western spirit." He theorized that European civilization was dying, that the equatorial climate was a source of spiritual vitality, and that he might usefully travel to Gabon to see what energies might be retrieved. His revivals of Bach tallied with wider ethical projects to treat, resuscitate, and renew. This final chapter returns to framing questions about climate-race relations, and the mission to "make human" by "curing" environments. It questions the logic of the humanitarian project—at once biomedical, raciological, religious, and musical—to free every living creature from their perceived enslavement to air.

Gasping for oxygen, to return to the Chiloango River in 1875, Pechuël-Loesche certainly invested in the concept of music as a means to achieve freedom from air. Although Pechuël-Loesche would later be commissioned by Leopold II's brutal Belgian colonial regime to survey the Congo for its plant and mineral wealth, the scientific charge of the Loango Expedition was explicitly antimodern. "The dark-skinned inhabitants of Africa don't need our civilization; rather, we need them," Pechuël-Loesche explained in view of booming Euro-American demand for rubber latex. The mission of the Loango Expedition extended from ethnographic salvage to human salvage. "We need this country's products as much as the country itself," he wrote, "in order to give the world economy ever greater expansion."[96] Among the aims of the expedition was to collect specimens for ethnological museums and recover "humanity at its most elemental." Pechuël-Loesche sought to rescue traces of the sacred purity of Naturvölker before their annihilation by white industrial modernity.[97]

Pechuël-Loesche's personal report of his J. S. Bach experience, written in the fog of 1875 delirium, suggested that the fugue of BWV 548 provided, if not salvation, then comfort in the midst of crisis. Not only Bach but all music carried this curative or resuscitative potential. Take the massed songs of the Vili-speaking peoples. In his *Volkskunde von Loango* (1907), Pechuël-Loesche made his own extractivist objectives plain when he coined the term *Kautschukmelodie* (rubber-latex melody) to describe his transcriptions of Bavili song. He marveled at how "singers managed to process the same motif equally well both without *tempo* and alternately in all possible *tempi*," improvising around "loose sequences of tones," and belying the prejudice that "the basis of music is rhythm."[98] It is true that discourses of human salvage only supplied greater urgency to the colonial imperative for expansion. But, for the Bavili-song hunter who was possessed by Bach on March 27, 1875, music, so aestheticized, was life-giving. This music not only acted as a means by which to salvage the human spirit; it offered the promise of autonomy. In the modernity Luce Irigaray names as the "Age of Breath," music no longer required air; it replaced air, compensating for when breathing was hard, or when conditions pressed in.[99]

CHAPTER 1

White "Genius"
Ngango, Gabon Estuary, 1817

Against World Spirit

The first story to tell is a story about the fantasy of the globe itself. The "genius" in the chapter title does not refer to, as the *Oxford English Dictionary* puts it, "The tutelary god or attendant spirit allotted to every person at birth to govern his or her fortunes and determine personal character." Nor does it suggest the genius loci of classical Roman religion, that "spirit of a place" that presided over local territories. Rather, my topic is the *genius globus* of pan-European mythology—the eighteenth-century sense of the word "genius" as a solitary hero of exalted or exceptional creative power. The *genius globus* was a voyaging figure, a roving spirit beholden to the emerging white sciences of nature.

This chapter shakes its fist at the globe. It tests the extent of humanity's subjection to the atmosphere, to a global medium supposedly all-determining of human variation, natural-born diversity, and earthen creativity. It takes seriously Achille Mbembe's claim that "there is no domination without a cult of spirits."[1] The pages that follow introduce the language of a discourse devoted to anthropopoiesis. Anthropopoiesis refers to "an art of the human," or latterly humanitarian project to "make human." This project to "make human" involved rituals of song and music making; but it also involved cosmopoiesis (cosmopoiesis referring to acts of world-making) and to struggles over environment. The chapter asks how environments might be woven together in song and storytelling. Relating the poetics of world-making to multiple states of song, it opposes the power of the atmospheric mass above with the power of stories and songs sung from below. At issue is the unquestioned sovereignty of the inexorably rotating orb. How might storytellers, while materially dependent on its chemical provision, speak back into the total sphere of utterance? Can they speak back?

A single case study orients this analysis of ca. 1817 world-making: the

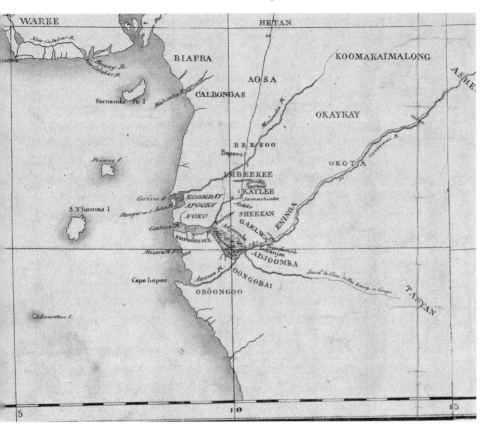

FIGURE 1.1. Detail of T. E. Bowdich, *A Map of North Western Africa dedicated to the African Association* (1820). Note the location of "Naängo" above the equator in the territory of the Empoöngwa (Mpongwe), the land of the "Kaylee," and, nearby, "Imbeekee." Toward the top right in small script, the "Ogooawai" (Ogooué) River will feature in chapter 6. Source: gallica.bnf.fr / Bibliothèque nationale de France.

"air" of a master musician recorded in the colonial archive as "the white negro of Imbeekee." The chapter relates the power of his storytelling, not as a singularity or exceptional event, but as evidence of the ritual force of narrative schemas sung over and over again. Later, that air—both the song and the locality of its production—will be narrated in three competing ways. A comparison of the stories and interests laying claim to this perifluvial environment—forest, water, air—lends itself to a comparison of three contending spiritual ontologies. These narrations constitute the argument of this chapter. But, for the moment, the disputed political ecology of the harpsong will be submitted to thick description. What follows, then, is a lengthy account of the battle for possession of this territory—a struggle for narrative supremacy over medial surrounds, as much as elementality itself.

The Story

Naängo/Ngango appears, on European maps, less than a degree north of the equator near the Pungue/Black Point or *Empoongoua*, where the Remboué River joins a large body of water (the Como) flowing down from the Crystal Mountains. The names that proliferate in this territory attest to the struggle to colonize it. The settlement, forty-five miles inland from the sea, is situated off the Gabon Estuary, named (they say) after the Portuguese "Gabão," a fifteenth-century word suggesting the shape of a hooded cloak.[2] A waterway known to Europeans as "Creek Georges" (Abååga/Avazza/Ava), only navigable by pirogue, ran south from the estuary toward what maps called "a conspicuous tree." A short uphill walk from the creek, to just more than forty meters above sea level, led to the settlement, indicated as Nnängo in Figure 1.1. I make this site, in view of period French cartography, at 0°06′01.8″N 9°43′22.1″E.[3]

Here, among the Myene-speaking Agulamba of the so-called Mpongwe, Sarah Wallis Bowdich, African explorer and English naturalist, bore witness to a prophecy of the world to come.[4] She heard a sign of hope for enlightenment. This at least was the gist of what she described as hyperpoetic oration—"an oratorio"—witnessed in 1817. Her firsthand accounts of the musical rite were printed in several forms and several publications before midcentury. These publications included "Sketch of Gaboon and its Interior" (1819), *Friendship's Offering* (1833), *Stories of Strange Lands* (1835), *African Wanderers* (1846), written for a mix of audiences and translated into numerous European languages as contributions to scientific, serious, and juvenile knowledge.[5] The twenty-six-year-old Bowdich was an author-scholar devoted to the "discovery of Africa." John Keats described her as a "beautiful little sylphid woman."[6] Alexander von Humboldt and other servants of global enlightenment at the Institut de France knew her well. Georges Cuvier "received her as a daughter" at the Jardin des Plantes in Paris during several periods of intensive study in the early 1820s, where she had access to his extensive library and collections.[7]

Bowdich was also a pianist.[8] In middle age, she frequented one of the most highbrow musical circles in Europe. The diary of the wife of Ignaz Moscheles records her as a regular at the composer's home in London, a haven for Anglo-German conversation, listening, and music-making. In 1832 Charlotte Moscheles described Bowdich as a "constant visitor at Chester Place" and "keen enthusiast for good music [who] took pleasure

FIGURE 1.2. Mendelssohn's 1833 sketch in *Letters of Felix Mendelssohn to Ignaz and Charlotte Moscheles*, ed. Felix Moscheles (Boston: Ticknor and Company, 1888), 91.

in instructing and amusing the children." A year later, off Regent's Park, Bowdich introduced Henry Chorley—art critic, friend of Felix Mendelssohn, and later cult leader for that composer—into the Moscheles circle.[9] How different her depiction of deadly Gabonese air to the atmosphere of figure 1.2: 3 Chester Place, Regent's Park, as sketched by Mendelssohn that year in his godson Felix Moscheles's album. (Mendelssohn is chief protagonist of chapter 3.)

The Mission

Sarah and her husband, Thomas Edward Bowdich, "penetrated" what they called "the rudest part of Africa" aboard the *Lord Mulgrave*, a ship chartered by the African Committee of the Company of Merchants, London.[10] Their mission was enlightenment: to gather the testimony of traders and enslaved peoples in order to determine "the geography, history, language, natural resources, and the moral and local state of the nations of the interior of western Africa." "I promise," the Bowdich prospectus read, "to prove myself, as long as such a climate may spare my life, the devoted and laborious envoy of Europe, and the firm and compassionating friend of Africa."[11] The goal was "to become intimately acquainted with the interior of Africa, and to tranquillize it[—]the first great steps towards commercial intercourse and civilization."[12] This involved bringing to light the dense riverine trade routes of the interior and testing the "Congo hypothesis" (proved false) that "the Gaboon River" might veer into the Congo, and thence into the Niger and Nile. In addition, they would "collect the remains of Arabic literature as may exist only in the Occidental Dialects," Sarah's husband being a philologist of Islamicate languages.[13] The Bowdiches were among the first to claim that the languages and music of sub-Saharan Africa could be traced back to the prehistoric source culture of ancient Egypt, their quest being for the lost (Hamitic) roots of white civilization.[14]

On one hand, as historical anthropologists in the school of Belgian ethnographer Jan Vansina teach, the geographies of the estuarine world involved structures of communication that "for thousands of years" formed along pathways on the forest floor. The gridwork of stream and elephant tracks beneath the equatorial canopy traced ancient kinship lines and a "migratory consciousness," routes of migration, that in Christopher Gray's romanticizing phrase, "knew no limits."[15] This was a "poetic cartography" of teeming ethnic and linguistic fluidity.[16] For Vansina the vast canopied ecosystem of the Congo Basin, stretching from southern Cameroon past Cabinda, "remains terra incognita for the historian." Yet the *forêt natale*, "almost as large as western Europe," was no virgin source. The term "rainforest," for these writers, does little to capture the biodiversity, range of cultural repertoires, and forms of knowledge available to its myriad inhabitants. The picture of an Edenic "first world," Vansina points out, is wrongheaded, as much as the idea of "the primeval forest." Long before the "land use model," these forests—whether semideciduous, lowland, montane, mangrove, evergreen—played host to a rich network of experiential paths and temporalities. These habitats were hospitable, sustaining a dense history of long-distance interethnic alliances, dialects, and social imaginaries.

On the other hand, gridded over the free-flowing rhizome was a flat bureaucratizing order that encountered the rainforest in fear. Imposed by colonizers, this system of power-knowledge sought "tranquilization." The Bowdiches brought with them an array of territorializing instruments useful to the project—"instruments for determining the latitude and longitude of places," thermometers, barometers, chronometers, astronomical equipment, logbooks, and so on. These tools and techniques served colonizing orders of perception, ones suited to a managerial ethos of ethnic classification and surveillance. These were the practices of biopolitical government, ones that involved, not so much a way of getting about the forest, as a way of governing it—or perhaps negating it by naming names on whited-out spaces on paper. The African Committee was committed to territorialization, preparing ground, as it were, for the ownership structures of "legitimate commerce." In the era of the so-called abolition of the trade in slaves (though not slavery itself) the committee sought to open the Gabon Estuary to circulation. The imperative was to clear the atmosphere of malaria (literally, "bad air"), in ways that would open the way to latter-day arguments for rampant deforestation.[17]

The Bowdiches spent nine weeks at the Pungue, while the Africa Company negotiated the trade of a supercargo of ebony and barwood (padauk), both harvested in these forests. These "musical woods" were prized on the European market. "Gaboon Ebony" was traditionally used for black piano keys, organ stops, fingerboards, and tuning pegs for stringed instruments of the still-consolidating Anglo-German orchestra. (In 1998, the International Union for Conservation of Nature listed the hardwood *Diospyros crassiflora* as "endangered.") Meanwhile, the vermillion color and vibrational properties of barwood (*Pterocarpus soyauxii Taub*) made it useful, according to an 1843 trade magazine, for violin bows and wool dyes.[18] Across the Atlantic world, these tropical environments furnished the raw materials necessary to the establishment of pan-European musical standards. (The new Erard presented to Moscheles in 1828, for example, was likely of Senegalese or Honduran mahogany.)[19] Civilization itself was at stake. Those aboard the *Lord Mulgrave*, at least, committed themselves to opening the territory to trade, after which such firms as Bristol's Richard & William King or Hatton & Cookson could at once meet market demand and serve the need for clearing.[20]

The Gabon Estuary had been a "cloak" for English slavers, pirates, and traders since at least the 1770s. It was normal for maritime adventurers to suffer protracted stays at the site the Bowdiches termed "Naängo."[21] Now disappeared, this one-street settlement still prospered because of its strategic access to both offshore Atlantic and inland trading empires. At least half of its five-hundred-strong population were purported enslaved persons in 1817, though the definition of the slave subject at the estuary remains a topic of scholarly dispute.[22] By the time the Bowdiches arrived, the Mpongwe coastal trading aristocracy were loath to get their hands dirty. Instead, as foreign tradeships docked, local custom was to trigger a chain reaction of mediations with interior groups, first with peoples Bowdich erroneously named (after local disinformation) Kaylee/Bakele. These middlemen—the Bowdiches thought them "cannibals"—in turn allegedly exchanged goods, women, and the enslaved further inland with the so-called Adyumba on the basis of the *ewonjo* or the *ropi ñ'osaka* (that is, the "head" or "price of a slave"). Historian Henry Bucher claims that this trading chain reached back and forth along the great Agulamba-Bakele-Adyumba caravan routes toward the Ogooué, the Poubara Falls, and Samkita.[23] The Bowdiches, according to later accounts, were "first to direct attention to the importance of the Ogowe or Ogovāwai, as [Bowdich] calls that river, which he expressed a wish to explore."[24] It was alongside this river (discussed in chapter 6) that Albert Schweitzer would establish his medical mission. This "heart of darkness"—Schweitzer's Ogooué—was a site where ideas about "the humane" were fraught, and where humanitarians would work out what it meant to be human.

The White Man's Grave

The rainy season was imminent when the Bowdiches landed. Sarah recalled the moment when "our thermometers, after the mercury had risen to 124° Fahrenheit, in the shade, were unfortunately broken." The white visitors began to die. Only weeks before entry at "the Gaboon," malaria had killed Florence, the Bowdiches' infant daughter. Now within the estuary proper, the first mate of the *Lord Mulgrave* succumbed in Sarah's arms "after five days fever," she reported, "while I was in the act of putting medicine within his lips." "A common sailor soon followed," she wrote, and "the hand of death was evidently laid upon our carpenter," who died on the voyage home.[25] Thomas, Sarah's husband, was killed "by land breezes" six years later during another journey to the African tropics. While making astronomical observations off the coast of what is now Banjul in the

Gambia, the thirty-year-old agent for the Royal African Company died suddenly. Stranded several weeks from home, Sarah Bowdich was left shouldering her husband's debts and three children (Teddie, Hope, and Eugenia) thus forcing her to make her living as a writer and essayist on the London literary market.[26]

The red mangroves [*Rhizophora mangle*] and "thick black stagnant liquid" spawned the most dangerous atmospheric environment known to Enlightenment man. This "white man's graveyard," so later named, was pathologized by European science, even after the chemical isolation of Andean "quina-quina" (quinine) by French apothecaries in 1820. "We are in the midst of His wonders," wrote Sarah Bowdich, "these glorious trees, in their silent majesty . . . reared their gigantic heads as if to say. *We live in splendour and beauty, where man cannot even breathe* [her emphasis]."[27] The silence of forest bespoke suffocation. "From the sickness which prevailed on board the vessel, the climate must be very insalubrious," Edward Bowdich observed, "the density of the atmosphere from exhalation [being] even more oppressive than the heat."[28] In white mythology, malaria—not yet understood as a mosquito-borne infection—was viewed as a contagion borne of the sin-soaked moral climate. The stench of evil and slavery, so heavy in this air, was thought to cause it. According to miasma theory, the forest mangrove wall presented a historical barrier that buffered the temperate winds of European civilization, the white spirits of free trade, and the saving power of circulation.[29]

The myth of the hostile jungle worked to explain African resistance to civilization. "The whole ludicrous nightmare of rainforests as a dump for the rejects of humanity," Jan Vansina memorably argued, was born of "environmental racist determinism."[30] Yet, in the 1810s, in the minds of such naturalists as Sarah Bowdich, the imperative to cure climate, particularly in the torrid zone, was a biblical injunction. "Wherein in time past ye walked according to the course of this world, according to the prince of the power of the air [Satan]," it is written in New Testament Ephesians: "the spirit now worketh in the children of disobedience."[31] According to scriptural law, the aerial realm—air itself—was the domain of Satan, though the Christological promise was that sanctification was near. Though these environments were death zones (where humanity was at its limit), the Bowdiches lived in the expectation of as much the abolition of slavery as the abolition of climate. The evangelical hope was that environments could be overcome, and that (in the last days) the children of Africa might break free from their physical and moral enslavement to the elements.

Journey and Arrival at Ngango

Sarah Bowdich's description of the approach to the village of Ngango/s'gaDgo—also George's Town—is typical of the ways in which the African explorer penned herself into being. "No jungle grew so near the water," Bowdich wrote, "and the straight and mighty trunks, visible to a great distance, and the gloomy stillness of the dark vistas, conveyed the idea of some vast cathedral."[32] She wrote of fabulous sights on the Remboué, including "oysters growing on trees," stories about a mountain to the east made of diamonds, and anthropophagist hordes just beyond the swamps. Informants told her that the "Kaylee," then supposedly inhabiting the mountainous forests northeast of the estuarine shore, fed not only on their prisoners but also on their dead: it was said that "Kaylee" fathers also consumed their own children.[33] Historians know that Mpongwe speakers spread unlikely myths about cannibalism to protect their trade monopoly. The disinformation campaign worked to deter white traders from engaging with either the "Bakele" or northern shore groups (in ways that eventually failed), as well as vice versa, deterring rivals from direct contact with the white spirits from across the sea, who had been known to eat those they enslaved.[34] François Ngolet expertly identifies the "Kaylee," "Kele," or Bakele as an ethnicity fabricated by Europeans in service of the colonial project. The Bowdiches were the first to "create" the Bakele in 1819, misled by their informants, the name deriving from the Ongom verb *U-kelekwe*, which means "suspended." Ngolet notes that Bakele means "those who are suspended, those who no longer have roots" and that these communities, attracted to the coast by the Atlantic slave trade, had lost their connection to a precolonial Ongom consciousness to the east.[35]

Though Ngango has long since been swallowed by the forest, and no longer appears on postcolonial maps or satellite images, in 1817 its "well-constructed houses of [*raphia*] bamboo [were] thatched with palm-leaves, and most of them decorated with carved doors, painting with red and yellow ochre."[36] Its single street stood in an elevated clearing on top of a hill above high mangroves, "an air of comfort and neatness pervading the whole," as Sarah Bowdich put it. A crown of tall and ancient trees, seen from some distance off, marked the location.[37] Since the 1790s, the wealth of the settlement owed to a prosperous trade with English, French, American, and particularly Portuguese and Spanish slaveships bound for Cuba and Brazil, as the center of the slave trade moved south to avoid antislavery patrols.

According to the Bowdiches, the chief trader at Ngango was Rassondji,

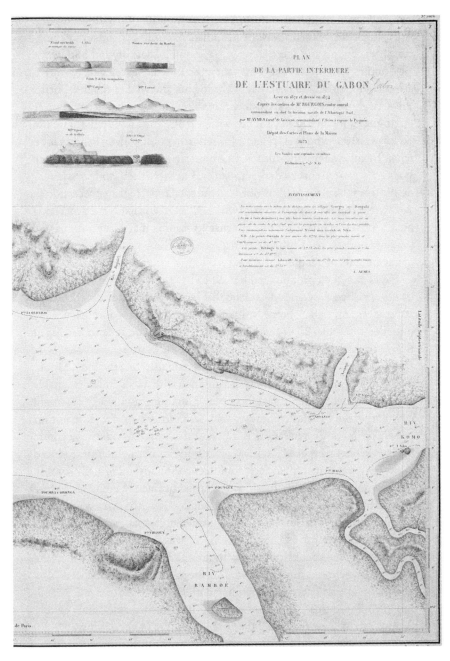

FIGURE 1.3. Map detail showing the precise location of the village "Georges"/ Ngango (below Pte. VIDJOUÉ at the mouth of the Ramboé/Remboué), the nearby Georges Creek or Avazza, and a picture of a prominent tree to the top right ("Arbre et Village Georges"); "Plan de la Partie intérieure de l'estuaire du Gabon" (Dépot de Cartes et Plans de la Marine, 1875). © The British Library Board, H.F.SEC.8.(3414).

a businessman complicit in Euro-American transatlantic trading empires. At Ngango, cargoes had always been human. According to the seventeenth-century accounts of Olfert Dapper, slave traffic allegedly ran both ways. Rassondji's predecessors at the estuary, the Bowdiches alleged, imported as well as exported the enslaved.[38] During her stay in 1817, Sarah reported the arrival of at least six slaveships: one French, two Spanish, and three Portuguese, including a schooner with a Black crew led by the "mulatto Yellow Gaston" who was "richly adorned with gold."[39] Even by the 1840s, when Ngango was on the decline, an American missionary named William Walker estimated that traders shipped two to three thousand persons annually from the estuary. Two-thirds of the total reportedly passed through settlements on the south shore, of which Ngango was likely the processing post. Given this history, it makes sense to assume that many who passed through here were eventually transported to the equatorial Amazonian environments of chapter 4.

Sarah Bowdich pronounced herself to be "the first white woman that had ever visited the Gaboon," a claim that served the market for "encounter anthropography" back home.[40] The inhabitants at Ngango were anything but encounterable. Their firsthand knowledge of Europe far outstripped European knowledge of the Pungue. Multiple European languages—English, French, Spanish, Portuguese—were in use.[41] At the time, Mpongwe speakers built sixty-foot vessels equipped with masts and sails capable of carrying eight to ten tons of cargo and up to eighty men.[42] Rassondji may have been bedridden in ways that Sarah interpreted as a sign of his people's climatic degeneration. But he had also traveled widely as a youth, having visited Liverpool.[43] At least two Mpongwe-born traders introduced to the Bowdiches had spent their adolescence, for upward of eight years, in France—one, named "Richard," being raised in Caen.[44] French furniture and European dress was common, as when the Bowdich party was greeted by the brother of Rassondji, in a long brown greatcoat and a cocked hat. Known to the English as "Tom Lawson," he was the same trader who historians speculate spent twelve months around 1769 being educated at the Catechizing School of the Society for the Propagation of the Gospel in New York City, "as part of an understanding with English slave traders."[45] Sarah Bowdich found this "Governor" to be "mild," "respectable," and "gentlemanly," in ways that frustrated the "encounter" arc of her narrative.[46]

The Performance

Sarah's opportunity to describe "first contact"—reenforcing the claim to her husband's "genius"—arrived on the evening of their first overnight stay. On the night, a terrifying thunderstorm broke overhead ("with a fury unknown out of the tropics"), and a twilight creature appeared to Sarah Bowdich. Having agreed to hear music that evening, she witnessed a miracle: and an instrument now stereotypically associated with the autochthonous spiritual traditions of the "first people." After a meal at Lawson's (with knife and fork at table), a musician was brought into "the middle of the room, which was lighted by a large torch stuck upon a pole, and composed of sweet-smelling gums tied up in palm leaves." Bowdich identified the musician as enslaved: a "homme de bois" reportedly acquired by Rassondji during wartime. In his hand, the singer carried an eight-stringed *ngombi* harp, which the Bowdiches would be among the first Europeans to study. It was an instrument of "full, harmonious, and deep tone." (As early as 1620, Michael Praetorius had printed an image of a comparable "Indianische" instrument—here seven stringed—in his giant three-volume *De Organographia*.[47]) The *ngombi*'s anthropomorphic design was typical of what later-century French-American explorer Paul Du Chaillu (who came of age at Libreville) would call "a monstrous and indecent figure of wood of the feminine sex."[48] The resonator represented a woman's body, the soundboard her skin (covered in goatskin), the soundhole her sexual organ, the neck her spine, and the strings her intestines. Its form tallied with descriptions made by leading ethnomusicological authority on the instrument, Pierre Sallée (see figure 1.4).[49] Sarah Bowdich, who inspected and later played the *ngombi* for an eavesdropping local audience, was fascinated. "The figure head, which was well carved," she wrote, "was placed at the top of the body, the strings were twisted round long pegs, which easily turned when they wanted tuning, and, being made of the fibrous roots of palm wine tree." "Both [the musician] and the harp," Bowdich alleged, "came far from the interior."[50]

Bowdich described the musician as a *nègre blanc*, adapting the language of enlightenment raciology. The so-called albino (a bowdlerization of a Portuguese term and only adopted in France in the 1830s) presented a challenge to prevailing European race-and-climate theories. The harpist, she claimed in one account, was "the most hideous and disgusting form which had yet met my gaze, accustomed as I had been to scenes of horror." In another Bowdich story, the musician surprised her on first entry to Ngango's elevated clearing, suddenly appearing beneath a great hilltop tree "enwreathed with Ipomeas in full blossom" as if the Edenic Tree of Life.[51] "The tree was covered," she observed, "to a great height with large convolvuli [plants traditionally associated with fecundity in Gabon], of every kind of hue." (This was probably the sacred pearwood *Adzap Baillonella toxisperma*, as indicated in figure 1.3, the tallest tree in the forest.)[52]

FIGURE 1.4. Anthropomorphic harp (*ngombi*); Gabon, Tsogo- or Lumbu-speaking peoples; early twentieth century; wood, hide, pigment, metal, nylon strings; 27 x 7 x 22 inches. Collection Neuberger Museum of Art, Purchase College, State University of New York. Gift of Lawrence Gussman in memory of Dr. Albert Schweitzer; 1999.06.39. © Jim Frank.

Ngangans told Bowdich that the musician had been captured at a river location (Mondah?) amidst an ocean of mountain systems to the northeast. Informants named this place "Imbeekee," marked on period maps as Imbiki/Mbiki/Imbékie and "two days journey" from "Kaylee."[53] (As seen, the harpist was likely supplied to Rassondji by Ngolet's ethnicized Bakele.) Though the Bowdiches avoided speculating about white tribes somewhere in the interior, they nonetheless related the musician's origins to a "whiteness" at the heart of the forest. "There are people inhabiting a mountain [at "Imbeekee"], Edward Bowdich reported, at a site of plentiful ivory inhabited by "a people that are said to see best in the night time, when they travel and work, sleeping most of the day, because the light hurts their eyes."[54] According to the writings of Malpertuis, Buffon, and others, that mythic albino race retained the vestiges of an "original whiteness," the idea being that all humans were originally white, and were indeed still born white, their complexions darkening after exposure to the corrupting powers of air. As Voltaire put it of Malpertuis's position, "Blacks are a race of whites blackened by the climate."[55]

All "unsightliness" was forgotten once the harpist-singer sat down to his instrument. Bowdich heard a "rapid and perfect succession of chords, from a sweet-toned harp" and registered her astonishment "as the music increased in beauty." The performer began with what Bowdich described as "a low recitative, as if to preface what followed," using his "melodious and powerful" voice.[56] What came next was difficult to transcribe. Bowdich could only offer what was told to her. In a musical journey, the harpist progressed from a lament for the death of a mother, to the protest of a man led to execution, to the imitation of the call of a forest woodpecker. It was "a rhapsody of recitative, of mournful, impetuous, and exhilarated air," she wrote, "wandering through the life of man, throughout the animal and vegetable kingdom for its subjects, without period, without connection, so transient, abrupt, and allegorical, that the Governor of the town could translate a line but occasionally, and I was too much possessed by the music, and the alternate rapture and phrenzy of the performer, to minute the half which he communicated."[57] The musician, to recall Vansina, chose paths of imaginative expression that Bowdich found inexplicable. This was the "hyperpoetry," according to Sallée, of a migratory consciousness: the improvised oratory of a fluid network of languages and dialects, metrical overlays, and shifting ostinatos.[58]

With pen and paper, Sarah Bowdich—it must have been her rather than her husband—notated a music without measure. Figure 1.5 reproduces a latterly published transcription of "Notes Sung by the White Negro from Imbeekee." On the voyage back to England, the Bowdiches likely gathered an earlier transcription into the manuscript for *Mission from Cape Coast Castle to Ashantee*, a book printed in 1819.[59] Sarah stowed a guitar and piano aboard ship, which likely assisted.[60] Kofi Agawu, in his *The African Imagination in Music* (2017), hails these Bowdich transcriptions as the first in European history to deal not only "with the external morphology of instruments" but to record actual "musical elements." Agawu notes the multipart thirds and fifths of Akan music in particular, evident in their published notation of Asante and Fante airs as well as the music of the

42 CHAPTER 1

FIGURE 1.5. T. Edward Bowdich, "Notes sung," *Mission from Cape Coast Castle to Ashantee* (London: John Murray, 1819), unnumbered page between 448 and 449. The Bancroft Library, University of California, Berkeley, DT507.B67.

seperewa, or harp lute.[61] Sarah Bowdich herself expressed skepticism, not merely with her own transcriptions but with the act of textual transcription itself. When figure 1.5 was printed and reprinted after 1819, it was always alongside the disclaimer that the task of sonic inscription was impossible, since "every notation must be far inadequate."[62] This song, she admitted, resisted European attempts to reterritorialize it.

Narration I: The Breath of the Forest

There are multiple ways to narrate this performance. One way would be to adopt a "rainforest acoustemology," after Steven Feld, and interpret the rite as an emanation of the spirit of the forest—even as the first music of the forest.[63] If Sallée and ethnographers of the so-called *Bwiti* cult are correct, what Sarah Bowdich witnessed was an invocation of the sacred wind that purportedly first animated the world. Sallée speculates that the Gabonese *ngombi* was originally forged in encounters between the aforementioned Bakele, forager Baseke, as well as other "bush peoples" (that is, so-called Pygmies). Bowdich herself sourced it deeper within the forests, among a mythic white tribe of "Mbiki." (Without mentioning albino tribes, in 1853, missionary James L. Mackey described the "Mbikoo" as a "scattered" people of once-numerous nomadic "bushmen" decimated by the slave trade and roaming "a belt of country from the Muni southward to the Gaboon" in the area of the Noya River.[64]) Whatever the source from whence it sprung, the *ngombi* of "Mbeekee" was held, by white travelers, to awaken the spirit of the forest.[65]

In more local myths, according to the oral tradition of Tsogo-speakers, inland peoples now intimate with the harp, the instrument originated with Ngolet's "suspended" Bakele, the same "forest people" whom Bowdich thought "cannibals." For Sallée, the evidence of "the music itself" suggests the truth of Kele origins. The disenfranchisement of these now near-extinct "anthropophagists," who have supposedly inhabited these forests for millennia, he suggests, is audible in the death motives and sadness of traditional harp-song lamentation. Sallée quotes the nineteenth-century explorer Du Chaillu, who marveled at the "almost always plaintive airs" of a "savage and treacherous people."[66] The sounds of the mythic harp, for Sallée, conjures something of the dying spiritual traditions of an always-already threatened existential ecology.[67]

In this narration, that pole in the center of the room incarnated the aboriginal Edenic tree, by which, according to *Bwiti* genesis myths, the "first people" descended to earth. These *batwa* were "the people that fell from the sky."[68] The arch of the harp was made from the flexible wood *kuta*; the aerial cords of the *roang* (*géoko*) palm and the resonator of the *raphia obanza*. Its strings, extended upward, formed a metaphorical umbilical cord connecting earthly men, who imagined themselves as tenants of the forest, to the higher life forces that sustained it. In terms of the narratives of *Bwiti* genesis myths, the harp vibrated with sounds attuned to an unimaginably potent acoustic ecology. The energies emanating from her resonator were a narcotic, inhaled with the psychoactive fumes of tree barks to produce altered psycho-physical states, characteristic of *ngombi* initiation rites.[69] The sounds of this instrument were intoxicating, apparently, in that they at once drew upon and awakened the verdant power of the living rainforest.

The term *Bwiti* has multiple meanings.[70] According to precolonial historian and linguist Kairn Klieman, ethnographic evidence suggests that *Bwiti*-inspired "initiation societies" originated in the forest world of peoples called Bakele (or Baseke). The esoteric cult of *Bwiti* is now recognized as one of the three official religions of Gabon, practiced there by the late-arriving Tsogo-speakers, having purportedly been birthed among "suspended" Bakele and other "forest people." It may be defined as a set of practices dedicated to the veneration of first-comer ancestors or spirits of the land. One meaning, Klieman writes, might be derived "from the standard reconstruction of [*-yìtí] as a proto-Bantu noun meaning "tree" or "medicine.'" Also possible, the term *bwiti* (from *bu-yiti*) means "the one/spirit/entity who calls." In this sense, the musician-visionary invoked the creative powers of the ancestors, by stirring the sexual entrails of the *ngombi*.[71]

Thus the anthropomorphic sculpture that Bowdich saw carved into the resonator of the harp (as in figure 1.4). To extrapolate Klieman's argument, in *Bwiti*-derived mythologies, the female form of the instrument bore the breath of life, while her bloated belly bore procreative pneumatic power. The first ancestor and "mother, origin of all things," her large belly and cheeks were no abstraction. They symbolized the blowing out of air, evoking associations "between breath (wind, air) and the original creation, for many Central African genesis accounts consider human life to have been engendered through the sacred breath, or 'wind' of God."[72] In *Explorations and Adventures in Equatorial Africa* (1858), Du Chaillu printed an image of a "Harp of the Bakalai [Bakele]." This Kele harp was an angular instrument without the humanoid carving upon its shoulder. The image appeared above a detailed description of a life-size wooden idol of a "cloven-footed" woman venerated at the large Bakele center at Njali-Coudié (near modern-day Ivanga). Du Chaillu reported that this fetish with copper eyes—a statue with "one cheek painted red, and the other yellow"—was named "Mbuiti."[73] No doubt he meant for his harp to be an object charged by a similar spirit, this forest site being "a sacred place, one that houses ancestral and territorial spirits that serve as intercessors to *-yambé, the 'first spirit' and 'first creator' of all things."[74] The sounds heard at Ngango in 1817, according to these intrepid travelers, emanated from deep within the interior. They originated among the swollen-bellied "first men."

Narration II: Transatlantic Sounds

A second way to narrate the harpist-singer's performance suggests withdrawing from the "sacred trees" and returning to the open trading waters of the estuary at Ngango. Here, at the edge of the swamps, the musician's "extraordinary vociferations" appear less an inspiration of "deep forest" origin than an act of allochthonous Mpongwe creation. Our second narration imagines "transatlantic sounds," human trafficking, and sonic circulation oriented around a powerful trading empire centered at Ngango.

In 1851, the aged Rassondji himself offered an oral history of his coastal people to yet another American missionary: Rollin Porter. Porter painted a picture of inexorable decline since the heyday of Rassondji's father. Not long ago, Porter alleged, "the Mpongwes lived far back in the bush; and it used to be thought that if one of them saw the salt water, he would soon die."[75] The first occupants at the Estuary, according to Porter's Rassondji, were the "Divwas"/Ndiwa, who were reportedly extinct but for a single individual living with Tom Lawson.[76] Like Ndiwa speakers, Mpongwe groups were purportedly also dying out by the 1840s, as were Seke peoples, who had "literally sold themselves out as slaves." Indeed, according to Porter's colonial account, every wave of race flooding in from the vital interior had succumbed—one by one—to the same climatic-degenerative state.[77] The swamps purportedly drained these once noble ethnicities of their virility, or so Porter claimed. The European slave trade was a likelier cause.

Yet if the Bowdiches were critical of the Ngangan's capacity for "indigenous music," this "deficiency" owed little to climatic conditions. Rather, it was the "inferiority" of coastal latecomers and the ways in which they revitalized *Bwiti* myth to advance the politico-religious concerns of the white man's commerce. The Bowdiches, in fact, claimed that Mpongwe speakers themselves were only musical to the extent that they forced subordinated peoples to make music for them, coastal music being "very inferior to that I have noticed before."[78]

Our second (and no less problematic) narration imagines that the poetic cartography established at Ngango was not animated by the earth spirits of *Bwiti*-inspired practice, as invoked by the myth of forest-dwelling autochthons. Instead, it recounts, after Klieman, that in *Ombwiri/Mwiri*-inspired societies, late-on *batwa* were water spirits (often coded white) understood to inhabit estuaries, creeks, rivers, lakes, ponds, and oceans.[79] For Klieman, the powers of ancestral water spirits arose among coastal settlers as a way for men like Rassondji to legitimize territorial precedence. The movements of these white spirits, in other words, functioned to animate ethnic linkages along the flow of oceanic trade routes radiating toward and outward from Ngango. To maintain triangular flows from Europe to the Americas, new creation stories were required to discriminate those who owned the land from those who had been marginalized from it. As such, coastal aristocracies invented an aboriginal *Bwiti* mythology in order to establish kinship systems useful to the relational structures of slave exchange. According to "a principal of precedence," late-comer populations throughout sub-Saharan Africa separated themselves from imagined "first-comers," that is, those who took precedence over the environment because their ancestors were buried in the land first.[80] An appropriation of the powers of "the first men," proved vital, not only to coastal genesis myths but to coastal acts of circumatlantic world-making.

More than this, Klieman claims, groups engaged in ocean trade imagined *batwa*, not in the abstract, as wooden figurines or invisible spirits of the forest. Instead, "the people from the sky" were personified. Klieman cites a process of ideological "rejuvenation" by which *Bwiti* sources were transubstantiated in the politico-religious terms of *Ombwiri/Mwiri* institutions— the prefix "om-" generally denoting embodied persons. Thus a new cast of flesh-and-blood subjects was birthed into the world: "creatures of the air" to be enslaved, bought, and sold to British, French, or Portuguese plantation masters. Thus the humanoid anthromorphic harp (figure 1.4)—as opposed to the plain Kele harp (figure 1.7)—so characteristic of late-comer *Ombwiri/Mwiri* practice. The word *batwa*, that is, became a stigma affixed to individuals and groups absorbed, or better invented by resident latecomer populations. The bodies of "bush peoples" were reimagined as a kind of "detritus" to be harvested from the interior. True, disenfranchised individuals were feared for their deep spiritual knowledge. True, they were afforded special powers, charged with mysticism, and granted a spiritual birthright to the environment. Yet they were also enslaved by client Mpongwe speakers, ostracized, and driven to the inner reaches, which is to say that these "forest" or "Pygmy" people were always-already mythic, even as they were invented. These fugitive beings were at once human and nonhuman, gods and commodities, according to the synoptic genesis narratives of how the world came to be. By this account, the musician described by the Bowdiches and the female figure emerging from the sacred harp were spiritually charged in equal measure. At Ngango, both were *batwa*.

The harpist-singer that appeared before Sarah Bowdich, in this second narration, was the means by which "big men" expropriated the "enchanted power" of the perifluvial forest. Rassondji, who owned the musician as "slave" (according to Bowdich), represented a new type of chieftainship produced at the Gabon Estuary in the era of transatlantic slavery, a wizard-like figure (complete with bell) who evoked authority, not only by a ritual appropriation of the powers of territorial spirits, but by literally taking possession of their bodies. In *Ombwiri/Mwiri* ideology, it should be emphasized, *batwa* came from an unspecified interior. These nomad musicians were without fixed genetic or geographic location. The designation *batwa* might refer to marginalized individuals as diverse as infants born breach or with the umbilical cord around their neck, children who left missing limbs in the netherworld, twins, individuals with sexual bimorphism, those with dwarfism, and, of course, persons with albinism. At once feared and fetishized, these marginalized subjects were absorbed into "late-comer" cosmologies that served the territorial imperatives of circumatlantic trade.

According to Sallée's informants, these white spirits habitually made their presence felt both in the sounds of the *ngombi* harp and the rush of wind on a waterborne pirogue, a dugout not unlike the one that bore the Bowdiches to Ngango. The shape of the "sacred harp" itself, in the terms of a genesis myth recorded at the coast by Sallée, was an analogy for the "pirogue of life." In *Ombwiri/Mwiri* oral tradition, the shape of the pirogue, thus, could be associated with the shape of female sexual organs, while the wind symbolized "the original animating force or 'breath of God.'" It was in a vessel such as this that the first humans were supposed to have journeyed to "the landing stage of world."[81] Certainly, if you exhibit the *ngombi* on its back, it can resemble an ocean-going boat, as in the nonanthropomorphic example pictured in figure 1.6.

In her vocal transcription reproduced in figure 1.5, Bowdich inscribed these "landings" perfectly, taking note of a cadential "leading phrase" or "sentence" (as she called it) that finished each "strain." (I take the descending scale of our eight-string *ngombi*, in her transcription, to be

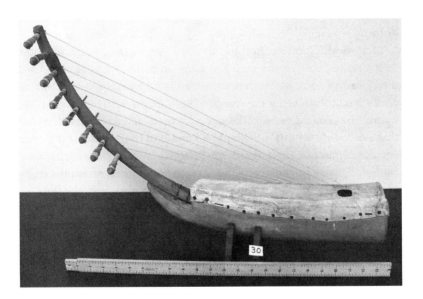

FIGURE 1.6. *Ngombi* harp collected by Albert Schweitzer and gifted to Maurice Kessler, fellow Alsatian, scholar of early instruments, and professor at Oberlin College Conservatory, before 1927. Roderic C. Knight Instrument Collection, Oberlin College Conservatory of Music, Knight-Revision Classification C42.13. From the Roderic C. Knight Musical Instrument Collection, Oberlin College, http://www.oberlin.edu/library/digital/knight.

E_5-D_5-B_4-A_4-$G(\#)_4$-$F(\#)_4$-E_4-D_4, following Sallée's theorization of an overlaid D and E bitonal system with "neutral thirds.") Note, for example, the cadential figures: the repeated descent to G in the first measure of the second system, and the four cadential turns (A-B-G) ending the "presto" phrase and repeated three times in the "andante" before the "long rapid recitative." These stopping points exemplify what Sallée, awkwardly, calls a *cadence conclusive*, by which he means a concluding formula attaining resolution on strings 2, 4, 6, and 8 of the harp. The remaining odd-numbered tones of the eight-stringed instrument, meanwhile, help the singer toward less decisive resting points: the *cadence suspensive*. The fermata achieved in the first system of figure 1.5 achieves such suspense. Sallée is rightly reluctant to associate the periodicity of this galant style—this improvised ethnolanguage of tension and rest, motion, and arrival—with Iberian syncretism or some "ancient Luso-Congolese source."[82] The presence of these Euro-African schema, for Sallée, shroud the genealogy of these "labyrinthine" harp-songs in mystery. The point, for Sallée, is that this musical language is waterborne in provenance. In this tradition, he writes, these cadential arrivals mimic "the action of the wind on the pirogue which, wind from behind, is carried upright and straight ahead [*cadence conclusive*] or, blown to the side, must tack [*cadence suspensive*]."[83]

Oratorical accounts of how the first men were birthed, Klieman writes, "often relate that humans were 'delivered' to earth in a pirogue, usually traveling on a current of water (amniotic fluids) and shepherded by a sacred wind (breath being the source of life)."[84] The very category of "the human" was vouchsafed for "those that journey," and narrated in the ways that evidently swept up an enraptured group of travelers on that stormy equatorial night in 1817. Here, in the rhetorical sweep of the harp sounds were stories that bound diverse listeners to maritime relationships reaching at once deep into the riverine interior and far out across the sea.

Narration III: White Genius

A final way to narrate this performance would be to plumb white mythologies, exploring systems suitable to colonizing orders of perception and domination. The whiteness of this "creature of the air," for the Bowdiches, misplaced him as a genius. In their view, he was tragically ill-adapted to the climatic terrors he was subject to. His displacement, for Sarah Bowdich, manifested itself as a divorce of sight from sound. The reported unsightliness of his body vouchsafed the beautiful purity of his music. One is reminded of the paradigmatic "our kingdom is not of this world" essays by Beethoven-devotee E. T. A. Hoffmann, written around 1813. "Orpheus's lyre," Hoffmann famously observed, opened the portals onto an "unknown realm, a world that has nothing in common with the external sensual world that surrounds him, a world in which he leaves behind him all definite feelings to surrender himself to in expressible longing."[85] One could cite Moscheles, touring Vienna in the year of the Bowdiches' sojourn at Ngango, who hailed the well-traveled Mendelssohn in his diary as a "young genius" and "one more prophet."[86] In 1817, Londoners commonly lauded Handel for his "originality" in drawing "all his stores from nature and from the force of his own genius, and was indebted to no one either for his style or his thoughts." The "genius" of Handel's music, the writer trumpeted, was most audible in the *Messiah*, since "all creation seems joining in the general chorus, and in strains of rapturous adoration; chaunting Hallelujahs and Hosannas, to him who sitteth on the everlasting throne."[87]

In white mythology, the spirits of genius were migrant and nonterritorial. The harpist-singer appeared, in this sense, as a spirit lifted out of time and space. "He was wholly abstracted," Bowdich confirmed, "from all around during the execution of his compositions."[88] That is, the terrible isolation of this "maniac," as Bowdich called him, was a sign of his heroic resistance to contingency. His whiteness was a relic of "original whiteness," and an indication of his isolation from the wretched effects of a long climatic enslavement. That isolation explained his deep immersion in the astonishing music. This vestige of the ancient world, as such, wielded his harp as a weapon against the forest.

It was Ptolemy, in first-century Alexandria, who first heralded a "pale, night-dwelling people living on the African continent."[89] Even in 1817, the existence of these people was still in scholarly dispute. A text published under the auspices of the Bowdiches' mentor in Paris scoffed at the myth of a white tribe in the deep equatorial interior, preferring to medicalize albinism as a pathological disorder in modern style. Yet even Cuvier-endorsed "Supplemental History of Man" (1824) blamed "the albino's" supposed hyper-sensitivity to light on a deficiency in "the coloring principle." (The clinicalization of albinism as a modern disorder, although it worked to free the condition from climatic explanations, advanced medical claims that something was wrong with hypopigmentation.) "Hence we find the eyelids of these people generally closed," one Cuvier disciple wrote, "but in twilight, dusk, or even a close approach to darkness, they see remarkably well."[90] The received wisdom was that their eyes were either possessed of a convulsive motion, or seemed to be "fixed in their heads, like people that lie a dying." Sarah Bowdich observed that the eyes of the harpist at Ngango seemed "small, bright, and of a dark grey" in one version but also "small and blue, and from seeing imperfectly in the daytime, they were constantly blinking, and had a vacant expression [since] his vision was imperfect in the light." "The light seemed to hurt [his eyes]," she explained, "and their constant quivering and rolling gave his countenance an air of insanity."[91] The eyes of the musician betrayed the extent to which he was out of place in the torrid zone. At the foot of the tree of life, the harpist-singer agitated against vitality itself.

Enlightenment science, that is, construed the *leucaethiop* (an eighteenth-century transliteration of Pliny's *leucæ Æthiopes* or "white Ethiopian") as deathly. "Pale as dead corpses," the influential *Encyclopédie* entry read, "their eyes are gray [and it] is said that they see only in moonlight like owls." The analogy to "bats and owls" was partly derived from Dapper, who also compared their flesh to "the skin of a dead corpse." Their eyes seemed to be "fixed in their heads, like people that lie a dying," Dapper alleged, which allowed them particularly keen night vision by "moon-shine." The *homo nocturnus*, according to enlightenment consensus, came into their own by night, taking bloodthirsty revenge on those who persecuted them by day. White anthropologists devoted to monogenesis and the unity of man seemed drawn to these myths. "Notwithstanding their being thus sluggish and dull in the day-time," went one old story quoted by such abolitionist ethnologists as James Cowles Prichard (1813), "yet when moon-shiny nights come, they are all life and activity, running abroad into the woods, and skipping about like wild bucks, and running as fast by moon-light."[92]

These twilight stories and fables were remarkably persistent. As late as 1861, French Navy officer and explorer Jules Braouezec printed a map indicating the country of "nomadic albino tribes named Bakouï" across the Crystal Mountains. He claimed to have seen "two or three" of this "small-sized people," who were called Akowa by the Mpongwe, and had "woolly red hair and eyebrows, albino color eyes, and pale yellow skin."[93] (The terms "Akowa," "Bakouyi," "Bakoya," "Baka," as well as a host of related names, are now generically affixed to a people designated as Pygmies.)[94] It is revealing that these white autochthons were invented first and in ways contiguous with the later "invention of the pygmies ... as a distinct racial category and then as a global substratum or frozen moment in human physical and social evolution."[95] An "albino paradigm," here, elides uncomfortably with a "pygmy paradigm" such as to buttress narratives about development, genesis, and Hamitic myths about original whiteness.[96]

Sarah Bowdich was struck by how the harpist, blinking against the world, seemed to push past the affordances of the musical instrument in his hands—how he transcended its crude materials. She heard universal Handelian genius:

> The running accompaniment served again as a prelude to a loud recitative, uttered with the greatest volubility, and ending with one word, with which he ascended and descended, far beyond the extent of his harp, with the most beautiful precision. Sometimes he became more collected, and a mournful air succeeded the recitative, though without the least connection, and he would again burst out with the whole force of his powerful voice in the notes of the Hallelujah of Handel. To meet with this chorus in the wilds of Africa, and from such a being, had an effect I can scarcely describe, and I was lost in astonishment at the coincidence. There could not be a stronger proof of the nature of Handel, or the powers of the [musician].[97]

Bowdich, that is, heard an oratorio, and a powerful argument for monogenesis: common ancestry, original purity, and whiteness. Here, at the beginnings of the Eurocene, is a mythology confident in the belief that the climate could be overcome. Such was their hubris—these roving white spirits of the Atlantic.

Conclusions

In myths still told, the *ngombi* harp marks the beginning of things. This was the instrument of the ancient world, whether born of the life-giving equatorial forest, "luso-congolais" (as in deriving from the precolonial Bavili court of Loango where Pechuël-Loesche was later engaged), or archaeologically rescued from the white dead-zone of ancient Egypt. It is often said, by those studying harp morphology and migration, that this southwestern-most example of the African harp belongs to an antediluvian family of arched lyres that can be seen in the pictographic rock art at the Ennedi Plateau in Chad and the Tassili n'Ajjer cave paintings in Algeria, as well as many even more antiquated Egyptian sources. Though they were never explicit about it, the Bowdiches clearly associated the *ngombi* harp, not only with *leucæthiopia*, but with the white-stoned necropolises of ancient Thebes on the Nile.[98]

The white genii of European music composed their own elaborate archaeologies of lyric genesis in Africa. Inspired by the excavations and writings of Napoleon's Egyptologist Guillaume Villoteau, Hector Berlioz famously introduced a "Theban harp"—"whose origin is lost in the mists of time"—into the trio for two flutes and harp played at Sias in the Nile Delta in *L'enfance du Christ* (1854).[99] Talk of Thebes brings to mind the onstage harps in the airless final scene of Verdi's *Aida* (1871), as well as many other orientalist depictions of suffocated antiquity. Figure 1.7 shows Gabriel Fauré strumming a Kele *ngombi* harp of exactly the sort described above, his long-suffering wife Marie looking on. Graham Johnson relates the photograph to Fauré's arrangement of a twenty-one-hundred-year-old song "discovered" during excavations at Delphi by archaeologist-philologist Théophile Homolle (the arrangement's dedicatee), and published as the *Hymne à Apollon* (1893–94), for voice, flute, two clarinets and harp.[100] Richard Taruskin reprinted the image in his *Oxford History of Western Music* above the caption "Gabriel Fauré with his wife, Marie, playing a reconstructed Babylonian harp (March 1883)." More accurately, this is a non-anthropomorphic Ongom (Kele) harp.[101]

Evocative of life as much as death, the *ngombi* harp has been found to be "the root of all popular music." This genesis myth is extraordinary. The literature seeking the true source of the blues in West and Central Africa is abundant and long-standing (Charters, Olivier, Evans, Coolen, Wald to name a few).[102] Gerhard Kubik's account blames the concept of "the blue note" on Erich von Hornbostel. Specifically Kubik names Hornbostel's transcriptions of phonograph cylinders brought back from the Gabonese forest in the wake of the Lübeck-Pangwe [Mpongwe] Expeditions of 1904–1909, and his publication "Musik" appearing in *Pangwe: Völkerkundliche Monographie eines westafrikanischen Negerstammes* (1913).[103] Kubik argues that the idea of the "blue note" dates back to at least 1925; but it was Hornbostel's concept of "neutral thirds," he claims, that most informed later academic constructions of the blues.

Kubik's idea is that Hornbostel's "neutral thirds" spawned "blues" discourse thirty years later, specifically in the writings of Arthur M. Jones on "Blue Notes and Hot Rhythm," Alfons M. Dauer (1955, 1958), and Kubik himself (1961).[104] (Kubik now prefers to seek the genealogy of a "blues" mental template in the "West Central Sudanic Belt.") An early demonstration of Hornbostel's concept occurred in the commentary to figure 1.8—a Gabonese "Harfenlied mit Chor. Spieler und Vorsänger" transcribed from a phonograph recording made during the 1907 Lübecker Pangwe-Expedition. Hornbostel noticed the independence of harp accompaniment from the vocal part, which is why he set the piece in two simultaneously sounding key signatures. Note the dissonance caused by the very first notes of the transcription. Hornbostel ascribed the cause of this continuously repeated dissonance—A naturals in the harp ostinato versus A flats in the choir—both to "polyphonic thinking" and to "neutral

FIGURE 1.7. Gabriel and Marie Fauré at Pruney. Fauré holds an Ongom (Kele) ngombi harp. Source: gallica.bnf.fr / Bibliothèque nationale de France.

thirds" tunings. Kubik later argued that Hornbostel's mishearing was due to period ignorance of "equiheptatonic scalar systems." In the same text, Hornbostel identified harps played in Gabon by late-arriving Fang speakers (see chapter 6) as the "descendants of the ancient Egyptian instrument that had penetrated farthest to the southwest [in Africa]."[105] Thus out of "more natural" divisions of the interval of the fifth, popular music was born. And it began, so this myth goes, in sounds that originated in the Gabonese forest.

I have invoked proto-blues discourse, but only to show how much the harp, which Sarah Bowdich saw under the hands of a master musician, provided common ground for multiple stories of cosmopoietic birth. In the three narrations outlined above, the performance of the harpist was

FIGURE 1.8. Hornbostel's transcription of a harp-song in "Musik," Günter Tessmann, *Die Pangwe* (Berlin: Wasmuth, 1913), 351, 329.

said to mediate the life-giving breath of the forest, the embodied *batwa* of transatlantic ritual, and the lost spirits of dissevered white genius. The master musician not only stirred up feelings of dependency or resistance in relation to disputed territories, but also called into question the very spiritual condition of those territories.

Talk about metropoles and peripheries fail in this context. This milieu was ever, to adapt Mbembe, "the nuclear power plant from which the modern project of knowledge—and of governance—has been deployed."[106] In a so-called "post-slavery era," abolitionists such as Bowdich fixated on the Gabon Estuary less for its human than for its environmental potential. The invention of ethnic categories, after Bowdich, only meant to "tranquilize" this climate further, since such narrative identifications established rules for its possession. Yet, pace myths about the lost souls of white genius, there is no such thing as empty space, as plotted so neatly on colonial maps. There is no nonideological background "out there" awaiting scientific disclosure. Neither is there some prediscursive global background providing one atmospheric infrastructure for the circulation of multiple cultural narratives. The geophysical erasure of such potent slave sites as Ngango notwithstanding, equatorial Africa was always a standing resource for Euro-American capital and wealth generation. Hidden in plain sight, the archive preserves, in stories told of the Orpheus of Imbeekee, evidence that the force of lyric genesis was always strongest at the center. It was here where the earwitnesses gathered at

Ngango traded kinship alliances with each other. It was here where competing narratives circulated amidst struggles over transatlantic patterns of exchange, mutual enrichment, alterity, and domination. It was here where power structures and divisions of labor were imposed, where the scale of ecological and economic exploitation was set, and where empires formed.

CHAPTER 2

A Falcon under Glass
Paris, France, 1838

Biopolitics begins in an enclosed structure.
PETER SLOTERDIJK, "A Crystal Palace"

Two Cases

In an 1838 article for *Revue de Paris*, François-Henri-Joseph Castil-Blaze recounted an anecdote about the excised larynx of Brigida Banti, then preserved in a glass bottle at a museum in Bologna. Those who remembered the furor caused by the Lombardic singer during the 1778 season in Paris, Castil-Blaze suggested, would also know the compass and range of the object. It was the same instrument for which Haydn had written his 1795 dramatic aria "Berenice, che fai?" for London's King's Theatre. But it was in Paris, Castil-Blaze wrote, that the talent of the great singer had been discovered. The story went that Jacques de Vismes stumbled upon this daughter of a humble Venetian gondolier on the street. Banti was an untrained singer, "gifted with more genius than science," when the director of the Académie royale de musique heard her performing outside a café on the boulevard du Temple. Exposed to the public, her success knew no bounds. By her death in Italy on 18 February 1806, Banti was so famous that her outsized larynx would be bequeathed to the Bolognese Academy of Sciences. "This organ, precious instrument of the *cantatrice*, of an extraordinary amplitude, phenomenal," Castil-Blaze explained, "was enclosed in a jar."[1]

Around the time that Castil-Blaze put pen to paper, also in Paris, Cornélie Falcon, the creator of Valentine in Giacomo Meyerbeer's *Les Huguenots*

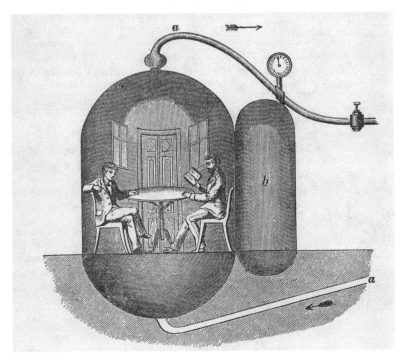

FIGURE 2.1. Paul Louis Tissier, "Tabarié's Pneumatic Chamber," *A System of Physiologic Therapeutics*, ed. Solomon Solis-Cohen, 11 vols. (Philadelphia: Blakiston, 1902–1905), X:90.

(1836), entered the interior of a giant glass sphere. The early life-support system or *bain d'air comprimé* (compressed-air bath) was built by Emile Tabarié, childhood intimate of the father of the sociological sciences Auguste Comte, as well as leading technologist for several of the first fully artificial climates and heating and air-conditioning systems. In addition, the chemist-engineer masterminded the emerging metropolitan fashion for luxurious aerotherapeutic establishments.[2] The exact circumstance of the enclosure of the French dramatic soprano in Tabarié's sphere is difficult to surmise. What is known is that Falcon experienced serious physical difficulties with her voice in 1837 and that the original "sphere de Tabarié" was erected in Chaillot and then transported to Montpellier before being rebuilt again in Paris, on the rue de Pyramides. Also in 1837, Charles-Gabriel Pravaz, the same Montpellier physician who hired Frédéric Chopin as instructor of "perfectionnement de piano" for his Institut orthopédique near the Bois de Boulogne, constructed the largest "compressed air bath" then in existence.[3] The first reports of Falcon's enclosure under glass appeared at the time of Castil-Blaze's rumination on Banti's embottled larynx.

FIGURE 2.2. "Chambre aéropiésique," in Arthur de Bonnard, *Description des Néothermes, et relation des principales guérisons obtenues par l'emploi des appareils médicaux de toute nature établis dans cette maison de bains et de santé* (Paris: Pollet, 1842), 8. Source: gallica.bnf.fr / Bibliothèque nationale de France.

La Cloche-Tabarié was a "pneumatic chamber" approached through a series of anterooms. The interior was fitted out with all the domestic accoutrements of a private boudoir: festooned with carpet, walls upholstered in leather or silk, writing desk and couch, books, papers, other reading and writing materials, and even musical instruments. A writer for the *Journal des débats* reported in March 1839 "that the apartment itself is not less than eight to ten feet high, with room enough to furnish a bed, a table, seats, a small piano, etc."[4] The reporter enthused that physiologists were now equipped to observe everyday life; patients, on the other hand, might be charmed by as-yet-unknown sensations. "Every precaution," according to later descriptions of Tabarié's structures, "is adopted to render the patient at ease, and to prevent all the unpleasant conceptions of confinement—to make the *séance*, in short, a pleasant and agreeable conversational gathering in an ordinary room."[5] Individual treatments, reports tell, lasted around two hours.

Tabarié's later iron-braced apparatuses accommodated up to twelve people. Falcon probably entered a more modest, copper-reinforced apartment. A steam engine supplied the flow of air while a double-acting pump and series of valves controlled the degree of compression. The environment was regulated at a distance by a male engineer, who found that when Falcon started singing, her extinguished "middle voice" flickered back into life when the mercury barometer rose above twenty-eight pounds per square inch and evaporated again when it dipped below.[6] Other reports confirmed the extent to which the life of Falcon's *médium*, or middle register, depended on the requisite atmospheric pressure. Théophile Gautier went so far as to allege that during the day, the "biting copper" timbre sounded effortlessly. But at precisely five o'clock every evening, presumably as the air thinned, the voice's sonorousness—"argentine like a glass harmonica"—dissolved.[7] Tabarié's artificial atmosphere, that is, filled in for an organ that was no longer there.

Tabarié's moment of glory came in 1838, when he presented a paper at the Academy of Sciences on the "effects of variations of atmospheric pressure on the surface of the body." His report described the effects of compressed air on "greater or smaller surfaces of the body." And he introduced several medico-therapeutic apparatuses, detailing the technology that restored Falcon's voice.[8] Tabarié's work caused enough of a stir to attract the attention of the most powerful scientists in France, including François Arago, the surveyor for the Bureau des Longitudes in Paris being an expert on the thermometric state of the globe. (Alongside Jean-Baptiste Biot, back in 1806, Arago had measured the weight and density of atmospheric air relative to that of a mercury.) The natural philosopher went so far as to submit a report detailing Tabarié's "dome of glass" to a March 1839 meeting of the Academy of Sciences. The scholarly concern, for Arago, was to address the relation of meteorological matters to questions of public hygiene and the sciences of man.

Prestige structures like Tabarié's were all the rage in 1838 Paris. Singing experts, including professor of "vocalization" at the Paris Conservatory Auguste Panseron, were enthusiasts. When Berlioz, himself suffering from bronchitis, visited Nicolò Paganini in the wake of a December 16, 1838, concert at the Conservatoire, he did so at the Etablissement hygénique des Néothermes at no. 48 rue de la Victoire. (Falcon herself lived at no. 17.) At least one of Tabarié's spheres was installed in situ.[9] When Paganini was resident at the Néothermes, Berlioz met the violinist in the air-conditioned billiard room. "This man-eater, this murderer of women, this ex-convict, as he's always been called," recalled the composer, could communicate only through mute gesture, due to a throat infection that would eventually kill him.[10] Paganini's residence at the temple of air-pressure therapy (*aéropiésie*) meant to heal his aphasia by "the application of vapors."

The Néothermes stood near the Opéra, on the site of the old Théâtre-Olympique. (The street has been renumbered, but the ornate wrought-iron back entrance of the "Bains Chantereine" still stands at 39 rue de Châteaudun.) The bathhouse was finished in 1830, where "during winter," the prospectus boasted, the beau monde might avoid "exposing themselves to the exterior air."[11] Its central attraction was a glass-covered gallery and air-conditioned arcade, designed by polymath, chemist, and authority on theatrical sanitation Jean-Pierre-Joseph d'Arcet. D'Arcet was the brother-in-law of Alexandre-Étienne Choron, music historian, choral pedagogue, briefly general manager of the Paris Opéra, and founder of the Institution royale de musique classique et religieuse. Parisians knew d'Arcet for his work on the salubrity of urban theaters, including the Salle Le Peletier.[12]

The Salle Le Peletier—the Opéra—was in fact turned into a pneumotherapeutic hothouse under d'Arcet's supervision. The chemist, who had been elected to the Academy of Sciences in 1823 and had worked for the Comité consultatif des arts et manufactures under the Ministry of the Interior, conceived labyrinthine systems of "steam heating." He also formulated the first study of the "sanitation of theaters" in Paris, publishing his findings in that important inaugural volume of population and economic statistics, *Annales d'hygiene publique et de medicine legale* (1829). His report on theatrical ventilation was commissioned by the Conseil d'Hygiène publique et de Salubrité. The council, the first of its kind, was founded in 1802 under the city's prefecture of police. D'Arcet thus spearheaded what Alain Corbin identifies as a social movement devoted to "purifying public space."[13] He conducted research on safe materials related to theatrical fire curtains and mine ventilation. He also researched the health risks of tobacco, public latrines, and bath houses, while conceiving safe methods to exhume Napoleon's body. His reports added to the almost five hundred documents a year received by the council between 1802 and 1848—reports that addressed diverse concerns related to factories, cemeteries, abattoirs, prisons, prostitution, water provision, sewage, policing, and theaters, not to mention disinfected city streets. The mountain of paperwork solicited by the council laid the foundation for biopolitical forms of public governance, as well as for the monumental volumes of sociological research by Adolphe d'Angeville, Louis-René Villermé, H. A. Frégier, and Alexandre Parent-Duchâtelet.[14]

The Opéra, following on from d'Arcet's success in the disinfection of the nearby Paris Stock Exchange (1826), was powered from within by a central heating infrastructure (or *calorifère*), first installed in 1822. A "complete system of steam-engines" beneath the amphitheater eventually humidified the house by means of twenty-four hundred pipes and shafts coursing through the foyer.[15] Ingeniously, d'Arcet designed a smokestack above the Salle Le Peletier, which took advantage of the heat of the illuminated chandelier-luster to discharge bad air through the central dome of the auditorium, as figure 2.3 shows. In addition, d'Arcet oversaw the installation of gas lighting systems at the Opéra in 1822 for the production of Isouard's *Aladin, ou La lampe merveilleuse*, and was consulted about their improvement in the 1830s. He played a pivotal role when the administration of the Opéra obtained permission in 1821 to construct Paris's first "gasometer," gas reservoir, or gasholder. Bankrolled by the July Monarchy's future minister of finance, the gasworks facility on the rue Richer functioned to illuminate the theater. It allegedly serviced some twenty-five kilometers of piping, suffusing every nook and cranny of the building by the time of the notorious moonlight ballet of Meyerbeer's *Robert le diable* in 1831.[16]

Jean-Baptiste Fressoz argues that gas advanced Orleanist political ideals under the Restoration.[17] The gasholder of the Compagnie Française d'Éclairage par le Gaz was briefly shut off after 1823 by ultraroyalists, who argued against the polluting effects of coal gas and warned of explosion. Good ventilation, d'Arcet insisted, implied life support for democracy. It meant designing technologies to support fully air-conditioned interiors with all doors and windows sealed; ideally, artificial climates were controllable at will and powered by combustion enough to continuously purify air. The campaign for coal-fired gaslighting and air-conditioning, Fressoz observes, went beyond purely aesthetic concerns. The integrity of the social order was at stake, to the extent that good politics, according to the logic of holistic medical discourse, depended on a constantly renewable supply of oxygen.[18] Certain public buildings, of course, required more diligent atmospheric regulation than most.

The Opéra was one such structure, renovated with a new ventilation system and thickened atmosphere after the July revolution of 1830. Critics were divided about the modified experience of the auditorium's dreamy interior. When the first director-entrepreneur of the Opéra, Louis Véron, a medical doctor who made a fortune in throat syrup, inaugurated his public-private enterprise, he did so with a performance of a truncated three-act version of Rossini's *Guillaume Tell*.[19] (Véron's operation benefited from government subsidy and was overseen by a committee appointed by the Ministry of the Interior.)[20] His workers installed a deep-red stage curtain and suspended giant gas-lit candelabras of opal-colored glass from each of the columns. "The parterre boxes (*baignoires* or 'bathtubs'), formerly vast and open to view," reported *Le Constitutionnel*, were "mysterious (*mystérieuses*), and reduced to the size of elegant loges."[21] Against a white ceiling and encircling the flaming-hot luster were "twelve semi-nude women or muses, elegantly draped and crowned with flowers," replacing

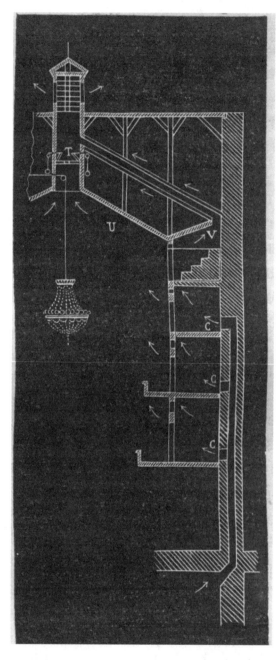

FIGURE 2.3. "D'Arcet's system," in Gaston Tissandier, "La Science au nouvel Opéra," *La nature: revue des sciences* (Paris: G. Masson, 1875): 123–26, 125.

images of the divinities of Olympia. A system of mirror reflectors heightened the media-saturated ambiance.[22] "The auditorium," wrote a correspondent for *La Gazette de France* when the Salle Le Peletier reopened for the first time, "resembles a lady's boudoir."[23] In the era of technologically rooted supernaturalism, admitted a journalist for *l'Entr'acte*, "there is nothing there except for gas."[24]

"The Opéra can no longer be a temple of the arts [but] should be a branch of life (*une succursale de la vie*)," the writer for *La Gazette de France* concluded: "It is a novelty fashion shop (*magasin de nouveautés*)."[25] And, indeed, the interior courtyard of the Salle Le Peletier opened out onto the earliest glass-covered Parisian arcades. In 1823, workers completed the Passage de l'Opéra, administered by the House, which led to the old Boulevard des Italiens. In Walter Benjamin's celebrated Marxist analysis, these passages instantiated newly immersive forms of consumerism. The arcades hosted such stores as music publisher Marguerite, arms manufacturer Caron, purveyor of handkerchiefs Lemonnier, pastry chef Rollet, and the perfume shop of the Opéra. They merged the spatial idea of the salon with that of the Oriental bazaar, where the flaneur might enjoy the air-conditioned immanence of the aptly named Galerie du Thermomètre (Thermometric gallery), or the aromatic provisions of the great western arcade, the Galerie du Baromètre (Barometric gallery).[26]

Glass-and-metal endospheres increasingly enframed Parisian life. In the 1820s, these dreamy structures betrayed disciplinary infatuations with atmospheric knowledge. D'Arcet and Tabarié's innovations, besides furnishing new systems for buying and selling at the Opéra, also afforded new barometric ways to study the effects of the great aerial ocean. In the language of the period, the bringing together of the health sciences with the climatological sciences represented more than a means of sanitizing public and private space. It represented, as one expert on compressed air baths put it, a "victory over the air."[27]

The Evaporation of the Larynx

This chapter recounts the fate of an object "melted into air," to quote Karl Marx.[28] It tells the story of *the evaporation of the larynx*, or its displacement as the true organ of voice. Its objects of study are what appear under glass: in the case of Banti, a showpiece of singular flexibility; in the case of Falcon, an organism on life support. First was a hard object displayed in an airtight jar—an entity preserved in death. Second was a living organism enclosed in a hyperbaric chamber—an entity sustained in continuous atmospheric homeostasis.

So far, I have concentrated on such air structures as the Néothermes, the interior of the Opéra auditorium, shopping arcades, botanical gardens, and so forth, thematizing the kinds of fascinations indexed by d'Arcet's statistical studies of public health. Men like d'Arcet applied their infatuations—thermoregulation, reconditioning, hothousing, humidification, acclimatization—as much to the well-being of individuals as to the welfare of the entire social body. Made possible by advances in steam engineering, these air-conditioning systems served the imperatives of atmospheric science. Their purpose was to treat life in ways opposed to vitalist configurations of isolated organs as instruments to be excised, mastered, and played. It was to address more systemic or organic concerns by directing attention to the intangible problem of the environment.

Placed side by side, then, jar and chamber animate two very different visions of vocal materiality—comparative visions that overlap historically and are not easily periodized according to neat political categories (Consulate, First Empire, Bourbon Restoration, July Monarchy) or administrative regimes at the Opéra (Duplantys, Lubbert, Véron, Duponchel, etc.). Where once vocal sound belonged to a singularly spectacular physical organ; vocal sound now belonged to a bewilderingly complex media system. This is not to say that the history of vocal culture underwent a blanket phase transition from matter to spirit, corporeality to incorporeality, physics to metaphysics. To juxtapose Banti's larynx and Falcon's life (in solid and gaseous phase, respectively) is not to assume the supplanting of a mechanistic era of Italianate laryngeal display by some more dynamic model of French artistic transcendence. Such distinctions only rehearse old-hat nationalistic narratives. Rather, these cases contain two different theories for voice and two different orders of materiality, one being no more or less mechanistic or ideological than the other.

True, in the case of Banti's larynx, the object of vocal understanding was a singing tube or *tube à chanter*.[29] But the artifact itself was eloquent by dint of its powers of extension, or at least was so when the great performer on the larynx—Banti—still controlled it.[30] In the case of Falcon, by contrast, vocal expression (coded female) depended on the remote application of air pressure (coded male). Here, atmospheric intensity and force of breath governed all aspects of vocal production. In the world of thoracic and diaphragmatic support, the imperative was no longer to target the vocal organ and its movements. Instead, it was to manage breath, which is to say the degree of compression above and below the glottis. Subject to continuous decomposition and recomposition, the larynx was regulated according to a myriad of thermodynamic values. The body part itself was ancillary to vocal function.[31] For such midcentury voice scientists as François Achille Longet, who cast doubt on the theory of "sound pipes" ("la théorie des tuyaux sonores"), the earliest pressure-puff conceptions of voice relied on fluid mechanics, as well as ideas of "sonorous waves," "flows of gas," and "periodicity." If there was a exemplar for this new appreciation for atmospherics, it was either Charles Cagniard de la Tour's double siren (which he proposed as a model for voice in 1840), or Tabarié's pneumatic machine.[32] The vocal folds, in these systems, fell under the physical government of air pressure, according to the principles of what was later called the "Bernoulli Effect."

The atmospheric frame would prove life-changing for such singers as Falcon. Here was a form of "no larynx" vocalization, where singing meant far more than the display of corporeal prowess. Far more than a skill, singing was a living process. And her art involved a practice without a tangible object of study. The expressive capacities of the *artiste* hinged on more than fabulous manipulations of some extraordinary organ. Rather, her genius hinged on external factors. Falcon's artistry, in short, was an effect of her relation and adaptability to unseen conditions. The measure of her prowess was how she coped: with the salubrity of the air, the crushing weight of audience expectation, institutional demands, the authority of published scores, the intentions of the composer, the contingencies of gender, the nervous electricity of her own body, stage fright, conceptions of voice type, and so on. The pressures were endless. Subject to stresses and strains too numerous to name, she was plunged into the drama of a natural and spontaneous event.

One way to interpret Falcon's vocal predicament would be to imagine Tabarié's sphere as a metonym for the bourgeois structure of human interiority, a structure built in service of the authority of "the milieu." The very concept of *milieu*, a reading of Leo Spitzer suggests, owed to the prominence of such structures. Spitzer relates a three-stage historical process wherein the word "milieu" shifted from its origins as a laboratory concept (denoting "the media in which experiments with bacteria-culture were carried out") to its modern usage as an article of faith. In its second stage, for Spitzer, the term denoted a physical "surrounding element" as "that which surrounds," in ways that only ever referred to organic beings, not inert substances. Only in the 1830s did the word bend to modern sociological understandings, by indexing "the total ensemble of exterior circumstances, of whatever sort, upon which the existence of a given organism depends."[33] No doubt the naturalization of this latter sense of "milieu" informed the atmospheric obsessions described above and spurred the investment in such contraptions as Tabarié's sphere.

King Louis-Philippe himself adopted the neologism *juste-milieu* as the watchword for his political reign in January 1831—a "golden mean" located centrally along a right-left axis between "the tyrannical despotism of sovereigns [and] the despotism of the multitude."[34] The politics of the just milieu proved particularly favorable to such liberal royalists as Pierre Paul Royer-Collard, who feared the despotism of absolute monarchical rule as much as the tyranny of revolutionary violence. Hercule de Serre, Victor de Broglie, Pauline de Meulan, and François Guizot, to name only a handful, felt the same. The prestige of Royer-Collard's doctrinaire philosophies, even in the lead-up to the 1830 Revolution, expanded the cause of those elites arguing in favor of moderation at any cost. The anti-extremists worked to achieve "balance" by endorsing only those governmental measures as would prevent change. For those devoted to the nonpartisan status quo, the best path to homeostasis was to commit to political toleration and "middle of the road" compromise, while also investing strategically in the most indecisive leadership money could buy.

Jan Goldstein expands on the political utility of *juste-milieu* indecision in her *Post-Revolutionary Self*, wherein she describes the ostensibly noninterventionist style of government incubated under the July Monarchy. She quotes Victor Cousin, high priest of the period's eclectic political philosophy: "I ask, when everything around is us mixed, complex, commingled, when all the opposites live and prosper together, if it is possible for philosophy to escape the general spirit."[35] The imperative of Cousinian metaphysics, Goldstein explains, was to engender forms of subjection where the private environment of the "individual" was sacrosanct. In question, here, is the effort to shape "that intangible, even ethereal thing called a self," by the practices of aesthetic contemplation, silent reading, or listening quietly to music.[36] She describes Cousin's project to construct this "entirely interior world" by reorienting politics to the pedagogical institutions of soft power—colleges and schools, theaters and shopping arcades, hospitals and asylums, factories and clinics, music conservatories and hyperbaric chambers. Cousin himself envisaged a politically moderate citizenry wherein subjects "voluntarily inserted" themselves into an "entirely interior world of introspection." "The psychological method consists in isolating oneself from any other world but that of consciousness," explained Cousin in 1826, "in order to establish and orient oneself there, where everything is real but whereas reality is exceedingly diverse and delicate."[37] The plan was to engineer social environments that acted not so much to outlaw political dissent legally as to ameliorate political tension through a process of "de-politicization."

In his *Urbanization of Opera*, meanwhile, Anselm Gerhard describes the *juste-milieu* concept both as an index of the ideology responsible for "no touch" forms of sociopolitical government and as a formulation useful to understanding the indecisive heroes of Meyerbeer's period-defining grand operas. Notably, Gerhard situates Meyerbeer's characterization of Robert in *Robert le diable*, Raoul in *Les Huguenots*, or Jean in *Le Prophète* in view of their consistent refusal to act. These vacillating heroes, Gerhard writes, "know nothing of what is going on around them" and seem bereft of "absolute principles" of any sort.[38] Gerhard cites Victor Hugo's preface to *Cromwell* (1827) to explain why these characters appear so will-less. "The drama," Hugo urged, "should be radically impregnated with the color of past ages; it should permeate the atmosphere in such a way that we only realize that we have changed centuries when we enter or leave the theater."[39] Hugo's ideal was that the audience should feel themselves under pressure, confused by historical milieux beyond their understanding and equivocating, like Meyerbeer's protagonists, in the midst of it.

The triumph of the aerotherapeutic movement, to conflate the summative analyses of Benjamin, Goldstein, Gerhard, and Foucault, was a sign that power was now exerted not by and through violent rule but by and through the powers of aesthesis. Hyperbaric chambers, grand opera, glass-covered arcades, and centrist government suggest that the behaviors of individual bodies (including excised vocal apparatuses) were best controlled by attending to the general structures wherein those individual bodies breathed.[40] In Foucault's account of biopolitical reason, the governmental strategy was less to quell dissent by the theatrical display of punitive legal power. Under the banner of the disciplines of public hygiene and political economy, instead, power worked to manage the life of restless populations by inventing more invisible systems of coercion. The strategy of the political elite was to shift surveillance from disciplining the body to statistically studying and regulating its entire field of operation.[41]

The very roundness of the Cloche-Tabarié suggests the extent to which the tempering powers of the *juste-milieu* mattered under the doctrinaire compromise—how much the discourses of wholesome physical, mental, and social equilibrium won out. On one hand, the engineer's "dome of glass" could be interpreted as a technology of inclusion. The glass seemed to promise political openness, transparency, and a perfect egalitarian atmosphere. (If ever there was an airtight model for social justice, this was it: from the outside, the interior appeared "open to all.") On the other hand, Tabarié's sphere was a sphere of privilege, allied with bourgeois efforts to stratify the urban populace into a series of strictly partitioned domains. Indeed, the Cloche-Tabarié was a "container structure," developed at once to incubate political conduct tout court and to segregate elites from the moral and physical pollution experienced by Parisian underclasses. The building without walls framed the experience of liberal autonomy according to the closed logic of total political containment. In situ power—subtle yet pervasive—operated in the most immaterial and yet tyrannical of ways.

The Instrument of Cinti-Damoreau

A very different system of enclosure occurred in the case of Banti's larynx, the difference being that any renewal of the oxygen supply would, necessarily, cause decomposition. Banti's organ was one among many remarkable synthetic objects of vocal display identified in pedagogical and scientific discourse on singing technique. The idea that the voice was a conical wind instrument was ancient, but also surprising durable, persisting deep into the nineteenth century and beyond. No less an authority than Georges Cuvier, the French naturalist who mentored Sarah Bowdich (see chapter 1), compared the vocal organ to a flute, imagining the glottis as the mouthpiece, the mouth as the body or tube, and the nostrils as lateral openings. His opinion drew not only upon the research of Denis Dodart's influential early eighteenth-century account of this amazingly divisible woodwind instrument of 9,632 parts, capable of at least 300 sounds within the octave. Cuvier incorporated the more up-to-date research of acoustician Félix Savart, who argued in 1825 that the ellipsis formed between the vocal cords formed an adjustable aperture that directed the passage of air.[42] The number of artificial larynxes—of rubber latex mostly—constructed in this period betray similar theories. For Félix Despiney, writing in 1822, the vocal tube was trombone-like, its remarkable extendability and contractility following the rise and fall of the larynx in the throat. The mobility of the organ accounted for the fact of vocal range, as well as the basic instrumental capacity for pitch modification.[43]

The century's most celebrated and influential scientist of singing was spellbound by Banti-like larynxes. Manuel García *fils* was so fixated with the larynx, so keen to see phonation live, that he constructed his patented laryngoscope. In the celebrated *Traité complet de l'art du chant* (1847), he marveled at how "every passion, however subtle its shade, affects the vocal organ individually, modifying its power, its conformation, its tonicity, in sum, its entire physical character." "The organ is a mold," he eulogized, "transforming itself incessantly according to the action of a myriad passions, and communicating the imprint of said actions to the sounds that it shapes."[44] García's earliest 1840 publications enumerated the diversity of forms this magnificent cartilaginous object was capable of. "Any modification in the timbre of a sound has its origin in an analogous variety of the internal disposition of the tube that conveys the voice," García argued in the first previews of his treatise (which appeared in *La France musicale*): "For, if a flexible larynx can undergo a subtle and infinite number of modifications," he continued, "it follows that minute differences of sound multiply to infinity."[45]

A close reading of García's work reveals that the larynx was conceived, in his view, as the *fons et origo* of voice. Airs were dispensed, he taught, by delicate threads of tone. These were molded into delicate aerial forms at the slit of the glottis. The practice of spinning out the sound—*filare la voce, filar il tuono*, or in French *filer la voix, filer le son*—was key to any beautiful cantilena. The *son filé* (or spun-out tone), so named "because the note is evenly drawn forth from the throat like the thread from the distaff of a spinning wheel," led the phrase.[46] Guided by the poetic thought, the glottis widened and narrowed to form air currents, which could be aimed hither and thither by an expert practitioner. These currents were threaded through an *embouchure* and directed by skilled manipulations of the membranous cone. In the "Italian" school of García, vocal mastery hinged on the laryngeal mobility necessary to shape what he called "sonorous rays." The pharynx, as well as nasal and oral cavities, in their turn, were "reflectors or modifiers of sound." The singer forms the instrument, García explained, "such as to direct sonorous rays (*les rayons sonores*) against the bony portions of the palate and to reflect these rays in the direction of the hinge of the mouth, which forms the sound and improves emission."[47] This was a vision of singing that had nothing to do with atmospheric theory. Airs, for García, were made, not given; music, by definition, was a variety of air.

As late as 1866, Edouard Fournié—builder of artificial larynxes— echoed García in hailing the agency of the organ: "The larynx possesses a special table of harmonics; but, even so, it is distinguished from other instruments by this remarkable fact: that the resounding cavity can modify its form and dimension according to every note emitted. It is a marvelous phenomenon, one which art has never been able to imitate! Each note corresponds to this particular table of harmonics in ways that secure the scale degree with exactitude and clearness, which is an adaptation that is not dependent on the will of the singer."[48] For such larynx-only theorists, every aspect of the harmonic art depended on the instrument—on its size, shape, and flexibility. The organ was no morbid appendix. Long associated with revolutionary, youthful, liberal, and Italianate ideals, the wandering larynx was in fact the alpha and omega of vocal study. The fabulous thing literally made airs, weaving vital spirits into the world in ways that validated the necessity for the audiovisual display of the most remarkable of them.[49]

Here follows, then, an "it-narrative" about the larynx (to borrow the story label typically affixed to eighteenth-century "circulation novels" that followed the fortunes of a singularly quirky commercial object), belonging not to Banti but to fellow soprano and close friend of Cornélie Falcon, Laure Cinti-Damoreau.[50] The biography of her instrument supplies a welcome foil for the heavy atmosphericism and psychologism soon to be associated with Falcon.

Cinti-Damoreau's larynx—more delicate than Banti's—was never displayed in an air-evacuated glass bottle. Yet critics hailed the instrument of this prima donna as "the most marvelous organ ever afforded since there were singers in the world."[51] Castil-Blaze went so far as to imply that this thing inaugurated the reform of French song more conventionally associated with the revolutionary arrival of Rossini in 1825.[52] The organ of this "singer on the larynx" (*joueuse du larynx*) was adaptable enough to flourish at the Théâtre-italien, Académie royale de musique, Théâtre national de l'Opéra-comique, and (later) on the concert stage.

These were the most expensive pipes in France. At Cinti-Damoreau's 1826 debut at the Opéra, in Louis-Sébastien Lebrun's *Le Rossignol*, her fee was already 25,000 francs per year. By 1829, that figure had ballooned to 44,200 francs, over 12,000 beyond that of her closest rival. "Have you ever fixed your eyes on a diamond which reflects a thousand refractions of a thousand different colors?" asked Léon Escudier of her scintillating vocal style: "The eye is dazzled by a myriad elusive forms; it cannot analyze; it falls into ecstasy; it admires without thinking; but when the glare subsides, when the vision evaporates, the soul is warmed, the spirit exalted, and you are filled with enthusiasm by this magical effect of nature."[53] Writers often resorted to metaphors of commercial exchange to describe the unmatched splendor of her embroideries (*richesse dans ses broderies*)."[54]

Cinti-Damoreau's was "the most agile larynx ever formed in nature" borne by the "most perfect cantatrice yet born to France."[55] Fans hailed her grace and the finesse of her impeccable diction. "Accuracy, softness, charming flexibility, she unites these in one, and sums it all up," exclaimed one aficionado, "she is the most perfect ensemble."[56] Docility was as much a feature of her delicate organ as of her person. For Maurice Alhoy, writing in his *Biographie dramatique*, a tiny publication no larger than a deck of cards, she was a "pretty little thing, who has a pretty little voice, a pretty little face, a pretty little foot, a pretty little waist."[57] Enthusiasts extolled her suppleness (*souplesse*), aerial arabesques, detail, and smallness.

This singer was never so atmospheric a *creature of the air* as Cornélie Falcon was. "Talent had come to her," Escudier explained, "as it would a nightingale."[58] The avian trope was commonly applied in descriptions of her person. As Mary Ann Smart has shown, Cinti-Damoreau excelled in *oiseau* or bird idioms, a speciality displayed best in such episodic lyrical flutterings as Béringer-Mompou's celebrated romance "Si j'étais petite oiseau," or "Dès l'enfance les mêmes chaînes" from *Le Serment* by Auber.[59] In this repertory, her organ divided, multiplied, and took flight, as in Marguerite's bathing aria "O beau pays" from Meyerbeer's *Les Huguenots*, with its famous flute introduction.[60] The singer seemed light, filled with air, and apparently in possession of a double syrinx. "The very breath of Madame Damoreau is sort of a song," exclaimed Escudier, "since the smallest accents of her voice carry a simplicity, a grace, and a charm that caress your ear as on the breeze."[61] Ornithologists of this period, indeed, were only just beginning to discover the extent to which their preferred objects of study depended on air. The bones of the feathered race, the pioneering research of Petrus Camper showed in 1803, featured pneumatic cells and hollow pockets that filled with air during acts of respiration.[62]

Cinti-Damoreau's critics were insistent. "Charming nightingale, warbling with grace and method, she pairs well with the flute of Tulou [who was flautist at the Opéra]," wrote Pierre Hédoin, "whilst cutting words into two, into three, such that often not a single syllable makes it to the ears of her listeners!"[63] Berlioz muttered that Cinti-Damoreau "sings like the flute of Tulou; unfortunately, she wants to play a concerto, and the ornaments slip out, so to speak, unwittingly. True, they are always perfectly charming, but in such original music, these vocal frolics are nonetheless the cause of unspeakable torment."[64] "We await action," huffed Berlioz's friend Joseph d'Ortigue, while Cinti-Damoreau "sings to us of streams and fêtes, nightingales and warblers, whilst echoes of love reverberate over and over again in the mountains."[65] Idealist critics like Berlioz and d'Ortigue *would* complain. The aerial qualities of Cinti-Damoreau's style posed a threat to the atmospheric purity of the sacred musical art they claimed was only just coming into view.

Cinti-Damoreau's style—particularly her way of "filating" breath—was especially a matter of dispute when it came to her performance in Rossini's *Guillaume Tell* (1829). For critics writing in *Courrier des théâtres*, for example, the *romance*, "Sombre forêt," especially written for Cinti-Damoreau's act 2 entry, was spun out too much in aria style. In Rossini's opera, an amorous Austrian princess, Mathilde, has just managed to separate herself from her hunting party; she frantically awaits her lover (the Swiss peasant revolutionary Arnold) in the high-altitude forests of Rütli. The princess knows that her love object is nearby and listening, as she reveals in her recitative. She goes so far as to call for him—"Arnold, Arnold, is it really you?"—over seductive D-flat-major brass harmonies.

It was at the downbeat to the *andantino*, Cinti-Damoreau's antagonists felt, that her melismatic display shaded into harlotry. The folksy introduction to the romance proper is accompanied by a wheezing A-flat drone marked *forte*. Moreover, Mathilde's vocal entry is announced by the showiest of introductory devices: a drumroll. Mathilde, in other words, far from singing spontaneously to the forest as her words suggest ("Sombre forêt, désert triste et sauvage; je vous préfère aux splendeurs des palais"/ "Dark forest, savage and sombre wilderness, I prefer you to the splendor of palaces"), was seen to be making a crass sexual exhibition of herself. For her critics, this scene staged the scandal of a princess flirting with a thirteenth-century Peeping Tom in the most whorish of ways. Figure 2.4 illustrates how to manage breathing while performing such spun-out melodies. (García's *Traité complet de l'art du chant* tended to relegate the whole question of "the breath" to detailed explications of "half-breaths."[66]) Rossini, here, appropriated Cinti-Damoreau's style to suggest a princess roaming the Swiss mountains in search of a peasant boy—or so male critics fantasized.

The figure shows how the princess brought the romance to a climax, having spun out the *melodie lunghe, lunghe, lunghe* of her opening four

FIGURE 2.4. Note the proliferation of "half breath" indications, in García, *Traité complet de l'art du chant*, 2 vols. (Paris, 1847), II:21. Source: gallica.bnf.fr / Bibliothèque nationale de France.

lines. Mathilde reaches her high note (A-flat) by repeating the phrase "my heart." After the "respiration entière" (full breath) at the end of the excerpt, as annotated by García, things heat up. Having dutifully dueted with a solo clarinet, Mathilde casts naturalism aside, noisily insisting, over and again, that "only the forest shall know my secrets." The final syllable of "secrets" announces a fortissimo tutti and the full return of D-flat major. The princess's indiscretion could not be more brazen; and indecency gathers as she launches into a series of gratuitous cadenzas. Several sources surviving from the nineteenth century supply *points d'orgue* for these improvisations. Austin Caswell reproduces only five of Cinti-Damoreau's patented variants for the final cadence of each strophe, in ways that hint at her circuitous lines of flight.[67] The naïve way to think about these "echoes and reverberations" is to imagine them merging with the soundscape of the Swiss countryside—ricocheting across mountains and forests. Yet few contemporaries, when they heard Cinti-Damoreau, were convinced they heard anything so wholesome.

Critics lampooned the erotic display. Mathilde was "a still-born princess," according to one author.[68] She was "a parasitical personage," in the words of another, peripheral to the work itself. *Le Constitutionnel* called the princess "futile" and scoffed at her taste for republican farmboys. Several writers lambasted the ridiculous love pairing, which mutilated historical fact in the name of the obligatory amorous tryst. One journalist blamed Mathilde on Rossini's librettist, Étienne de Jouy. "There is nothing more ridiculous than to see a princess jumping precipices," he scoffed. "In *Guillaume Tell*, Mathilde is just as badly conceived and has the same morals," the complaint continued, "assuredly, at the Opéra, M. Jouy is fond of sluts [*dévergondées*]."[69] For all the antagonists, it was beyond the pale that the daughter of the emperor of Austria should be sexually attracted to the son of a common laborer.

"They have the voice, the musical knowledge, an agile larynx," Berlioz lamented of *dévergondées* like Cinti-Damoreau, but "they are lacking in soul, brain and heart."[70] The singer's larynx, in other words, was sexually profligate and the display of it, moreover, a disgrace. Thank goodness, therefore, according to chauvinist narratives, that the age of the larynx was on the wane, and that Cinti-Damoreau's fortunes at the Opéra were on the decline, her husband wrangling with Véron over pay from as early as 1832. The arrival of Falcon (who played Mathilde at the Opéra in May and June of 1834), and the replacement of Cinti-Damoreau heralded a dramatic epistemic shift. For such male critics as Berlioz, the old Italianate spectacle was gone. An atmosphere had entered the scene.

The Atmosphere of Falcon

"That Miss Falcon succeeded Mrs. Damoreau was no easy task," wrote *Revue et gazette musicale de Paris*, "light vocalization is not her *forte*."[71] Véron's administration spared no cost to smooth the transition, launching a concerted press campaign in favor of "deep inner expression." Falcon was the archetypal *soprano de sentiment*. She was, critics observed, a product of the system: hothoused at the conservatoire before graduating to the stage of the Opéra. Véron imagined that she would bring a newly moral vision of bourgeois interiority to his productions. Though lacking facility, though shy and silent, this inspired chanteuse was not prostituted to the god of vocal display, or so they said. In the presence of such beauty, as Gautier put it, "Who cares about her voice?"[72]

Falcon was an enraptured singer, puffed as the paragon of French dramatic values. She expressed herself rather than sang, and she did so with pressure rather than line. Castil-Blaze described the Falcon organ in nationalistic terms as "a well-characterized *dessus*, a white voice and of beautiful metal, as the Italian say," observing that if her larynx lacked the agility to compete with more fashionable virtuosos, then so much the better.[73] The category—*chanteuse falcon*—became a quintessentially Gallic voice type, referring at once to a kind of *spinto* or pushed quality in the sound, combining free top notes with a dense, heavy quality in lower tones. The voice itself was an ideal: something imagined rather than real; and the archetype was defined, significantly, in terms of air pressure. That the *falcon* should disappear so soon after its appearance seems appropriate, since the myth was defined, right from its debut, in view of dissipation. It was the original atmospheric voice, one recalling the vision with which this chapter began: the fragile life of a soprano incubated under glass.

This story is well known. Falcon lost the most personal part of her voice on 6 March 1837 during a performance of Louis Niedermeyer's *Stradella* at the Opéra. One version of the legend pinpointed the precise measure at which the soprano's organ evaporated. Disaster struck during the second-act balcony scene, where the cantatrice failed to answer "Demain nous partirons—voulez-vous?" with the expected "Je suis prête."[74] Later reports alleged that the fatal moment constituted divine punishment for a sole sexual misdemeanor, carried out by an *ingénue* who was otherwise, in the words of romance that introduced her in *Les Huguenots*, "whiter than the whitest ermine" (*plus blanche que la blanche Hermine*). Another rumor held that Falcon's loss was the debt paid for the sin of a recent abortion, or the moral cost of an exhausting adulterous tryst with her future husband

François Malançon, who was still married on the tragic night.[75] Another went so far as to observe that, along with her *médium*, she had died onstage, or had at least died from the public's point of view: "Her beautiful voice stopped in her throat. She staggered and fell, as if thunderstruck. She raised herself up, [to reveal] her face awash in tears. The audience sat up too, anxious and overwhelmed—plunged into a deep and respectful silence. Mad with distress, Adolphe Nourrit [her mentor and teacher] pressed her in his arms such as to console her, and covered her with kisses as a father would his child. . . . La Falcon died tonight at this theater."[76]

The feuilletons of 1837 noted less of a catastrophe. (The facts show that Falcon continued to appear regularly at the Opéra throughout March and left to perform at Rouen in April before returning for the Parisian debut of tenor Gilbert-Louis Duprez on May 15, 1837.) One reporter who attended on the fateful night merely heard "weak sounds" before the soprano's exit.[77] Another complained that the curtain was raised again to reveal that Falcon had been replaced by Maria Nau, a Spanish-American singer who had been, in Louis Gentil's words, torn from the lesbian method of Laure Cinti-Damoreau (*méthode lesbienno-cinthienne*), with whom she studied.[78] According to Berlioz, Falcon sounded more vibrant than ever on this fabled spring evening, though her voice had mysteriously transmogrified into an intense contralto. It exhibited a "volume and timbre" particularly in "the lower cords," in ways that were "rare in France." The *contre-alto*, indeed, was an anomalous voice type under French climes, at least according to Escudier's influential assessment of a decade later.[79]

More mythic evenings followed. On March 14, 1840, after a sojourn in Naples to drink in its "balsamic and velvety air," Falcon was forced to attend her own funeral, as it were, when her comeback at the Salle Le Peletier was announced. Gautier reported that all of Paris attended. He added that, on Falcon's reentry, her physical beauty was more otherworldly than ever: "the same oriental passion of her black eyes, the same warm Jewish pallor [Gautier was convinced she was Jewish], the same melancholic oval of her beautiful face, the same abundant and superb hair, the same anxious and nervous ardor."[80] Two decades later, Charles Baron de Boigne remembered how her partisans rejoiced at the announcement of "a performance in which she was to sing the second act of *La Juive*." He recalled their fanaticism: "They believed in a miracle, in resurrection."[81] But the sound of Falcon's voice failed to materialize. At the words "O mon père!" early in the first act of *La Juive*, according to one report, "the poor girl could not overcome the emotion that so visibly tormented her; she fell unconscious into Duprez's arms, and had to be carried offstage."[82]

At the fatal moment, reportedly, "un mal de gorge universel" overcame, not just Falcon, but the entire collected assembly.[83] *Le Figaro* reported that Madame Cinti-Damoreau, observing from her box, also fell unconscious. She too had to be removed from the scene.[84] Berlioz heard Falcon's middle register asphyxiate in auscultive terms. He detected "raucous sounds like those of a child with croup, guttural, whistling notes that quickly faded like those of a child full of water."[85] "This performance, which was to be a family celebration to celebrate the return of the prodigal voice," wrote Charles Baron de Boigne, "was transformed into an evening of mourning, when two thousand spectators grieved the irreparable loss."[86]

These scenes staged the spectacle—night after night—of an actress suffocating and being resuscitated over and again, as if subject to the torture of some cruel ventilator. Theaters rehearsed this obsessively: the drama of a woman struggling to breathe. Falcon's "strong voice, colossal, with supernatural brilliance," which "like all that is great and beautiful, crushes, annihilates" confirmed one biographer in 1837 "addresses itself to the masses."[87] The soprano under pressure, indeed, became a stock in trade, not just of the popular theaters but of the 1830s operatic stage. A new kind of victim mentality overtook those productions so beloved of Véron's administration, and then of Duponchel's, from 1835. Repeatedly brought back to life, these women were forced to sing without air, without enough air, or perhaps too much air. This was why the chanteuse was so often rendered mute on stage: because her existence was subject to invisible forces she could not know or see. If she struggled to breathe, it was because she was immersed in a system that both persecuted and sustained her.

Another of Falcon's passionate failures took place, appropriately, at the home of a man now universally hailed as "the father of toxicology." Mathieu Orfila was a brilliant tenor who presided as much over matters of chemistry as he did over matters of singing. Orfila's wife, meanwhile, was "a little brunette woman, dry, trotting, milling, and fidgety" who ran possibly the most salubrious literary-artistic salon in Paris. Anne Gabrielle Orfila (née Lesueur), daughter of the famed sculptor and accomplished singer, guarded the exclusivity of her domestic sanctuary in the Latin Quarter with jealousy. The story goes that it was on the rue Saint-André-des-Arts, at the time of Falcon's comeback in 1840, that the operatic soprano was solicited to sing. Charles Bouvet recalled that she volunteered "Il va venir," the romance from the second act of *La Juive*, which Halévy had written for her and for which she was most celebrated:

Il va venir... il va venir!	He comes... he comes!
Et d'effroi je me sens frémir!	And in terror, I feel myself shake!
D'une sombre et triste pensée	Overtaken by a dark and dreadful thought
Mon âme, hélas! Est oppressée.	My soul, alas! Is oppressed.[88]

Falcon's matchless skills in declamatory acting were on show. In the opera, the salon-goers knew, Rachel finds herself alone (for the first time) in the closeted world of her ultra-orthodox fifteenth-century home at a time of insufferable religious persecution. Indeed, for the opera's denouement, the young girl will be submerged alive in a cauldron of boiling oil. In the episode under review, Rachel is as much the victim of a merciless Hebrew God as the victim of a love she does not understand. The Jewish girl is caught between "her enslavement to necessity and passions that will consume her."[89] She awaits her lover.

Thirty years later, close friend of Berlioz and prominent voice teacher Stéphen de La Madelaine published a forty-three-page memoir of "the dramatic style" in the second volume of his *Études pratiques de style vocal* (1868) wherein he recollected, in laborious detail, the circumstance of Falcon's "moral torture." In La Madelaine's measure-by-measure guide to the performance of "Il va venir," Falcon appears as an *artiste exagéré*, and mistress of "imposingly tragic situations." *La Juive*, recalled the aging voice coach, was "the most well-made and well-mounted work I have known in my long career as a critic and musician." His study, though written decades later, presents an intimate view of this living model of anguish (*angoisse*) and suffering (*souffrance*).[90] Having been so close to her, La Madelaine claimed to have insider knowledge, particularly in questions of high La melodrama.

The score of "Il va venir" (figure 2.5), La Madelaine knew, fixates on a single note: a B-flat. (In Mary Ann Smart's and Benjamin Walton's analysis, Falcon's registral break occurred at precisely this pitch.)[91] The romance begins with an eight-measure scene of hearing, as Rachel listens attentively for the arrival of her lover. On the one hand is her perception of the opening horn call (exterior world); on the other is the sound of her beating heart (interior world). La Madelaine described the bifurcated introduction as "three chords, played pizzicato on the bass strings, and separated by meticulously-indicated quarter-and eighth-note rests [indicating 'sighs' and 'half-sighs'], [which] represent heartbeats wracked with fright." "Their quietness," he observed, "suggests the taking-shape of a mysterious interior (*mystère intérieur*) within the young girl."[92]

La Madeleine counseled that the soprano forget the notated rhythms of Rachel's opening outburst, singing not just *mezzo voce*, but *sotto voce*. He taught that the first notes at the end of the first system of figure 2.5 should be delivered via a radical neutralization of the sound—an effect achieved by full dilation of the glottis. Similarly, the words "Et d'effroi je me sens frémir!" were not to be sung but *recited* with "dark energy." Meanwhile, the consonant Fs of "effroi" and "frémir" were declaimed in defiance of Halévy's notation. All of this was to be colored with an instinctive passion, since "it is after all nature, rather than its imitation, which is the proper business of art."[93] Falcon's auditors, La Madelaine recollected, were summoned into a private interior. The fantasy was of "going under," of gaining exclusive entry to the inner feeling world of the tragic actress.[94]

The ensuing seven measures (mm. 9–15 in figure 2.5) switch to the parallel minor and orient around the half-step above B flat, rather than the half-step below. Rachel's breathing now supplies metricality and power to the pulsing low B-flat heartbeats. For the phrase "D'une sombre et triste pensée; mon âme, hélas! Est oppressée," La Madelaine presented no less than six pages of commentary. The depth of Rachel's struggle was to be embodied by a technique of vocal darkening and covering (*assombrissement ou couverture de la voix*) that was supposedly, physiologically speaking, impossible for women and could only be attained by sheer force of will. La Madelaine taught that every nuance of sound should be matched by appropriate body movements.

Gesture, he recalled, altered Falcon's voice. La Madelaine remembered how the stare of the great cantatrice was fixed as she sang "D'une sombre," and how her hand stretched out before her, index finger raised to the sky, pointing to the unfathomable powers that terrorized her. At "mon âme," according to La Madelaine, she took two steps upstage, arched her back violently, and protected her chest with her hands, as if to signal to the invisible conditions that oppressed her.[95] (La Madelaine went so far as to reproduce a line drawing of this claustrated pose.) For the repeated rising vocal line ("Mon coeur bat mais non de plaisir") that followed, Falcon assumed another attitude: her left hand closed on her breast before for being raised in despair to her head. This time, however, Rachel's high G-flat, reached by a *rinforzando*, failed to resolve to the expected dominant seventh. Instead, Falcon let out a "muffled cry rather than a sound" rudely interrupted by a phenomenon La Madelaine claimed to have studied closely: *éloquence des silences*.[96]

It was here, when the music returned to the major, that the eyes of Orfila's guests reportedly teared up. At the flowering of adolescent love ("et cepedant, il va venir!" where figure 2.5 leaves off), Falcon "suddenly stopped, and without being able to utter another sound, communicated her helplessness with a few sad gestures."[97] La Madelaine remembered more of

FIGURE 2.5. Piano-vocal reduction of "Il va venir," Fromental Halévy's *La Juive* (Paris: Maurice Schlesinger, 1835), 167. Jean Gray Hargrove Music Library, University of California at Berkeley, M1503.H35 J8 1836 Case X.

"Il va venir," writing of Falcon's use of such extended techniques as sighs, sobs, "cries of the soul," speech song, as well as other nonmusical sounds. When finally a voice emerged, according to myth, Falcon contented herself with a few simple words: "You see," she said, "I warned you."[98]

Falcon's laryngeal voice had evaporated. A void had opened where her organ once was. Hers indeed was "a young soul emerging from her very pores, and coming out" (*une jeune âme qui sort par tous les pores*).[99] She was a singer whose larynx was absent, or at least whose loss positively affected the expressive intensity of her performance. The spectacle was of an overcharged actress locked in a battle with unseen circumstances. Male audiences, evidence suggests, craved the sight of her body gesturing in mute protest. Bereft of a vocal medium, fighting her way back, she struggled just to breathe. When the drama continued, at "Et cependent, il va venir," Falcon finally achieved relief, the function of the richly orchestrated E-flat-major background in the final measure of figure 2.5 being enough to provide beneficent healing.

It remains to explain, by way of conclusion, the fervor for inner expression over extrovert perfection, atmospheric enclosure above uncontained aerial freedom, Falcon over Cinti-Damoreau. One way to rationalize the preference would be to unpack its gender implications. The scene of Falcon's voice, operated at a distance by men, indexes the extent to which the *juste-milieu* sought to manage the lives of women by means of high-pressure control systems. (Indeed, the detail of La Madelaine's analysis provides yet more evidence of the imperative to contain.) A second way to narrate the change would be to focus on the space of "the self," a media form quite literally constructed in service of an "apolitical" *juste-milieu*. A third way might be to blame the social sciences and their associated disciplines: positivism, political economy, statistical method, the health sciences, and so on, as above. To be sure, advances in public hygiene had powerful implications, not only for the social management of populations but also for the social governance of voices. The explanations mount.

In the end, it may prove more useful to settle at the level of the everyday. What is clear is that it was precisely in this milieu that it became possible for singers to experience voice, less as the consequence of their own individual skill, than as the organic development of a bewildering multiplicity of unseen external factors. Indeed, the admittance of conservatory students into the hallowed interior of the opera house was controlled according to ecological law, respiratory technique, breath management, and gendered understandings of vocal health. This chapter has gone in search of the media conditions of bourgeois expression. It has described a range of atmospheric structures necessary to the production of interiority, and made a study of perhaps the first voice in history to be expressive of its social context.

CHAPTER 3

Moral Atmospherics in Elijah
Black Country, Britain, 1846–1860

Prologue

The prologue to the first part of Felix Mendelssohn's *Elijah* opens with four chords sounded by a brass choir. Elijah steps forward. His words precede the traditional instrumental-choral introduction. (Mendelssohn composed the work in German and had it translated into English for the premiere.) The prophet's bass voice lifts majestically over a rising arpeggio, echoed repeatedly throughout the work and symbolic of the sovereignty of God. He recites the biblical text from 1 Kings as printed in figure 3.1. "As the LORD God of Israel liveth," Elijah recites, "before whom I stand." The curse follows, Elijah declaring his sacred anointing as a soothsayer with power over the weather. "There shall not be dew nor rain these years," he sings, ascending by step to a melodic sequence of interlocking falling diminished fifths. "There shall not be dew nor rain," Elijah insists. The tritones he sings this second time—called the "curse motive" only since the 1890s—recur throughout the work as a "reminder of Divine wrath."[1] So does the ninth-century BC Tishbite prophet, identified in Christian folk traditions with pagan thunder and sky gods, foretell the catastrophe. He prophesies drought for a sinful people. The air will lose moisture. The earth will burn. His voice curses the environment.

A critic at the English premiere of the oratorio in Birmingham observed that "Herr [Josef] Staudigl, accompanied by the low mysterious tones of the oboes and bassoons, delivered in a voice of thunder, the awful predictions of the prophet Elijah."[2] Another critic reported that, as the curse sounded, so-called tower drums accompanied Staudigl's "stupendous voice." These Victorian tympani were descendants of the French double bass kettledrums captured by the Duke of Marlborough at the Battle of Malplaquet in 1709. In 1784, George Frideric Handel, reportedly, used these lionskin instruments, held by the British Board of Ordnance in the

ELIJAH,
A SACRED ORATORIO.

PROLOGUE—(Elijah.)

As God the Lord of Israel liveth, before whom I stand, there shall not be dew nor rain these years, but according to my word.—1 *Kings* i, 17.

OVERTURE.

CHORUS—(The People.)

Help, Lord! wilt thou quite destroy us?

The harvest now is over, the summer days are gone, and yet no power cometh to help us! Will, then, the Lord be no more God in Zion?—*Jeremiah* viii, 20.

RECITATIVE CHORUS—(The People.)

The deeps afford no water; and the rivers are exhausted!

The suckling's tongue now cleaveth for thirst to its mouth; the infant children ask for bread, and there is no one breaketh it to feed them.—*Lamentations* iv, 4.

FIGURE 3.1. *Birmingham Musical Festival* [prospectus] (Birmingham: John Tonks, Hill Street, 1846). © The British Library Board, 7894.s.1.

Tower of London, for the Handel Commemoration Festivals in Westminster Abbey.[3] The descendants of these behemoths would resonate still louder in the quake of Henry Distin's "Monster Gong Drum" or "Great Leviathan Drum," designed for the Crystal Palace. Used there for the giant 1860 performances of *Elijah*, the tympanum of this seven-foot *bodhrán* was "made from the largest buffalo-hide ever imported [from Africa] into

England."[4] The first performances of the prologue, that is, added rolling tympani, to dramatize, in the words of a critic, "the notion of the prophet's edict being delivered in thunder."[5]

The Austrian bass was majestic.[6] Staudigl was noted for his enormous top hat and for the "purity of his style and judgement of his readings."[7] His sermonic style was typical in the venues that first made *Elijah* popular: Birmingham Town Hall, Exeter Hall, the Crystal Palace (London), and St. George's Hall (Liverpool). These urban gathering places were incubators for millenarianist speech. Riding the wave of evangelical revivalism and nonconformist enthusiasm, the leading public orators of the milieu forged prophetic reputations in these halls, inciting fiery atmospheres of feeling (to reframe Raymond Williams's "structures of feeling").[8] Like so many modern Elijahs, a new generation of preacher-prophets made prognostications of world-ecological doom to enthralled audiences of "the thousand." "Then did the prophet Elijah break forth like a fire," so goes a chorus in Part 2 of *Elijah*: "His words appeared like burning torches."

Elijah heralds an environmental crisis. It declares a postlapsarian world—a scorched earth redolent of human sin. The curse of the prophet sweeps audiences into what Carolyn Merchant, in a book subtitled *The Fate of Nature in Western Culture* (2003), calls a "Recovery of Eden" grand narrative, where modern nature is sick—or rather where Nature is idealized as a lost tropico-botanical idyll.[9] Capital-*N* Nature, as opposed to lowercase-*n* natures, refers to an ideal representing, by its pristine wholeness, the promise of a world freed from politics or human intervention.[10] Kristin Asdal, for one, calls capital-*N* Nature an aesthetic construct, an ideal representing by its very perfection the denial of politics tout court.

Parables of fall and redemption, Lawrence Buell suggests, in his account of the "long-standing mythography of betrayed Edens," precipitate "totalizing images of a world without refuge from toxic penetration."[11] Edenic narratives, Buell points out, engage listeners, as the curse of Elijah does, in "the end of Nature." At the same time, they project an ecological holism that acts of the imagination have the power to reconnect to.[12] Buell diagnoses what he calls "toxic discourse," by which he means a plot archetype yoked to the biblical story of the contamination of a lost sacred purity. *Elijah* traces the oratorical arc from a moral desert laid to waste by human action, to the annihilation of the world, to the final recovery of Paradise. But that cultural narrative, one archetypal to protestant evangelical reform, takes as its initial premise a modern world beset by the evils of moral and industrial pollution.[13]

The Time of the Seventh Angel

> And the seventh angel poured out his vial into the air; and there came a great voice out of the temple of heaven, from the throne, saying, It is done! And there were voices, and thunders, and lightnings; and there was a great earthquake, such as was not since men were upon the earth, so mighty an earthquake, and so great. And the great city was divided into three parts, and the cities of the nations fell: and great Babylon came in remembrance before God, to give unto her the cup of the wine of the fierceness of his wrath. And every island fled away, and the mountains were not found.
> Book of Revelation, 17–20 (King James Version)

This chapter makes three observations. First, *Elijah* was premiered amidst heavy air pollution in Birmingham, the birthplace of the steam engine. On August 26, 1846, an energy regime, or the then-fifty-year-old institutions built from the profits of fossil fuel extraction, paid for its production. As a case study, *Elijah* stands in for all catastrophist oratorios of the period and an industrial cosmology devoted to the reproduction of musical artworks. *Elijah* manifested a cosmology—a way of narrating Nature—founded on a very real experience of ecological crisis. The "thousand" felt themselves to be breathing in intoxicants poured into the atmosphere by the burning of a black subterranean fuel mined from the graveyard of organisms buried millions of years ago.

Second, this epoch was an epoch of fanatical and pervasive prophetic utterance. There are many Elijahs in the pages that follow: Straudigl, Mendelssohn, Alexander von Humboldt, Karl Marx, James Glaisher, John Pyke Hullah, John Cumming, David Boswell Reid. These prophets professed to speak, like Elijah, on behalf of Nature. Take Mendelssohn, composer of Nature music, hailed in what follows as a modern Elijah. Humboldt, established his claim to authority by virtue of travel the forests of the Orinoco basin and the Peruvian deserts. The Reverend Cumming thundered sermons of such thunderous force as to be difficult to contest. Reid, soon to be introduced, manufactured air-conditioning systems that claimed to rescue humanity from the pollution they themselves caused. These "prophets"—whether artist, scientist, prophet, or architect—worked on behalf of Nature. They brought about its Truth.

Third, *Elijah* was at once financed by the profits generated from the coal-fired energy system and produced by that very same system to mitigate against environmental decay. On one hand, governing elites admitted heavy pollution as a necessary feature of the carbon economy; on the other, they developed public health measures to offset the costs of industrial advances. The "Great Sanitary Awakening," so-called by scholars, gathered momentum in the 1840s to counter the effects of a ruinous fossil fuel regime.[14] A whole bureaucracy was built, including hospitals, schools, concert venues, churches, and botanical gardens. These structures of moral and physical care intended to sustain laboring populations in productive balance. One such reformist initiative was the "singing class" movement, introduced among many such sanitation schemes to offset the health effects of atmospheric pollution in the 1840s. Middling-class choral societies—led by Hullah, Joseph Mainzer, and John Curwen—aligned with what Bill Luckin calls Britain's "medico-environmental public sphere," a sphere of social government that widened considerably in the decade of *Elijah*'s production.[15] Choral singing sounded the keynote in the Victorian war against filth. The movement taught resilience, eventually spreading the gospel of clean living and healthy lungs to such far-flung British colonies as New Zealand, Madagascar, Canada, South Africa, India, and the South Sea Islands.

The "onset of the Anthropocene" dates to Birmingham—at least according to the 2000 argument made by Nobel Prize–winning chemist Paul Crutzen and marine biologist Eugene F. Stoermer—and the invention of steam power by James Watt, Matthew Boulton, and those who financed *Elijah*. (There has been pushback against the Crutzen-Stoermer thesis, Will Steffen redating the "Great Acceleration" to the spread of radioactive fallout in the wake of the Trinity Nuclear Test of 1945; Bill Ruddiman, in his "Early Anthropogenic Hypothesis," proposed an earlier onset, citing mass forest-clearing activities and agrilogistic processes begun five thousand to eight thousand years ago.)[16] The term "Anthropocene," famously, was coined by Crutzen-Stoermer in a 2000 article for the *IGBP* (*International Geosphere-Biosphere Programme Newsletter*). Yet they only echoed prophetic proclamations by Victorians themselves, including remarkable Scottish science writer Mary Somerville. As early as 1848, Somerville described how "man" was asserting himself as a geological force in the earth system. "The change produced in the civilized world within a few years, by the application of the powers of nature to locomotion," Somerville wrote, "is so astonishing, that it leads to a consideration of the influence of man on the material world, his relation with regard to animate and inanimate beings, and the causes which have had the greatest effect on the physical, moral, and intellectual condition of the human race."[17] Somerville recognized long ago, from within the nascent energy system, the epochal consequence of the triumph of steam.

The workshops of Birmingham and the commercial markets of London powered the global transition to fossil fuels. (Music publisher Novello steam printed four thousand copies of the octavo piano-vocal score of *Elijah* in just the first eight months of 1860.[18]) The first atmospheric engines, sources of power derived independently of prevailing climatic conditions, were developed for mining operations. Steam proved the motive benefits of energy conversion; yet it also produced "plague-winds"—the external by-product of internal combustion. By virtue of energies achieved by burning carboniferous rock, goods and services could now be moved across vast distances and on industrial scales. Industrialists at the center of empire had learned to seize an intangible asset. They had learned to capitalize on air.[19]

For human geographer Mark Whitehead, the three years before the premiere of *Elijah* saw the institution of "atmospheric government" by the British state. Whitehead argues that the administrative determination was, not merely to govern air but to govern populations by governing the content of their breathing. The year 1843 not only saw the first appointment of a Parliamentary Select Committee on Smoke Prevention, "established in order to discuss the ensuing problems of atmospheric pollution in industrial Britain."[20] That year also witnessed, according to Whitehead, the first logistical attempt to solidify working ties between governments and scientists in the crusade against air pollution. Earlier public health initiatives had also defended against toxicity: the 1836 General Register Office (GRO) formed to register births, marriages, and deaths; the Poor Law Commission of 1838; the Health of Towns Association, set up in 1844; and the 1839 Committee of the Privy Council on Education, which directly advocated for the advancement of choirs through John Hullah at Exeter Hall. (Hullah claimed Mendelssohn as a friend, the latter having attended a party at the choirmaster's home in May 1844, for a performance of his newly revised *First Walpurgis Night*.)[21] Other measures followed, such as London's Smoke Nuisance Abatement Act of 1853, devised to reduce "nuisance from the smoke of furnaces in the metropolis and from steam vessels above London Bridge" or Joseph Bazalgette's sewage system for London, built in response to the 1858 Great Stink.

The first use of the word "sanitation" appeared in the 1848 National Public Health Act, the first national legislation to incorporate a clause on smoke abatement. (Michael Angelo Taylor, member of parliament, railed against "smoke nuisances" as early as 1819 and 1820.)[22] The adjective "sanitary," to be sure, had been coined in 1842, for the purposes of Edwin Chadwick's *Inquiry for the Poor Law Commission into the Sanitary Condition of the Laboring Population of Great Britain*. In the mid-1840s, discourses around civic pride mushroomed into what George Muntz, industrialist of Muntz Steel and member of parliament for Birmingham, would call "the mania for sanitary measures." The era's "sanitarian narrative," as Ralph F. Smith calls it, was founded upon the doctrine of the epidemic air, which held sway until at least the 1880s, when (as argued in the next chapter) germ theories of disease finally turned medical attention away from the sky.[23]

The 1842 report lauded the 1838 work of Poor Law Commissioners as the first to make statistical surveys of air quality standards and to warn about the evils of "decomposing animal and vegetable substances, damp and filth, and close and overcrowded dwellings."[24] A mountain of facts enumerated the extent of the problem: mortality rates, unemployment numbers, urbanization statistics, medical records, and birth rates; while air chemists quantified the toxic effects of effluvia, sewage, cesspools, decomposed matter, and coal gas. The data amassed through governmental surveillance reports both served the cause of "statistical enthusiasm" and expanded the biopolitical reach of the modern disciplinary state. Encouraged by strong evangelical backing, the facts gave impetus to the project to cleanse and civilize.[25]

Chadwick himself identified miasma (as much as smoke) as the chief evil besetting working populations. "The annual loss of life from filth and bad ventilation," his inquiry found, are "greater than the loss from death or wounds in any wars in which the country has been engaged in modern times."[26] An 1846 study submitted to Westminster by the related Health of Towns Association, a broad-church organization launched at Exeter Hall in 1844 to lobby for comprehensive public health regulation, was explicit. "The ultimate end of sewerage, drainage, and a supply of water adequate to the cleansing of sewers, drains, and streets," wrote leading physician of the London Fever Hospital, Southwood Smith, "is to maintain the air, wherever human beings take up their abode, in a fit state for respiration."[27] The air, for these reformers, was a domain for political action and struggle.[28]

Mendelssohn as Prophet

In the planning stages of *Elijah*, Mendelssohn wrote to Pastor Julius Schubring that he envisaged "a thorough prophet, such as we might again require in our own day, strong, zealous, and, yet stern, wrathful, and gloomy." Schubring was Mendelssohn's librettist-collaborator, fellow disciple of Friedrich Schleiermacher in Berlin, evangelical minister at Dessau, and a long-standing friend. In that same letter of November 2, 1838, Mendelssohn insisted that his Elijah be "a striking contrast to the rabble, whether of the court or the people—in fact, in opposition to the whole world, and yet borne on angels' wings."[29] The pair agreed that the curse of the prophet precede the narrative. (The overture is absent from the manuscript parts used for the premiere and was not part of the composer's initial conception.)[30] Yet they fell out over the question of the portrayal of the Hebrew prophet—whether Elijah should receive objective depiction as an historical character, or as a Messianic prefiguration of the living Christ.

Their falling out belied a mutual investment in Schleiermacher's "theology of feeling."[31] These friends exalted collaboration and the possibility for universal consensus. Mendelssohn's genius, many scholars note, was to use the experience of sensitive listening to direct the citizens of the Prussian state and the Kingdom of Saxony, as much as Lutherans and Catholics in German-speaking lands, toward a common artistic polity. *Gefuhlskultur*, that is, invoked higher affective unities. Petty language and religious divisions were soothed by the cultivation of a *Gefuhlssphäre*, a circle of sentiment. Melody, in particular, according to the latter-day apostles of the Berlin Enlightenment, was a political balm. Mendelssohn himself believed melody to be a definite purveyor of meaning. "Only melody can say the same thing [to different people]," the musician wrote in 1835, "[and] can arouse the same feelings in one person as in another, a feeling which may not be expressed."[32] Radiated upward and outward, melody healed social division, assuaged dogma, and unified the human spirit. It worked to humanize.

The necessity for a good music education was no less important to the politics of reconciliation. "The nineteenth century's most important—and successful—civic musician," as Richard Taruskin calls Mendelssohn, played no small part in inspiring art-religious enthusiasm for institutions of "classical music."[33] Myth tells us that the modern rituals of public concert culture—conservatory training, massed amateur choral singing, orchestral conducting, Bach worship—the very forms of the European orchestra and the concert hall itself—crystalized under Mendelssohn's baton, whether in Berlin, Leipzig, Birmingham, London, or Boston. John Sullivan Dwight, American evangelist of the Mendelssohn cult, put it well when he wrote that "music delivers us from actual bondage; it buoys us up above our accidents, and wafts us on waves of melody to the hearts' ideal home."[34] Mendelssohn's inspirations "ameliorate[d] the ceaseless conflict of opinions, civilized the savage, toned down self-assertion, and softened angularity of character." Dwight insisted that "music must become a part of our common, we may say our atmospheric education."[35]

Mendelssohn widened the sphere of feeling most on his visits to London, alighting no less than ten times on that "smoky nest" between 1829 and 1847.[36] The Berliner had been drawn into what Celia Applegate has called an "Anglo-German symbiosis."[37] Applegate describes this political formation as a shared cosmopolitan ethic, reconciling such diverse constituencies as the dissenting evangelicals of the Sacred Harmonic Society, the members of the Philharmonic Society, and the Anglican noblemen of the Ancient Concerts. The artwork unified the efforts of such diverse international actors as patrons, musicians, architects, librettists, theologians, instrument makers, engineers, listeners, long-dead composers, even ancient Hebrew prophets. In Mendelssohn's messianic vision of the life of Elijah—and this was the point of contention with Schubring—Christianity would appear as the final universalization of Judaism. The story was still a nineteenth-century story, because *Kunstreligion* had yet to cast off all its false prophets but also had yet to unite the world's people under a single monotheistic dome.[38]

Not everyone breathed so freely within the oratorio's *Gefuhlssphäre*. As early as December 1847, Eduard Kruger of the *Leipzig neue Zeitschrift* and *Neue Berliner Musikzeitung* condemned *Elijah*'s text for being "crassly Jewish" and "narrow-mindedly pious."[39] Later generations found the moralizing tone of Mendelssohn's sermons cloying. "Until we have got far enough to recoil from Elijah flippantly rattling off his atrocious 'God is Angry with the Wicked Every Day,'" George Bernard Shaw opined in the 1880s, "we shall never fathom the depths of truly great music." Shaw moaned that "the enemy" excelled at "the chopping to pieces of the prophets of the grove with his richest musical spice to suit the compound of sanctimonious cruelty and base materialism which his patrons, the British Pharisees, called their religion."[40] George Grove complained, similarly, of the same preachiness that tarnished Mendelssohn's first success, the oratorio *St. Paul*, which premiered in Düsseldorf but was soon being performed as far afield as Liverpool, Riga, Rotterdam, Moscow, Prague, Rome, Boston, Baltimore, and New York. The Schubring-Mendelssohn attitude in both *St. Paul* and *Elijah*, Grove moaned, was "in essentials, that of the preacher taking for text a portion of history different in kind from all other history, and applying the lessons he desires to draw from it in the form of a direct sermon, with just so much scenic background as will make the sermon interesting."[41] "A weak potpourri of religious fanaticism and sanctimonious preacher's piety" is how Eric Werner famously lambasted *Elijah*'s apocalyptic panorama. These tirades betrayed the pressures of anticosmopolitan dissent, as cracks began to appear in the glass sphere of consensus.

Not that Mendelssohn was a pusillanimous do-gooder. He had no reputation for piety around the time of his fateful illness in 1847. Nor was his compositional style associated with what Grove called "shallow respectability," or what George Bernard Shaw called "Sunday-school sentimentalities."[42] Mendelssohn's music was hardly genteel, even after the 1850 publication of Wagner's notorious *Das Judenthum in der Musik (Judaism in Music)*.[43] James Garratt, for one, interrogates the so-called Mendelssohn Problem as an anti-Semitic construct that has obscured the reasons why he was, for his contemporaries, "the musician who most clearly appreciated the contradictions of his age."[44]

For most, as he neared his tragic death in late 1847, Mendelssohn was the milieu's most exalted modern prophet. No less a figure than Prince Albert, himself a skilled composer, described him as a "Second Elijah," while attending the oratorio's second Exeter Hall performance in London on April 23, 1847: "To the Noble Artist, who, surrounded by the Baal-worship of debased art, has been able, by his genius and science, to preserve faithfully, like another Elijah, the worship of true art, and once more to accustom our ear, amid the whirl of empty, frivolous sounds, to the pure tones of sympathetic feeling and legitimate harmony: to the Great Master, who makes us conscious of the unity of his conception, through the whole maze of his creation, from the soft whispering to the mighty raging of the elements."[45] The Prince Consort jotted these words into his personal program book for *Elijah*, before they were translated into English by the Prussian ambassador to London, Christian Bunsen. Bunsen was himself a learned Indo-European linguist and ethnological and philological writer, who led the pan-European struggle for a universal orthography: "an alphabet so comprehensive as to include the sounds of every known language."[46]

Mendelssohn's universal language, in Albert's conception, assuaged the disunity of a sinful world. *Elijah*, after all, narrated the grand historical passage from Yahweh, the storm-and-fire god of a small Bedouin tribe to the world-god, creator of the heavens, divine lawgiver, and god of charity.[47] By the ways they stirred up "the elements," these melodies resonated with projects of empire building. They wielded the powers of "science" and "genius" against the noisy pronouncements of such minor Canaanite weather gods as Baal.

The Great Enframement

The image at figure 3.2 is of Wyld's Great Globe, a *Gefuhlssphäre* illustrative of the ways in which Nature was enframed at the height of *Elijah*'s popularity. The building was erected just a short walk from Exeter Hall on London's Leicester Square. James Wyld, a Charing Cross cartographer and map publisher as well as politician and geographer to Queen Victoria, inaugurated the installation on June 2, 1851, one month after the opening of the Great Exhibition of the Works of Industry of All Nations. The giant sphere provided a multisensory experience of being-in-the-world. It immersed paying viewers in a wraparound *Umwelt*.

The Great Globe encapsulates a key moment in processes of globalization: of a globe being made, or of globe making. The topography of the earth was depicted to scale on the inside of the orb. Visitors in search of geographic enlightenment entered from the South Pole. Climbing the

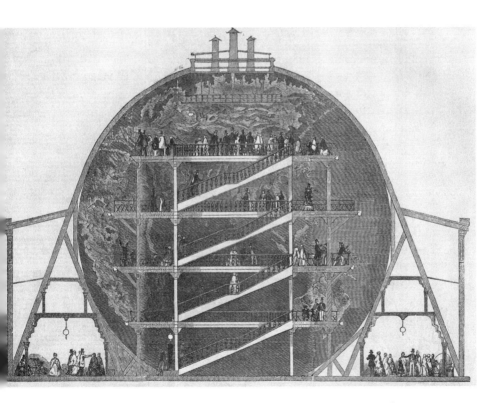

FIGURE 3.2. "Mr. Wyld's Model of the Earth," *The Illustrated London News* (June 7, 1851): 511.

stairs, they experienced biodiversity from within, though the interior was stiflingly hot in summer and hotter the further you ascended. Recall the rainmaking episode ending Part 1 of *Elijah*, where, atop Mount Carmel, the voice of the prophet's youthful servant reports repeatedly to the audience that "the heavens are as brass, they are as brass above me" and later "the earth is as iron under me." Soon after opening, this "globe that was itself a building" had to be artificially air-conditioned because of a lack of oxygen.[48]

Alexander von Humboldt served on the committee (the Cosmos Institute) that maintained the Great Globe's integrity. The explorer, biogeographer, and pioneering climatologist is often hailed today, for his work on deforestation and industrial emissions, as "the man who predicted climate change." The "father of environmentalism" was certainly prescient when he suggested that mankind's industrious know-how was having catastrophic effects on global ecosystems. The Prussian naturalist was also a close family friend of the Mendelssohns; after his expedition to South and Central America, Humboldt had been extended a line of credit by Felix's father. At the time of *Elijah*, Humboldt was publishing his five-volume "portrait of Nature" entitled *Cosmos: Sketch of a Physical Description of the World* (1845–60). Like his brother Wilhelm, whose study of languages strove for "a conception of the world in its individuality and totality," Humboldt theorized the earth system as what the ancient Greeks called a *kosmos*—"a beautifully ordered and harmonious system."[49]

Humboldt, famously, was the figurehead for a new unified science of the environment. His vision reached for "a point of view from which all the organisms and forces of nature may be seen as one living active whole, animated by one sole impulse."[50] The cosmos, he wrote, was "the assemblage of all things in heaven and earth, the universality of created things constituting the perceptible world."[51] His confidence in its immanence was vouchsafed by a globally distributed effort of knowing. Empire, that is, allowed for an expanded range of climatic readings and a broader geographic base of study. The Great Globe itself would not have been possible without the international spread of bureaucratic techniques of statistical measurement, telegraph systems, transnational programs of scientific data collection, and the fossil-fuel-powered technologies of the world system. From his base in Berlin, with his associate Carl Frederick Gauss of Göttingen, Humboldt had already established a network of stations for the simultaneous measurement of magnetic storms across the Russian Empire. In 1836, he explicitly appealed to the English scientific community to expand that network southward into the farthest reaches of the British Empire.[52]

Sociability, as much as imperialism, John Tresch writes, "was central to Humboldt's conception of scientific knowledge," as much as it was to Mendelssohn's objective conception of musical art. A who's who of observers, field stations, and observatories made possible the magnetic crusade that traced the distribution of polar intensity, inclination, and declination around the world. "Humboldt in Curana, Saussure in Geneva, Dalton in Kendall, Arago in Paris, Euler in Petersburg, Young in London, and Playfair in Edinburgh": this network of investigators worked to identify Humboldt's famous "isothermal lines," regions of shared average temperature in bands across the earth. "Humboldt was composing a cosmic symphenomenony," Tresch writes, imagining musicians and instruments in cooperation, "and helping to assemble the worldwide orchestra needed to perform it."[53] International actors came together in patient, intimate, and serious cooperation to achieve global consensus.

Let us take a breath. Before our eyes is an aestheticized spherical interior. Conjured under the sign of industrialism, indeed under the sign of the steam engine, this vision of unity served ideologies of progress and capital expansion. So many prophets emerged to warn of its consequences, and insiders knew that this Nature would not last, even as it was erected. (The Great Globe, after all, had to be dismantled in 1862.). Take, for example, Louis Spohr's oratorio *Fall of Babylon* (Norwich, 1842), a middle-English apocalyptic predecessor of *Elijah*, associated with painter John Martin's giant panoramic canvas of the same name. The message conveyed by these artworks was that the cosmology itself was engineered to fail, it being well understood that Nature and industry were coconstituted. The globe itself was doomed.

Weather Prophets

Mendelssohn was one of many prophets. He was certainly not alone in raising his eyes to the ominous sky. The scale of scientific activity established to gain knowledge of the atmospheric threat, as Katharine Anderson has shown, grew exponentially in the 1840s, particularly regarding weather prediction and atmospheric chemistry. (Anderson observes that the prophet was an enchanted figure for Victorians; she describes "the prophet's mantle of authority, and at the same time, its distasteful associations with enthusiasm, dogmatism, and false claims to knowledge."[54]) One reason for the development of public health administrations was to gather predictive meteorological data. The General Register Office, for instance, was founded under dashing novelist Thomas Henry Lister in 1838, "to gather statistics of mortality and, as a related activity, collected and published comprehensive weather information."[55]

The science of midcentury Victorian weather prediction, Anderson shows, was a controversial enterprise. It was a practice "poised between divination, opinion, and calculation." The readers of meteorological signs could be "weather prophets," chemists, astrologers, almanac writers, geomagnetists, catastrophists, or street preachers. The modern prophet, she writes, "was one of the rhetorical terrains on which the contests between religious and scientific authority were played out."[56] They were spiritual guides in "an era of social and political upheaval." Anderson demonstrates how metereologists struggled to transform a diverse collection of predictive behaviors into an authoritative science of prophesying: "a science not of weather prophets but of weather networks." The challenge was to submit the ever-changing air to laws. An increasing number of precision instruments assisted in the institution of a "science of detail" dependent on "laborious and continued observation."[57] The hope was that some modicum of scientific authority could be exercised over Nature by collecting data and making statistical surveys.

It was the industrial network itself, ironically, that facilitated an expansion in the scale of scientific activities directed toward air quality control. In part, this was an effect of the broader institutionalization of meteorology and "the growth of specialized societies and journals, the assertive presence of men of science in cultural life after midcentury, the movements for scientific education and research funding."[58] Another impetus for the popularization of weather prediction was widening interest in cyclonology, aerostatics, magnetism, and other meteorological phenomena. The public health movement, meanwhile, disseminated a growing concern for air. Works of such varied reputation as *Zadkiel's Almanac*, *Murphy's Weather Almanac* (from 1842), or *Illustrated London Almanack* (from 1845) competed with the authorized forecasts of the Magnetical and Meteorological Department at the Royal Observatory, Greenwich (from 1840). Meteorology was fast gaining a reputation as a popular science within the grasp of every mind and suitable to barometric study in the drawing room.

Debates raged about the health benefits of smoke, the question of whether storms rotated, whether atmospheric electricity was a cause or effect of rain and winds, and the chemistry of rain. Anderson goes so far as to address the manifestations of such premillenarians as Edward Irving and the prophetess Joanna Southcott at the Scotch Church on London's Regent Square, some of whose congregants began to speak in tongues in 1830: a sure sign of the End of Days. Anderson examines debates between catastrophists (who believed that the earth's history was marked by a series of violent atmospheric upheavals, instigated by God) and uniformitarianists (who believed that the planet's geology was the result of incremental shifts occurring over millennia). "The problems of weather forecasting in Victorian Britain," she concludes, "are hard to interpret without a consideration of this spectrum of ideas about prediction, prophecy, and prophets."[59]

The reminder of the chapter attends to four buildings—four "atmospheres of feeling"—that hosted early productions of *Elijah*. At this stage, the priority is to observe how these structures were air-conditioned and to explain the spiritual values circulated in them. The consensus inspired by sacred song formed part of a rising tide of religious and governmental reforms launched to ensure the welfare of the laboring populations under global industrial capitalism.

I. Town Hall, Birmingham, 1846

Elijah was premiered in the interior pictured in figure 3.3. The building, originally a purpose-built "Musical Hall," had been erected in 1834 at the

FIGURE 3.3. "The Birmingham Musical Festival—The Great Music Hall," *The Illustrated London News* 9 (August 29, 1846): 137.

top of New Street (recently refurbished with raised paving and gas streetlights). A picture of sanitary health, the hall was surrounded to the south and east by a maze of narrow streets: the slums of the Old Inkleys, the New Inkleys, Tonk Street, Peek Lane, the Froggary, which was cleared for the New Street Railroad Station in 1854. From under 60,000 people in 1800, Birmingham's population had grown to nearly 200,000 by 1846. Again, Dickens comes to mind: "a town of unnatural red and black like the painted face of a savage," he wrote of Coketown in *Hard Times* (1854), "of machinery and tall chimneys, out of which interminable serpents of smoke trailed themselves for ever and ever, and never got uncoiled ... where the piston of the steam-engine worked monotonously up and down."[60]

The Town Hall was the sanctuary of a region to its west named (by Tractarian divine William Gresley), precisely in 1846, as "the Black Country." An area of urban sprawl in the West Midlands, the Black Country was bounded by Wolverhampton and Walsall to the north; Smethwick, Halesowen, and Stourbridge to the south.[61] Industrial labor made this region the home of mass extractive industries: coal mining, coking, iron foundries, glass factories, metal-bashing, brickworks, and steel mills. Brass manufacture and gun making, the latter at its height during the Napoleonic wars and now funding colonial expansion overseas, had long ago helped to establish the Black Country's very own microclimate. Billions of tons of carbon dioxide were to be poured into the atmosphere by the burning of fossil fuels.[62]

Birmingham industries powered midcentury globalization. The stage was set for *Elijah* forty years earlier when James Watt's business partner Matthew Boulton, a music lover and patron of the Oratorio Choral Society (who sold engines), encouraged the early music-philanthropic efforts of Joseph Moore.[63] Moore's charitable zeal was legion. This son of a builder of hothouses was also *Elijah*'s commissioner.[64] (The mastermind behind the Triennial Music Festival had made his fortune in die sinking and machine-powered button making.) He and such Birmingham industrialists as John Taylor, Richard Spooner, Joseph Walker, and Joseph Frederick Ledsam, who acted as orchestral steward at *Elijah*'s premiere, took the lead in fund-raising for the Hall, completed in 1834. A new breed of "humanitarians" (a word coined nine years later, in 1843, according to the *Oxford English Dictionary*) added support. Among them was Joseph Sturge, a Quaker devoted to "anti-slavery, peace, free trade, suffrage extension, infant schools and Sunday schools, reformatories, spelling reform, teetotalism, hydropathy, and public parks."[65] Music was held in such high civic esteem that the municipality granted the Committee of the Birmingham

Triennial Musical Festival permission to seize the Town Hall whenever the artistic need arose. This was the third time Mendelssohn had traveled to Birmingham at Moore's behest.

Elijah was an industrial object seized from the toxic sky. One might say that the iron infrastructure of the 1838 London and Birmingham railroad was integrated, not only into the oratorio's "actor network" but into the raw materials of its composition. A special steam train was requisitioned to depart from London Euston at 2 p.m. on August 23, 1846. It transported Mendelssohn himself, Ignaz Moscheles (who was originally slated to preside), the vocal soloists, 125 players from the London Philharmonic and opera orchestra, 62 extra choristers, music critics for propaganda purposes, and several instruments necessary for performance. These included that "tower drum" played by Thomas Chipp and a "monstre ophicleide" transported for French virtuoso Jean Prosper Guivier.

For the morning premiere, 396 musicians gathered beneath the pipes of the Hall's organ, "richly illuminated in vellum colour and gold," framed in "dark oak, with gilt ornaments and mouldings."[66] They included organist Henry Gauntlett, 271 chorus members with 60 male "bearded altos" (as Mendelssohn called them), 68 violins and violas, 26 cellos and basses. "A dense mass of human beings" amounting to around two thousand audience members congregated within the concert room.[67] The hall's richly decorated interior boasted a style of polychromatic coloring that celebrated the glories of republican free trade by being modeled at once on the Roman Temple of Jupiter Stator and the interior of Mendelssohn's beloved Sing-Akademie zu Berlin.[68]

A critic at the premiere marveled at the immense organ engulfing the performers, "with its thirty-two feet pipes, looking like gigantic rolls of oil cloth, [which] rose up from behind till its head touched the roof, like some vast animal of mysterious form."[69] This Leviathon, as the chorus master that morning called it, featured the first thirty-two-foot front built for an organ in England. In preparation for its construction, Moore had traveled with Sigismond Neukomm—King of Brumagem [Birmingham] as Mendelssohn once dubbed the author the oratorio *David* (Birmingham, 1834)—from Haarlem to Hamburg to compare the bellows on rival instruments. A Grand Ophicleide stop, "probably the first true high-pressure reed," was added in 1840, voiced by an immense fifteen inches of wind pressure. The 1834 instrument, by William Hill, was trumpeted as the most advanced musical technology then in existence.[70] The makers intended for Birmingham's status as a global technological powerhouse to be measured and made audible in the strength of its pneumatic power.[71] This was, by common consent, "by far the best constructed, as well as the most splendid, music room in Great Britain, if not in the whole world."[72]

Critic Julius Benedict reported that, as Mendelssohn entered at around 11:30 a.m., "the sun, emerging at that moment, seemed to illuminate the vast edifice in honour of the bright and pure being who stood there, the idol of all beholders!"[73] Mendelssohn's appearance that morning caused the haze to lift. "During the whole two and half hours that [*Elijah*] lasted," the German-Jewish composer wrote to his brother, "I could sway at pleasure the enormous orchestra and choir, and also the organ accompaniment." "He possesses a remarkable power over the performers, moulding them to his will," wrote the *Birmingham Journal*, "and though rigidly strict in exacting the nicest precision, he does it in a manner irresistible."[74] Mendelssohn himself marveled at his godlike atmospheric powers, and the docility of this "impressionable, kindly, hushed, and enthusiastic audience—now still as mice, now exultant."[75] The artist-prophet was heard to bring enlightenment, his angelic countenance shining forth as Jerusalem's builder among dark satanic mills.

Elijah had an explicitly medico-environmental raison d'être. Moore secured a £4,800 profit from the 1846 Festival, which he then funneled into the General Hospital Fund. This was the point of the Mendelssohn enterprise: to counter the heterodox atmosphere, as Moore worked alongside the Hospital Committee, Ratepayers Protection Association and the Town Commissioners in service of sanitary improvement. The efforts of the festival committee, that is, were remedial. They were aligned as much with the efforts of the 1843 Parliamentary Select Committee on Smoke Prevention, as with James Watt's age-old "smoke consumption" inventions.

Moral hygiene was no less urgent to the project. The municipality of Birmingham was incorporated as recently as 1838, instituting works programs expanded after the passing of the Public Health Act of 1848. Surely the loudest advocate of sanitary reform in the city was Rev. George Dawson, the charismatic nonconformist preacher and Mendelssohn fanatic. "The greatest talker in England," as Charles Kingsley called him, preached a Civic Gospel from his nonsectarian pulpit in the Church of the Saviour (built in 1847), as if oratory itself—clean talk—could sanctify Black Country air. Dawson encouraged his congregations to roll up their sleeves for Birmingham. He spoke of sacred song, alongside God-breathed speech, as a civilizing force. "If a man loves music," this advocate of civic renaissance, universal education, and the public library movement sermonized, "he generally loves charity."[76] Mendelssohn's popularity in the provinces, for him, was a sign that artisans had absorbed a moral capacity for feeling. This fountainhead of all that was "patient, laborious, learned, mystical, tender, loving, true-hearted" taught that even "tinkers and weavers [might become] the lords of light and truth."[77] German-Jewish oratorios were especially uplifting. "A town is a solemn organism," Dawson proclaimed, "through which shall flow, and in which shall be shaped, all the highest, loftiest and truest ends of man's moral nature."[78]

Elijah was the state-of-the-art product of a carbon regime that targeted the air for global industrial capitalization; yet it also served public health initiatives that targeted the same air for reform. Art, for social reformers, was an instrument of reparation, one that furnished immersive environments for sanitary living. "Governments may stamp the manners [of urban populations]," wrote the first historian of the steam engine, Robert Stuart Meikleham in 1845, "but it is the air they breathe which moulds the form, temper, and genius of a people."[79] Armed with atmospheric knowledge, municipalities labored alongside health practitioners, scientists, amateur choral societies, and religious leaders to enact smoke-abatement measures, slum-clearance programs, and ventilation schemes. Sacred song, for them, encouraged men and women to decontaminate circumstances for themselves. The crusade for better living conditions, in this sense, emerged as the handmaiden of progress, one that arose in lockstep with the capitalist tenet that sustainability and development could be had at the same time. The patrons who packed the aisles of the Birmingham Music Hall, in other words, sought in mass choral song a means of improvement. They aimed to achieve a higher, purer, future Nature, both within their own bodies and without, in the world.

II. Exeter Hall, London, 1848

Figure 3.4 depicts a second important building for *Elijah*, reached by taking the train back to London. Exeter Hall loomed large on the north side of the Strand above the Thames, a few steps from Wyld's Great Globe. It was at the gathering-place of the so-called Puritan world, where the most authoritative English version of Mendelssohn's oratorio was first heard, with thirteen of the original movements from Birmingham substantially altered or recomposed. This occurred on key dates in April 1847 (when Prince Albert pronounced Mendelssohn a modern rainmaker), and then in December 1848, when soprano Jenny Lind made her celebrated *Elijah* debut.

Exeter Hall stood at the epicenter of global evangelical reform. The Sacred Harmonic Society, an amateur choral organization that sponsored

FIGURE 3.4. "The New Orchestra, Exeter Hall, London," *The Illustrated London News* 13 (November 4, 1848): 277.

the London premiere of *Elijah*, moved their offices there in 1836. The building, wrote an early chronicler, "has accommodation for over four thousand persons, and it is the great Protestant forum and centre of attraction for all those who anxiously desire the spread of the Gospel, the dissemination of Christianity, and the evangelization of the world."[80] Thousands upon thousands gathered here to hear fiery sermons and speeches: lectures on science, God in Nature, and religion. No venue assembled so many: philanthropic revolutionaries, bible-protestants, humanitarian do-gooders, abolitionists, sanitary campaigners, evangelical crusaders, and singers. Exeter Hall hosted the great May meetings: the religious conventions of such pious bodies as the Bible Society, Temperance League, the Protestant Association (1835), the Sunday School Union (1803), Society for Promoting Christian Knowledge, the London City Mission, the British and Foreign Bible Society, the Religious Tract Society. The Society for the Recovery of Persons Apparently Drowned, or Humane Society (thus the word "humane") gathered annually to promote artificial respirators. (This society had long blown smoke up the public's ass, literally, by installing life-saving kits, including tobacco smoke enemas, at regular intervals along the Thames.) The great orators of the epoch delivered thunderous lectures to these crowds, hailed by some for their intensity of feeling, lambasted by others for submitting to the hall's stupefying atmosphere.[81]

"It is like living on a steamship," wrote Giuseppe Verdi, having arrived in May 1847 for the purposes of composing his opera *I masnadieri* for the voice of the Swedish nightingale. "The city of London resembles the face rather of Mount Etna, or the suburbs of hell, than an assemblage of rational creatures," agreed Meikleham in 1845, paraphrasing John Evelyn's classic account of the British capital in *Fumifugium* (1661).[82] Evelyn complained of "foul mouthed issues, and curls of smoke": the circulation of "infernal vapour" gathered "such a cloud of sulphur that the sun itself, which gives day to all the world beside, is hardly able to penetrate and impart it."[83] "I find all this smoke and smell of coal disagreeable," Verdi echoed in a letter to Countess Clara Maffei in Milan. "The diabolical climate takes away all desire to work," he muttered, "Blame the climate ... blame the climate."[84]

Though London did not have the worst of it, 1848 was a year of unprecedented atmospheric terror. According to pioneer of English weather forecasting James Glaisher of the Royal Observatory (down the Thames at Greenwich), the first signs of revolution were detectable in the air. (In 1862, Glaisher would offer a series of lectures to the Exeter Hall faithful on "Aerial Scientific Research" and "Scientific Experiments in Balloons.")[85] In the first quarter of 1848, according to Glaisher, London alone had experienced more rainfall than in the previous six years combined. It had been both unusually hot and unusually cold. By March 31, Glaisher warned that "great fluctuations in the readings appear to have been general, and differing from any period since 1800."[86] A worldwide disturbance, Glaisher claimed, was observable on the basis of meteorological data collected from across the global telegraphic network. He blamed the tide of political violence sweeping the continent on a great magnetic storm.

Whirlwinds were recorded in Penzance as early as December 12, 1847. Vesuvius erupted the following March and would do so again in April. Ice formed in Poona on February 16, only a few days before Paris's *révolution de Février*. Extreme cold hit Madrid at the same time as early hawthorn in Lancashire. Bombay was inundated on April 6. By June 13, the *Times* reported a "perfect tornado" at the heart of the Enlightenment in the vicinity of Berlin. "Trees have been uprooted," the newspaper recorded: "On whole tracts of garden ground the produce is ruined, the cherry harvest is nearly annihilated; the hailstones cut up every kind of tender vegetation, and the fields of corn are beaten flat." "Mob manifestations and tumult" in the region of Mendelssohn's beloved Singakademie followed the night after, with students facing down five battalions of the *burgherwehr*. The agitators barricaded Alexanderplatz, tearing down the palace gates and storming the arsenal.[87] By July, similar political outbreaks were being reported in Vienna, Prague, Budapest, Moscow, Milan, and Venice. For Glaisher, a mass of magnetic readings, made known through the news cycle of an industrial telecommunications network, explained the cause of the violence and the scale of the climatic event.

Recollecting the tumult of 1848, Karl Marx gave a speech at the Bell Hotel on the Strand, in the shadow of Exeter Hall eight years later, wherein he described "the revolutionary atmosphere enveloping and pressing from all sides." The Berlin-educated philosopher borrowed the language of atmospheric theory to account for the surge. "All that is solid melts into air," Marx wrote in *The Communist Manifesto*, published in London the day before workers gathered at La Madeleine to protest the ban on "banquets." All "fixed, fast-frozen relations" were "swept away" by the bourgeoisie's "constant revolutionising of production, uninterrupted disturbance of all social conditions, everlasting uncertainty and agitation." He decried the "subjection of Nature's forces to man, machinery, application of chemistry to industry and agriculture, steam-navigation, railways, electric telegraphs, clearing of whole continents for cultivation, canalisation of rivers."[88] Marx complained that bourgeois forces, now assimilating "the entire surface of the globe," sought to "nestle everywhere, settle everywhere, establish connections everywhere."[89] "Beneath the apparently solid surface," Marx told the Chartist banquet in broken English: "[the 1848 revolutions] betrayed oceans of liquid matter, only needing expansion to rend into fragments continents of hard rock." The earth itself was disintegrating. "Noisily and confusedly," Marx observed, "[the masses] proclaimed the emancipation of the Proletarian, i.e. the secret of the nineteenth century, and of the revolution of that century, the atmosphere in which we live weighs upon every one with a 20,000-pound force, but do you feel it?"[90]

The great evangelical preacher John Cumming agreed. The events of 1848 were a sign that "the last vial is now trembling in the angel's hand."[91] Cumming, pictured in figure 3.5, was in fact the most charismatic Victorian preacher-prophet on the Strand. The dissenting minister of the Scottish Church and orator in chief at Exeter Hall was "eminently handsome: his figure slight, but beautifully proportioned: his dress decidedly of the Genevan school."[92] Many found "his coal-black hair and eyebrows" sexually attractive. From the pulpit of Exeter Hall, every successive Sunday evening in 1847 and 1848, at the height of the *Elijah* craze, Cumming delivered catastrophist sermons to thousands of congregants. He was the leader of a vast antipopery movement, the British & Foreign Bible

FIGURE 3.5. "Rev. John Cumming," *The Drawing-Room of Eminent Personages*, 8 vols. (London: J. Tallis, 1860), II.

Society, and the Society for Promoting Female Education in the East. Cumming enjoyed lecturing on "speech loaded with music" in view of the greatest orators of his time, including Hugh M'Neile, Robert Hall, and Thomas Chalmers. His "clear and silvery" voice had just enough provincialism to pronounce him a native of the "land of the mountain and the flood."[93]

All classes flocked to hear his thunderous voice: pauper widows, prime minister John Russell and his wife, the Duchess of Wellington, even Queen

Victoria, who invited the prophet to Balmoral. Cumming foretold the fall of Islam. He claimed that the insights of meteorology and geology cast light upon the biblical processes by which "whole races have been suddenly destroyed and new races have been instantly created."[94] His lectures in evangelical science found God's footprints in "the red sand-stone, in the subterranean mine, in the fossil realms, in the mineral kingdom, in the saurian monster and in the ancient petrification."[95] George Eliot called Cumming the "Goshen of mediocrity, in which a smattering of science and learning will pass for profound instruction, where platitudes will be accepted as wisdom, bigoted narrowness as holy zeal, unctuous egoism as God-given piety."[96] (Eliot attended the second Exeter Hall performance of *Elijah* on April 23, 1847, the same witnessed by Prince Albert; she joked, as someone "who'd been guanoing her mind with French novels," that the event represented "a kind of sacramental purification of Exeter Hall.")[97] This "voluble retail talker," Eliot called him, preached that the telegraph had been foretold in Daniel, the steamship in Isaiah. Yet his lectures sold like hotcakes, commanding streamprint runs of up to sixteen thousand copies.

Cumming prophesied that the end of the world would take place on a day in 1864. "The seventh angel pours out the seventh vial," he thundered in a series entitled Apocalyptic Sketches presented to packed Exeter Hall audiences from August 1847 to January 1848. "And that vial, we are told," the prophet continued, "is not poured out, like the others, upon definite localities, but upon the air, or that atmosphere we breathe."[98] Cumming was a premillennialist; he was obsessed with the earth's sin-saturated breathable envelope. By the following December, Cumming could lecture on "1848: or, Prophecy Fulfilled." In this series, the preacher cited the language of newspapermen as evidence of the polluted orb. "'Our social atmosphere' is the language of one," he noted, "'our political atmosphere' is the language of another."[99] For him, the chain of revolutions sweeping Europe in 1848 heralded the second coming of Christ. "The Apocalypse speaks of contagion in the air as its source," Cumming boomed before one Exeter Hall assembly: "Science adds it Amen to Scripture, and says it is so."[100]

In contradistinction to his opinion of air, the preacher loved choral music, hailing Mendelssohn's *Elijah* as a magnificent and yet dim pre-echo of the great Grand Oratorio that would unify Creation on the Day of Days. "The insect upon the wing and the cherub beside the throne," he foretold, "all voices of sea and sky, and wind and wave, shall swell together the mighty harmony of that mighty song."[101] Mendelssohn's *Elijah*, for

Cumming, was a barely audible manifestation of that great Song of the Apocalypse, a Nature Music already roaring on the other side of silence. "We are to enter a new world, to breathe a new atmosphere, to hear new sounds, to come in contact with new objects, to behold intenser splendours, and brighter visions of joy and glory," he announced in his second series of *Apocalyptic Sketches*, "and we must be fitted for it by the Spirit of God, before we can enter or enjoy its happiness, or sing its songs, or breathe its air, or gaze upon its glories."[102] In his "Music in its relation to Religion," delivered in January 1850 to the Young Men's Christian Association at Exeter Hall, Cumming announced that "man's soul is audible, not invisible, as God gave an apocalypse of himself of old, not in the blazing fire, nor in the bursting earthquake, but in the 'still small voice.'" (Mendelssohn's chorus "Behold! God the Lord passeth by" was apparently still audible in the room.) Cumming extolled Mendelssohn's "rapturous flights of sound" and the solitary voice of Jenny Lind in the aria written for her, "Hear Ye, Israel" heard "as if a lull had occurred to the hurricane." According to his prophecy, those attuned to the "still small voice" would enter, after the destruction of Armageddon, into the full experience of Creation as Creation was intended.

Song, for Cumming, was the harbinger of Eden, an "inspiring power" that, though corruptible, "keeps off pulmonary disease."[103] "The atmosphere was meant as truly to be the vehicle of song and sweet sounds as to supply the lungs with oxygen," he thundered in a lecture on "Sacred Music," also delivered to the YMCA at Exeter Hall and illustrated by performances from a four-voice choir: "It is a mark of the goodness of God that the element He has made essential to life, He has made the element also of the very richest enjoyment."[104] Creation, that is, though out of tune in 1848, was a "living hymn" awaiting the Great Tribulation. "[Great works of music are] not the devil's property, and so to be left in his possession," Cumming explained, "but God's fallen things."[105]

At the same lecture:

> [Music] is a great leveler—this is a mistake—it is a great dignifier and elevator; it brings high and low nearer to each other. The wind which rushes through the organ at St George's Chapel at Windsor, has first passed through the barrel-organ of some poor Italian boy. The organ of church, and chapel and meeting-house, the voice of Jenny Lind, and that of the street-singer, have but one common capital to draw on—the unsectarian and catholic atmosphere, the failure of which would be the extinction of Handel, Haydn, and Mozart.

The air sometimes calls up Handels, and Haydns, and Mendelssohns, on the ocean, in the forest, and on desert winds; and these, like invisible, but not inaudible musicians, make glorious music. Sometimes the shrouds of a ship, as she rolls on the tempestuous deep, raise wild sopranos to the skies; sometimes the trees and branches of a forest of gigantic pines become mighty harp-strings, which, smitten by the rushing tempest, send forth rich harmonies,—now anthems of joy, anon dirges over the dead; sometimes the waves of the sea respond like white-robed choristers to the thunder bass of the sky.[106]

The "unsectarian and catholic atmosphere," that is, bound saints and sinners—the highest to the lowest—in a shared Humboldtian circle.

By these words, Cumming paraphrased the Ninth Bridgewater Treatise of 1837, the influential essay famously penned a decade earlier by Charles Babbage. God, for Cumming as for Babbage, was a divine meteorologist and the atmosphere a "vast library"—an ever-gathering datacloud of world-historical knowledge:

What a strange chaos is this wide atmosphere we breathe! Every atom, impressed with good and with ill, retains at once the motion which philosophers and sages have imparted to it, mixed and combined in ten thousand ways with all that is worthless and base. The air itself is one vast library, on whose pages are for ever written all that man has ever said or woman whispered. There, in their mutable but unerring characters, mixed with the earliest, as well as with the latest sighs of mortality, stand for ever recorded, vows unredeemed, promises unfulfilled, perpetuating in the united movements of each particle, the testimony of man's changeful will.[107]

Babbage's text was key to the making of modern climate—perhaps the first to recommend statistical and even computer modeling for analyzing complex weather systems.

"The atmosphere we breathe," Babbage famously wrote, "is the everyliving witness of the sentiments we have uttered."[108] Virtuous or evil deeds in one region of air had relational consequences, even at great distances, for virtuous or evil deeds in another. Every sound, the very "pulsations of the air, once set in motion by the human voice," in Babbage's reading, had global repercussions. For Babbage, those responsible for the cries of the 611 Africans suffocated in the hold of the slaveship *Felicité*, or the 150 souls thrown overboard the Portuguese slaver *Adalia* in 1837, would be held to account on Judgment Day. The "waves of air... that perambulate the earth and ocean's surface" were permanently impressed in the Book of Life.[109] Nothing shall pass.

Exeter Hall was the epicenter for choral reform in London. Besides the Amateur Musical Festival meetings of the Sacred Harmonic Society, the first class of the Exeter Hall "Normal School of Singing" under John Hullah was given here in February 1841.[110] Earlier experiments had occurred at a Normal School set up at Battersea in London for workhouse boys in green uniforms. The success of Hullah's "green birds" led the Committee of Council on Education to engage the same choirmaster to teach the fixed-doh system used by Guillaume-Louis Wilhem's Orphéonistes in Paris. (Wilhem was the father of those choral societies devoted, since 1833, to the pacification of the French laboring classes). These men developed an environmental approach to pedagogy. They applied Pestalozzian styles of active learning to music instruction, deducing theory from practice via a monitorial system involving hand gestures, reading machines, and "letter cases."[111] By the end of the first year, according to contemporary estimates, at least fifty thousand children of the laboring classes had begun to receive instruction in singing.[112] Hullah's reputation was such that, by the time of his "upper singing school" performance of *Elijah* at Exeter Hall on June 20, 1849, he was professor of vocal music at King's College London and a national treasure.[113]

For Hullah, an intimate of Mendelssohn and Henry Chorley, music was the "handmaid of Divinity." (Chorley, the music writer, had been introduced to Neukomm and then Moscheles via chapter 1's Sarah Bowdich; for him, in 1847, *Elijah* was the "sacred work of our time—a work for our children and our children's children."[114]) Instruction in choral singing, for Hullah, allowed the "town-bred mechanic" to "taste the breath of Heaven, fresh, blowing, pure and sweet," since singing tended "to unite and blend and harmonize all who may come within its sphere."[115] A key moral concern was to use air economically on the principle of "waste not; want not." Every breath was precious. "Every particle of air," Hullah charged, "which a speaker or singer (in action) exhales silently, is wasted—is something taken from the force and volume and ease of his utterance."[116] The imperative was not only to fortify the lungs by productive use of the atmosphere. Singing, according to an 1844 Committee of Council on Education report "relating to [Hullah's] Manual of Vocal Music," was an "important means of forming an industrious, brave, loyal, and religious working class."[117] As a reviewer of Hullah's *Part Music* in 1842 attested, choral song was a "great moral engine for softening the manners, refining the taste, and raising the character of the industrious community."[118] It allowed even the lowliest sinner to tune into that sacred Nature—as yet only faintly perceived—to which they all ideally belonged.

In the summer of 1848, the roof of Exeter Hall was raised, and the giant Joseph Walker organ of 1840 pushed back to improve aerial circulation. The architect on the project, Henry Daukes, insisted that the roof be arched, in ways that required the support of eighty tons of iron. Daukes preferred "tactile" to "forcing power," which is to say fewer steam engines. But it is fair to say that the necessity for reventilation would not have been felt without the participation of David Boswell Reid, the "Father of British Air-Conditioning," and a man closely associated with Exeter Hall (more about him soon).[119] Acoustics and ventilation were improved, following the advice of the new conductor of the Sacred Harmonic Society. Michael Costa recommended a domed instead of flat-paneled ceiling, and a larger orchestra, now seventy-eight feet wide, "eleven feet more than Birmingham Town Hall." A performance of—what else?—*Elijah* inaugurated the venue on November 1, 1848.[120]

A critic reported that "some two or three hundred members of the chorus are extricated from what was not much preferable to the blackhole at Calcutta. They can now breathe freely, and use their lungs without danger of suffocation."[121] The three-manual organ, on which Mendelssohn had played Bach's "St. Anne" Prelude and Fugue in E-flat Major BWV 552 in 1842, was augmented "with the view of increasing its power and efficiency."[122] Its 2,187 pipes were now relieved of harsh mixtures and tuned to equal temperament in order to "sweeten the whole body of choral sound."[123] Critics lauded the "powerful and brilliant" stringed instruments and the "delicacy and clearness" of horns and woodwind; they also wished that the trombones and drums had been less noisy for an *Elijah* that was "so far superior to anything ever previously heard at Exeter Hall."[124] The orchestra was rearranged: the basses and cellos were removed from the very front of the stage to the sides and back; the old iron railings were removed; and the conductor turned toward the players rather than outward toward the audience. Costa insisted upon "rigid discipline."[125] The old English "bearded altos" were replaced by women dressed in white on one side, with men in black on the other. One effect of introducing "a number of female voices into the alto part of the chorus" was that the sound acquired "a richness and mellowness it never had before."[126] The goal, in short, was Nature.

The "twin columns [of Exeter Hall], emulating those of Hercules," explained Undersecretary of State for the Colonies James Stephen in 1844, "fling their long shadows across the street through which the far-resounding Strand pours the full current of human existence into the deep recesses of Exeter Hall."[127] Stephen wrote of "an impetuous tide of sound" welling up within Exeter Hall: "a ceaseless swell of exulting or pathetic declamation." "The changeful strain rises with the civilisation of Africa," he explained, "or becomes plaintive over the wrongs of chimney-boys, or peals anathemas against the successors of Peter, or in rich diapason calls on the Protestant Churches to awake and evangelize the world."[128] (Stephen had recently overseen the implementation of the Slavery Abolition Act.) Buildings like these, the colonial administrator surmised, existed to stir up the song of global atmospheric Pentecost. "Gently and imperceptibly," wrote Charles Dickens of Exeter Hall ideology, "the widening circle of enlightenment must stretch and stretch from man to man, from people to people, until there is a girdle around the earth."[129]

III. St. George's Hall, Liverpool, 1854

Under construction for thirteen years, St. George's Hall in Liverpool—allegedly the "World's First Air-Conditioned Building"—was built in imitation of Birmingham Town Hall.[130] It too was a purpose-built concert venue paradigmatically associated with *Elijah*. Dickens called it "the most perfect hall in the world."[131] The structure boasted a ventilation system designed by aforementioned architect-engineer Boswell Reid. Predictably, a grand performance of *Elijah* consecrated the building the day after its ceremonial opening on September 21, 1854, with Pauline Viardot singing a memorable "O Rest in the Lord."[132]

Reid—also a composer of atmospheres—requisitioned four large steam-driven fans to force air, filtered and warmed, into a cavernous reservoir beneath the floor of St. George's Hall. Three more steam engines powered the oversized organ, two of them for the bellows and another, placed in the vaults below the floor, for supplying "the grand source of wind." Conceived by Bach fanatic Samuel Sebastian Wesley and built by Londoner Henry Willis, this nine-thousand-pound instrument, with an innovative radiating pedalboard, trumped its Birmingham rival in power.[133] "The grand object of the architect is to treat the room as if it were itself a part of a musical instrument," Reid explained while discussing the acoustics of the building. "Ventilation in a crowded assembly," he clarified, "is like the management of a musical instrument, which must not only be tuned to a proper key, but sustained continuously with an impulse apportioned to the strength and tone which it ought to breathe."[134]

Reid, as mentioned, engineered the first fully artificial climates in Britain, using a technique he called "systematic ventilation." Acoustic design or "the communication of sound" served his definition of architecture as "the act of enclosing and servicing an interior atmosphere." Reid's systems exploited the drawing power of the heat of large coal-fired steam boilers, which fed labyrinthine networks of pipes, ducts, and valves. The "mighty volcanos" stoked beneath his buildings supplied ventilation to such sealed governmental interiors as the state apartments of Buckingham Palace and Windsor Castle, London's Italian Opera house, Brighton Pavilion, the Old Bailey, prisons in Edinburgh, Perth, and Belfast, the Royal Yacht, as well as several floating chapels and hospital ships. Reid was famed for his work on the Houses of Parliament, where the maze of steam pipes ran for an estimated fifteen miles. Until recently, Reid claimed, "aerial agents, having in their control life and death, health and disease, comfort and oppression, floated almost unknown around the person, their power being neither fully recognized nor rightly understood."[135] Reid worked tirelessly to identify and eliminate these toxic agents.

Not that everyone was enthused. "There is something really tragic," wrote one critic of the effects of "ventilating mania" and "blasts from hell" at the House of Lords, "in a stately Baron exclaiming 'Air, give me air,' and the order to the usher to ask Reid's man to pump a few more cubic feet."[136] Others alleged that the provisions supplied to the leader of the opposition were not conducive to the proper conduct of democracy. "This would-be god of winds," protested another antagonist in 1846, "is nothing but a flatulent hobgoblin."[137]

Like sanitary reformers before him, Reid loved statistics. In his *Illustrations of the Theory and Practice of Ventilation . . . with remarks . . . on the Communication of Sound* (1844), Reid estimated that the inhabitants of the earth "respire annually 3,327,000,000 of tons of air, and evolve 109.5 million tons of carbon," the total weight of the atmosphere amounting to "about 5,261,000,000,000,000 of tons." The population of London, he estimated, evolved "annually, from their lungs, about 220,000 tons of carbon," whereas at any sitting of the House of Commons "on a very leading question, when 800 persons, members and strangers, are present for twelve hours, air is required for 11,520,000 respirations."[138] The "great and primary object of architecture," Reid argued, was "to afford the power of sustaining an artificial atmosphere."[139]

St. George's Hall was a work of civic purification, financed by Liverpool's historical involvement in the transatlantic slave trade—or rather the profits of the 1833 government bailout—the Slavery Abolition Act supplying the equivalent of a 16.5-billion-pound payout to British slave-holding families in compensation for their loss of property. Originally, over the grand southern portico was a sculptured pediment, since removed, featuring the stock abolitionist image of the figure of "Africa, in a posture of gratitude and humility, with her sons in her arms; the breaking of chains is the work of Britannia."[140] The organ, like the Minton tile–decorated interior, was conceived by architect Charles Robert Cockerell, who had assisted in rebuilding London's Covent Garden Theatre and whose wealth was based on his family's former slave holdings in Jamaica; his brother had been compensated for the "forfeiture" of no less than ten slave plantations in 1834.[141] Cockerell intended for the interior to re-create the thermal Roman baths of Caracalla.

Sanitation campaigners were implicated, such as Robert Rawlinson, then assistant surveyor to the corporation of Liverpool. But the kingpins of its planning were former slave traders, who were now among the wealthiest men in the city. On the original finance committee of the project were such luminaries as George Hall Lawrence, lord mayor of Liverpool from 1846–47, who was "compensated" by the Slavery Abolition Act for the loss of 218 enslaved persons and two plantations in Jamaica. William Earle, who served on the building's Improvement Committee, received payouts for the loss of 314 emancipated individuals and sugar plantations in British Guiana and Trinidad. Married to the granddaughter of antislavery campaigner MP William Roscoe, Henry Robertson Sandbach, also on the Improvement Committee, was compensated for the loss of 2,415 enslaved souls on more than eleven estates in British Guiana.[142] These were the men—harbingers of high culture—dedicated to Roscoe's vision of Liverpool as the Florence of the North. They both financed their own sanitary absolution and whitewashed the city's past in preparation for glorious postabolition profiteering.

Figure 3.6 shows another of Reid's claims to fame: his design for three air-conditioned steamships, launched in 1841 to penetrate the malarial swamps of the Niger River. The impetus for their design dated to the celebrated June 1840 meeting of the Society for the Extinction of the Slave Trade and the Civilization of Africa at Exeter Hall. Cumming was on the Select Committee, John Russell an advocate, Humboldt a foreign corresponding member, and Thomas Fowell Buxton occupied in the chair. Prince Albert, elected president, gave his first public address here. It was at this meeting, introduced by the sounds of the Exeter Hall organ, that it was decided to launch an antislavery mission and geoengineering project, one involving three air-conditioned steamships built to penetrate the malarial swamps.[143]

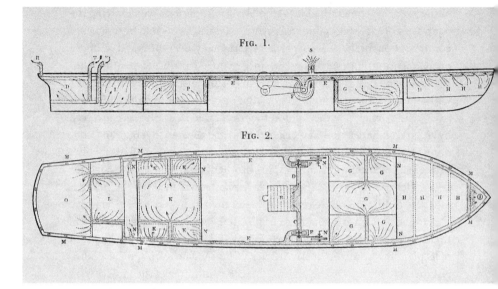

FIGURE 3.6. James O. McWilliam, *Medical History of the Expedition to the Niger During the Years 1841–2* (London: John Churchill, 1843), 255. Note how the transport of whiteness contrasts with that of figure 4.3. Wellcome Collection, https://creativecommons.org/licenses/by/4.0/legalcode.

Reid's space capsules, built in the wake of the so-called abolition of slavery, were Victorian precursors of moon units. All three vessels were assembled at the docks in Liverpool. Reid calculated for the amount of air per person required, on the basis of his claim that healthy individuals breath twelve hundred times per hour. The system of valves and tubes under the gunwales worked according to Reid's "vacuum principle" and "plenum principle." At times of malarial danger, as when entering the poisoned atmosphere of the Niger Delta on August 13, 1841, a "medicator or purifying chamber" was activated to pass the "sulphureted hydrogen" over tanks of lime and chlorine. The point was to cleanse vitiated air. Antislavery leader of the Africa Civilization Society Joseph John Gurney explained that steam vessels, "if brought fully to bear, may wonderfully facilitate all our dealings with Africa—carry its visitors swiftly and easily through the unhealthy deltas, and introduce them to those spots in the interior, where they may act on the population, for its temporal and spiritual welfare, with the greatest advantage."[144] These lifeboats were the civilizing technologies by which self-proclaimed abolitionists carried their own environments into malarial zones. The medical topography required that they isolate themselves from the slave reservoirs they had once engineered to build their cities.

One key aim of the Niger expedition was to defeat the harsh climate by cultivating commercial trade in the Gulf of Guinea. An attendant goal was to establish model plantations in the interior, to be overseen by West Indian farmers. In order to circumvent the suffering of the enslaved, additionally, the air chemistry mission would need to collect statistics on hygrometry, disease, botanical life, ethnographic data, demography, geology, climate, air pressure, and terrestrial magnetism. In this, in collecting and collating scientific knowledge of the medical topography of West Central Africa, Philip D. Curtin argues, the expedition can be counted a success.[145] Otherwise, the mission was disastrous. Only a month after the HMS *Wilberforce* had penetrated the bar at the River Nun, the expedition's "geographer of plants," Berlin-based Theodor Vogel, recommended to the expedition by Humboldt himself, fell ill and died. Soon after, malaria killed almost a third of the 150 Europeans, whereupon the expedition was pronounced a failure. This seriously damaged the cause of global humanitarianism. "A great antislavery expedition goes to Africa," historian of the mission Howard Temperley wryly observes, "and establishes—a slave plantation."[146]

IV. Crystal Palace, London, 1860

Finally, the Crystal Palace in Hyde Park, London—arguably the birthplace of classical music—hosted the largest performances of *Elijah* ever.[147] The Palace was a 1.2-million-cubic-meter greenhouse, lifted for the Great Exhibition in 1851 and built in conjunction with Wyld's Great Globe, for the paradigmatic World Fair; in 1854, it was rebuilt on a larger scale near Sydenham Hill. Of glass and steel, the interior shown in figure 3.7 was conceived, according to the modular design of horticulturalist Joseph Paxton, as an imperial global museum. A glittering cathedral, the edifice symbolized the ideological triumph of fossil-fuel industrialism. It raised the ideals of sonic immersion to intoxicating levels and all within an immense artificially climatized interior.

Dostoevsky, the Russian novelist, felt suffocated by "all the world" when he visited in 1862:

> You feel a terrible force which has united all these numberless people here, from all over the world, into a single herd; you become aware of a colossal idea; you feel that something has already been achieved here, that there is victory, triumph here. It's even as if you begin to feel afraid of something. No matter how independent you are, for some reason you feel terrified. "Hasn't the ideal already been achieved?" you think,

FIGURE 3.7. "The Great Orchestra inside the Crystal Palace, London," *The Illustrated London News* 30 (June 27, 1857): 630–31.

"isn't this the end? isn't this already in fact "a single herd." Aren't you forced, in fact, to accept this as the full truth and grown numb once and for all? It's all so solemn, triumphant and proud that you begin to gasp for breath. You look at these hundreds of thousands, these millions of people obediently streaming here from all over the earth—people coming with a single thought, peacefully, insistently and silently crowding into this colossal palace and you feel that something final has been accomplished, accomplished and brought to a close. It's a kind of biblical scene, something from Babylon, some kind of prophecy from the Apocalypse being fulfilled before your very eyes."[148]

The pollution necessary for the manufacture of this structure was barely in evidence, since, in the house of enlightenment, one barely heard the wind and rain rattling at the glass.[149] For Dostoyevsky, the building presaged the end of history.

Elijah's popularity at the Crystal Palace culminated in the Mendelssohn Festival performances of 1860, involving at least twenty thousand participants. It was inside this glass house that the first modern concert program notes were written (by August Manns to celebrate the centenary of Mozart's birth in 1856); where classics were incubated, particularly in the 1860s and 1870s; where, at the Handel Commemoration of 1859, the preserved manuscripts of the *Messiah*, *Israel in Egypt*, *Acis and Galatea*, and the *Dettingen Te Deum* were displayed under glass. It was here that the autograph of Schubert's Symphony no. 7, purchased by George Grove from Mendelssohn, was exhibited similarly in the Center Transept in 1883; where the high-pressure 4,568-piped, 16-reservoir organ by Gray & Davison (1854–57) loomed large; where the "African Mahler" Samuel Coleridge-Taylor first received music lessons in 1880; where fragments of a live performance of Handel's oratorio *Israel in Egypt* conducted by Manns on June 29, 1888, with 4,000 singers and 500 musicians was captured by George Edward Gouraud's Edison phonograph. It was here, flanked by the palace's indoor trees, that critics grumbled about the individual parts of *Elijah* being indistinguishable and lost to reverberation, though most agreed that the numbness of the environment was beguiling. It was at the palace that the audience rose from their seats (as was traditional at least since the Gloucester Music Festival of September 1850) for the culminating "Sanctus" of Mendelssohn's *Elijah*.[150] "Holy, Holy, Holy is God the Lord, the Lord Sabaoth!" chanted three thousand choral singers, for the monster Mendelssohn performance of May 1860, the Part 2 quartet ringing antiphonally across the center transept.

Conclusion

"Holy, Holy, Holy" provides a fitting climax. But it is "Yet doth the Lord see it not," another chorus resonating in the wake of Elijah's introductory curse, that narrates the progress of the "Recovery of Eden" archetype best. "Yet doth" is an expanded cyclic variation of the musical materials first exposed in Elijah's prologue. The chorus captures the narrative arc of both the oratorio plot and the first tableau of Mendelssohn's *Elijah*. It progresses from fire, suffocation, and drought—to rain, precipitation, immersion, and Nature recovered, by which I mean Nature "covered over" or "discovered again." It moves from catastrophe to healing.

Dwight, who probably heard a September 1852 performance *Elijah* with Viardot again in the Birmingham Town Hall, described a chorus in C-minor "full of diminished sevenths and of discords from bold overlapping of one chord upon another."[151] The critic noted how "Yet doth the

FIGURE 3.8. Proof copy of *Elijah* prepared for Ewer's 1847 piano reduction, with corrections and alterations in several hands, some by Mendelssohn and William Bartholomew. The Hanna Holborn Gray Special Collections Research Center, The University of Chicago Library, call number: alc M2003.M5E4 18–b.

Lord see it not" prefigures the grand fire and rain choruses of Part 1, and identified three sections. The first section, begun in figure 3.8, takes the rising arpeggio first heard in Elijah's prologue over the words "As God the Lord of Israel" and throws that arpeggio between vocal parts over a string tremolo. The two-note sighing figure, "I stand" now heard chorally as "at us," leads to several iterations of the diminished-fifth curse, indicated on page 28 of the figure: "His curse has fallen upon us!" A cyclic expansion of the stepwise rising minor thirds at "his wrath will pursue us" completes this first section, with the curse motive now repeatedly heard. The five repeated notes of "till he destroy us" correspond to the "-ccording to my word" that had once concluded Elijah's opening prologue.

The middle section of the number is a Bachian chorale, expressive of congregational joining in, where diminished fifths steadily resolve into descending perfect fifths. While proofreading the first English-language piano-vocal score, Mendelssohn asked to retranslate the English words, from "For He is Lord and God" to, as Dwight described it, "'FOR HE, THE LORD OUR GOD, HE IS JEALOUS GOD,' &c., thrown up like a mountain range of the primeval granite in the midst of this great musical creation."[152] The third section anticipates the great "rain chorus" in the parallel major at the end of Part 1. "Yet [the mountain range] is not all barren," wrote Dwight of this anticipatory end, "for erelong its sides wave with the forests sprung from the accumulated soil of ages, and the solemn procession of the clouds in heaven passes in shadows over their surface; the key shifts to the major; the accompaniments acquire a freer movement; rich, refreshing modulations succeed each other smoothly, and the vocal parts diverge in separate streams of perfect harmony, at the thought: 'HIS MERCIES ON THOUSANDS FALL.'"[153] At these words, the rising lines, once expressive of suffocation, turn into descending ones, falling across the interval of a fifth again, indicating precipitation. This third section proffers total aesthetic immersion. "You feel the changing temperature of the air in some of those modulations," Dwight wrote of the rain chorus, soon to be expanded into "Thanks be to God!": "What a *gusto*, what a sense of coolness.... There are certain chords there which we would call *barometrical* or atmospheric."[154] Once again, the concluding "-cies on thousands fall" echo the five-note termination of the prophesy. By this expansion of Elijah's prophetic-thematic materials, Nature breathes back to life.

And so, rain falls.

In his *Carbon Democracy* (2011), Timothy Mitchell argues that "fossil fuels helped create both the possibility of modern democracy and its limits."[155] "Democracy in its best sense is merely the letting in of light and air," abolitionist James Russell Lowell agreed as early as 1884. "All free governments, whatever their name, are in reality governments by public opinion, and it is on the quality of this public opinion that their prosperity depends," Lowell pronounced as he accepted the presidency of the Birmingham and Midland Institute: "It is, therefore, their first duty to purify the element from which they draw the breath of life." He continued: "With the growth of democracy grows also the fear, if not the danger, that this atmosphere may be corrupted with poisonous exhalations from lower and more malarious levels, and the question of sanitation becomes more instant and pressing."[156] The question of perfecting sanitation and artificial ventilation touched upon more than just the concerns of prosperity. For

Lowell and his associates, true government provided life support for the very possibility of goodness. Democracy itself was a form of compensation: it was useful but only in the sense that it provided relief to a dying system, prolonging, insofar as it was possible, the life of an accursed energy regime.

In the same way that the health of democracy depended on the afflictions of the carbon economy, so *Elijah* at once manifested the causes of global warming and the prognosis for its cure. The artwork was at once financed by coal-fired energy profits and delivered to the world in order to offset the costs of industrial progress. The nature of art, when produced under the sign of the steam engine, was fraught. Prophets knew this, and those within the circle, Mary Somerville for one, recognized, from the onset, a chaos internal to the energy regime. Prophets like her understood very well that the world system taking shape all around was cursed, even as it formed. If there were those who sought to hasten the second coming of Christ, there were many more who worked to resist pollution, if only for the purposes of continued financial gain. *Elijah*, that is, was an artwork invested in atmospheric reform, but only insofar as it was also invested in atmospheric contamination. It was an eschatological work, in that it was devised not merely to strengthen lungs but also to provide moral fortification in failing conditions.

Historically speaking, then, industrialism and environmentalism emerged alongside each other. The worship of Nature and the worship of Industry developed in parallel as dialectical and mutually reinforcing opposites. The need to care for the environment would never have arisen without industrialism; industrialism, in turn, necessitates colonial projects of environmental, moral, and ethnic cleansing. Were it not for imperial expansion, the threats of global warming or greenhouse gas emissions would not exist. (French mathematician Joseph Fourier famously identified greenhouse gas effects as early as 1827.) Without big data, the transnational spread of techniques of atmospheric and statistical measurement, telegraphic communication systems, global programs of scientific collection, the emergence of the life sciences, and the violence of capitalist and imperial conquest, such concepts as "the climate crisis" or "the Anthropocene" would be unknowable. Industry and Nature, toxicity and healing, evil and good, colonialism and environmentalism: the inconvenient truth is that these ostensibly contrary poles in the cosmology turn out to be mutually reinforcing. Which is to say that the solution to the crisis of the carbon economy was never available or reproducible within the cosmological structure itself.

CHAPTER 4

Black *"Possession"*
Santa Maria de Belém do Grão-Pará, Brazil, 1871

Equatorial Milieu Redux

The air of these countries dictates the making of slaves.
(Per commorationem iis in locis, ubi aër dicitur servos facere.)
JOHANN-GOTTLIEB HEINECCIUS, *Elementa iuris civilis secundum ordinem Pandectarum: commoda auditoribus methodo adornata*[1]

Music and fireworks sounded to ward off evil spirits on January 20, 1871, when Joseph Beal Steere waded ashore. It was full moon: the last night of the Festividade do Glorioso São Sebastião. (Sebastian was patron saint of pestilence and plagues at the mouth of the Amazon.) A wooden chapel, raised on posts, stood near Rebordello, a site indicated exactly on the line of the equator in figure 4.1. Rebordello was a remote settlement logged in mid-seventeenth-century Jesuit records as the epicenter of Arawak-speaking Aruã resistance.[2] Newcomers here feared so called African tropical fevers. Supposedly originating in equatorial Africa, yellow fever in particular routinely contaminated the holds of foreign ships, merchant cruisers, and steamers. Early in 1870, tropical epidemiologists narrated how this specific scourge—this time incubated at the African slave ports of Gorée and Saint-Louis—overtook Cape Verde, swept through Cuba, Jamaica, and Guadeloupe, before forcing Buenos Aires, Rio de Janeiro, Bahia, and much of the Brazilian littoral into lockdown.[3] By 1871, the fever was endemic to the area in ways that threatened Euro-American plans to transform the rainforest ecology of the equatorial basin—a giant carbon store romanticized in this period as the lungs of global organic life—into the perfect commercial resource.

Steere entered the life-rich zone at a propitious moment. Under US pressure, on September 7, 1867, the Brazilian Empire had opened the Amazon and its tributaries to "the flags of all nations."[4] Steere—naturalist,

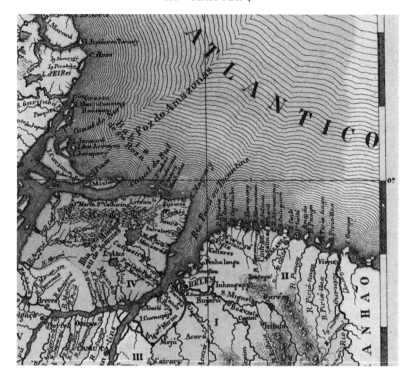

FIGURE 4.1. *Atlas do Império do Brasil*, ed. Cândido Mendes de Almeida (Rio de Janeiro: Lithographia do Instituto Philomathico, 1868), IV. Library of Congress, Geography and Map Division.

anthropologist, song hunter—collected human and nonhuman specimens for museums at the University of Michigan. He catalogued and shipped dead birds, reptiles, mammals, and plants, while his "Language and Music of a Few Tribes of the River Purus, Brazil" (November 30, 1871) transcribed "girl songs" and "boat songs" of the Hypurinas (*Apurina*) and Pamarys (*Paumaris*) within the Amazon.[5] As a philologist, he salvaged dialects and made phonetic transcriptions of several languages. Inspired by his Swiss-American mentor Louis Agassiz, Steere's observations on the modernity of interracial types honored avant-garde theories of racial *métissage*.

The introduction of steam navigation was rapidly transforming this ecosystem. Steere took four days to travel to Caviana Island from Santa Maria de Belém do Grão-Pará, a city sixty-two miles inland and a gateway to the Amazon River system. His steamer skirted the western edge of the largest fluvial delta island on earth, indicated as both Marajó and Joannes Island in figure 4.1. Cowboys, river dwellers, the enslaved, and maroon communities lived among cattle estates in the archipelago.[6] Many were Black, as Alfred Russel Wallace, progenitor of theories of evolution and natural selection in this territory, observed twenty-four years earlier. Wallace had landed at Mexiana, a smaller island fifteen miles to the east.[7]

Having climbed a bank to enter "a large low hut," Steere recorded two violins, banjos, guitars, and a clarinet—instruments "played alternately by nearly all the men present, there being no regular musicians." Women wore "costly dresses and gold beads" (perhaps in the green and red associated with the cult of Saint Sebastian). Men dressed in white. Dancers "of nearly all colors and conditions" went barefoot. "The only regulation" for participation, Steere surmised, was "that they should all be free."[8] Activities began innocently enough: secular French dances, with African couples-within-a-circle dances inserted as interludes. Steere noted the frequent exchange of partners during the latter and "a series of mysterious movements about the room of turning in unison as if in pivots and of strange passes as if they sought to magnetize each other, all the time snapping the fingers."[9] The room was lit by "little rough clay lamps, made by the [Africans] and filled with the oil of the andiroba, which grows in the forest here."[10] The oil released a sweet-smelling mosquito repellent that worked to ward off illness.

After midnight, according to Steere, the *festa* took a turn. The circling movements went viral as profane conjoined with sacred. A curtain opened to reveal an alcove filled with "grotesque figures." A wooden casket was revealed containing images and icons of Catholic saints as well as other idols. Steere heard "a song, or a pro nobis, in mixed Latin and Portuguese, which seemed to include a pretty large scale of all the saints in its supplications; the female part of the congregation kissed the images." There were signs, Steere added, of "scrape of the foot"—an indication, he felt, of this racialized class's "loss of self."[11] Having honored "the household gods," the ritualists grew possessed. "The dance went on with renewed zeal," Steere complained, especially when the overconsumption of cane brandy perpetuated disturbing scenes of sexual violence. At this, Steere withdrew, and tried to get some sleep, even as "the music clash[ed] away within a few feet of my head." The festivities continued through the night, in fact until four o'clock the following afternoon. Though his diaries betrayed a love for syncretic music, a mystified Steere waded back to his boat at this point, lamenting "the loose system of morals" existing in this milieu.[12]

Celebrated in popular festivals in the nine days before January 20, Saint Sebastian manifests the combined ritual practices of folk Catholicism/

Kardecian spiritism, Amerindian shamanism/*Pajelança*, and African fetishist animism. Then as now, Saint Sebastian presided as the spirit warrior of the Marajoran wetlands. Historians tell that his cult emerged during the 1340s, when bubonic plague devastated Afro-Eurasia and the Mediterranean world, killing, by some estimates, 60 percent of the European population.[13] In Marajó, Sebastian interceded against infection, offering solace to the sick; the arrows piercing his body explained outbreaks of lesions and swelling.[14] He was provider, protector, and advocate. Brought across the seas, his white body, injured and bound to the stake as if a beaten slave, iconized the suffering and survival of a persecuted and displaced people.

In the early 1960s, American anthropologists Seth and Ruth Leacock described the syncretization of Sebastian in the Amazon region with the *encantado* Rei Sebastião, an ancestral entity of white rather than Black or Amerindian inspiration.[15] *Encantados* are the enchanted ones—thousands of spirits who live below or above the earth in hidden dwelling places beneath bays, rivers, beaches, streams, and forests. Rei Sebastião, the former king of Portugal, battled the Lisbon plague of 1569 and went missing while crusading in what is now northern Morocco. His spirit, together with those of his family and warriors, presides at several beaches on existing islands along the coast between Belém and São Luís. In particular, he enchants Pará's "Salgado Paraense" (in figure 4.1, the coastal shores to the northeast of Vigia).[16] The Leacocks described so-called spirit possession cults at a *terreiro* (or place of worship) in the Pedreira neighborhood of Belém, where they were told that Rei Sebastião, together with his family and warriors roamed the Lençol dunes and salt marshes farther to the east at Maranhão.[17] If one walks that beach on dark nights, the Leacocks learned, the sounds of the spirits preside: one hears Sebastião's enchanted children crying, while at New Moon the king himself takes the spiritual form of a bull.[18] (Extraordinarily, with chapter 1's discussion of leukopathy in view, the Praia do Lençol is today officially recognized as the location with the highest recorded population of persons with albinism, these "children of King Sebastião" or "children of the moon" purportedly cursed to live with skin disease under a hostile equatorial sun.[19])

In metropolitan Belém, the Leacocks witnessed entities of the Rei Sebastião pantheon "possessing" spirit mediums, at "drumming ceremonies" of what they called, in the 1960s, the *batuque* religion. Sebastian has many names. He might "ride" spirit mediums as Xapanan, the Yoruban god of smallpox, an irascible deity with power over insects and mosquitos. He might be Omulu, the *orixá* (an *encantado* of high status) of pestilence: yellow fever, smallpox, and cholera. Alternatively, he might be received by children of the saint as Baluaé (the disfigured *orixá* of healing), Oxossi (a Yoruban forest deity), or the *coboclo* deity Sete Flechas (Seven arrows), endowed with power to prevent or contain disease.[20] The Leacocks recorded the *doutrina*, still frequently danced and sung in the 2020s to these words, inviting the *encantado*'s "possession":[21]

Rei Sebastião, guerreiro militar	King Sebastian, military warrior
Rei Sebastião, guerreiro militar	King Sebastian, military warrior
O Xapanan	O Xapanan
Éle é pai de terreiro	He is the father of the terreiro
Éle é guerreiro	He is a warrior
Nesta guerra imperial	In this imperial war[22]

According to oral accounts collected for the American Museum of Natural History, the first "spirit possession" ceremonies in urban Belém dated from only around the 1890s. A *mãe de santo* (female cult leader) named Dona Doca reportedly brought her spirits with her from Maranhão. Later literature, however, disputes this claim, noting deeper and more eclectic histories of African spiritual practice and musicking in the region.[23]

Ex-appropriation

This chapter invokes the spirit of King Sebastian, a wounded white crusader who, to cite Nietzsche, emerged "in the age of disintegration in which the races mixed, who has in his body the legacy of diverse origins, which is to say contradictory drives and standards [whose] fundamental desire is that the war, *which he is*, should finally have an end."[24] It narrates the absorption of a "colonial wound"—an *élément noir*—into the corpus of lettered music and white musical knowledge in the equatorial Atlantic.[25] Kim Sauberlich, whose scholarship on dances of the enslaved in the Luso-Brazilian Atlantic follows Barbara Browning in diagnosing a contagious Afrodiasporic musicking, provides a model for this work.[26] A prepossessing environmental approach, in what follows, proves useful to a dense description of the war for spiritual control of Black Amazonia. An awareness of ecological matters defined medical discourse about and public articulations of what the previous chapter called "the doctrine of the epidemic air." At issue is a Euro-American struggle to ex-appropriate African popular vitality and absorb that vitality into the environmental management systems of white settler populations. The story of the shift from agricultural slave societies to modern urban control societies after 1867 is complicated in view of the ways in which fossil capital strategically ex-appropriated slavery into steam navigation industries in this equatorial milieu.[27] In question is not the growing popularity or outbreak of the kinds of injurious festive musics Steere described in 1871. Rather, it is the outbreak of a biomedical discourse, evinced in the colonial archive, that was applied, as much to the government of racial mixing as to the government of epidemic musics. For such white crusaders as Steere, it was becoming possible to be wounded à la Saint Sebastian. It was becoming possible to be prepossessed by the sounds of a syncretic religious festivity.

For Steere, the fact of "possessed" Afro-Catholic festivity was due to the atmospheric presence of Blackness, which explained the prevalence of infectious disease among nonacclimatazed whites. His research was informed by such American Confederacy expatriates as the Louisianian sugar and cotton planter with an estate across the bay from Belém and Romulus John Rhome, a former Texas cattle rancher with a slave plantation four hundred miles upriver. Disgruntled slaveholders from the southern United States had been granted land and assisted immigration as compensation for their losses during the American Civil War (1861–65). Spurred to counter race-based arguments that the climate was uncivilizable, Brazilian elites approved plans for the *branqueamento* or whitening of the Amazon. A rival project, mooted by US Consul-General J. Watson Webb in Rio de Janeiro, was to exploit the site as a dumping ground for formerly enslaved African Americans. "All the freed negroes of the United States shall be transplanted to the region of the Amazon," Webb proposed, "at the expense of the United States, and there be endowed with land gratuitously."[28] "I do not know in the world of a country richer, fuller of attractions, healthier, fitter to be the focus of a population of 20 million white Euro-American immigrants," Steere's mentor Agassiz protested, "than this magnificent valley of the Amazons." By the time of Steere's visit, however, many white *confederados* were so demoralized by disease that they begged for financial assistance to return back to the United States.

By the 1870s and 1880s, as Steere's field notes on the festival of Saint Sebastian at Rebordello suggest, discourses about "loss of self" served a legitimizing function. The epigraph of Heineccius that introduces this chapter suggests that "the air of certain countries" ipso facto "makes" slaves, slavery being endemic to those climates where conditions were deemed to have enslaved first. Those creatures of the air subject to the *terreiro* were already "possessed," according to the legal terms of discourses of natural possession or *usus* (so termed under Roman law). Talk about music-induced trances, in other words, was hardly new.[29] Pro-slavery advocates had long used "possession state discourse" to make claims about the peoples they dispossessed. Steere clearly interpreted the fact of Blackness as a sign both of lack of self-possession and of climates that purportedly caused race in the first place. If it is true that the concept of subjectivity itself was formed in relation to modern concepts of property, then the fact of "spirit possession" in dance and music proved that nonwhites were predisposed to enslavement, therefore legitimizing "recursive dispossession."[30] The stereotyping of nonwhite peoples as essentially "unfree" worked to establish the conceit of their ill-suitedness to owning property as much as to justify the continuance of slavery.[31] Discourses about "spirit possession," that is, validated dispossession, while the Amazon was restructured as property, the supposedly virgin rainforests being mythologized as "free for use" whether by modern Brazil or the international economy.

The "opening up" of this territory coincided with the final intensifications of the three-centuries-old institutions of slavery, the establishment of antislavery (but also anti-Black) emancipationist societies in Belém, the strategic manufacture of such endo-epidemic threats as yellow fever, as well as the institution of public health strategies to quarantine those threats—government measures imposed on Paraense populations in the name of sanitation and infectious disease control. (Anything "Paraense" comes from the state of Pará.) The corollary to the establishment of antislavery societies at the Amazon gateway was the emerging disciplinary prestige of modern biological race sciences.[32] One striking fact revealed below is how much music and sound reputedly infested the region. In the spiritual race war for this environment, rhythms and sounds were imagined as both poison and cure, degenerate and civilizing, virus and vaccine.[33] Steere's project was to quarantine musics in view of a perceived racial essence, integrate these musics into the ever-widening circle of white knowledge, decry the modernity of ethnic mixing, and struggle toward the biopolitical enclosure of global environmental life.

The most celebrated activist in the liberal Brazilian struggle against slavery, Joaquim Nabuco, in *O Abolicionismo* (1883), enamored of the doctrine of the epidemic air, invented entire histories on the back of the myth of racio-environmental war:

> Slavery enveloped our entire populated space from Amazonas to Rio Grande do Sul in an environment destructive to all the manly, generous, humanitarian, and progressive qualities of our species. It created a crude, money-grubbing, selfish, and backward national vision, and for centuries it cast in this pattern the three heterogeneous races which

today constitute the Brazilian nationality. In other words, it made the air itself *servile*, to use the medieval legal phrase, like the air of the villages of Germany where no free man could live without losing his freedom. *Die Luft leibengen war* is a phrase which, when applied to all of Brazil, best sums up the national legacy of slavery. It created an atmosphere that envelops and stifles all of us, and this in the richest and most admirable of the world's dominions.[34]

The spirit of slavery, in other words, plagued breathing. "Wherever it goes," Nabuco wrote, slavery "burns the forests, and mines and exhausts the land; and when it moves on, it leaves behind a devastated countryside in which a miserable population of wandering vagrants is just able to survive." For such abolitionists as Nabuco, African belief systems asphyxiated the lived experience of a sterile and indolent populace. There were two paths to redemption: either to institute a national project of whitening, or to bioengineer an altogether different habitat. "The Brazilian people need a new environment," Nabuco concluded of this second plan, "an entirely different atmosphere in which to develop and grow."[35] This chapter addresses the "war," as imagined by abolitionists as much as anyone else, to cultivate that "entirely different atmosphere" at the gateway to the Amazon.

Santa Maria de Belém was a city built "in the midst of the living waters," generations of engineers having worked to push back the feverish seasonal tides of Guajará Bay, the Guamá, and Tocantins rivers. Sugar exports declined precipitously from 1867, though slave labor still serviced steam-powered plantation mills processing molasses and cane brandy. The population had doubled since the first modern appearance of yellow fever twenty years earlier. From 1865 to 1869, the annual value of exported raw rubber shipped from Belém nearly tripled from 3,959,036 to 9,698,721 milréis.[36] Scraps formed by coagulations on the "weeping tree"—*caoutchouc/caá-uchü* from the Tupi for "wood that weeps"—were collected and transported as "negroheads" from Pará.[37] With global demand for rubber soaring, extraction would require brutally ethnocidal forms of racial capitalism on both sides of the Ethiopic Ocean. Consider the Cabinda coast, a territory with strong ties to Pará, as introduced alongside Eduard Pechuël-Loesche at the beginning of this book.

In Belém, slave labor and industrial capitalism were codependent. The 1872 census, itself a sign of growing faith in public health surveillance and statistical reason, recorded the presence of 5,087 enslaved persons (2,609 men and 2,738 women) in a total city population of 34,464. Approximately a third of the estimated 22,443 enslaved Africans imported to the state of Pará between 1816 and 1841 were shipped from West Central Africa.[38] The proportion of urban slaves never fell in the two decades before the passing of the *Lei Áurea* ("Golden Act") in 1888, when Brazil finally declared itself free of slavery.[39] The exemplary work of social historian José Maria Bezerra Neto shows that the city streets were a refuge for fugitive slaves after 1867, as the police turned a blind eye to legal enforcement. Fugitives found opportunities for social insertion in Belém, often in Amazon steam navigation industries.[40] "Unlike the other northern and northeastern provinces of Brazil," writes Oscar de la Torre in his *Black Amazonia* (2018), Pará absorbed more of the enslaved than it lost to coffee-producing southern states. Belém, in particular, cultivated an extraordinarily flexible system of domestic slavery, becoming the commercial hub for slave exchange in the province.[41]

The dependence of fossil energy industries on slave labor was exemplified during a reported *batuque* outbreak in Belém central in early February 1869, "not heard in the city center for a very long time."[42] *Batuque* is a generic word often speculated to have Portuguese origins. (*Bater* means "to beat," "to strike," "to hammer"; *batucar*, "to hammer," "to drum.") Some scholars say the word has *bantu* roots, the noun *batukue* referring to "they who have become excited."[43] More accurately, the term was used by white writers to stigmatize Black Atlantic musical ceremonies from Cape Verde to Cuba to Cabinda, as we saw in the description of "the batuco" in the introduction to this book. The Leacocks, who we met earlier, folklorized *batuque* as "the principle public ceremony of the Batuque religion." They observed practitioners moving in a slow counterclockwise circle within an open three-walled pavilion concealing a curtained alcove, which served as a chapel. "The trapped tropical night air, heavy with humidity, seems to inhibit the normal outward ripple of the sound waves," they poetized: "The monotonous boom of the drums, the rustle of the gourd rattle [*maracá*], the metallic clatter of the *cheque-cheque* (an elongated metal cylinder or *ganzá*), all seem held in oppressive suspension directly over the *terreiro*."[44] Drum patterns called forth "winds of divination," summoning *orixas* and whole pantheons of spirits. "Treatment by maraca," (*tratamento do maracá*), meanwhile, was a phrase often applied to *Pajelança* healing rituals around 1871.[45]

On February 2, 1869, as Bezerra Neto has shown, the *Diario do Gram-Pará* printed an open public letter of complaint signed by seven prominent city residents about "batuque" practices occurring at a *sobrado* or

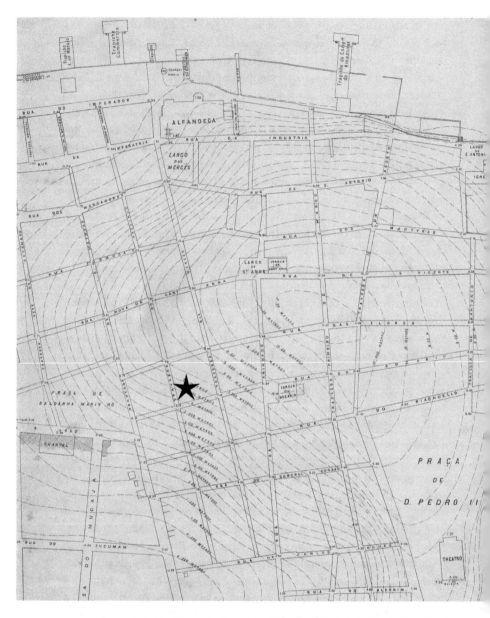

FIGURE 4.2. Detail in Edmundo Compton, *Planta da Cidade de Belém do Gram-Pará* (1881). National Archives of Brazil, BR RJANRIO F2.0.MAP.69.

Portuguese colonial-style residence in the Campina neighborhood of the "Bélem da belle époque."[46] According to the letter, a "slave camp" flourished on the travessa do Passinho (now Campos Sales) between Flores (Ó De Almeida) and Rozario (Aristides Lobo), marked as a star in figure 4.2. The travessa do Passinho was a rapidly gentrifying "French" commercial street with high-end clothing, including boutique shoe and elegant fabric stores. The sounds of drumming erupted at a site soon to be equidistant from the iconic "Paris N'America" department store off the Largo das Mercês founded in 1870 (the current art nouveau building dates from 1909) and the nearby Theatro da Paz. The neoclassical opera house, its foundation laid in March 1869, would eventually boast ornamental facades in imitation of Paris's Opéra Garnier. Only a block east of the disturbance was the low-lying swampy Piri, a historic source of "mephitic miasmatic exhalations" and perennial target of sanitary improvement, that once divided this neighborhood from the Old City. Two blocks east was the historic Igreja Nossa Senhora do Rosário dos Homens Pretos, recently built for Black Catholicism by the enslaved, "the materials [having] all been purchased by their own savings."[47] Every Saturday and Sunday night, the letter contended, "many blacks congregate to dance the batuque," the "disturbance" lasting "late into the night." The 1869 complaint made no mention of "spirit mediums" or possession states. Instead, the practice of *batuque* was classed as a criminal activity, city laws proscribing gatherings of slaves "in stores, taverns, butcher shops, streets and squares."[48] Public health was another concern, since such practices contradicted the imagined norms of productive modern life. For a city "so advanced in civilization," the *Diário de Belém* griped, police should be expected to "repel from its bosom" such "barbarous" sounds.[49]

Two aspects of this complaint were remarkable, as Bezerra Neto observes. First, a public health discourse framed the official criminalization of the musical practices of the enslaved population, as ordered in city municipal codes. These codes barred "loud sounds, loud voices, and shouting with no need," "*batuques* or *sambas*," or "playing of the *carimbó* or any other instrument that disturbs the nocturnal peace."[50] Though fear of insurrection was an urgent motivating factor for legal prohibition, historians such as Paul Christopher Johnson have argued similarly: that a public hygiene discourse rather than moral or abolitionist arguments prevailed in the fight against Brazilian slavery. "Paradoxically," he writes, "in a pattern developed even prior to abolition (1888), the increasing liberalization of the state appears to have been correlated with the development of repressive police institutions."[51] The eradication of these sounds, in fact, aligned with those medical discourses developed to address the eradication of epidemics; demands for public quiet went hand in hand with the sanitary demand for paved streets, gaslighting (installed by a British company as early as 1864), theater-going, and refuse collection.[52] Second, extraordinarily, the complainants expressed frustration, less with *batuque* practices themselves than with the police chief. City authorities, it was implied, not only tolerated but *supported* African musicking, legal codes notwithstanding. The police were accused of complicity, which is to say that the outbreak provided leverage for antimunicipal critique.[53]

The patron and facilitator of this particular *batuque* disturbance, according to *O Liberal de Pará*, was José Vellozo Barreto (born 1831) of 46 travessa do Passinho. Though evidence is sketchy, "Vellozo" was a white merchant, steam navigator, and Amazon pilot. He had been a local player when the Amazon basin was incorporated into the Brazilian internationalist imaginary. As an immigrant Portuguese teenager, he privateered on the river before being enlisted, in 1854, by the Amazon Steam Navigation Company. The imperial treasury subsidized the private firm, in the wake of US Navy Lieutenant Mathew Fontaine Maury's famous narration of great riches in *The Amazon and the Atlantic Coasts of Southern America* (1853). The first projects of the Amazonian opening profited from Vellozo's skills as a river trader, cartographer, and hydrographer.[54] He was "consulted by the presidents of the province" providing them "them valuable information, making reports and maps, descriptions about the Indians of the Amazon valley, inhabited sites, commercial ports, and other details of public interest."[55]

Vellozo's enslaved workers, integrated into Amazon Steam infrastructures, sowed havoc in Belém. Evidence suggests that the travessa do Passinho was an epicenter of informal Black resistance. Just in September 1871, for example, one Liberato was arrested for fighting, while another, Affonso, was arrested for "hurling insults."[56] Two years later, curses thrown at the ex-wife of a certain Firmino Porciano dos Santos led to Vellozo's Firmina being violently beaten and injured, before being arrested.[57] A few months after the *batuque* outbreak, in November 1869, two more of Vellozo's enslaved men (Séraphim and Thomé) were imprisoned for throwing stones at the brand-new tramway, financed that year by the US consul to Pará and pulled by small steam locomotives. Séraphim was arrested again a year later for escaping, only a few days after Leopoldino was held for fighting.[58] Another two (João and Tibucia) were detained for fleeing in January of 1871. On October 29, 1868, Vellozo's Bernardo was even arrested for attempting to commit suicide. In the long discourse on effective slave management, Gabão captives from the Gabon Estuary, in particular, were alleged to be prone to suicide, often through self-asphyxiation by swallowing their own tongues.[59]

Vellozo was active in slave trading after September 1869, when the public auction and display of slaves was forbidden by law. In March 1871, he advertised a "good" woman, "twenty years old, beautiful figure" and "without vice" for private viewing. Two Vellozo "slaves of good conduct," twenty-two and thirty years of age respectively, were made available at his premises two months later, along with a thirteen-year-old *moleque* houseboy, and two Black women, one thirty and the other only fifteen.[60] Five years later, another teenage girl, this time an eighteen year old, was listed for sale.[61] Examples of Vellozo's slave activities were numerous. Preparing for the birth of his daughter Anna, for example, Vellozo sent out a call for a wet nurse to rent.[62] At the end of his life, despite his paltry education, he was hailed as "a delicate and intelligent man of proven honor." Curiously, in April 1882 at the Opera House (Theatro da Paz), the venerable Associação Philantrópica de Emancipação de Escravos reportedly honored him at an abolitionist conference, in the presence of Manaus-born Paulino de Brito, firebrand journalist and agitator against the institutions of Amazonian slavery.[63]

The backlash against late-night musicking on the travessa do Passinho was led by the *Diário do Gram-Pará*. The signatories of the 1869 complaint included James de Vismes Drummond Hay, British consul, advocate of mass white immigration to the Amazon region, and biopirate later implicated in smuggling seeds to London's Kew Gardens to break the Brazilian monopoly on rubber supply. Five months later, the *Diário do Gram-Pará*, under the headline "Emancipation of Slaves," listed the founding principles of the aforementioned Philanthropic Association for the Emancipation of Slaves.[64] The first meeting of its Administrative Council took place on October 26 that year at 6 travessa do Passinho; the home of the Scottish-Brazilian secretary Samuel Wallace MacDowell was only two blocks down from Vellozo's. The international association was spearheaded by Austrian-born Carlos Seidl. Other members included city musician and cathedral organist Adolfo José Kaulfuss (who oversaw the installment of the largest Cavaillé-Coll organ in Brazil, see chapter 6) and Antônio José de Lemos, the sanitarian who would later lead in the medico-hygienic aestheticization of the city. The humanitarian project was to raise funds for slave manumission by organizing charity benefits, shows, balls, music concerts, and gift auctions.[65]

There were other ways for the city to whiten. Another strategy involved incorporating the quarantined essence of racialized "song-and-dance" routines into official metropolitan life. Take, for example, Círio de Nazaré activities planned for October 16, 1869. (In 2013, UNESCO listed the Círio de Nazaré or Taper of our Lady of Nazareth as intangible cultural heritage; the festival hosts some two million pilgrims annually in October for the largest religious procession in Christendom, honoring the Virgin of Nazaré, patron saint of Pará.) Back in 1869, "Dances of Africans" were programmed for the Pavilhão de Flora in the up-market eastern suburb of Nazaré.[66] The bandstand (demolished in 1891) stood alongside the then chapel of Nossa Senhora de Nazaré do Desterro. In addition, mock Tupi dances were scheduled alongside fireworks and pyrotechnics, gymnastic routines, and religious music conducted by an orchestra under Teodoro Orestes, including "the best musicians in the city." Later in November, as part of the festival of São Brás, patron saint of throat infections, a *bamboula* occurred alongside a spectacle in imitation of the 1863 Parisian outstanding feats of aerial photographer and *aéronaute*: "a great balloon of the kind Monsieur Nadar adopted in his mission to conquer the immense beyond, [leaving for] the nearest planet to our earth." The balloon in view, listeners heard "the melancholy tones of the marimba" (later a so-called "thumb piano") as performers made "nostalgic reminiscence of their beautiful Congo."[67]

This chapter began with accounts of similar processes of heritage making, as in Steere's description of Marajoran musical festivity two years later, in 1871. On one hand, Steere's ethnographies inscribed superabundant scenes of freedom: vignettes on racial and sexual *mestiçagem*. His celebration of the early-evening interludes anticipated the great tourist studies of Amazonian regional cultures in the 1920s by such folklorists, newsmen, and writers as Abguar Bastos and Teixeira Monteiro. Antonio Maurício Dias da Costa's perceptive critique of the tranquilization of a dance music later identified with rural festivities—*carimbó*—applies here, that word being useful to the period's invention of a healthy and secular "popular environment." (*Carimbó*, like *bamboula*, is only the word for a kind of drum.)[68] On the other hand, excessive musical festivity and racial interaction made Steere feel ill. Exactly a month after his experiences on Caviana Island, Steere described a particularly orgiastic *entrudo* at Belém. Held in March, this annually awaited shrovetide festival marked "the last and maddest part of the Carnival." The facts of the event confirmed to him the evil of "superstitions and customs brought from Africa." Steere noted how people threw "little waxen balls filled with water of various colors" at each other across balconies. Black men reportedly gathered around city fountains to toss *limões de cheiro* (balls of lemon-scented water) at women, often filled with tapioca, but also sometimes with urine and feces.[69] He found the region's celebrated mania for large-scale religious festivity disturbing.

Let us pause to look at the scene: a city trying, not merely to build its own belle époque, but to cleanse the air; emancipationists calling for the eradication of sounds coded "African" from an urban epicenter; a slave master patronizing *batuque* practice; police officials reportedly reluctant to enforce public health laws; "African" and "Tupi" dances neatly incorporated into official city events. I have argued that the *batuque* outbreak of February 1869 betrayed an interdependent relationship between slave labor and industrial capitalism. Also, there is the question of how to narrate the *batuque* disturbance historically. The atmospheric frenzy stirred by the energy of drums and maracas, on one hand, sounded for some like the irruption of an insurrectionist "slave" essence drawn from an archive of suffering. On the other, the fact that authorities tolerated and even enjoyed these sounds suggests that for others they were matters usefully absorbed into a globalizing white economy—so that the economy might profit by their inclusion.

Yet there must be alternatives to troping Black sound as only either resistance or acquiescence.[70] The figure of Saint Sebastian in view, the lesions that pockmarked his skin never healed, and he did not profit by his wounds. The fact of his festive commemoration, year after year, in interracial batuque practice suggests that his wounded body functioned as a lasting memorial to failure. The permanence of his injuries, to be clear, was a sign of an as-yet incomplete and always injurious crusade. One might say that the stigmata on his iconized body pierced the mythical perfection and plenitude of whiteness itself. As such, the racial epidermal schema turned against itself, the celebration of Sebastian's mutilated body was also the celebration of that which will never fully be assimilated. This is why complaints show up in the lettered archive in 1869: because of the violent and unresolved ways in which an essentialized "race element" was ex-appropriated into modern biomedical systems of surveillance and lockdown.

GRANDES EPIDÉMIES CHORÉIQUES

The moment of the plague at the mouth of the Amazon, now imagined in a state of atmospheric war, was also the moment of *grandes épidémies choréiques*. Medical science, in particular, theorized equatorial dancing epidemics as endemic phenomena, liable to cyclic meteorological resurgence. They were first identified in 1860s French tropical medicine after psychiatrist Jules Baillarger's work on *folie communiquée* and later French sociologist Gabriel Tarde's celebrated theories of "mathematical" crowd suggestion. In 1867, Brazilian doctors noted the prevalence of endo-epidemic "affections of a choreic nature" or "a general inability to control motor functions"—*beribéri de tremeliques* near Manaus on the inner Amazon, for example.[71]

Late in the century, specialist in Afro-Brazilian animist fetishism Nina Rodrigues gathered evidence that "Abasia coreiforme epidêmica" or a special form of "dancing beriberi" (lethargy, restlessness, cramps, seizures) had spread from the Amazonian North through Belém and São Luís do Maranhão in the early 1870s. The disease affected Blacks more than whites and women more than men.[72] Rodrigues focused on a spike occurring in 1882, when mass dancing broke out on the Itapagipe peninsula in Salvador's industrial district at Bahia. He described how an outbreak swept through the ultra-modern French-owned Nossa Senhora da Penha fabric factory, where racialized textile workers operated automated spindles and looms driven by fifty-horsepower steam engines and imported boilers. "The affected people, after walking normally for some time," one newspaper reported, "will suddenly bend one or both legs, or their torso to one side for a few minutes, as if they were lame, paralytic, or staggering, then proceeding with their regular walk."[73] For Rodrigues, the "most powerful causal agent" of "shaking disease" was the environmental effect "of the contortions in African sacred dances."[74] By the 1880s, he suggested, *chorea*—from the Greek χορεία for dance—was an endemic malarial condition absorbed into populations along the entire equatorial northeast.

For settlers, the most dangerous transnational choreic condition was yellow fever, the infernal disease having spiked in Belém whilst Steere was at Caviana Island, killing his friend and research partner, Lyman, and many Europeans in Belém.[75] Patients progressed from lethargy and jaundice in the first stage to a phase of remission; finally, massive organ failure led to the loss of motor skills, galloping arrhythmia, and a frantic end, where bodies had to be tied down. It was not a quiet death. Doctors called the endemic form of the disease *dengue* (possibly from the Swahili word for a "cramp-like seizure caused by an evil spirit"). Here, I quote James O. McWilliam, the naval surgeon (responsible for figure 3.6 in the previous chapter) who actually piloted Reid's medico-humanitarian steam-powered ventilation systems up the Niger in 1841. In Brazil, according to McWilliam, the "aborted form of the yellow fever" was named "polka fever." The name, he explained, occurred because the disease was "nearly coincident with the introduction of the well-known *dance* of that name" and because of "the almost invariable twitching in the limbs for some hours at the first attack."[76] The endemic nature of *dengue*, it follows, perpetuated a whole nosology of low-level pathological disorders in

Belém after 1867: the *maxixe, choro, polca-lundu, polca-tango, polca-cateretê, tango-brasileiros*, and so on. Some commentators, according to one English period critic, went so far as to attribute the post-1846 popularity of Afro-Bohemian "trembling dances" across the world "to an exhalation from the earth, in some degree analogous to azote or nitrogen gas."[77] The first piece of printed music ever published in Belém, appropriately, was a "brilliant polka for piano" (1858) by the same Prussian organist Kaulfuss we discovered earlier patronizing the Philanthropic Association for the Emancipation of Slaves, entitled "A Cidade de Belém."

The great modern visitation of yellow fever south of the equator occurred during the tropical summer of 1849/1850. Not in living memory had that protective barrier once thought to shield the tropical south from transatlantic colonial plagues been breached.[78] When the plague struck Belém, Wallace's collaborator, Henry Walter Bates, reported that "this moving vapour was called the *Maî* [*Mãe*] *da peste* ("the mother or spirit of the plague"). "The first cases of fever occurred near the port," Bates wrote, "and it spread rapidly and regularly from house to house."[79] The authorities took every sanitary precaution, including "the singular one of firing cannon at the street corners, to purify the air." At such times, it was usual to mark the hours, as happened night and day on Good Fridays at Belém, "by the dismal noise of wooden clappers, wielded by [African men] stationed near the different churches." "Within a few days," Bates wrote, "thousands of persons lay sick, dying or dead." The fever fell "most severely on the whites and *mamelucos* [of European and Amerindian parentage]."[80] Bates, like Steere, blamed the devastation on music and festival-going, since it "tended much to demoralize the people" with "degrading notions of religion." Others contended that the *Mãe da Peste* meted out divine punishment for a climate of Black insurrection, prevalent since the Cabanagem Revolt of 1835–40, when Belém was temporarily conquered by peasant rebels.

Ten years later, Bates marveled at the speed by which post-epidemic city mitigation measures had been implemented. He lauded the clearing of "irregularly-built houses," the draining of the "large, swampy squares," as well as their planting with rows of almond and casuarina trees. Equally commendable, for him, was the strategic settlement of twenty thousand white Portuguese, Madeiran, and German immigrants. Besides noting the increased presence of steam technology and foreign merchants, Bates was struck by the decline of old religious holidays in favor of such amusements as "social parties, balls, music, billiards."[81] The drive to secular rather than religious musical festivity was very much a part of a metropolitan sanitarian agenda. The authorities addressed themselves as much to bourgeois amusement as they did to urban redesign, water management, gaslighting, and slave reform.

Yellow fever came with many names; it would take years before it was established as a mosquito-borne rather than miasma-induced virus. In 1724, Portuguese historian Sebastião da Rocha Pita dated an outbreak of what he called *bicha* [*bicha* being a misspelling of *bicho*, meaning "animal"] to 1686, when a contagion was conveyed by ship from São Tomé off Gabon, as punishment for the sins of the population of Pernambuco.[82] In the colonial Atlantic, the pestilence was named *vómito negro* (black vomit), *xekik* (blood vomit), "the invisible enemy," "the visitor," *maladie de Siam*, *typhus miasmatique, putride jaune*, or *febre amarela des acclimatados*. French military physician Mathieu Andouard called yellow fever an *infection des bâtiments négriers*, finding that the virus was incubated in the holds of middle-passage slaveships, where the enslaved died, he wrote, "in the midst of their own filth," rebreathing the air of their own suffocated exhalations.[83] "The organization of the [African], and the more extensive functions of the skin of this race," Scottish medical historian and follower of Andouard reasoned, "give rise to the most offensive and foul state of the atmosphere when numbers of this race are confined in a limited space, and particularly in humid and warm atmosphere."[84] The *croisement* of bodies packed in close proximity allegedly brewed the unholy conditions that engineered the virus. Andouard called it the "African fever" or "African Plague." His scientific tendency was to reach for the most banally racist explanations.

The Racial Element

Liberal champion of antislavery and statesman Rui Barbosa, spokesperson for the Brazilian emancipationist movement, bemoaned the unassimilability of the yellow fever virus: "Sparing the African element, an exterminator of Europeans, the yellow plague, negrophile and xenophobic, attacked the existence of the nation in its marrow, in the very source of the vital fluid which would regenerate its good African blood, since immigration has come to purify our veins from the effects of primitive miscegenation, and it [the "yellow plague"] gave us, in the eyes of the civilized world, the airs of a slaughterhouse for the white race."[85] According to the doctrine of Black immunity, for such advocates of mass European immigration and African erasure as Barbosa, *l'élément noir* was a disease vector for yellow fever.

For Christina Sharpe, in her exemplary disquisition on breathing for *In the Wake: On Blackness and Being* (2016), the slavehold was the first machinery of racialization, engendering "a form of *consciousness*" engineered under extreme hypobaric duress.[86] If the trauma of slavery was the founding moment of modernity, as Kodwo Eshun's Afrofuturist writings contend, then those subjects who survived the Middle Passage were the original moderns. The critical knowledge and consciousness attendant to Blackness, for Eshun, was long ago awake to the problem of air.[87] For racist liberals like Barbosa, trafficked Africans posed a threat to white purity, in part because these abstracted lives were purportedly invulnerable to the virality of the breath-taking musics they purveyed en route. Frantz Fanon's famous words about "the zone of non-being" come to mind, as do Ashon Crawley's words on "the [white] theology-philosophy, that produces a world, a set of protocols, wherein black flesh cannot easily breathe." Revolution, for Fanon, though here he was talking about "Indo-Chinese" revolt, occurred "quite simply," because "it was, in more than one way, becoming impossible for him to breathe."[88]

The sounds of steam power and African labor emanated from the same waterborne source along the Amazon, slave exploitation working hand in glove with industrial capitalism. "Ugh! ugh! ugh! ugh!" or "Eh! Eh eh eh," wrote one chauvinistic United States traveler in 1868, of his experience of Black stevedores working Brazilian ports.[89] Writing from São Luís in Maranhão southeast of Belém, John Upfold Petit, US consul, expressed his surprise at hearing such "Ethiopian melodies" as "Poor Old Ned," or "Oh Susannah!" in the street. "The melodies of the North American plantations (the African-born airs of Virginia and Tennessee, long since threadbare in the United States)" Petit wrote, "are, like the smallpox, contagious through all ranks of [Maranhense] society."[90] Paraense historian Vicente Salles reports that, in the mid-nineteenth century, the workers of the aforementioned Amazon Steam Navigation Company, working the docks and steamboats at Belém, sang "Chô! Fly, don't body my."[91] In 1872, that same "African-American melody," used to shake off insect infestation, was sung by "black men of the Amazonas Company"—"naked from the waist up, and shining with sweat"—two thousand miles away at the western Peruvian edge of the Amazon basin on the Huallaga River near Yurimaguas.[92]

Not just African American but West Central African links were strong, not least to the power centers described earlier in this book. In 1861, Manuel Antônio Pimenta Bueno, director of the same Amazon Steam Navigation Company in Belém, abandoned operations upriver at the colony of Serpa/Itacoatiara, partly after the reported ill-treatment of the company's so-called free Africans and the striking of a director by one "Black Paulo." A scandal had arisen with British diplomats over the "re-enslavement" of sixty-eight individuals, illegally shipped from West Central Africa to northern Brazil and then legally transported to the Amazon as "free laborers" to work for Amazon Steam.[93] Twenty-five men in particular had been among the 145 enslaved of an original 450, who survived the Middle Passage in 1856 from Ambriz (near the site of this book's introduction) aboard a Massachusetts-built slaver. The military interception and unloading of sick Africans at Salvador, according to one historian, "caused terror among the population of the city," spurred by the belief that the presence of "ill Africans" would corrupt the prevailing racial climate.[94] Another ten men and two women indentured to Amazon Steam had been "rescued" farther north by Pernambucan authorities after 209 Africans, most of them children shipped from the Congo River, were confiscated from a diseased schooner "in the most deplorable state of nudity and complete state of debility."[95] The remaining thirty-one, all single men, arrived in October 1861 from the House of Corrections in Rio de Janeiro, transported as "slaves" in all but name. No doubt a few ended up musicking at Vellozo's early in 1869.

Circling outward, figure 4.3 is an illustration of slave incubation statistically quantified, parts of which were reprinted by David Boswell Reid, the atmospheric sanitarian we met in the previous chapter's discussion of *Illustrations of the Theory and Practice of Ventilation* (1844). The image was itself imitative of Thomas Clarkson's more famous and larger abolitionist diagram of Middle Passage suffocation widely circulated since at least 1787. Clarkson's antislavery research was inspired by the 1772 Lord Mansfield judgment that "the air of England is too pure for any slave to breathe." Mansfield pronounced that any enslaved person who set foot in England was automatically free by virtue of the purity of English breathing. Reid's intention, when he discussed the barometric implications of Africans packed into slaveholds, was more analytical. He offered a statistical measure of the minimum quantity of air necessary to the maximum containment of African life. "The hold of a slave-ship presents a spectacle of disgusting wretchedness and piteous woe, which cannot be equaled, and completely beggars description," Reid wrote, quoting Thomas Fowell Buxton's at once abolitionist and racist position: "It is often filled with masses of living corruption."[96] Since these bodies purportedly excited "fevers and fluxes," Reid recommended that humanitarian slave interceptors be equipped with portable ventilators, "useful to removing the atmosphere before the sailors enter below deck." Other accounts echoed

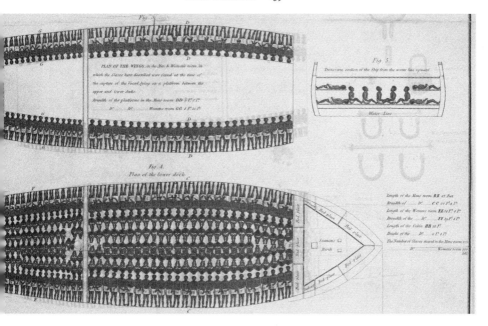

FIGURE 4.3. John Hawksworth and S. Croad, "The representation of the brig *Vigilante*, from Nantes, a vessel employed in the slave trade, which was captured by Lieutenant Mildmay in the River Bonny, on the coast of Africa, on the 15th of April 1822" (1823). Library of Congress.

chemist Robert Boyle's classic experiment for measuring the quantity of air necessary to sound, flame, and breathing. In one oft-quoted account, the enslaved "drew their breath with all those laborious and anxious efforts for life, which are observed in expiring animals, subjected by experiment to foul air, or in the exhausted receiver of an air pump."[97] Generally, these writers took excessive delight in the barbaric calculus.

Figure 4.4 illustrates another technique of Black containment, devised not much more than a year before Steere arrived in Brazil. The aim of the technique was to measure comparative statistical differences in the vital capacity of races. Black and brown bodies, according to Jousset's pneumometric measurements, naturally used less air. Jousset's work, borrowing from the graphic methods of experimental psychology, studied "the living man." Here, racial life power was differentiated by spirometer and pneumograph, devices I will discuss in more detail in the chapter to follow. The Frenchman's experiments borrowed from the pioneering racial records made by naval medic and tropical pathologist Alexander Rattray. From 1869, Rattray made anthropometric studies of variously stereotyped men, including two Sierra Leonean sailors, over the course of a three-

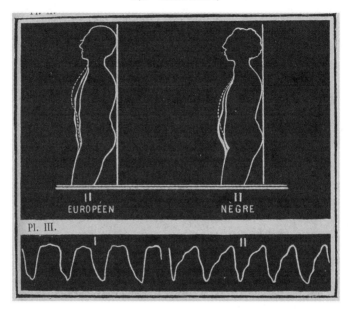

FIGURE 4.4. Alfred Jousset, *Traité de l'acclimatement et de l'acclimatation* (Paris: Octave Doin, 1884), 91. Wellcome Collection, https://creativecommons.org/licenses/by/4.0/legalcode.

month journey from Plymouth (England) to Bahia (Brazil) and back again aboard HMS *Bristol*. At eight degrees below the equator somewhere in the mid-Atlantic on August 13, 1869, for example, the vital capacity of "pure black" Benjamin Campbell measured a full twenty-five cubic inches higher than it did in "temperate" Plymouth. This is to allege that Campbell was less alive when in England. For such racial fatalists as Rattray, graphic experiment "proved" that the worldwide acclimatization movement was ill-conceived. For him, the races were less far less adaptable to travel than the enthusiasts of massed immigration and settler colonialism supposed.[98] Jousset racialized breathing similarly. At top left in figure 4.4, a picture of wholesome European breathing is contrasted, to the right, with the lower abdominal disorder of "l'homme des régions tropicales." The latter caused jagged needle tracings, the lines meant to inscribe the nature of disordered breathing attendant to life in the torrid zone.

Conclusion: Infection-Contagion

In this equatorial milieu, infection and contagion paradigms (embracing the concerns of environment and foreign pathogenic attack, respectively) were intermixed. On the one hand were the infectionists, acutely aware of the dangers of *vapores pestíferos*, especially when the Amazon Delta discharged sediment loads of more than 750 metric tons annually. (The contribution of French and British infectionists of the 1820s and 1830s had been to narrow the concepts of atmospheric influence to that of "miasma".) For them, the slaveharbor at Belém was reportedly "impregnated with the fomites of yellow fever" and plagued with noxious exhalations.[99] When two British agents for the Amazon Steam Navigation Company overnighted near the docks in 1873, the London-based corporation having recently been restructured, they were puzzled by "a mysterious noise, which was heard at intervals every night." They speculated that "[the noise, which] resembled a slight explosion against the bottom of the ship, producing a vibration of the air in the hold, and filling the whole ship with a weird ringing sound" was due "to bubbles of gas produced by decaying vegetable matter."[100] The accumulated deposits of thousands of slave ships, later infectionist thinkers explained, had "entered into the composition of the mud and tinted the sea water," and now threatened to be sucked back into the unsuspecting hulls of visiting commercial ships.[101]

On the other hand, besides infectionists, were an increasingly prestigious band of contagionists, who advanced germ theories of disease, birthing the modern fields of tropical bacteriology and parasitology (after Louis Pasteur). Contagionists were microbe hunters. They were essentialists devoted to the isolation and study of animacular bioagents. There would be many names for the "yellow fever germ" or "African fever germ" in Brazil by the 1880s: microbiologist João Baptista de Lacerda's "polumorphous fungis," Domingo Freire's "bacillus spores," "micrococcus amaril," or "black ptomaines." Speculation about the animacular or insect origin of yellow fever dated back at least to a groundbreaking 1848 article by Josiah Nott, notorious Alabaman anthropologist and American translator of Arthur de Gobineau's *An Essay on the Inequality of the Human Races* (1853–55).

Widely regarded the founding father of biological essentialism and modern race science, Gobineau himself was struck ill with the African Plague in Brazil, three days after surviving the transatlantic Lisbon-Dakar-Recife-Salvador trip in March 1869, to take up a diplomatic position at the French Embassy in Rio de Janeiro (at precisely the time of our *batuque* complaints in Belém). "A degeneration of the most tragic aspect," a terrified Gobineau cried, suffused his body, after exposure to "a mulatto population, degraded by blood, [and] vitiated in spirit."[102] Gobineau could not be sure whether the cause of his fever was animal or human, because it was only really in the 1880s when the female genus of the *Aedes aegypti* mosquito was scientifically identified as the enemy of European acclimatization in the Black Atlantic.[103]

The Brazilian littoral was a hothouse of primitive tropical infestation, "twisted, messed, ragged." "Physical nature here," Gobineau wrote, "is not impregnated with moral nature."[104] "We have come to know," agreed Swiss traveler Charles Pradez in 1872, discussing the "constitution du nègre" in his *Nouvelles études sur le Brésil*, "that the air we breathe contains a myriad of beings which, by the infinity of their smallness, escape our eyes, penetrate into our lungs, and are drawn into the torrent of our circulation." The reality of swarming equatorial life, Pradez contended, was that "the air is saturated with eggs, dippers and germs of all kinds, which act on the [darker] blood of the [African] and requires a secretion, an elimination which is carried on the skin."[105] A newfound conception of the intensity of aerobotanical life, that is, came to inform racist theories about everything from tropical disease transmission to processes of Black enracement, "mucous tissue, composed of infinite vesicles" purportedly explaining the smell and pigmentation of African skin. According to the logic and language of epidemiology, racial fomites saturated the content of human breathing in such mephitic regions as the Amazon Delta. Life, in the contagionist conception, no longer served or was composed of a single life force (*Lebenskraft*) oriented to a single end. Rather thousands upon thousands of bioagents—viruses, bacteria, parasites, spores, antibodies—necessarily suffused even the whitest of bodies. A swarm of contending elementary organisms coexisted and struggled in a perpetual state of politico-organic war. Life was infested with death; death was infested with life. In this choreic conception of modern being, swarming parasitic air enslaved all living matter.

Transatlantic racial capitalism reached a stage of mutation after 1867, in other words, where "black elements" were introjected into "popular culture" as necessary evils. A microbial theory of life was yoked into a biopolitics of rapacious inclusivity. The white social body worked to embrace the negative modalities of all its imagined dialectical opposites. It *required* war, as much as it began to show the pockmarked wounds of its increasingly infested life world. In musical terms, the most expressive social body would need to relinquish some aspect of possession over itself and develop discourses dramatizing its own intermixture with the supposedly enslaving fevers of African life. Thus the love for the abject sounds of the enslaved's dances and what one late-century German musicologist and pianist called Black rhythms that "literally bore themselves into the consciousness of the listener, *irresistible and penetrating to the verge of torture*."[106] It is often said that the move from "slave societies" to "control societies" was accelerated by expanding global markets, which drove liberal emancipation. It would be better to say that slavery was not so much abolished as incorporated under conditions of modern liberalism. Fanon diagnosed that neocolonial situation long ago when he remarked that the "presence of the negroes is an insurance policy on humanness."[107] The presence of African suffering, in other words, allowed for white "humanness" to continue to assimilate. Following Saint Sebastian, the body of whiteness began to learn how to live with its multiplying racial wounds.

Foucault narrated the history of global enclosure and quarantining in these terms:

> We pass from a technology of power that drives out, excludes, banishes, marginalizes, and represses, to a fundamentally positive power that fashions, observes, knows and multiplies itself on the basis of its own effects.... It is not exclusion but quarantine. It is not a question of driving out individuals but rather of establishing and fixing them, of giving them their own place, of assigning places and of defining presences and subdivided presences.... Plague is the moment when the spatial partitioning and subdivision (*quadrillage*) of a population is taken to its extreme point, where dangerous communications, disorderly communities, and forbidden contacts can no longer appear. The moment of the plague is one of an exhaustive sectioning (*quadrillage*) of the population by political power, the capillary ramifications of which constantly reach the grain of individuals themselves, their time, habitat, localization, and bodies. Perhaps plague brings with it the literary or theatrical dream of the great orgiastic moment. But plague also brings the political dream of an exhaustive, unobstructed power that is completely transparent to its object and exercised to the full.[108]

These words name the difference between "negative" regimes of power (traditionally associated with the expurgation of lepers) and inclusive "positive technologies of power" (advanced since the seventeenth century that found special focus at "the moment of the plague").

The microbial theory of being served a "fundamentally positive power" because it rationalized why white bodies should tolerate the "slings and arrows" of modernity, and why racial wounding was necessary to progress. Microbial logics were elaborated as early as Marx's classic critique of commodity fetishism, where animist idolatry was revealed as the primitive driving force of Euro-American market exchange.[109] In Nietzsche, of course, the tranquil codes of enlightened morality and the scruples of civilization were fatal to authentic experience, his project being to "realize life, your life, integrally, wholly, fully."[110] "Does it not seem that there is a hatred of the virgin forest and of the tropics among moralists?" Nietzsche wrote in *On the Genealogy of Morality* (1887): "And that the 'tropical man' must be discredited at all costs, whether as disease and deterioration of mankind, or as his own hell and self-torture? And why? In favor of the 'temperate zones'? In favor of the temperate men? The 'moral'? The mediocre?"[111] Nietzsche's embrace of "tropical sin" explained his famous preference for such music as the habanera-infused and ethnographically sourced melodies of Georges Bizet. The vital force and sexual depravity of these super-heated sounds, Nietzsche wrote, "makes me productive." The potency of "tropical man" was audible in "a music that knows how to live amongst beasts of prey," a "savage" kind of dance "whose supreme charm is the ignorance of good and evil." The sadomasochism of colonial pillage, he argued, was more life-affirming than the humanitarian pieties of what he called "slave morality." The only way for good music to progress, in his view, was to infest it with danger.

Even Gobineau, reportedly the most paradigmatic racist who ever lived, argued that no race was more musical than "the black race," claiming that the African "possesses in the highest degree the sensual faculty without which there is no art possible." "Assuredly," he wrote, "the black element is indispensable for developing artistic genius in a race, because we have seen how much fire and flame, enthusiasm and inconsiderateness, dwells within it, and to what extent imagination, that mirror of sensuality, along with all the cravings towards matter, make it calculated to receive the impressions produced by the arts, in a degree of intensity utterly unknown to the other human families."[112] Nott, in his American edition of Gobineau's *Essay on the Inequality of Human Races* neglected to translate this paean to the passion and power of Black musical genius, likely because the American had never so keenly embraced the genetic presence of the *élément noir* moving within. In France, it was more common to think, as Gobineau did, "that the Negro stands forth as the lyrical poet, the musician, the sculptor *par excellence*."

Remarkably, Gobineau's "black element" insinuated itself into the "heart of whiteness" at the bosom of musical art in the Francophone world on a day in 1875. The sculpture displayed in figure 4.5 still stands today in the "Bassin de la Pythie" beneath the grand staircase of the Opéra Garnier, a building erected in service of Napoleon III's dream for an imperial temple to the arts. In order to better adorn "the capital of the nineteenth century," Garnier himself approached the sculptress Adèle d'Affry (a.k.a. "Marcello") for the purposes of installing the Pythia on her operatic tri-

FIGURE 4.5. Adèle d'Affry (a.k.a. Marcello), "Pythian Sibyl," Opéra Garnier, Paris. https://creativecommons.org/licenses/by-nc/2.0/legalcode.

pod. D'Affry was a companion of Gounod and Liszt; she had sculpted the work while in Rome, six years prior to installation. D'Affry cast her own writhing upper body and breasts for the sculpture, but *une femme africaine*, likely one "Zingara Marie," provided the model for the twisted head and neck of the oracle of Delphi, which still today sits in the basement of the Opéra Garnier.[113] According to Greek myth, the African Pythia, frenzied Delphic prophetess, and high priestess of the Temple of Apollo sits near the Omphalos (ὀμφαλός, or "navel" stone), which once marked the geophysical center of the ancient Greek world. Still today, she breathes in the sacred fumes, her tripod placed above a fissure vent in the earth, from whence escaped the fumurole gases that purportedly inspired her oracular song. (D'Affry's sculpture depicts the rising ethylene as bronze plumes snaking beneath her feet.) The presence of African genius—*une femme africaine*—within the very engine room of French expressivity attests to the ways in which *l'élément noir*, prepared by myths of elemental musicality, inspired the advance of pan-European cultural production. In 1875, Garnier's state-of-the-art steam-heated ventilation system (powered by no less than fourteen furnaces and burning an estimated ten thousand kilograms of coal per day) provided the stimulus for this primal scene of Pythian spirit possession.[114] Night after night, the bourgeois operagoer immersed himself in her elemental song in ways that he hoped would deepen his humanity and awaken his dying creativity.

CHAPTER 5

A Spectral Image of Breath
New York, United States, 1901

White Light

The cylinders are no longer playable, but the New York Public Library has two peculiarly historic brown wax examples in its archives. They are stored inside cardboard canisters in a tray containing similar objects, labeled with typewritten markers. Both were made on the night of March 29, 1901, using an Edison "home" phonograph. The music of these cylinders, played back on digital equipment today, competes with what sounds like the passing of one of Manhattan's elevated trains ca. 1900, or one of Charles Cretor's ferocious steam-powered popcorn machines. The term *aura* applies, invoking Walter Benjamin on "the unique apparition of a distance" in "a strange tissue of time and space." (The word originally referred to the halo that formed around photographed objects in early daguerreotypes.)[1] Barely audible, spiraling in the distance, are orchestral instruments, the voice of the legendary tenor Jean de Reszke, and the chorus of the old Metropolitan Opera House in New York City. The roundelay of sound, etched in wax, preserves a once-in-a-lifetime moment.

The moment was recorded in other media formats too. Newspaper critics reported a mood thick with anticipation. An unprecedentedly large crowd, spilling from the foyer onto the street, awaited "the strongest cast which can be brought together," including bass Édouard de Reszke, Adolph Mühlmann, soprano Milka Ternina, and Bohemian-German contralto Ernestine Schumann-Heink.[2] The performance, offered as a bonus to subscribers, made a special feature of Reszke. This was the final night in which the aging fifty-five-year-old Polish Apollo would appear in New York for a complete opera.

Figure 5.1 shows Reszke-as-Lohengrin, fixed here as an engraved print, backstage at the Met, and readying himself. Born in Russian Poland, this

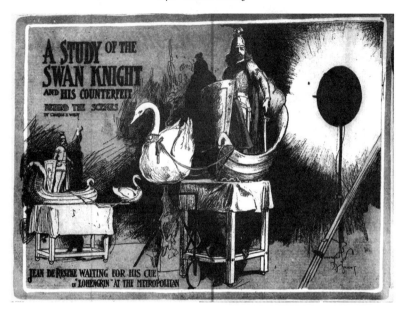

FIGURE 5.1. "Jean de Reszke waiting for his cue," *New York Herald* (January 13, 1901): 16. Image produced by the Library of Congress.

not-quite-European figure was the star of the show, his sonic presence introduced by a bright white light, as the figure suggests. Since the 1880s, Reszke had been Europe's chief publicist for Richard Wagner's *Lohengrin*, though mostly in its French and Italian translations. In 1901, the tenor would sing Wagner's "bel canto opera"—as he had since 1896—in the original German. To capture Reszke's swan song, Lionel Mapleson moved a giant horn under the hood of the prompter's box. (Late the following year, the patrons complained that the outsized recording horn was distracting, which forced Mapleson, the librarian of the Met, to move his obtruding machine to the catwalk in the rigging above the stage.)[3]

Many historians of what Emily Thompson calls "modern sound" have shown that, before commercial consolidation, talking machines served a bewildering variety of functions.[4] Edison phonographs could be dictaphones, parlor instruments, music boxes, medical devices for diagnosing vocal health, tools for teaching elocution, apparatuses for learning foreign languages, vehicles of public instruction, and so on. In 1877, Edison considered many names for his "phonograph," including "the atmophone" (a recorder of the atmosphere) and "the climatophone" (a device for recording the weather). The machine was sold with a shaving knife to smooth away old tracings. Horns could be made and exchanged to suit requirements. Patrick Feaster writes that sounds were recorded "at different speeds or backwards, layered one over the other into elaborate patterns, and otherwise manipulated to create interesting artistic effects."[5] These wax cylinders, then, are best thought of as art objects, creations imbued, as much with feelings of loss, as with the "tissue of time and space" inscribed into them.

Mapleson's records, to be clear, are artworks of perfect fidelity. The librarian did not freeze the air, so to speak, for the purposes of future thawing. Every replaying modified the soft cellulite of the original. And he never imagined that his records would last forever or that they would be immortalized in the way they were after their transference to disc in the 1930s. Instead, the cylinders were fixed to be souvenirs of a time passed. Mapleson not only hoped to salvage the "voice of the nineteenth century" and Reszke's "lost" style. His plan was to record the last throws of a passing era—a sonic image of the nineteenth century itself—and to archive that spectral image, itself sealed up, in the Metropolitan library.

Mapleson dropped the needle deep into act 3, at the dissolution of the bridal chamber scene, the penultimate scene of the opera. A failed Italianate love duet has preceded this moment in Wagner's score ("Fühl'ich zu dir so süss mein Herz entbrennem, atme ich Wonnen, die nur Gott verleiht"). In an extended slow movement, the divine knight presses Elsa (here sung by Croatia-Slavonian diva Milka Ternina) to follow his long-breathed phrases. The hero encourages her to inhale the rarefied air wafted in from afar ("Atmest du nicht mit mir die süssen Düfte?"). "When [Lohengrin] led Elsa to the window," novelist Willa Cather had written when she saw Reszke and Nordica perform the scene in Italian a year earlier, "I assure you he brought the stillness and beauty of the summer night into the hot air of the playhouse."[6]

Elsa, by her failure to respond, proves herself unworthy of the hero. The lovers do not breathe the same air, a fact made clear by Elsa's fitful and distorted cabaletta where she pesters her husband to reveal his secret identity ("Hilf Gott, was muss ich hören!"). She demands to know his name. At this, the duet's formal structure disintegrates. So much so that the scene admits the worldly intrusion of the evil Telramund (played here by American baritone David Bispham) and four knights with swords drawn. Here, Mapleson's first cylinder seized a snatch of a controversial moment for Reszke, who, rather than striking Telramund to the ground as directed in the score, raised his sword in a magic gesture as if to compel his foe "by some supernatural power to fall to the ground vanquished."[7]

Reszke played Lohengrin as a sorcerer. In the description of Cather, he was a singer "whose tenderness is wholly without effeminacy, or whose voice can rise clear, melodious and true, to the full measure of tragedy, and then there is, undeniably, a deep sentimental quality, that baffling minor tinge that is in the acting of Modjeska and the music of Chopin."[8] After a few seconds, Mapleson stopped the cylinder, waited, and started it again to catch the spectral sounds of Reszke, doubled by a distant oboe, weeping he second half of the so-called *Frageverbot* motive at his characteristically slow tempo ("Dort will ich Antwort ihr bereiten"). The first cylinder, then, ends with Lohengrin looking outward toward the final scene where he will reveal himself before Elsa and the assembled court.

Mapleson's second cylinder also anticipates Lohengrin's moment of truth. Skipping into the finale, after the grand arrival of the assembled Brabantine armies, the record captures the Italian chorus of the Metropolitan Opera (who sang out of tune "with dogged persistence") proclaiming Lohengrin's entrance in full.[9] Reszke's opinion that Wagner's scores were best performed with heavy cuts (to alleviate tedium) is borne out in what follows. The denunciation of Elsa's betrayal was edited out to speed the dramatic flow.[10] Thus the hero's request to be exempt from guilt for Telramund's murder skips to the grand set-up: "So hort!" and the chorus's expectant "what mystery must I now hear?" Which is where the cylinder leaves off . . . but for Mapleson sealing his creation by shouting into the horn the following day: "De Reske! Last night! March the 29th 1901! At the Metropolitan Opera House! New York!"

The Art of Atmosphere

Reszke's greatest moment—which Mapleson left to the beyond—was the "grail narration," a scene in which the singer came into his own. Singing "In fernem Land," Lohengrin reveals his identity: he is a grail knight from the sacred castle of Monsalvat. It was in this scene, according to reports, that Reszke showed off why he was reputed as perhaps the greatest master of breath control who ever lived. The air itself stilled for Lohengrin's farewell song. Critics marveled at "the attitude of the audience which hangs breathless on every note of Jean de Reszke."[11] Reszke formed his voice, not by projecting tone outwardly but by holding breath in. His practice was to manage rather than emit air, to condition rather than use it. The whole collected assembly held their breath.

The grail narration, relatedly, provided the opportunity for Reszke to display his spectrum of celebrated high pianissimo colors. These timbres were the goal and result of the complex breath-management system he himself developed. First was Reszke's rock-solid posture, which maximized sympathetic resonance by the so-called fixed high-chest method. Next came his system of breath support, where the singer "drank in tones," which is to say that he formed voice, not by projecting tone outwardly but by resonating within. A third technique involved a method of breathing called "inferior costal respiration," soon described.[12] Fourth was Reszke's method of singing *dans le masque*, which allowed for tones to be "painted" in vibrant shades and colors.[13] At base was a pressurized system of voice management where lights and timbres resonated in sympathy to form into a subtly shifting sound image.

In what follows, the origin story told of mechanical sound reproduction is as much a story belonging to the history of technology as a tale involving the history of breathing. A host of techniques and technologies, developed in this period, served the spectrographic project to conjure ambiances, particularly such sound-imaging equipment as became useful to recording the spectra of standing wave patterns, resonance vibrations, and harmonics. A concern to stay air, at the turn of the century, related to a need to create atmospheres—indeed, to package, reproduce, and sell them. The artistic imperative was to paint tone worlds, literally. Breath control, that is, allied with the modern project to arrest the flow of air with both body and machine techniques. In question here are not only phonographic technologies and breathing techniques but also wider social apparatuses, air-conditioning, storage, and environmental management systems. What does it mean to make atmospheres? What does it mean to conjure sound images according to modern theories of standing resonance?

The Incorporation of Opera

Jan Mieczysław Reszke sang with a spectrality—a *sound qua sound*—that depended upon sloughing off provincial associations with nations, languages, or styles. Though he could speak little German and even less English, he was at the forefront of the movement for "Polyglot Opera" or what he himself called "Russian Salad."[14] "Polyglot Opera" was a phrase popularized in London by Augustus Harris, the operatic impresario, who used it most during his 1889 season, when Reszke persuaded him to produce Gounod's *Romeo* in French at the "Royal Italian Opera," Covent

Garden.[15] The "polyglot" singer himself had made his debut as an Italian baritone in Venice by the name of Giovanni di Reschi. He then gathered a formidable reputation in Paris during a five-season stint, as the "tenorized" Jean de Reszké (1884–1889). This was the same Reszké for whom Jules Massenet composed the tableaux of *Le Cid* (Théâtre National de l'Opéra, 1885). By 1889 the dream of all three schools of opera (Italian, French, and German) exploited by a single company still seemed far off. Progress would be made five years later, in the summer of 1894, when Jean, Édouard, and Harris made the pilgrimage to Bayreuth, following in the footsteps of dramatic soprano Lillian Nordica, who on July 20 that year sang Elsa in the first ever *Lohengrin* to be staged at the Festspielhaus. The success of the American in this landmark production "as the author conceived it" was such that critic William James Henderson, at the *New York Times*, proclaimed that "the twilight of the so-called Wagner singer is at hand." Nordica's supporters gushed that this was the first time Wagner had been "actually sung," rather than barked in the usual guttural Teutonic tone speech.[16] Wagnerphiles meanwhile, lamented "the downfall of Bayreuth," which had become just another "holiday resort for rich Americans."[17]

The toast to victory was made in New York on November 27, 1895. At a celebratory dinner in mock medieval style, Reszke raised his drinking horn to "International Opera" after a triumphant all-German performance with Nordica (Italian chorus excepted) of *Tristan und Isolde* at the Metropolitan Opera.[18] The Pole spoke in four languages that night— English, German, Italian, and French—though he showed little interest in the Anglo-American dream of a permanent native-language tradition on home soil.[19] The previous May, Henderson had already caught wind of a future "Opera in Three Tongues" at the Metropolitan Opera House: "'The French operas in French, the Italian operas in Italian, and the German in German' has been the De Reszke war cry all Winter." Reszke's German-language *Tristan*, according to Henderson, was a "genuine musical event" and "a triumphant demonstration of the universality of Wagner's genius."[20] Gone were the usual "discordant shouts and ejaculations" of an Ernest van Dyck, Max Alvary, or Albert Niemann. Instead, Reszke preferred a dreamy fusion of the best of three sound worlds: Italian melody, French tone color, and German sublimity. The battle against the frenzied *voix blanches* of such singers as van Dyck or Lola Bleeth was won, their "eiffelesco-babelesco-pyramidal grunts" supplanted by Reszke's own matchless timbral shadings and commanding "breadth of style, perfect intonation, and deep emotion."[21] The project, for the invited dinner guests, was to crystallize an enduring international standard.

In preparation for Bayreuth, Reszke had reportedly taken twenty days off during the summer of 1894 to work with Cosima Wagner's musical advisor, Julius Kniese, in the resort town of Karlsbad. For five hours a day, the Pole trained, though the singer still expressed himself opposed to such German declaimers as Niemann who failed to "give the words their proper softness in singing."[22] A month after toasting "Opera in Three Tongues" in New York, on January 2, 1896, Reszke advanced the internationalist cause by singing his first German Lohengrin opposite Nordica. The New York press lauded his "strange and potent" Wagnerian speech song. "Spectral, magical and the wonder of another world," he "poured forth," in the words of one writer, "singing for the first time the part as it should be sung, without soft Tuscan 'cignos' and saccharine 'iot'amos.'"[23] The old toyshop Italian figure, apparently, had been exchanged for a creature of universal power: "no longer a sentimental chevalier, but a devoted hero."[24] The French-German-Italian merger on English-speaking terms with a Polish singer, many agreed, had "opened a new era in the style of Wagnerian performance." The system had illuminated a new status quo and a new standard for sound.[25]

Reszke appeared both in London and New York under the auspices of the Maurice Grau Opera Company: a multinational conglomerate managed by a French-based Austrian-born "monarch of the operatic world" with signatories including Edward Lauterbach, Chairman of the Republican County Committee in New York, railway magnate Frederick W. Sanger, and "Bonanza King" industrialist John William Mackay. From 1896 to 1903, Grau oversaw an operatic plutocracy under the autocratic thumb of Jean de Reszke and his sibling Édouard, a bass who made his mark singing the King of Egypt in the first Paris performance of Verdi's *Aida* under the composer's baton.[26] The company product was international grand opera on an impossibly lavish scale, it being "the most brilliant operatic government that the world has ever known from a financial point of view." Jean garnered stipends in excess of $3,000 a night.[27]

Grau's scheme functioned according to a lucrative "star system" according to which, in the words of Hermann Klein in 1903, "what Covent Garden does this year, New York does the next," though he qualified that in Wagnerian matters it was the American city that led the way.[28] In London, every summer, the smooth-operating businessman ("with heavy-lidded eyes that seem lost in reverie") was director of Covent Garden's "Grand Opera Syndicate Ltd.," a corporation bankrolled by the Marchioness of Ripon, Lord Esher, Lord Wittenham, and (of course) the Reszkes.[29] In New York, late every following winter, Grau leased the rebuilt opera house from its property owners: the Metropolitan Opera and Real Estate

Company. The real estate in question was the thirty-five parterre boxes of the so-called Diamond Circle, bejeweled by an oligarchy of thirty-five shareholders of unspeakable wealth, who had rebuilt their playhouse after the fire of August 1892. In the remodeling, as if to reflect rising inequities in US wealth and new concentrations of corporate power, the number of boxes was reduced to accommodate only the richest patrons, while space for standing room was increased.

The fumes and stifling heat of the old gas burners were gone. Instead, the "plenum ventilation" system of Frederic Tudor, which air-conditioned the original building, was expanded, with the additional installation of myriad personalized vents through the parterre floor and chair legs from below. (Tudor was the son of the "Ice King" of the same name, who made his fortune shipping New England ice to the Caribbean, Europe, and India.) The object was compression: to "have an excess of air entering the building beyond that escaping by the regularly provided foul-air outlets, thus insuring an internal atmosphere pressure slightly in excess of the air without the building."[30] Many still found the system suffocating—though not so much as the oppressive Festspielhaus in Bayreuth, where Carl Brandt's steam-generating boilers and Wagner's "endless melodies" asphyxiated the captive audience.[31] 1890s New York saw a veritable explosion in proto-air-conditioning or "refrigeration" techniques as an addendum to several smoke and noise abatement campaigns. Elites worked to keep the nuisance of foul gas, smoke, and cinders in Midtown Manhattan where they belonged—on the streets, and in the lungs of the working poor. The luxuriant interior of the Met, meanwhile, was enriched, not only by pressurized conditioning but also by the fragrant fumes of Turkish tobacco and ivory-tipped De Reszkes, the patented "Aristocrat of Cigarettes" (see figure 5.2).

"The Greatest Tenor of the Nineteenth Century"

"Jean de Reszke's voice is dead," or so the newspapers announced five months before his comeback on December 31, 1900, billed as "the last night of the nineteenth century." In the days leading up to the event, bull-baiting subscribers anticipated a fracas.[32] Word had it that the fifty-year-old had lost his mojo in London. Singing the role of Walther in Wagner's *Meistersinger*, Reszke battled on bravely in German even though his voice had run aground. "The wreck is beautiful," the critic wrote, "but a wreck it is, and the performance could not but excite painful memories."[33]

Rival critics knew that fans would applaud even "if he but moved across

FIGURE 5.2. "Equally as mild and harmless a cigarette as was specially blended for and always smoked by that great tenor," De Reszke Minors, the Aristocrat of Cigarettes (London: J. Millhoff & Co.). © The Board of Trustees of the Science Museum, https://creativecommons.org/licenses/by-nc-sa/4.0/legalcode.

the canvas [as] a fascinating though voiceless apparition." Fortunately for New Yorkers, the sound of Reszke's voice flickered back to life one last time at precisely 8:26 p.m. on New Century's Night. Reszke was "greeted by an immense audience." Pulled into the third scene by the Metropolitan swan, Lohengrin competed, as Henderson of the *New York Times* put it, with "a burst of applause which was with difficulty stilled soon enough to permit his adieu to the bird of transportation to be heard."[34] "He began his farewell to the swan," according to the *New York Evening Post*, "and ere he had sung six bars the fact was established that the London rumors were once more proven false." His voice was "a trifle thinner," in the words of the *New York Sun*, but he still sang with "the voice of a healthy, mature [and] impregnable artist." For Hearst's *New York World*, there was an audible sigh of relief when Jean's first "few notes confounded his detractors and reveled the fact that his voice still possesses ... its indescribable spirituality, its dignity and its pathos." The *Morning Telegraph* spoke of Reszke's patented "mystic, almost divine suggestion."[35] "When the opera was over, at 11:30," another critic concluded, "the fact was clear that Jean de Reszke had remained to the end the greatest tenor of the nineteenth century, and that he would set a standard for the twentieth which coming generations will find it difficult to live up to."[36]

Superhuman Breathing

But it was in the grail narration where Reszke most came into his own. To paraphrase Nietzsche on Wagner, this would be the moment when "the musician himself suddenly grew in value to an unheard-of extent: from now on he would be an oracle, a priest, even more than a priest, a kind of mouthpiece of the 'essence' of things, a telephone from the world beyond."[37] Here, the Polish visitant brought into the opera house the more precious ether of a distant heaven. And the scene would end with Elsa's gasping for air—"O Luft! Luft der Unglücksel'gen!"—as she realizes that she can no longer breath on Lohengrin's level. One is reminded of Nietzsche's experience of Wagner's aesthetic: "I should like to open the window a little," he protested in *The Case of Wagner* (1888), "Air! More air!"[38]

Lohengrin's dramatic transfiguration, as the Italian-English-German piano-vocal score of figure 5.3 suggests, was introduced by the brightly colored return of the shimmering high strings of the hushed opening of the opera's prelude. Divisi first and second violins produce radiant A-major sonorities, their incandescent pianissimos morphing first into high flutes and oboes before evaporating into four solo violins playing harmonics high on the bridge. Here, as Theodor Adorno would have it, Lohengrin's rapt vocal pianissimos were allied with a coeval transmogrification of orchestral instruments, achieved by obscuring their timbral difference one from another. Wagner's ideal, Adorno argued, was a sacralized sound-image scrubbed clean of the traces of instrumental labor. The sonic phantasmagoria, in his view, occurred by a process of occlusion, wherein all social relations necessary to the means of production evaporated.[39]

Liszt described the music of the orchestral prelude less critically. He wrote of an ether that "extends outward, in order that the sacred tableau may be painted before our profane eyes," the colors, overtones and resonance of sacred delirium roused by "indescribable perfumes" wafted in "from the dwellings of the Just."[40] Baudelaire, having read Liszt, described a state of "solitude with vast horizons and bathed in a diffused light" when hearing Wagner's sounds. He heard "burning whiteness." "I became aware of a heightened brightness, of a light growing in intensity so quickly that the shades of meaning provided by a dictionary would not suffice to express this constant increase of burning whiteness," Baudelaire gushed: "Then I achieved a full apprehension of a soul floating in light."[41] One thinks of that light fixture used to introduce Reszke in figure 5.1.

For one pupil of Reszke, who studied the score in detail, Lohengrin's recitation had always seemed "rather dull, another of Wagner's interminable sermons." This was until he heard Reszke invoke the sacred courts

A Spectral Image of Breath 157

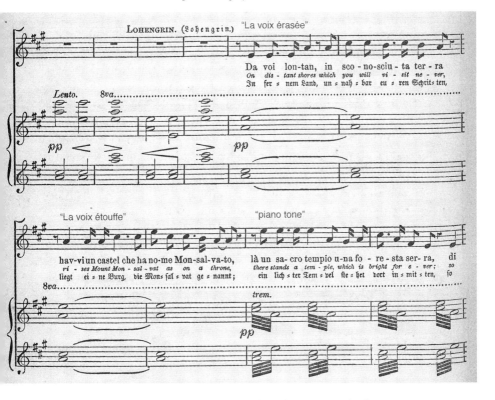

FIGURE 5.3. Grail narration in Italian, English, and German, Richard Wagner, *Lohengrin: A Romantic Opera in Three Acts*, ed. Arthur Sullivan and J. Pittman (New York and London: Boosey, 1872), 342, with my annotations after Reszke.

of Montsalvat. "As soon as he began 'In fernem Land unnahbar euren Schritten,'" wrote the pupil, "I realized that there was an otherworldliness about it all that had been hidden from me."[42] Reszke's art, his acolyte reported, was beholden to the practice of so-called *appoggio*, a technique of "fixing the voice" or "leaning on the breath" promulgated by Francesco Lamperti in Milan. To "drink the tone," Lamperti claimed in 1864, was to support "a column of air over which the singer has perfect command, by holding back the breath, and not permitting more air than is absolutely necessary for the formation of the note to escape from the lungs."[43] The breath, one pupil explained, "though vigorously pressed out, still remains inside the body." Lamperti's practice was to make his disciples sing in front of lighted candles, the nonflickering flame being confirmation of perfect breath management.[44]

To Lamperti's system of pressurized containment, Reszke added his own brand of vocal hypostatization, by fostering sensations of "placing," "focusing," or "directing compressed regions of air" to various parts of the head, nose, cheekbones, teeth, soft or hard palate. At the opening phrase of the narration ("In fernem Land")—where the singer extends the orchestral invocation of the harmonic series—Reszke instructed his pupil to "draw back the uvula, pinch the tonsils, [and] push the diaphragm," to achieve sounds devoid of head and chest resonance. This was a version of what Reszke elsewhere called the "crushed voice" (*la voix écrasée*). In the score, the indication *appuyer la poitrine* (press the chest) implied that the singer focus vibration behind the soft palate such as to physically embody Lohengrin's atmospheric detachment from earth.

"Plus loin, plus loin, further back, further back," Reszke would exhort at the second phrase: "liegt eine Burg, die Montsalvat genannt." "How hopeless to try to get the sort of passionate reverence he got into the word *Monsalvat!*" his pupils lamented: "A sort of *ripæ ulterioris amor*, very simple, very personal, but all accomplished by a definite technique: a tiny upward *portamento*, a half-smothered M, a sudden piano, his marvelous *voix étouffée*; it was like a recipe, shake the bottle and apply the Elixir of Life." The *voix étoufée* or "asphyxiated voice" was yet another Reszke *pianissimo* technique, achieved, according to reports, with an "almost closed mouth and low palate, the larynx being rather high, but the support [*appoggio*] as deep and strong as possible."[45] There were a myriad of other coloristic Reszke placements, such as his patented "echo voice" or "piano tone," the latter used at "Ein lichter Tempel stehet dort inmitten," where the instruction was to "throw light into the voice, strike right above the uvula." "Take your time," Reszke directed throughout the narration, and at its climax— "es heist der Gral!"—he drew back even further: "Get your support on the note preceding the high note, and just carry the resonance of the high note further up by drawing back the uvula as far as possible, and when on the note itself, expand the ribs to support it 'like the pinions of a bird.'"[46]

Breathing Wars

No critics disdained Reszke's colorist aesthetic more than exponents of traditional voice science, though singers—to this day—have never stopped singing "in the mask" or "placing" voice, or singing by sensations or images. "What 'goes on' above the throat are illusions no matter how real they may feel or sound," wrote W. E. Brown, professing to speak for his teacher Giovanni Lamperti.[47] "I do not believe in teaching by means of sensations of tone," agreed a spokesperson for the eighty-nine-year-old Manuel García in 1894, apparently in response to "modern theories" of Reszkeian breath control. García complained that earlier in his career he "used to direct the tone into the head, and do peculiar things with the breathing, and so on, but as years passed by, I discarded them as useless, and I now speak only of actual things and not mere appearances." "All control of breath is lost the moment it is turned into vibrations [at the glottis]," García protested in an 1894 article, "and the idea is absurd that a current of air can be thrown against the hard palate for one kind of tone, the soft palate for another, and reflected hither and thither."[48] The singer, so far as physiological science was concerned, had no business "making timbre," since timbre was not within his power to control. Timbre was a property of brute pharyngeal fact, a quality to be observed by science rather than confected by art. The color and beauty of various sounds, they insisted, had nothing to do with byzantine internal patternings of air. For García's twentieth-century apostles—most prominent among them French mezzo Blanche Marchesi (daughter of Mathilde)—the naïve mysticism of "the sensation school" was dangerous. These Reszkeians decried physiological reality.

At the head of the "Nasal Method" movement, Marchesi complained, stood "the Triumvirate": Jean and Édouard de Reszke, as well as their personal physician, New York socialite and medical doctor, Henry Holbrook Curtis. Marchesi called these three men "ignoramuses" because they failed to locate voice in nature. For her, the one true source of sound was the glottis: the "tongue" (after the Greek *glôttís*) or "inner mouth" that García had famously first seen live through his patented laryngoscope some forty years earlier.[49] The reality of vocal folds and glottal strokes, Marchesi scoffed, could never be wished away as the Reszkes dreamed, merely by cultivating vocal onsets begun with a consonant "h" or the consonant "m." (Reszke developed an influential set of daily exercises that softened plosive attacks.) The clouding of laryngoscopic objectivity, Marchesi lamented, had led to "the foundation of a New Religion," which, having declared war on science, "spread like a prairie fire" "from the North Pole to the South." The speculations of the Triumvirate, she bristled, wreaked "havoc in the singing profession."[50]

Yet Reszke was hardly opposed to science. At least two specialists in the emerging field of oto-rhino-laryngology were full-time disciples of his "new gospel." The first was Joseph Joal, an amateur musician and doctor at the bathhouses of Le Mont-Dore, a high-altitude spa in the Massif Central frequented by European singers and other fashionables over the summer.[51] Joal specialized in "thermal therapies." He was the inventor of the *pulvérisateur*, an improved spirometer, and a device for the inhalation of carbonic acid. His expertise allowed him unparalleled access to the finest singers in Europe—Emma Albani, Rose Caron, Josephine de Reszke,

FIGURE 5.4. "Source des chanteurs" beneath the central gabled portico under a glass roof at Le Mont-Dore.

Victor Capoul, Jean Lassalle, Léon Melchissédec, Jean-Alexandre Talazac, and François-Pierre Villaret among them, who featured in the publication of his spirometric writings. In 1888, Jean de Reszke attended the mountain retreat beneath the dormant Puy-de-Dôme where Joal lived. There, at Le Mont-Dore's great Neo-Byzantine thermal bathhouse was the famous "Source des Chanteurs," as photographed for figure 5.4. That hot volcanic spring—still bubbling away today under the hothoused glass roof of "Le

Hall des sources"—was thought to contain such minerals as would restore any fatigued singer to health. (Today, the establishment is one of the last remaining to specialize in *des inhalations des gaz thermaux* through specially designed tubes.)[52] Reszke was the inspiration for Joal's "On Forms of Breathing in Singing," which appeared in a specialist French journal four years later.[53] Joal's publication was a blistering attack, "telephoned in" from the Monsalvat of mainstream French medicine, on the encroachment of mainstream medical science into matters of artful song.[54]

The main target of Joal's scorn was not so much García as the Parisian doctor of Hungarian extraction, Louis Mandl. Mandl's long-standing insistence on the supremacy of "abdominal breathing" had been folded into the vocal curriculum of the Paris Conservatoire since 1866. According to Joal, Reszke himself was a resolute defender of so-called costal, rib-cage, or clavicular respiration. Joal cited recent research that used his favored graphic method (rather than laryngoscopic probes), to illustrate the vulgarity of Mandl's "low" methods. Like Joal, Mandl had been concerned with identification and classification of *types respiratoires*. (Here, he followed Beau and Maissiat, who as far back as 1842 had given the first scientific descriptions of the "superior costal type," "inferior clavicular type," and "lower abdominal type.")[55]

Thanks to the *pulvérisateur*, any subject's vital capacity (and hence level of civilization) could be measured with unprecedented accuracy. Joal cited the 1890 study of Dr. Thomas Jefferson Mays of the Philadelphia Polyclinic. As figure 5.5 shows, Mays racialized breathing by applying pneumographs to the chests of eighty-two Indigenous Native American girls between the ages of ten and twenty-two. Thirty-three were "Indian of pure breed" and thirty-five "half-breeds." The majority of these purported "savages," Joal reported of the pneumographic results, breathed according to Mandl's vulgar abdominal descent. Only a few girls from "tribes comparatively civilized, such as the Mohawks and Chippawas" were found to be of "costal type."[56] Similarly, Dr. John Harvey Kellogg—eugenicist, future founder of the Race Betterment Foundation, and originator of Kellogg's Cornflakes—conducted research on forty women, again divided equally and racially: twenty Chinese and twenty Indigenous Americans. As Joal reported, "primitive breathers" proved to be of the same abdominal type. European women, meanwhile, were often more of the costal variety. For that fairer sex, apparently, this type constituted "a true secondary sexual characteristic," one that circumvented impediments to genital and uterine function. Feminists such as Elizabeth Chamberlayne, English composer and member of the Royal Musical Association, disagreed. "I have by nature, and always, as far as I know," Chamberlayne protested, "breathed

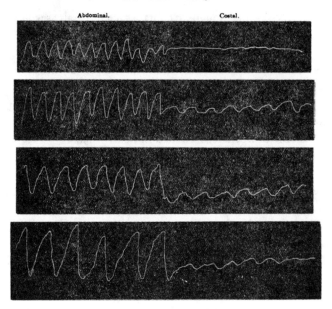

FIGURE 5.5. "Tracings taken from the Chests of Indian Girls," in Thomas J. Mays, "An Experimental Inquiry into the Chest Movements of the Indian Female," *The Therapeutic Gazette* 3, no. 5 (May 16, 1887): 298.

from the abdomen."[57] Joal countered that of the thirty-three he had tested pneumographically, not a single chanteuse of value was a stomach breather. Higher forms, he insisted, used higher breathing.

An even greater proselytizer for the health benefits of Reszkeian breathing was Holbrook Curtis, a doctor key to the international dissemination of the laws of sound imagery, nasal resonance, timbral shifting, and "forward tone." Like Joal, Curtis acted as Reszke's personal physician and friend. After the singer's New York debut, the specialist rhinologist-surgeon was invited to the singer's estates and stud farm near Klomnice in Russian Poland. Curtis had made his name in the operatic world in December 1889 after surgically removing a tumor on the vocal cords of Italo Campanini, pupil of Lamperti in Milan, notable early exponent of Radames, and the original Italian Lohengrin (in the version witnessed by Verdi). Curtis was a powerful advocate of "voice culture," a social and artistic movement launched in service of fine elocution and singing instruction, as well as for the cultural, economic, and political well-being of New York State.[58] He was also a physician to the stars, with a clientele that by the end of his career included Enrico Caruso, Ignacy Jan Paderewski, Ellen Terry, William Faversham, Antonio Scotti, Emma Calvé, Johanna Gadski, Luisa Tetrazzini, Pol Plançon, and Teddy Roosevelt. In 1906, he embroiled himself in the celebrated "adenoid riots," when massed adenoidectomies were rolled out in the New York public school system, and parents in the Lower East Side and Brooklyn revolted. Throughout, Curtis stood firm in his conviction that congested nasal passages prevented some seventy-five thousand children from breathing properly, which explained the cultural ubiquity of poor voice tone, speech defects, retarded intellectual development, and "depraved and ungovernable" behavior.[59]

In a paper read to New York State Teachers Association in Rochester in 1893, Curtis introduced Joal's findings to an American audience, adding that in his laryngological work with singers he had been struck by the deleterious effects of different schools of training on the vocal folds. (Those schooled in García's notorious glottal attack, for example, presented cords with disfigured convex bulges, "the center showing the result of attrition.") Instead of inspiring with Mandl's advancing abdomen, Curtis recommended girding the loins. Reszke's system was to flatten the stomach, fortify the lower regions, and expand laterally. He taught that the only way to unleash the mysteries of compound vibration was to use the high-chest method, "a clever trick which maintains great resonance even when the lung is nearly exhausted of air."[60] Curtis recommended that singers fix their chests in the puffed-out manner made famous by Reskze's portrait photographs of the period. The elevated rib cage worked to add "secondary resonance to the voice from below—a sort of complementary timbre—the fixed upper thorax allowing of the least possible change of color during tone production."[61] To assist in the production of resonance, he recommended the use of a Sbriglia belt (named after Reszke's teacher, Giovanni Sbriglia) strapped tight around the waist in order to "cure [oneself] of the bad habit of so-called abdominal respiration."[62] In modern times, such singers as Franco Corelli, Plácido Domingo, and Lauritz Melchior forced air against the higher chest using similar reinforcement. Abdominal braces were yet another means by which to set the chest, thicken the sonic haze, and hold breath within.

Together with Reszke, Curtis devised possibly the most painterly conception of singing ever. He preached that there was far more to singing than García's tiny vocal folds, advising singers to study the "ingenious mingling of pure spectrum colors" and "color harmonics in music in the same way that they must be studied in painting." To follow Reszke, apparently, was to "cultivate tone harmonies and sympatica in the voice at the expense of brilliancy of execution." "There is no rule [other than the magic rule of feeling]," wrote Curtis in reference to the famous painter who was also a regular at bathhouses of Le Mont-Dore, "for the palpitating sunlight effects and prismatic play of colours in the school of Claude

Monet."[63] Adapting Helmholtzian theories of sympathetic vibration, Curtis imagined singers building tone by the addition or subtraction of "those harmonics, which are added to the original tone by intervibrations within the accessory cavities of the nasal passages."[64] Rather than zeroing in on the glottis, in other words, Curtis directed attention upward and outward toward the facial resonators. The glottis, after all, was only a void, an "orifice glottique" in the words of Mandl, a reverberant space that (in Curtis's conception) was activated as much by secondary vibration from above as direct air pressure from below. "I find that the great question of the singer's art becomes narrower and narrower all the time," Reszke (who sniffed cocaine to open the airways before performance) declared in an interview with Curtis, "until I can truly say that the great question of singing becomes a question of the nose—*la grande question du chant devient une question du nez.*"[65]

The best sounds, for Reszke, were produced by "forward placement." This was the point of Curtis's aptly named treatise *Voice Building and Tone Placing*, showing a new method of relieving injured vocal cords by tone exercises, published in 1896.[66] In Curtis's vision of "forward placement" and "timbrated sounds," the practice was literally to paint a sound image "against the mask." It was to "put on" tone, or give vocal sound "a face." Lilli Lehmann, alongside Reszke principal exponent of international opera (who in 1899 sang opposite him in "the ideal *Tristan*") agreed. Figure 5.6

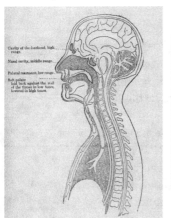
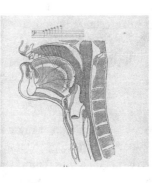
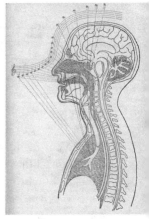

FIGURE 5.6. Images from Lilli Lehmann, *How to Sing* [*Meine Gesangskunst*] (London: Macmillan, 1902), 81, 111, 126. Jean Gray Hargrove Music Library, University of California at Berkeley.

shows images from her vocal tutor of 1902. Here, she extolled the cultivation of living tones: "perfect tones" forged from "continuous streams" and "whirling currents and vibrations," which filled the spaces artfully prepared for them by a raised soft palate. She wrote of "soaring inner sounds" vivified by directing breath toward focal points on the palate and sensations of a "very elastic rubber ball" above and behind the nose and toward the cavities of the head. Sometimes, she imagined a balloon that she shaped to suit the desired sound form. "In order to bring out the color of the tone the whirling currents must vivify all," Lehmann explained, the vowel sounds that enter into it, and draw them into their circles with an ever-increasing, soaring tide of sound."[67] These animated tides circulated "in unbroken completeness of form" as swirling arabesques or overtone patterns resonating in the region of the brain. In her vision of singing, the most perfect sound images were always imprinted against the sounding boards of the palate.

Lehmann's ideal of tonal life achieved full graphic expression in such voice-printing technologies as Curtis's tonograph, as pictured in figure 5.7. Curtis's invention was an instrument devised in 1897 for photographing "tone forms" and for observing the coming-into-being of "ravishing beauty of sound."[68] It consisted of a circular turntable-sized membrane stretched over a metal tube and covered in a mixture of salt and emery. When activated by the standing vibration of a singer's vocal sound, the tonograph produced phantasmic tone figures or, to put this in Wagnerian terms, "deeds of music made visible." With the aid of his invention—"recording in geometrical figures the vibrations of the voice"—Curtis published vocal records of such illustrious singers as Calvé, Caruso, Plançon, and (of course) both Reszkes. These "copies of the will," which looked remarkably like Berliner's gramophone records, were the products of just another next-generation voice-imaging technology. Curtis explained the tonograph's usefulness to the project of building out tone in these terms:

> A tone, to make a perfect geometric figure, must be sung well forward, with no forcing or tension, and with absence of shock or breathiness of tone. In other words, perfect production must be employed to make a harmonious figure, in the same way that it must be studied to make an agreeable impression upon our ear; and, for the same analogy, may we not reason that the little membrane of our ear drum may be divided up in the same exquisite arrangement of nodal lines by audible tones, and thus communicate to the brain, by means of the auditory nerve, the impression of agreeable quality in tone.[69]

PLATE I—TONE PHOTOGRAPHY.

MR. PLUNKETT GREENE SINGING INTO THE TONOGRAPH.   MISS PECK SINGING INTO THE TONOGRAPH.

FIGURE 5.7. Holbrook Curtis, "The Tonograph," *Scientific American* 76, no. 22 (1897): 345.

Curtis admitted that the most influential precedent for visualizing tone was not the tonograph but the eidophone, as shown in figure 5.8 and developed by the remarkable British soprano Margaret Watts-Hughes. Exhibited at the Arts and Crafts Exposition in London in 1889, the eidophone deployed standing wave patterns and color pigments on glass in order to animate strange "voice flowers," "tree forms," "serpent forms," a myriad of strange organic forms come to life. According to Curtis, the eidophone opened up new worlds of voice, one where the resonant cavities of the head were analogous to "weird caverns at the bottom of the sea, full of beautiful coloured sea anemones and mussel shells, headless snakes, entanglements of flower and leaflike forms, all seemingly vital with the same laws of growth as those which inspired the creation of the designs in Nature which they suggest."[70] These self-organizing forms, produced by the magic of cross-vibration, purportedly illustrated the tone's psychophysiology. And they could be imprinted visually: either upon the roof of the mouth, the diaphragm of the ear, as well as on membranes of glass or wax.

The images of figures 5.6, 5.7, and 5.8 presaged an international and absolute standard. At once French, German, Italian, English, American, and Polish, the sound forms that Reszke divined were never fully localizable. Expression, ideally, was placed in the realms of atmospheric resonance broadly conceived. The organ of voice, in other words, was remote; or at least the source of voice was located as much at the ear or mouth as it

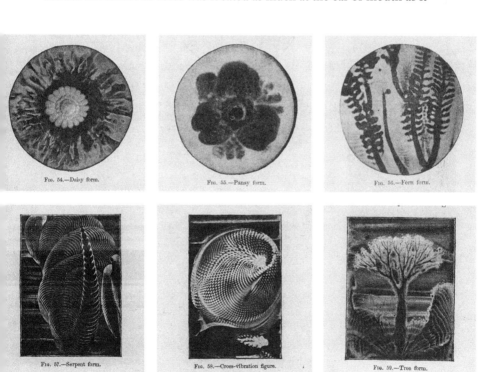

FIGURE 5.8. Watts-Hughes's voice-prints in Holbrook Curtis, *Voice Building and Tone Placing, Showing a New Method of Relieving Injured Vocal Cords by Tone Exercises* (New York: D. Appleton, 1896), 227–31.

was located atmospherically. The implication of Reszke's work was that vocal tones were airborne and spectral. As if to prove their atmospheric provenance, these living forms could be summoned into visible life by means of techniques of sonic capture. Their cultural production depended on highly rarefied levels of technical and technological expertise, which is why it mattered little that Reszke arrived in New York with no voice. "Jean de Reszke is more than an artist," Gounod reportedly agreed. "His is the richest and most marvelously colorful of palettes."[71]

The capture of vibration through projection and sonic placement was the common goal of a range of nascent cultural techniques in this period. When Mapleson seized that small portion of the vibrating world on March 29, 1901, he was invested in far more than arresting time. In making the recording, the librarian was also devoted—as much as the assembled audience was—to an *atmosphericization* of air. His work served in the project to make what was once intangible tangible. This was also the point of Reszkean breathing: to venerate not breath itself, but the image of breath. Its function was to recruit extraordinarily complex forms of environmental control to the task of abnegating the most basic means of human production and reproduction. The highest music, that is, required a denial of air. In the drive to evacuate contingency, sound became image. Or perhaps it would be better to claim that the will to thickness and color required that air, wherever possible, be removed.

CHAPTER 6

Albert Schweitzer's Equatorial Piano
Lambaréné, Gabon, 1913

An Ethical Instrument

A hemisphere: in the foreground, forming the first of three concentric circles extends the land of exile, colorless Europe; then comes the dazzling circle of the Islands and of childhood, which dance the roundelay around Africa; the last circle is Africa, the world's navel, pole of all black poetry's dazzling Africa, burnt, oily like a snake's skin, Africa of fire and rain, torrid and tufted; Africa's phantom flickering like a flame, between being and nothingness . . . beyond attainment, disintegrating Europe with its black but invisible rays; Africa, an imaginary continent.
JEAN-PAUL SARTRE, "Black Orpheus" (1948)

The piano with organ pedals, pictured in figure 6.1, was built for Africa. It was presented by the Paris Bach Society to Albert Schweitzer in 1913. Schweitzer received the gift, with which he planned to continue his Bach studies, on the eve of his departure for the Paris Missionary Society's mission at Lambaréné, pronounced "Lembareni" (meaning "try and see" in Galwa/Galoa). The mission stood on the banks of the Ogooué River, in Gabon, West Central Africa, near to where this formal photograph was staged and taken.

The Paris-based firm of Gaveau finished the piano in 1912, a year before Schweitzer's trek. The instrument has been restored to life several times, notably in 1967 and 1976. It can be found today in Schweitzer's home village of Gunsbach, the piano retired to his living room in the Munster Valley in Alsace, northeastern France. Its construction materials, mostly of hard West African Sapeli mahogany, were selected for their resilient qualities. A double iron frame fortified the case, making the whole heavy and difficult to transport. The keys were affixed with screws rather than glue. Climate- and termite-proofed, the instrument was built to be as healthful

FIGURE 6.1. Black labor/white culture on the Ogooué. "Das Clavier im Einbaum, Lambaréné," © Archives Centrales Albert Schweitzer Gunsbach.

as the body of its possessor, Albert Schweitzer, leading scholar-performer of J. S. Bach, medical missionary, organist, theologian, philosopher, Nobel Peace Prize laureate (in 1952), humanitarian, mystic, and, according to *Life* magazine, "the Greatest Man in the World."[1]

Later, this instrument will be shown to be conceived for the optimization of life and that its raison d'être was at once biomedical and spiritual. For the moment, note that, in contradistinction to pianos, pedal pianos appear in the image of a durably sacred technology. Church organs, with multiple keyboards at hands and feet, furnish a structurally immersive experience for the player. To use a word coined in 1909 by Jakob von Uexküll, the instrumentalist is subject to a wraparound *Umwelt*.[2] The "piano with pedal attachment" domesticates the habitus and experience of the organ, which Schweitzer (in his voluminous writings) called a "holy instrument," best approached with the *heilige Gesinnung* proper to its ethos. "Anyone who studies organs is carried beyond the human and all too human, and purified into the pure joy of truth," Schweitzer opined in a 1926 letter: "[That player] reveres the organ and the sounds of the organ as among the great spiritual teachers and experiences the mind of eternity (*Ewigkeitsgesinnung*)."[3] The instrument on the Ogooué was certainly one such "ethical instrument," conceived in the service of humanitarianism. It was consecrated for the cause of advancing life, in ways that this chapter seeks to explain.[4]

Recent scholarship has been kind to such instruments. Roger Moseley, Emily I. Dolan, Deirdre Loughridge, Thomas Patteson, Eliot Bates, and others have long recognized the agential power of instrumental interfaces: the limits of technological setups, haptic engagements with so-called non-human entities, the digital life of cognition, and so on. The focus on "thing power" has been invigorating and a boost for the field. Yet there may be room, taking philosophical account of the affordances of musical technology, to be more materialist still and apply what Schweitzer called "elemental thinking" to the task. Temperature, for one, has an obvious physical effect on tuning. Consider the provenance of the materials that musical instruments are made of, as well as the climates and trade relationships that make them possible. An "elemental" approach might extend to invisible concerns besides the weather, like belief and value, also.

While this chapter attends to the "raw materials" that physically constitute the piano, it is more interested in the freight of values—the elemental meanings—that make such technological arrangements possible. The fact of Schweitzer's piano suggests that, when it comes to musical instruments, the power of the invisible casts the power of the visible into the shade. Though "non-human" layouts and the concerns of political ecology are important, physical setups are impotent as they stand alone. An assemblage like the one pictured in figure 6.2 only gains true conceptual, dare one say spiritual, power when touched by the player. It is precisely in active processes of engagement that the system comes to life. Any such entity, that is, only makes sense in view of the invisible investments imposed upon it, including investments in bodily training, techniques of performance, and the routines of everyday practice. The geopolitical tradeoffs that come together in the playing of the thing are no less implicated. Which is why, in what follows, I throw the physical matter of Schweitzer's tropical pedal piano into the air and think about the values it carries up there.

Elemental Thinking

One way to understand the piano would be to think about Schweitzer's "life philosophy" or what he called "reverence for life." The phrase in German was *Ehrfucht vor dem Lebem*, or "awe before the overwhelming sovereignty of life." (Schweitzer spoke Alsatian, German, and French.) Famously, Schweitzer's mature *Lebensphilosophie* involved a sacred duty: "to preserve life, to promote life, to raise to its highest value life which

FIGURE 6.2. *Piano à pédalier* by Gaveau at the Maison Albert Schweitzer in Gunsbach, Alsace. Note the screws in white keys. © Archives Centrales Albert Schweitzer Gunsbach.

is capable of development."[5] Schweitzer thought of this moral calling as his primary contribution to human history. "The most immediate fact of man's consciousness," he famously philosophized, "is the assertion 'I am life that wills to live in the midst of life that wills to live.'"[6] The ethical actor experiences all life as his own, Schweitzer argued, in the knowledge that his own life is bound up with the lives of all other lives, from the highest man to the lowliest plant. Goodness consisted in devoting oneself to the alleviation of the suffering of all life. The future of humanity, he sermonized, was in the care of the moral few who would act in service of life—succoring, advancing, fortifying, and lifting it up. All things with life and breath were best respected, not in a posture of self-righteousness but in an attitude of trembling and fear. Thus his celebrated motto: "My life is my argument."

Schweitzer embarked upon his mission of healing—abandoning his career as a philosopher, teacher, and musician to retrain as a medical doctor—having learned of "Les besoins de la Mission du Congo" (The needs of the Congo Mission) in the pages of the *Journal* des *missions évangéliques* (June 1904). Yet, in retrospect, Schweitzer admitted that his "reverence for life" owed first to an encounter with the Ogooué. He wrote that it was "at the edge of the primordial forest" that "thoughts that had been stirring in me since 1900" began to mature.[7] "That over which I have toiled since 1900," he observed in *The Decay and the Restoration of Civilization* (1923) "has been finally ripened in the stillness of the primeval forest of Equatorial Africa."[8] His *Lebensanschauung*, he wrote, emerged in that liminal zone between civilization and savagery, water and forest. The claim was that the unyielding brutality of the climate he was subjected to in the Gabon had tested, sharpened, and strengthened his moral psyche. It had exposed him to the truth of what he called "inviolable life."

The value of "elemental thinking" was revealed to him twice over in the lives of the inhabitants of the "primeval forest." These were the lives that Schweitzer was called to minister to in his medical work. On the one hand, reportedly, were the genteel Galoa/Galwa speakers: caught up in the history of slavery, related to the Mpongwe speakers of chapter 1, but purportedly "thinned by three hundred years of alcohol and the slave trade."[9] (It was often quipped that the Myene-speaking "Galoa" were honorary "Gallois," that is, civilized enough to thrive under the care and protection of the French.[10]) On the other were the vital products of the interior: the "cannibal" Fang, who were "savage," sharp witted, and easily offended, as figure 6.3 imagines. These newcomers to the Ogooué arrived around 1870, invading like a "raging epidemic" from the northeast. (Fang scholar and turn-of-the-century Catholic missionary on the Ogooué Henri Trilles predictably managed to trace the origin of the "Fang races" to the Upper Nile.[11]) Schweitzer's account was dramatic: the march of the Fang operated by predatory ingestion. These resilient people were proud and upright. Though they knew cannibalism, they knew nothing of slavery. Such was their European reputation. Schweitzer wrote that the slow death of transatlantic slave systems had created a void into which "swarmed from inland the cannibal Fans, called by the French Pahouins who have never yet come into contact with civilization, and but for the opportune arrival of the Europeans this warrior folk would by this time have eaten up the old tribes of the Ogooué lowlands."[12] "Tall, angular, bold, and singularly vain in the dressing of their hair," these people knew how to live.[13]

Black Orpheus

This is a little-known fact: Jean-Paul Sartre, author of "Black Orpheus" and the epigraph introducing this chapter, was the youngest grandson of Albert Schweitzer's uncle.[14] In the years before 1913, long before he contributed to anticolonial discourse, young Sartre went for walks with Schweitzer in Paris, testing the crisp urban air. The epigraph, to provide a sense of his mature thought, appeared in "Orphée noir," an essay devoted to the imagined binary between "black life" and "our whiteness[, which] seems to us to be a strange livid varnish that keeps our skin from breathing." Primitivist movements in France, of course, hailed (as they still often do) the élan vital of Sartre's "Africa of fire and rain." Life, in Sartre's modernist conception, thrives at the "navel of the world," where the reproductive powers of Blackness apparently respire from the sexed pores of central African skin. For "our black poets," Sartre wrote," "being comes out of Nothingness like a penis becoming erect; creation is an enormous perpetual delivery; the world is flesh and the son of flesh; on the sea and in the sky, on the dunes, on the rocks, in the wind."[15] Life, according to Sartre, breathed deepest in Africa.

The racial logic in this modernist strain of Sartrian "life philosophy," as Donna V. Jones has shown, was hegemonic enough in Europe to become the dominant discourse by which even anticolonial and Black power movements sought cultural and political emancipation. Cultural vitalism, that is, conditioned Francophone attitudes toward this peculiarly Sartrian understanding of negritude. (In 1961, for example, he would contribute the introduction to the first edition of Frantz Fanon's *The Wretched of the Earth*.)[16] When power turns to biopower, paradoxically, independence movements could only express resistance by primeval shows of ejaculative vitality. (Again, we are dealing with an Afrovitalist primitivist stereotype, where the products of equatorial climates purportedly possess a kind of hypersexual life power.) Life could only be resisted by displays of *even more life*. "Négritude's grounding of black oppositional culture in vitalism," Jones observes, is owed to an experience of social reproduction imposed by biomedical paradigms of thought. "Racialism has been central to our culture," she concludes, "and that this racialism has often been vitalist."[17] For Jones, the ecstatic celebration of "African Heat" as the source of life itself, while ostensibly countercultural, ends up feeding the very colonial politics it seeks to oppose.

Colonial Biointegration

The post-1910 period witnessed the absorption of Gabon, after the scramble of the fin de siècle, into the belly of a voracious colonizing beast. When Schweitzer's piano landed near the equator, there was no "traditional society" to speak of in the Ogooué region—so prone was the state to fissure, commercial upheaval, and forced migration. Before 1910, the river was officially governed under the thumb of the French Congo. Since then, it fell under the anarcho-capitalist fist of "Afrique équatoriale française" (AEF), a region four and a half times the size of France. In late 1911, Governor-

General Martial Merlin declared his AEF the French Empire's "Cinderella," having traded 270,000 square kilometers and approximately 1,118,500 people in negotiations over the wider territory with Germany.[18] (The Germans swapped territory north of Gabon close to the old Cameroonian frontier in exchange for a more populated swathe of land near Chad.)

Under Merlin's administration, France would begin to eat her Cinderella. On July 9, 1909, parliament announced the loan of 21 million francs for the purposes of an injection of investment capital.[19] A great extraction project was begun, one targeting such forest timber products as okoumé, ebony, and mahogany brought to the banks of the Ogooué.[20] Ivory was lucrative, too, Lambaréné being a center of operations for the growing rubber and timber trade. Predatory concessionary companies—such as the Société du Haut-Ogooué (SHO) (which by 1899 had already secured "over a quarter of the entire colony as its own fiefdom") or the Société Agricole, Forestiere et Industrielle pour l'Afrique (SAFIA) (reconstituted in 1911 to exploit its monopoly over okoumé logging on the Lower Ogooué and in the lakes around Lambaréné)—consolidated to procure forest products after the perceived failure of metropolitan officials in Paris to properly capitalize on its equatorial possession.[21] As late as 1915, official reports complained that 70,764 tons of wood still went to foreign countries. Only 12,531 tons went to France. (For a sense of Europe's growing appetite, consider that, in 1898, a mere 1,489 tons of timber besides ebony had been exported in total.)[22] The determination was to break the monopoly of nonstate actors and incorporate this image of "dazzling Africa" into a widening biopolitical order.

The introjection of the life of the rainforest, as Schweitzer himself noted in such writings as his 1914 essay "Social Problems in the Forest," perpetuated mass displacements of indigenous populations in the Ogooué region, taxation schemes, scorched earth tactics, disease, and total psychophysical reconstruction.[23] "From about 1909," Christopher Gray writes in his history of land transformation on the river, "labor migration to work in the timber industry started to radically alter the landscape of Southern Gabon."[24] Since 1900, as described by scholars beginning with Catherine Coquery-Vidrovitch's foundational analysis of the finances of concessionary firms, a per-capita tax was levied to force populations into *corvée* work (only outlawed in 1946) and to generate internal capital enough to run the colony autonomously. The collection of tax revenues, enforced by gunboat and the burning of villages, compelled communities into indentured labor. The abuse caused enough concern to instigate the formation of the 1905 de Brazza commission, Pierre Savorgnan himself (largely responsible for facilitating the system) now returning to Gabon to investigate. From

1911, colonial reports from the Lower Ogooué noted that labor migration was perpetuating a catastrophic neglect of village plantations. The consequences were the abandonment of settlements, food shortages, and the dispersion of the population into ever-smaller bush encampments. François Ngolet and Gray argue, using Catholic missionary reports, criminal records, and other sources, that the combination of raised taxes, a ban on the sale of gunpowder to quell rebellion, higher taxes, and irregular rainfall instigated "commercial and economic collapse." By the time of Schweitzer's first years, food shortages, famine, and outbreaks of disease were common. "The years 1915 to 1919," Ngolet and Gray conclude, "were the darkest of the colonial era for central and southern Gabon."[25]

Boycotts and violent rebellions ensued, as did an upsurge in spiritual *Bwiti* practices. Mysterious "leopard-men killings" were revived. (Leopard men were spiritualists, antecedents in modern Black Panther mythology, belonging to secret political societies—animal-human "superbeings"—who dressed in leopard skins and spread fear through acts of terror in an attempt to wrest back control of land.) Across southern Gabon, several figureheads emerged in the spiritual resistance movement, including Fang leader Emane N'tolé at Ndjolé, Adouma sorcerer Wandji of Lastoursville, and Punu leader Mavurulu Nyonda Makita of Moabi Koudou. As early as 1902, Catholic missionaries noted the revival of "yasi" practice (*Mwiri*-type spiritual traditions of renewal) among the Galwa at Lambaréné, fomented by a clansman named Rigondja.[26] At the time of Schweitzer's arrival, around 1913, these spiritual activities intensified. In the south that year, colonial authorities arrested a certain M'Bombé, a Tsogo-speaking *nganga*, who hailed from the banks of the Ngounié.[27] The charges against M'Bombé included trading *bounda* war fetishes and a potion that gave their owners the power to be invulnerable to bullets. The transcript of M'Bombé's interrogation, which took place less than a month after the arrival of Schweitzer's piano, indicates that the source of these fetishes was a Lambaréné-based specialist named Louemba. The witch substance of M'bombé's war fetish, apparently, was amplified by his personal possession of a white man's skull.[28]

These events were not merely by-products of colonialism. Rather, they indicated the incapacity of the state to fulfill its biopolitical agenda, which was to maximize the productive life of the colony. That drive—to optimize developmental health—was consistently frustrated. Gabonese life proved difficult to yoke, as the work of Florence Bernault shows.[29] A glance at the empire's schemes for economic transformation in the 1913 glossy pages of *Les Annales coloniales* or *La Dépêche coloniale illustrée* illustrates the extent of its failure to harness the colony's potential energy.³⁰ Grand state plans included giant capacity studies, hydrographic surveys, charts for a network of railways, radioelectric communication systems, road building, mining concessions, port construction, and so forth. On one hand, these richly illustrated special issues indicate how much equatorial Africa was absorbed into the French imperial mindset—the plan being to inject some of the hot blood of the colony into the cold veins of bourgeois Europe. On the other, such they show how much the fantasy of colonial bio-integration perpetuated yet more myths about the dazzling energy of this imaginary continent.

FIGURE 6.3. "Fang warrior," Robert Hamill Nassau, *My Ogowe* (New York: Neale Publishing Company, 1914), 681.

FIGURE 6.4. A power statue that Schweitzer was obsessed with as a boy: part of the 1864 Statue de l'amiral Bruat at the Champ de Mars in Colmar, Alsace, by Frédéric Auguste Bartholdi, designer of the Statue of Liberty in New York. "It is a Herculean figure with a thoughtful, sad expression.... Whenever we went to Colmar, I sought an opportunity to look at him. His face told me about the misery of the Dark Continent." Albert Schweitzer, *Memoirs of Childhood and Youth*, trans. Kurt Bergel and Alice R. Bergel (Syracuse NY: Syracuse University Press, 1997), 57–58. © Archives Centrales Albert Schweitzer Gunsbach.

The Cannibal Stage

The export of the insulation technologies of German art music to a former slave reservoir involved more than a provincial imperial navigation of the human. Earlier, this book adopted the term "anthropopoiesis" to denote an art of the human. That art worked to cultivate a more equitable and equal-tempered world, one delivered from the purportedly dehumanizing effects of the climate. One way to explain Schweitzer's piano would be to say that it was transported to the tropics for the sacred purpose of healing the tropics or that this humane instrument had something to do with the salvation of the Gabonese indigenes from their enslavement to air.

Yet there was more to Schweitzer's project than bringing civilization to an imagined heart of darkness. Rather, via Schweitzer, West Equatorial Africa was used (as it had been for centuries) as a wellspring for the exploitative purposes of European rebirth; colonists imagined the life energies of the equatorial rainforests as an elemental power useful to their own spiritual revival. European civilization, Schweitzer claimed in such apocalyptic publications as *Civilization and Ethics* (1923), was committing suicide.[31] (His nephew's view of "disintegrating Europe" was equivalent.) Europe was in precipitous Wagnerian decline. Thus the necessity to expose such obsolete technologies as the eighty-eight-keyed piano to colonial testing. The task was not so much to save African humanity. Rather, the purpose of Schweitzer's "penetration" of the Ogooué was to introject the carnal-atavistic power of the Gabonese forests for the purposes of the restoration of civilization. It was to traffic in life.

In Schweitzer's Nietzschean account (we know this from books he began to write while on the Ogooué), Europe's rapid technological advances had outstripped its spiritual progress. Despoiled by increasing industrialism, civilization had lost its true ground in ethics. Schweitzer's project was primitivist, modernist, and avant-garde—as his association with the radical *Orgelbewegung* and early-music movement suggests. His calling was biopolitical in that he was qualified as a medical doctor and would sacrifice his own life to better the lives of others. His mission was first to save old Silbermann organs and to save Bach. Next it was to save African souls and bodies. Most of all, it was to save Europeans from their own sterility. The point was not principally to minister to the life of threatened Galwa and Fang peoples in the rainforest. It was to reawaken the moral potency of what he called "the Western Spirit." If the equatorial climate was the simmering source of life itself, the philosopher-cum-musician-cum-doctor-cum-fetishman would travel to this tropical wellspring to reinvigorate Europe's lost humanity. This, at least, was his idea.

Schweitzer operated at the heart, then, of a "cannibal humanitarianism." He was caught up in a historical process involving the mass colonial ingestion of the forest. If not exactly cannibalistic, this symbolic "eating up" existed for the purposes of humanitarian gain. Fetishism, cannibalism, and the trade in human body parts were phenomena invariably associated in the European mind (at least since Charles de Brosses's invention of *fétichisme* in 1760s Paris) with the pathologized spiritual climates of West Central Africa.[32] Around 1913, Fang speakers were specifically implicated. Period anthropological and mission studies identified the Gulf of Guinea as the source of these tropical horrors, though the finger is best pointed back at Europe. Schweitzer certainly thought of himself in the middle of it. (By fetishism, I mean the paraphilia that invests spiritual powers in the physical substance of a treasured object. The word "fetish" was derived through the Portuguese *feitiço* from the Latin *factitious/facere*, meaning "to do, or to make.") Cannibalism refers to the occult process by which the body of a person is ingested so that the eater comes to possess the life properties that once belonged to that person. In view of the commerce in body parts, limbs might be amputated in order to feed on the life forces contained in the victim's flesh. The high colonial stage cultivated a rampant intellectual obsession with fetishism, as a cover for colonialism's own carnal drive to pillage, ingestion, and life absorption.

As many scholars have noted, W. E. B. Du Bois among them, fetishism was utilitarian. The point of these spiritual and material practices was to distribute life power through social structures, acting, as it were, in a "distribution of the sensible."[33] Life, in the perceived fetishist vision, is transferable. Medicine men equipped with strong enough musical powers, that is, were equipped to manipulate the location of that life, by causing life spirits to migrate from one thing to another. The possessor of a charm or amulet will feel strong. She will feel protected by the malevolent natural potencies in some witch substance. A musician-sorcerer's esoteric powers may play on a population's fears and thus exert control over entire communities. Whole governments can arise in relation to this commerce of things, spirits, and body fragments. More than this, the very natural order may be organized in relation to kinship systems at once human, animal, and vegetable. Schweitzer was only one of many servants of the occult project to move life power from one source to another, from Africa to Europe. As Du Bois put it: the fetish is "not mere senseless degradation," he wrote in 1915, "it is instead its own philosophy of life."[34]

That philosophy of life was at once powerfully projected onto the inhabitants of the Ogooué region (particularly the Fang), and absorbed into the lives of European traders, missionaries, even Franco-German philosophers. Colonialism was at what Freud would call "the cannibal stage." For Freud, who corresponded with Schweitzer, psychic introjection was basic to the healthy development not only of strong human subjects but civilization itself, it being vital to drive the cycle of oral replenishment by symbolic killings of the father and periodic returns to the mother's breast.[35] In the wake of his *Totem and Taboo: Some Points of Agreement between the Mental Lives of Savages and Neurotics*, published in the same year as Schweitzer's sacred piano arrived on the Ogooué, Freud observed that "the ego wants to incorporate this object into itself, and, in accordance with the oral or cannibalistic phase of libidinal development in which it is, it wants to do so by devouring it."[36] In question here is not only the need to feed off the equatorial forests for the purposes of European rebirth. As Bernault points out, it is not accurate to speak of the "gobbling-up" of the physical and moral life structure of the region by an all-consuming and globalizing Europe. Colonization involved a process of mutual feeding, one where whites, as she puts it, "interfered less as foreign purveyors of things and ideas that connected natives to distant horizons or as *dei ex machina* imposing market values and commodification on Africans than as partners in a mutual process of moral reconstruction."[37] This is to say that Europeans "ate up" the "lively" beliefs of the Gabonese, as much as the Gabonese introjected the mythologies of Europeans. They fed off each other.

Schweitzer himself folded this mutuality into his ethics. It was less that, by "returning to Africa," he was abnegating his own life for other lives, thus adding incrementally to global vitality. His position accorded with his favorite Bible verse that "whosoever tries to keep his life will lose it; but whoever loses his life will find it anew" (Matthew 16:25). His mission of self-sacrifice assumed an affirmative biopolitics, one devoted to the celebration of "life in its fullest"—his own life included. Medical procedures of immunization and defensive inoculation were certainly implicated. But, particularly in 1913, the young Schweitzer pursued life for the purposes of expanding his own *Lebenskraft*. This he would achieve by putting himself to the test, the idea being that, by exposure to sickness, disease, and the elements, life itself might become stronger. The energies of the Galwa and Fang, after all, were there for the taking. And, as Freud taught, cannibals only eat the ones they love.

Moving Life

The piano *qui résistera au climat tropical et aux termites* arrived by paddle steamer at the Catholic Mission Station and Hatton & Cookson's local factory on April 26, 1913, as light was fading. The captain refused to advance east, citing floating timber on the "right branch" of the Ogooué, named Ouzougavizaé/Onuranga. The final destination was Congoé Hill Cottage, located on a ridge above Andênde. This was still nearly an hour's paddle by pirogue around the head of the eleven-mile-long island dividing the river. Figure 6.5 indicates "Congoé" toward the top left corner and Hatton & Cookson's factory toward the bottom left. By 1913, on the opposite right bank (not yet indicated) was Lambaréné, a settlement that would grow amidst the soaring timber trade into what is now the third largest town in Gabon. The piano awaited the arrival of "a very large pirogue cut made from the trunk of a single tree" belonging to Hatton & Cookson to complete its journey from Paris. "One could port several such instruments at a time," Schweitzer wrote, "the pirogue being capable of carrying up to three thousand kilograms."[38] A heavy zinc-lined case—looking like a giant sacred reliquary—protected the keyboard. The metal box was addressed to Schweitzer, the white medicine man who first passed that way ten days earlier.

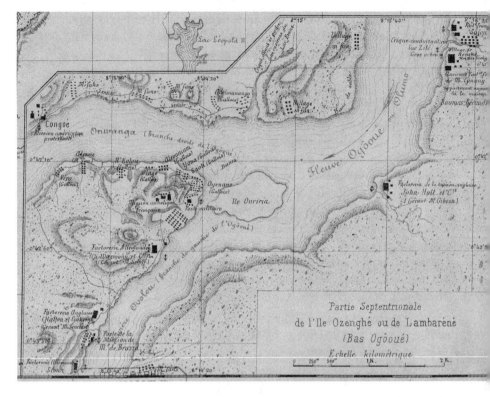

FIGURE 6.5. Detailed map of the head of Lambaréné, from *Colonie française du Gabon-Congo, 1/3 700 000 / dressée et dessinée par M. Payeur-Didelot* (1894). Note the many Fang villages surrounding the "mission américaine protestant" and the footpath to "Adolinanongo." By 1894, Hatton & Cookson's factory had moved from Adolinanongo. Renoké's village is indicated in the top right-hand corner. Source: gallica.bnf.fr / Bibliothèque nationale de France.

The Ogooué was a place of madness and cruel beauty in the colonial imagination. The most celebrated description of the approach to it came from the pen of explorer-ethnographer Mary Kingsley, who ascended this section of the river in 1895. "Doubtless, it is wrong to call it a symphony; yet I know no other word to describe the scenery of the Ogooué," she wrote in *Travels in West Africa*: "It is as full of life and beauty and passion as any symphony Beethoven ever wrote, the parts changing, interweaving and returning."[39] The air crackled with an affirmative will to live. Nights were filled with the deafening hum of insects. "Palms rustle an obbligato to the loud music of the crickets and the toads," wrote Schweitzer in 1915, "and from the forest come harsh and terrifying cries of all sorts."[40] Bush noise—screeching parrots, jabbering monkeys—assailed the air by day; it was difficult to tell human from nonhuman. Robert Nassau, the American missionary who founded Congoé (he called it "my prosperous and comfortable station"), suffered a kind of insanity before the "strange sounds" enveloping him, "the origin of which I could not always get an acceptable explanation from the natives." "Perhaps some where voices of birds, or insects; or, the wind in tree branches; or, echoes of cry of beasts, or call of human being," Nassau wrote. "Perhaps, in my highly-wrought mental and depressed physical state at that time," he continued, "I did really hear sounds that were not audible to others, or to myself in a normal state."[41] The web of "leitmotifs" (Kingsley's phrase), though it induced psychosis, always retained something of its fluid regal power. "And, through all these changing phases," she wrote, "there is always the strain of the vast forest, and the swift, deep, silent river."[42]

Schweitzer experienced the "antediluvian" flow with similar hallucinatory awe. The Ogooué, he liked to say, is "not a river but a river system." Crashing into the lowlands from the rapids above Ndjolé, the river sinks down to an almost sullen sea-level by the time it reaches Lambaréné, still two days steam journey from the sea. The island acts to disperse its course further, Gabon's largest river splitting from here on out into a maze of watercourses, bewildering for their myriad clan names, eventually spreading into a 100-mile-wide delta as large as the Nile, Niger, or Mississippi. "It is impossible to say where the river ends and the land begins," Schweitzer wrote in a delirium, "for a mighty network of roots, clothed with bright-flowering creepers, projects right into the water."[43] At the end of the rainy season, lasting from October until May, the humid climate has no range of temperature, the nights being as hot as days. The "absence of air movement," Schweitzer moaned, "made it seem as if one was "living in a prison." The sandflies at Andênde were legion. "The heat is intolerable," the doctor wrote in 1913, because on all sides," he complained, "rises the forest in an impenetrable wall nearly 100 feet high, and between these walls not a breath of air stirs."[44]

In his first reports back to Paris, Schweitzer observed the tragic fate of the young Swiss medical missionary, Maurice Robert, then gravely ill, who would quit the Ogooué with his family late that summer. Robert probably met Schweitzer in these first weeks, the former being a role model for the ambitious Alsatian newcomer. Before 1910, Robert also lived at Congoé Hill Cottage, introducing regular medical consultations, founding the first dispensary, and developing the small hospital (built around 1900 by missionary Paul-Elie Vernier) into a robust operation. Schweitzer's first infirmary in the Gabonese interior, that is, restored Robert's vision, the structure having fallen into disrepair after its interim use as a henhouse. Robert practiced a radically liberal theology, having decommissioned himself from Paris Evangelical Missionary Society (SMEP) two years earlier. This organization, though it sponsored his mission, found Schweitzer's avant-garde views equally controversial. But even Schweitzer had to admit that the original white fetishman of Congoé Hill had gone too far.

Robert and his family had "gone native" on his return from a sabbatical in Switzerland in 1911, founding a model village named Oroudanô or "the village of Robert" not far downriver. Here, near Ngomo Mission, Robert's "phalanstery" experimented with woodwork, brickmaking, pottery, soapmaking, basketry, and the equality of all members: men and women, white and Black, Catholic, Protestant, and pagan. Robert's goal was nothing less than the founding of a "new race," one that would rescue humanity at once from "moral misery," sectarian fundamentalism, and "odious exploitation" by timber and ivory traders (read: Hatton & Cookson) who operated "factories" around the head of the island.[45] According to one source, the rebel missionary named his commune the "Village of Love."[46] Robert determined, wrote Schweitzer, "to live among Africans as their brother absolutely." But his failure to maintain "the social interval," meant that "from that day, his life became a misery." "In this daily and hourly contest with the child of nature," Schweitzer rationalized, "every white man is continually in danger of gradual moral ruin."[47] Robert's psychosis was chastening proof, Schweitzer claimed later that year, of how hard it was "to keep oneself really humane" in this climate, "and so to be a standard-bearer of civilization." The difficulty of holding onto humanity, he explained, "is the tragic element in the problem of the relations between white and colored men in Equatorial Africa."[48] Robert was rushed to Europe mentally exhausted only a few months after the successful delivery of the "tropical pedal piano" on Congoé Hill. By December 18 of that year, at the age of thirty-five, he was dead. His heartbroken wife followed three years after, leaving their five children at a loss. The brave dreamer, that is, had suffered the consequences of failing to build the necessary moral fortitude to protect himself, or so Schweitzer thought.[49]

Schweitzer counseled that strong moral fortitude, regular intellectual labor, and a healthy diet of Bach was necessary to withstand the forest. The climate was all-consuming, and his sense of the need for assistance extreme, as evidenced by the prevalence of the "sleeping sickness" he so frequently treated in the first days of his arrival at Andênde. "Negro lethargy" was an illness thought to be exacerbated by a "natural weakness of the brain," one that was best resisted by mental exercise and continual psychic fortification. Schweitzer positioned himself at the forefront of research into this tropical disease, as he sought to awaken the land from sloth. He knew of the work of the Sleeping Sickness Institute at Brazzaville and the 1901 insights of English specialists Ford and Dutton on trypanosomata, or boring bodies, which had been shown to cause "chronic inflammation of the brain."[50] Even so, Schweitzer observed that even the most intellectually robust colonists, traders, and missionaries could remain in this environment for no more than two years before fatigue and anemia compelled them to return to Europe. The lowland Ogooué region was purportedly "the most unhealthy spot on the face of the earth."[51] He quoted the words of several of his native patients to prove the point: "'Here, among us, everybody is ill,' said a young man to me a few days ago. 'Our country devours its own children' was the remark of an old chief."[52] To survive here, one needed toughness.

Ntsé yi Nkomb'Ademba

The site that Schweitzer reclaimed had an occult history. Congoé Hill once belonged to a powerful trader and ritual specialist named Nkombé. The "Sun King" had gifted this "Hill of the Americans" to the aforementioned Nassau, a mission doctor and author of *Fetishism in West Africa* (1903). This occurred in the same year, 1874, that Nkombé was poisoned to death by a rival (in December). Nkombé had built his considerable power by gathering esoteric trade charms, enchanting potent sites, and controlling fetish-making rituals. He was a Galwa speaker, whose marriage and trade alliances with the Mpongwe gave him power over the northern overland slave route (passing up the Remboué through chapter 1's Ngango), and the western route (along the Ogooué to the coastal Orungu, also Myene speaking). Powerful Orungu traders long administered the slave barracoons at Cape Lopez off the Ogooué delta. (Cape Lopez was still processing an estimated three thousand to four thousand mostly Cuban-bound slaves per year in 1875.[53]) Nkombé himself was known to travel twice a year as far inland up the Ogooué as Lopé to the domain of Okandé-speaking pirogue specialists in order to procure his lucrative human cargos.[54] He was a man of strength.

Around 1868, Nkombé shrewdly expanded his power base by allowing Hatton & Cookson to build their first "trading factory" at Adolinanongo. The Hamburg firm of Karl Woermann as well as Senegalese trader Kerno Mahmadou-Seydiou joined soon after.[55] It was from this village indicated at the upper center of figure 6.5—the name derived from two Galwa words: *dolina* (to observe) and *anongo* (the peoples)—that the "Sun King" controlled the river. (In 1927, as will be shown, Schweitzer would absorb some of his spiritual power when he moved his hospital to this necromantic site.) Nkombé built his wealth by bypassing the Orungu slave-mongering middlemen at the coast. Ivory, rubber, ebony, and padauk began to be traded at this section of the river for salt, guns, ammunition, brandy, Manchester cotton cloth, crockery, and other "fetish" trinkets. After Nkombé's death, Adolinanongo was largely abandoned as European factories moved to the head of the island. Things fell quiet for several years before massive colonial reinvestments in 1911 and a resurgent timber market initiated the transformation of Lémbaréni/Ewondjwenenge into the dynamic trade center that is modern-day Lambaréné.[56]

From the window of Congoé Hill Cottage, Schweitzer wrote that he could see Pointe Fétiche, the fearsome site where the Ngounié River enters the Ogooué. That point, according to Nassau's *Fetichism in West Africa*, "was a sacred fetish, beyond which no white man might go." The promontory, 140 miles from the sea, was another "favorite dwelling-place of the spirits." Nassau wrote that Portuguese slave traders had been allowed there and no farther, for fear that they would destroy prevailing trade monopolies.[57] The first white man to travel the slave route from the Gabon Estuary was another agent for Hatton & Cookson, Robert Bruce Walker, who inadvertently emerged above Fetish Point after traveling overland from Ngango (see chapter 1). Walker was taken hostage by an even more powerful sorcerer, "blind King" Renoké, who ruled the eastern shore. A French gunboat had to come to Walker's rescue, thus breaking the fetish. (Renoké purportedly secured his occult power by blinding himself with a hot iron rod, an act that purportedly afforded him deeper access to the spirit world.) Walker was lucky. "Anyone who went beyond this point, further into the interior," Schweitzer observed of this sacred site in 1914, "was eaten."[58]

New Fetishes, New Spirits

The fear of the site was maintained by musical ritual, in ways that add poignancy to the final transport of Schweitzer's pedal piano by pirogue. Locals knew that the sacred piano had arrived to reconsecrate this territory for the high colonial era. Change was in the air. Nassau explained that when riverine clan members passed Fetish Point in canoes, they sang targeted rowing songs to propitiate evil. They "respectfully removed their head coverings."[59] Though Renoké's fetish was broken, pirogue crews often still refused passage until deep into the new century.[60] Alternatively, pirogue teams staged elaborate sung rituals in order to negotiate this part of the river safely. The practice of attaching bells to the front of the pirogue to ward off spirits may date from this period.

Bells were long-standing syncretic appropriations. The mission bell at Andênde rang every morning at six o'clock, and was followed, Schweitzer reported in 1913 of his first morning at the station, by "the hymn sung by the children in the schoolroom." It is likely that the Swiss folk song, especially arranged in two parts for his arrival that previous evening, was heard repeatedly. According to oral sources, the sound of various bells at Lambaréné was soon called "la voix du Bon Dieu" or "the voice of the Great Doctor." These *cloches du culte* were fetish charms, charged with life power. Sonic ritual, that is, possessed the power to call spirits to the land and move them around.[61]

Schweitzer noted that a vast repertory of songs had developed for placating the powerful spiritual life of the river and for entraining bodies to the task of safe navigation.[62] On his own first journey to Congoé Hill by pirogue in April 1913, the doctor wrote that he listened "avec ravissement" to the "les beaux chants des pagayeurs." He was told by Noël Christol that these songs were so ancient that "the indigenes themselves no longer understand the words."[63] Another missionary, Fernand Grébert, reported that even Schweitzer was unable to transcribe the music of Fang rowers because of the microtonal inflections and scale systems.[64] The slipping in and out of head register and between voice parts hardly helped. Schweitzer himself lamented that the repertory was dying and complained that Christian song was strangling the life out of a powerfully arcane *Musikbewusstsein*.

Only a year after landing in the Gabon, Schweitzer wrote to the Institute of Psychology in Berlin University and Carl Stumpf, founder of the Berliner Phonogramm-Archiv and doyen of comparative musicology.[65] Stumpf had previously contacted Schweitzer about Gabonese music before his departure. (Schweitzer was a student of Stumpf's experimental studies in *Tonpsychologie*, having worked with him in 1899 Berlin.) Schweitzer's words of April 3, 1914, are worth quoting at length:

> In this country, it is a question principally of rowing songs. They are very old and *wonderfully beautiful*: created in the style of motets with interesting counterpoint. Once upon a time a great culture, of its kind, must have held sway here. On the other hand it is time to record this music. In twenty years time, it will no longer exist, because the young people learn Christian songs from the Mission. Recently the children from the Catholic Mission fetched me to an ill Father and sang . . . Laudate pueri." Furthermore the motor boats are taking over *from the* rowing boats, as the foreign trading posts find them better for their purposes. Within the foreseeable future there will no longer be any

day-long journeys by rowing boat, where twenty men in a canoe stand one behind the other and sing, because otherwise they would not be able to keep in time with the rhythm of the rowing. Id est: end of the rowing song.[66]

In the same letter, Schweitzer lamented his own failure to make "phonogram recordings and studies" of this ancient repertory. Work on the second German edition of his book on Bach and the fifth volume of Schirmer's complete American edition of the organ works, he complained, had occupied the time. He could confirm, however, that "*the music here is extremely abundant*," and that this repertory of rowing songs needed urgent ethnographic salvage by phonograph.[67]

Although a purportedly dying art, rowing was a serious business on the Ogooué. "That people get into a boat without wanting to go on a journey or being obliged to forward goods, merely in order to row, and that they spend their leisure time in practicing rowing," Schweitzer wrote, "is quite incomprehensible for Africans." "I go on to tell them that in Europe people row for pleasure, a statement followed by uncontrolled laughter. Then come the questions, 'Who told them to row?' 'Nobody.' 'But somebody must give them a present for doing it?' 'No, they do it of their own free will, and for nothing, and often they row until they are quite exhausted. The comments on this second subject are endless.'"[68] This description was meant to be amusing, but it also shows the extent to which Schweizer was serious about the existential threat posed to the idealized native gestalt.

"My Grand Improvisation"

At this point, dear reader, know that the photograph labeled "Das Clavier im Erbaum," introducing this chapter as figure 6.1, was not taken in April 1913. Rather, the picture was staged for a later landmark event, occurring in May 1927, when Schweitzer began what he called his "great improvisation." That day marked the final move and rebirth of his hospital two miles up the river to the aforementioned Adolinanongo, the Ntsé yi Nkomb'Ademba or stronghold of the long-dead sorcerer. It was a move of high strategic and political consequence. The impression on the ground, according to oral testimony, was that Schweitzer was usurping or cannibalizing Nkombe's sacred power. (French authorities, after 1890 and the death of Renoké, appointed satellite leaders who presided over two decades of decline.) The importation of the sacred piano coincided with an age of revival, the timber boom, and the ascendant Fang. New representations of power and the sacred were in play. The photograph of the piano's removal to this occult site marked this moment of consequence. Schweitzer, aware of its potent history of the site, styled himself as the successor of Robert, Renoké, and Nkomb'Adembaon. The fetishman was the new grand purveyor and distributer of life.

Like Nkombé, Schweitzer—as a surgeon—had a reputation for dismemberment.[69] The medical missionary admitted that in "many districts of Equatorial Africa it is difficult, or even impossible, to persuade the natives to let themselves be operated upon for fear of what the white man would do to them." In view of the perception that he was harvesting body parts, Schweitzer claimed only to amputate when the patient's life was threatened. If Fang interpreter and assistant N'Zeng was unreliable (like all Fang, apparently), the thinking of his Galwa equivalent, Joseph Azowani, too easily betrayed his former occupation as a cook. Azowani's tendency was to refer to patient anatomy like joints of meat on a butcher's table: "This woman has a pain in her upper left cutlet, and her loin."[70] A human leg would be "a gigot." In his mission journal of late 1913, Schweitzer boasted of "the terrible conviction of my power" and how people shook in fear before him. A member of the girls school at Andênde took a more severe view still that year, writing to a pen pal back in France: "First, he kills his patients; then he heals them; then he wakes them up."[71] The anaesthetic medicines stored at the new dispensary had apparently bestowed upon this strange newcomer the divine power to take life or let live.

We know from oral testimony and Schweitzer's own account around 1913 that his "name among the natives in Galwa is '*Oganga*,' i.e., fetishman"— that is, a ritual specialist skilled in dealing with evil spirits. The words *nganga, onganga, ngang, inganga*, as we saw in chapter 1, referred to a doctor, medicine man, sorcerer, divine, doctor, witchdoctor, or necromancer. The presence of musical instruments—whether drums, *mvet*, or *ngombi* harp—aligned with the attributes and authority of the traditional healer-musician leaders. Boxes (reliquaries, phonographs, keyboard instruments) were thought to carry special power, fetishes being composed of "a number of little objects which fill a small bag, a buffalo horn, or a box." These things might include "red feathers, small parcels of red earth, leopard's claws and teeth," bells, or—most prized—body parts or skulls that once belonged to revered ancestors.[72]

Fetish Boxes, Musical and Nonmusical

In 1913, Schweitzer wore two human skull fragments probably in an amulet box around his neck—"of a longish oval shape [from the parietal bone of a

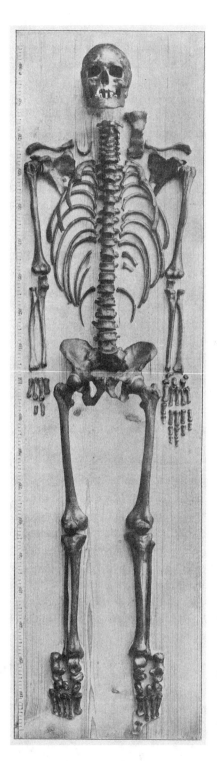

FIGURE 6.6. "Gesammtansicht des BACH-Skelettes," Wilhelm His, *Anatomische Forchungen über Johann Sebastian Bach's Gebeine und Antlitz* (Leipzig: Hirzel, 1895). Anatomische Forchungen über Johann Sebastian Bach's Gebeine und Antlitz: nebst Bemerkungen über dessen Bilder / von Wilhelm His. Wellcome Collection, https://creativecommons.org/licenses/by/4.0/legalcode.

cranium] and dyed with some sort of red coloring matter"—that had once belonged to a patient with sleeping sickness. "I am myself the possessor of a fetish," Schweitzer admitted in a 1914 letter back to Paris.[73] Eight years earlier, skulls had preoccupied Schweitzer, when he wrote about the exhumation of a much larger box, on October 22, 1894, containing the mortal remains of one of the most powerful ancestors in world history—no less than Johann Sebastian Bach (allegedly)—in the churchyard of the Johanniskirche in Leipzig. (Schweitzer's enthusiasm was palpable in the prose he devoted to figure 6.6 in his famous *J.-S. Bach: Le musicien-poète*, first published in Paris before his departure for Africa.) After an "exhaustive and scientific investigation," a team led by the noted anatomist Wilhelm His had exhumed "an elderly man, not very large, but well-built."[74] "Among the interesting peculiarities of Bach's skull," Schweitzer reported, "may be mentioned the extraordinary toughness of the bone of the temple that encloses the inner organ of hearing, and the quite remarkable largeness of the fenestra rotunda." The capacity of "the Bach skull," measured at 1479.5 cubic centimeters, particularly fascinated Schweitzer. A clue to the authenticity of the fetish was that the skeletal remains had been buried in an oak coffin, a historical detail ascertained from burial records and payments made to the original casket maker.[75]

Boxes such as these were signs of great power. On the Sundays when he was preaching at Andênde in 1913, Schweitzer laid claim to the forest musically by bringing out several music boxes. Instead of forcing his "congregation" to sing sterile European hymns, Schweitzer would "play on the small harmonium that has been carried into the open air." If not the harmonium, a gramophone—belonging to a Canadian volunteer dubbed "Mrs. Canada" (Lillian Russell)—was fixed to play a suitable religious piece. For example: the clanging of the Andênde bell at 9 o'clock in the morning on August 19, 1913, heralded an occasion for Schweitzer to remonstrate with latecomers for being slow to emerge from the forest. Russell transcribed the gist of Schweitzer's sermon. "This station must become a pure and holy place in this country," he thundered, "so that those who live in its vicinity notice that those who live here are struggling to become better; struggling to get rid of ideas of covetousness, lying, and adultery; struggling to be good and to forgive those who have done evil to them."[76] It was a battle to draw his patients out, and a battle to consecrate the site. "At the place where they are gathered," the preacher lamented, "some are in the habit of making their fire." Not only "congregational cooking," but while he was speaking and being translated, Schweitzer had to contend with Russell's two pet monkeys, bleating sheep, butting goats crossing in front of him, and weaver birds "situated in neighbouring trees, making a

FIGURE 6.7. Du Chaillu's box sounded the acousmatic interruption of Manrico from a breath-filled offstage during *Il trovatore*'s torture scene in act 4. The breathless onstage Leonore, meanwhile, bemoans her oppression, accelerating and then expiring in ways nowhere more melodramatically declaimed than in Rosa Ponselle's extraordinary 1928 Victor recording. I can think of no other *scena* in Verdi that better thematizes the physical struggle of breathing. Ethelreda Lewis, *Trader Horn: The Ivory Coast in the Earlies* (London: Jonathan Cape, 1927), 15.

deafening din."[77] It would take time for Schweitzer's fetish reliquaries to work their spiritual charm.

Other musical boxes—portable enough to allow for the transference of life power—had long since been absorbed into the ever-changing perifluvial soundscape. One example was Paul Du Chaillu's ancient music box, purportedly discovered "in a cannibal hut" by the notorious Trader Horn, who worked under Nkombé's protection at the Hatton & Cookson factory at Adolinanongo around 1884. Horn claimed to have identified the box of the legendary Franco-American explorer of the late 1850s (whom we met in chapter 1) in a village reliquary.[78] Stored amongst a fetish ensemble, the instrument could purportedly still play old tunes. Horn reported that it tinkled Verdi's ubiquitous "Miserere." Figure 6.7 only proves that the Italian composer was not joking when he wrote to a friend from St. Petersburg on May 2, 1862, that "were you to go to the Indies or to Central Africa, you would hear *Il trovatore*."[79] (A display case of Du Chaillu's "cannibal skulls" was viewable until recently at the Ipswich Museum in Suffolk.) As Jeremy Rich has shown, the American primate collector Richard Lynch Garner, meanwhile, seduced Fang communities with his "magical phonograph" from around 1906. Garner had ostensibly brought his phonograph up the Ogooué in order to record the speech of monkeys (and humans) and to further his "ingenious inquiries into the language of apes."[80] Schweitzer observed of 1913 that, where once these phonographs were encountered as instruments of evil, "there is hardly a village in this neighborhood from which no gramophone screeches into the jungle."[81] Phonographs, that is, had been fully naturalized, even ingested into the spiritual phenomenology of the forest.

Yet the most powerful box on the Ogooué was undeniably the one carried up Congoé Hill in 1913. Every night, Schweitzer played his piano until late, having decided early in his mission "to use my free hours in Africa for the very purpose of perfecting and deepening my technique" and "learn all of Bach's organ works by heart, even if I have to spend weeks or months on any particular piece." Oral sources suggest that these late-night practice sessions—which Schweitzer thought of as necessary for his own mental fortification—were heard in the forest as incantation rituals. The sorcerer-healer-organist on Congoé Hill, apparently, was understood to be calling the spirits to himself.[82] Augustin Emane quotes one informant (whom he dubs "Janvier N. M.") who remembered that Schweitzer's intentions were more malevolent still. "The *nganga* [Schweitzer] uses his *ngombi*," Janvier N. M. is recorded alleging, "to attract sickness and the sick."[83] The point of all that Bach was not merely to summon spirits, in other words. It was to "swallow up" patients. "When the colonized escapes the doctor, and the integrity of his body is preserved," explained Fanon in his condemnation of medical science as part of colonialism's governing apparatus in 1959, "he considers himself the victor by a handsome margin."[84] The locals, that is, heard Schweitzer's performances as a means to ex-appropriate not merely power—but life.

All-night music making defined Lambaréné in this period. Mission reports describe myriad musics intermingling as they traveled across the starlit water between adjacent riverside villages on the Ouzougavizaé. Often, these reports interpreted the nonstop drumming as the noise of body parts being compounded in secret, to the accompaniment of drug-induced dance. "I remembered the quietness of the Schweitzer hospital," countered James Fernandez, distinguished University of Chicago anthropologist who did fieldwork on the Ogooué: "It struck me that very often its founder must have gone to sleep with the church bells of Gunsbach in his mind's ear."[85] That said, as late as 1960, James Berman, an American doctor-volunteer, recollected an incident where a distant village drummer began to play "a duet" with Schweitzer one night at Adolinanongo. For Berman, "each seemed to harmonize with the other" until they apparently ended together. Schweitzer was so lost in his Bach that when the incident was reported to him, he claimed ignorance of it.[86] All that evening practice, that is, was heard as part of the white wizard's relentless struggle to take control of Gabonese life and ingest it.

A Political Ecology

As seen in figure 6.3, Gaveau affixed Schweitzer's piano (*entièrement tropicalisé* in the words of the 1976 restorers) to a double iron frame. The makers screwed the soundboard in, ribs and bridges built in rather than glued

FIGURE 6.8. "Stump of a Mahogany Tree," Albert Schweitzer, *On the Edge of the Primeval Forest: Experiences and Observations of a Doctor in Equatorial Africa*, trans. C. T. Campion (London: Adam and Charles Black, 1922), 101.

on. According to the restoration team, sapele mahogany was the chief wood used. The yellow-sheened, slow-growing hardwood is indigenous to the Gabonese rainforest and listed today as "vulnerable" on the International Union for the Conservation of Nature's "Red List of Threatened Species."[87] Trees of the *Entandrophragma* species apparently possessed the requisite indigenous resilience. In fact, the original timber may even have traveled down the Ogooué on its way to Gaveau's factory near Paris, before being shipped back as a piano.

Figure 6.8 shows that Schweitzer himself traded *Entandrophragma* as "raw materials supplier" for the reinvigoration of Franco-German culture, he being a "timber fanatic" as his wife called him.[88] The image of the mutilated mahogany tree was printed in his 1822 book, *On the Edge of the Primeval Forest*. The story behind the photograph goes that, in March 1915, at the height of the First World War, the organ at Mühlbach, indeed the majority of the town of Mühlbach in northeastern France, was destroyed by German shelling. An organ close to Schweitzer's heart was lost. That instrument, an 1736 Andreas Silbermann, had been played by his revered maternal grandfather, Johann Jakob Schillinger, pastor and organ builder at Mühlbach, the same who had first inspired Schweitzer to be a musician. Soon after hearing news of wanton European self-destruction, the distraught Schweitzer met with an unnamed Galwa "big man" who lived across the river at Lambaréné. When asked, "Oganga, why are you so sad?" Schweitzer tried to say what an organ was ("in my homeland they have destroyed things that are beautiful and dear to me"). This explained, Schweitzer asked for permission to harvest "the beautiful mahogany tree that stands there on the bank of the river [Ogooué], spreading out in such majesty" for the purposes of its resurrection. The "big man" agreed, and the tree was felled, though the project stalled after Schweitzer was taken as a prisoner of war by French colonial officials in 1916. Eventually, because the limbs of the tree were left to rot on the forest floor, another plan was devised for the organ at Mühlbach. That plan bore fruit in 1923, when an instrument matching Schweitzer's precise specifications was completed by Dalstein & Haerpfer of Alsace-Lorraine.[89] But the life of the "beautiful mahogany tree" on the Ogooué had been sacrificed, in yet another case of the Gabonese interior cannibalized for the purposes of European spiritual regeneration.

The pedalboard of Schweitzer's piano, built for Gaveau by Etienne Dalstein, proved most susceptible to tropical damage. Schweitzer reconnected the broken high-E foot pedal to the action stack with a crudely bent green wire—a sign of the fetishman's struggle to keep his suffering pianoware healthy. (In 1976, the restorers decided to leave just this one of Schweitzer's jury-rigged African repairs untouched.) Organ builders Dalstein-Haerpfer had a history with Schweitzer. In 1907, they helped him construct what he called "the first true Bach organ," which now stands in the L'église Saint-Sauveur in Strasbourg. Also around this time, Schweitzer's mission to stop "the slaughter of the old organs" began with a campaign to rescue the historic 1737 Silbermann organ at St. Thomas's in Strasbourg, then due to be overhauled. Its tracker action, in particular, was saved from removal after Schweitzer's last-ditch intervention. Legend has it that Dalstein-Haerpfer's historically informed restoration of this particular instrument set the tone for the authenticity movement and organ reform in Alsace. Even so, the Alsatian restorers raised the "diapason" to A435 Hz by using tuning slots, replaced the existing Quintaton with a III-rank Cymbale, added a pedal coupler, and extended the pedalboard to twenty-seven notes.[90]

The "first victory" for the fledgling *Orgelbewegung*, according to Schweitzer, came four years before his departure for the Ogooué River.

In 1909, the young firebrand was invited by Guido Adler to present a series of "International Regulations for Organ Building" at the third congress of the IMS (International Music Society) in Vienna.[91] The result was a veritable universal declaration for organ welfare and a human rights document for the humane treatment of organs. (I exaggerate.) Schweitzer was no antiquarian; his favorite instruments were the large modern Parisian organs built by Aristide Cavaillé-Coll between 1860 and 1880. For him, nothing matched the instrument of his teacher, Charles-Marie Widor, at Saint-Sulpice or the organ of César Franck at Saint-Clotilde. But the young Schweitzer opposed the "chaos of sounds in which I could not distinguish the separate voices" characteristic of newfangled electro-pneumatic machines.[92] (He preferred the tracker slider-chest or tubular-pneumatic systems.) He was shocked that German makers should favor push-button pistons above foot levers. He hated that manufacturers raised wind pressure by electric means. The "unnaturally strong bellows of the modern organ," he complained, was yet another sign that "we are living today under the sign of the collapse of civilization."[93] "The day is not far distant when the last of our beautiful Silbermann organs will be replaced, or renovated beyond recognition," Schweitzer protested in 1907, "and then the Bach organ also will be one of the unknown things of the past."[94] Spiritual decline heralded cultural extinction, since the "electric lungs" of factory-built instruments sustained neither life nor moral feeling. In one of Schweitzer's many tirades against "factories" and industrial-capitalist production, he admitted that "the struggle for the good organ is to me a part of the struggle for truth."[95] His friends, he used to admit, would quip: "In Africa he saves old blacks, in Europe old organs."[96]

Pedalware aside, more interesting for my purposes is Gaveau, the firm responsible for the keyboard of Schweitzer's equatorial piano. (Documents in the Gaveau archive indicate the date of completion of serial and sale number 55729 as March 10, 1913.[97]) In March 1913, the "Société Gaveau Frères" ran a model humanitarian social utopia: a piano factory and worker-welfare village to the east of Paris at Fontenay-sous-Bois. This 30,000-square-meter site, built along the Paris-Bastille railway line in 1896, hosted a 14,000-square-meter "usine modèle à vapeur" and a 16,000-square-meter worker's city, including onsite medical facilities and free health care.[98] It boasted five roads, each named after one of the Gaveau daughters. In 1913, Arnold Dolmetsch worked for the firm, building harpsichords, clavichords, and spinets, which is to say that Gaveau was a wellspring for the burgeoning early music movement. Back in 1907, the concert hall of the firm had opened on the rue de la Boétie in the eighth arrondissement, with an onstage organ built by none other than Cavaillé-Coll. Gaveau's workers, its reconstructed keyboards, and even newly energetic styles of Bach performance received life support under the company's care.

The salle Gaveau was the scene of several Bach premieres and revivals in Paris, including among the city's first St. John Passions, a work that obsessed the young Schweitzer. From 1907, Schweitzer would travel from Alsace on the train six to eight times a year to play the organ there, where he accompanied the Paris Bach Society, an organization that he helped found three years earlier. (The directors included Gustave Bret, Schweitzer's teacher Widor, as well as Paul Dukas, Alexandre Guilmant, Vincent d'Indy, and later Gabriel Fauré, the *ngombi* harp player of chapter 1.)[99] The society was renowned for its curation of Bach's secular cantatas. An epochal revival of the St. John Passion (in French) late in November of 1907, redirected the focus of the orchestra and choir to larger choral works. Schweitzer spent many hours making cuts and suggesting strategies for performance.

Bach: Wellspring of Life

Gaveau and the Bach Society commissioned a custom-built pedal piano for Schweitzer, because they felt indebted to his invigorating and invigorated conception of Bach. More than this, they honored the vitality he brought to their Bach concerts. The physicality of Schweitzer's playing may not be immediately apparent in the recordings that he made in the 1930s for EMI (London Gramophone Record Company), given the slowness of the tempos he tended to choose. (It was at the sessions for these electric recordings that engineers developed "the Schweitzer Technique" of microphone placements, an "enlivening" procedure where two condenser microphones were placed back-to-back and away from each other.) Careful listening to these recordings, however, betrays an approach to keyboard touch that was, Schweitzer believed, life giving.

In *J.-S. Bach: Le musicien-poète*, Schweitzer explained:

> If so many organists imagine that they play Bach "interestingly" by taking him fast, this is because they have not mastered the art of playing *plastically*, so as to give *vitality* to the work by bringing out its detail clearly. It is quite a mistaken idea that what Bach chiefly wants is a monotonous smoothness. He certainly favored the legato style. But his legato is not a mere levelling; *it is alive*. It must be filled by a fine

phrasing which the hearer need not perceive as such, but of which he is conscious as a captivating lucidity in the playing. Within the legato, the separate tones must be grouped into *living phrases*. [my emphasis][100]

Schweitzer's concept of "grouping" was related to ideas about keyboard touch and the haptic life of fingers that were developed under the tutelage of his erstwhile piano teacher in Paris (from 1898 to 1900), the great Alsatian pianist-pedagogue and Liszt pupil Marie Jaëll. (Schweitzer was in fact so much of a devotee that he found time to act as Jaëll's translator for the German edition of her 1897 *The Mechanism of Touch*.)[101]

Schweitzer reported that his own hands, as if severed from his person, were awakened under Marie Jaëll's musical tutelage. "I completely transformed my hand," Schweitzer wrote, its newly vivified power figured in these terms:

> The finger—so her theory goes—must be as *fully conscious* as possible. . . . As the finger prepares for a motion, it must always try to project the desired sound. A resonant touch is realized by the quickest and lightest possible depression of the keys. But *the finger must also be conscious*. . . . To achieve an *ever more conscious and ever closer relationship with the keys*, the finger must cultivate to the utmost its sensitivity to their touch. With the perfecting of this sensitivity the player will become at the same time more responsive both to tone color and to color in general.[102]

Although he was skeptical of Jaëll's thesis that with "the appropriate development of the hand nonmusical people could become musical," Schweitzer applauded when flesh became sentient, fingers were inspirited, tonal color vivified, and body parts vitalized.

One thinks of the many plaster casts made of Schweitzer's hands, including the craggily emotional pair dated "1928" and formerly in the collection of Emmy Martin, who worked as Schweitzer's secretary at Congoé and helped manage his move to Adolinanongo. Other hands of the milieu were those of the wife of a local French trader at Nkogo, Pierre Izak. Her hands were cut off near Lambaréné by Ekoro Mabizoro and Ndongo Nzigue, two machete-wielding missionary-educated men of Fang origin, early on the morning of November 19, 1917. (Such mutilations mimicked the myriad amputations of Leopold II's brutal regime in the Congo Free State.) At the cannibal stage in colonial history, severed hands carried sacred life power. The Fang attackers, as Bernault puts it, ignored "the immaterial, fantastic power of domination symbolized by the mortal body of their victim, thus transforming her into a fetish whose value derived from its material substance."[103]

Schweitzer shared a fetishist's belief in the phenomenology of conscious flesh, particularly as demonstrated in the living power of Bach performance. Indeed, he pronounced himself bitterly opposed to the sterility of that formalist vision of Bach so current after the publication of Philipp Spitta's late-century biography (1873–80). Famously, Schweitzer constructed the composer, in his best-selling *Bach, The Poet-Musician* (as per the French title), as a poet of Nature, using the chorale texts to explain what Schweitzer called "tone symbolism." That symbolism, purportedly, explained the extraordinary vitality of the chorale preludes as well as such texted works as the cantatas and the passions. For Schweitzer, Bach did not write art for its own sake. Instead, the music of the master teemed with life—with language associations, ideas, colors, symbolism, and the world:

> If the text speaks of drifting mists, of boisterous winds, of roaring rivers, of waves that ebb and flow, of leaves falling from the tree, of bells that ring for the dying, of the confident faith that walks with firm steps, or the weak faith that falters insecure, of the proud who will be abused, and the humble who will be exalted, of Satan rising in rebellion, or angels poised on the clouds of heaven, then one sees and hears all this in [Bach's] music.[104]

In Nietzschean terms, Bach's music manifested an elemental life force and an extraordinary will to live. Bach's music—so pictorial, representative, and suffused with tone painting—activated what Schweitzer called "the graphic power of music."[105]

Schweitzer's clearest statement on Bach appeared in response to a survey of musicians, which he entitled "what Bach is for me." These words appeared in an October 1906 issue of the widely read German journal *Die Musik*:

> Bach is an affirmation. . . . Under poorest material conditions, without getting tired or discouraged, without appealing to the world to take notice of his work, without doing anything to preserve it for the future, his single concern was to create what is true. . . . What he experienced survives in his music alone. It is there for all those who truly live. . . . Each voice has its own will, its own personality, all are free to meet in freedom, to go their own way, to hate or to love, and in the end work

together in order to create something that is alive because it is. A score of Bach is a manifestation of that elemental force that reveals the infinity of the universe. . . . . His work is truth."[106]

Bach's struggles with the Leipzig municipality, the miserable conditions in which he was forced to create, the less-than-perfect physical environment for performance, the doggerel verse that post-office officials like Picander forced him to set to music—these struggles had forged in Bach a musician of exceptional creative resilience. When it came to setting banal texts, "the music seems to confer a higher vital power on the words [and] divests them of their lowly associations."[107] The study of the very bones of this *coloriste-symboliste*, in Schweitzer's account of early century research on Bach's skull, revealed that he knew pain. The suffering of the man, reportedly, perpetuated an unsurpassed will to life.

Bach, of course, was the great ancestral life force behind the missionary's idea of spiritual awakening. "Bach is a terminal point," Schweitzer famously wrote in his biography, "nothing comes from him. Everything leads up to him." The trying conditions under which the composer labored saw the advent of the most life-affirming music attributable to the history of the human will. He was no narrow Lutheran, said Schweitzer. Instead, Bach "belonged to the history of mysticism" and the life of all religious humanity. For Schweitzer, the old master served in the relentless pursuit of truth, with an almost reckless determination to live life on the threshold of suffering and glory.

A Life-Giving Text

Figure 6.9 makes an epic account of that threshold. Schweitzer wrote that "a score of Bach is a manifestation of that elemental force that reveals the infinity of the universe" only seven years before his precious copy of Bach's St. Matthew Passion was stolen from his bookshelf at Congoé Hill Cottage (before February 1914).[108] That text, "into which I had written the organ accompaniment [and] which I had worked out very carefully," "went for a walk" with his piano edition of Wagner *Meistersinger*. "Blacks steal his things with a good conscience," Schweitzer moaned, though it is more probable that, rather than stolen, the thing was appropriated: in this cannibal stage of colonial history, writing, especially musical writing, was usually regarded as a form of magic.[109]

Schweitzer himself, like the ex-appropriators who stole his *Meistersinger*, invested in the life power of Bach scores. The Maison Albert Schweitzer in Gunsbach preserves Schweitzer's own annotated copy of

FIGURE 6.9. Johann Sebastian Bach, *Passionsmusik nach dem Evangelisten Johannes* (Leipzig: Bach-Gesellschaft, 1862), with Albert Schweitzer's annotations. © Archives Centrales Albert Schweitzer Gunsbach, MBA 12/1.

the St. John Passion (published by the Bach Gesellschaft in 1867), which survived the doctor's travels to and from the Ogooué. The book opens at figure 6.9: "Herr, unser Herrscher," the celebrated opening chorus of the definitive 1727 version. Schweitzer evidently performed direct from this score during those Bach Society concerts at the salle Gaveau on November 27, 1907, and again on the February 25, 1910. (In his Bach monograph, Schweitzer recommended accompanying the choir and band using piano vocal scores.)[110] This swirling introduction, so far as Schweitzer was concerned, bristled with *Tonsymbolismus* in ways that exemplified his conception of Bach.

For Schweitzer, the fearful, churning vitality of this music was best confronted in an attitude of *Ehrfurcht vor dem Leben*. The throbbing G-minor lamentation induced Holy Awe. In the German edition of his Bach monograph, Schweitzer explained that its composer recomposed the choral introduction to better reflect the "demoniacal" sweep of St. John's account of the Passion. ("In him was life, and that life brought light to humanity.") John's narrative demanded a music of sublime terror, one where the sacrifice of Christ paralleled the at once horrific and majestic experience of Nature Itself. As such, Schweitzer wrote, "The music seeks to express this double idea of suffering and glory."[111] Life is at once given and received, sacrificed in pain and then ingested in awe.

Numerous commentators have reflected upon the "dual nature" of the Passion overture, at once worldly and divine, linear and recursive, arrow-like and cyclic, modern and premodern.[112] On the one hand, Schweitzer noted the music's manifestation of suffering (Christ's body at Golgotha, the nails driven in, the blood poured out) expressed by the angular dialogue between two pairs of oboes and flutes that "sigh and wail incessantly" (executed by the right hand in this piano reduction). The dissonance of these jagged lines—expressing "thoughts connected to the Passion"—supplies "the music [with] a curiously bitter and gloomy character, which at first distresses the hearer, as he cannot reconcile it with the words 'Herr, unser Herrscher/ dessen Ruhm in allen Landen herrlich ist!' ('Lord, our Lord-Ruler, whose glory is Magnified in all Lands!'/ 'O Lord, our Lord, how excellent is thy name in all the earth!')." Schweitzer recommended that organists exaggerate the violence of the dissonant woodwinds. "Bach's figured bass," he explained in his Bach monograph, "indicates that the organ is to accompany, in a higher octave, the sustained dissonances of the flutes and oboes." (Sure enough, a glance at figure 6.9 shows that Schweitzer added figured bass.) On the other hand was the fearful churning of the strings, symbolizing the majesty of the Creator-Christ moving "in grave and tranquil semiquavers." "It is by this dual presentation," Schweitzer summed up, "that Bach's music, like the narrative in the fourth Gospel, conveys simultaneously the ideas of majesty and suffering."[113]

For Schweitzer, tone symbolism suffused these pages. Adding to their strength was a total accumulation of tones, Christ's magnification depicted by a kind of sonic massification of all twelve keys of the keyboard, as is obvious in figure 6.9's reduced score. The eighteen-measure ritornello of the opening chorus divides into two equal parts, the first nine bars sustained over a tonic pedal, the ensuing nine bars following a circle of fifths back to the tonic. Measure one of the figure presents a G-A-B flat-C-D cluster in the left hand, which is expanded outward by the addition of right-hand dissonances one by one. Over the next eight bars, notes amass in this order: E, F#, A-flat, F, B natural, E natural, and finally the tritone C# at measure 9. By the ritornello's midpoint, in other words, all twelve tones within the octave have sounded over the pulsing G pedal. In the second half, from measures 9 to 18, this "sound mass" is accumulated again over a circle of fifths. The process of accretion is easier to track in the piano reduction this time: the tritone C-F# high in the right hand of measure 9 descends by half-steps six times over until all twelve tones have sounded. At Schweitzer's steady speed and with his particular dynamic, the final "cluster chord" probably sounded immense, especially at the sound of the C# in the bass pedal at measure 17. Schweitzer highlighted the energy of the piling up toward the entry of the choir by adding several hairpin crescendos in blue crayon. He thus exalted the twelve-tone layout afforded to the hands by the instrumental interface, by expending all the tonal possibilities available to the European keyboard. As much, a *Lebensphilosophie* was manifested: an ethic oriented, not toward survival, but *Lebensverherrlichung*—positive life augmentation. "Philosophy has totally evaded the problem of man's conduct toward other organisms," Schweitzer wrote in 1922: "We might say that it has played a piano of which a whole series of keys were considered untouchable." With Bach, all tones required equal reverence, in ways that were achieved in the opening ritornello of the St. John Passion by a total exhaustion of means.

Schweitzer liked to point out that it was actually Bach in 1913 that had inspired his life-optimizing efforts at the hospital. "Two hundred years after his death," Schweitzer wrote, "Johann Sebastian Bach contributed to health in Africa."[114] As a servant of world vitality, Bach was not one to show off. But the first solo virtuoso concert that Schweitzer offered for the benefit of his medical mission occurred late in the afternoon of April 25, 1912, only months before his departure to Lambaréné. The concert took place at the salle Gaveau, Schweitzer seated at the hall's Cavaillé-Coll. Third Republic salon culture came out in force to support the cause. (Benefactresses included the comtesse de Béarn, Marguerite de Loÿs Chandieu, and the comtesse de Pourtalès, who no doubt owned private organs *chez elles*.)[115] Schweitzer's sacred-secular program was divided according to the liturgical year, with a small choir adding a cappella interludes: "chorals de la Passion et celui de la Pentecôte."[116] Many more such art-religious concerts would follow during Schweitzer's periodic returns to Europe in the coming years, in which Bach was honored as his humanitarian forefather. "I devoted what I had earned by giving organ concerts, together with the profits from my book on Bach, which had appeared in German, French, and English," Schweitzer explained in 1922. "In this way the old Cantor of St. Thomas, Leipzig, Johann Sebastian himself, helped me in the provision of a hospital for Africans in the virgin forest."[117] The ancestral spirit of Bach, that is, provided the financial capital that made Schweitzer's ethics possible, because the Cantor himself, it turned out, had been the first life worshipper on the Ogooué.

Conclusion

Famously, it was at sunset on a day in September 1915 when Schweitzer had his great Road to Damascus epiphany: *Ehrfucht vor dem Leben*. He was passing a stretch of the Ogooué aboard a steamer, near a village named Igendja, approaching Ngoma Mission 80 km downriver from the hospital at Andênde. "We were making our way through a herd of hippopotamuses," he wrote, when "there flashed upon my mind, unforeseen and unsought, the phrase 'Reverence for Life.' The iron door had yielded. The path in the thicket had become visible. Now I had found my way to the principle in which affirmation of the world and ethics are joined together!"[118] Late in his career, Schweitzer spoke the sacralized concept of Life arising at this location ("a music from the jungle") and the ethic of "the Reverence for Life" as "a grand, calm music roar[ing] within me."[119] Figure 6.10 depicts the scene.

This was a site on the river of suffering and glory. It was here, before the cannibal stage, that Nkombé, Renoké, and their ancestors used to carry enslaved persons before trading them to the Orungu, who then sold them on to circumatlantic slave traders. Many souls died on this island waiting for the transaction to take place. Locals considered site haunted by spirits of the dead. It was at Igendja that Schweitzer decided that "the fundamental fact of human awareness is this: *I am life that wants to live in the midst of other life that wants to live.*" It was here that Schweitzer determined to participate in the suffering of all other suffering life. Here, he decided to work to maximize life and make it sacred, with an imaginary association he called the "Fellowship of those who bear the Mark of Pain." "Elemental thinking" developed deep ecological roots in this environment; and, certainly, the environmentalist aspect of Schweitzer's thought continued to evolve through his career.

Thus the text of Schweitzer's "A Declaration of Conscience" broadcast over radio waves from Oslo, Norway, forty years later. On April 23, 1957, at the head of thermonuclear nonproliferation movements, the eighty-two-year-old Schweitzer used radio technology to warn that—in the wake of the uranium bombs dropped on Nagasaki and Hiroshima, and the hydrogen bombs tested by the United States in the Marshall Islands in March 1954—radioactivity threatened to destroy the conditions that sustained life itself. Stratospheric fallout threatened to weaponize the very oxygen that we breathe. Schweitzer spoke these words: "That radioactive elements created by us are found in nature is an astounding event in the history of the earth and of the human race. To fail to consider its importance and its consequences would be a folly for which humanity would have to pay a terrible price. We are committing a folly in thoughtlessness. It must not happen that we do not pull ourselves together before it is too late. We must muster the insight, the seriousness, and the courage to leave folly and to face reality."[120] Superbomb experiments, he warned, had spawned "radioactive clouds" that "will constantly be carried by the winds around the globe and that some of the dust, by its own weight, or by being brought down by rain, snow, mist, and dew, little by little, will fall down on the hard surface of the earth, into the rivers, and into the oceans." Even an "air mass 400 kilometers high" would not be enough to protect humanity from this global threat. Radioactive elements in rainwater were being "deposited in certain parts of our body, particularly in the bone tissue and also in the spleen and in the liver." The potential effects of this radiogenic environment on future generations were dire. A political state of affairs had plunged humankind into a new thermogeological epoch, "an astounding event in the history of the earth." Addressed to no specific state or nation, Schweitzer's godlike voice was perhaps the first to announce the Great Acceleration: the start date of the Anthropocene, as the 2019 Anthropocene Working Group (AWG) latterly decreed—the 1954 Trinity Tests.[121]

It is certainly true that, along with Schweitzer's tropical piano, goodness, compassion, the values of *Ehrfucht vor dem Leben* were carried up the Ogooué in 1913. But allied with those values came others: strength, resilience, and (as I have argued) a certain biopolitics. The traveling piano carried these values of struggle in its materials, in the way it was moved

FIGURE 6.10. The islands at Igendja, where Schweitzer had his revelation. © Archives Centrales Albert Schweitzer Gunsbach.

around, in the way it was touched, in the way it made Bach sound, in the texts or scores that it animated, in the way it revived the waning powers of the most reputedly sacred, primeval, and powerful of musical instruments, as well as in the way it fortified dying bodies (especially European ones).

It is true that a set of geopolitical or better elemental relations was also carried up the Ogooué. Such elemental relations were coded into the sound of Schweitzer's tropical pedal piano, as well as into the fact and matter of its construction. But it would be better to put it the other way around and say that the sounds of this climate-proof piano, heard every night on the Ogooué, were instrumental to those elemental relations themselves. The lesson that Schweitzer taught is a good one by which to conclude. The mission of the musician and philosopher would have been impossible had he not believed that it was within his power, through instrumental means, to move the world—even to change the moral makeup of the sky.

Epilogue

What does it mean to say that music making is mixed up in struggles over environment as much as creation itself? What are the implications of approaching the art of music as an art of the atmosphere? This book links nineteenth-century obsessions with air management to the emergence of a thickened consciousness of air's life-properties in the Eurocene. That consciousness converted air, to cite Latour one last time, into a matter and fact of concern.[1] The goal was to convert air into atmosphere.

In the "age of breath" (and here Irigaray returns) atmospheric resonance constituted music's elemental media system in ways that obscured the material presence of performing hands, vocal apparatuses, local audiences, and instrumental affordance. The European Romantics, Emily I. Dolan finds, fetishized sound, believing it to be *the* raw material for music.[2] As music was objectified as the art of manipulating timbre (sound understood as a natural resource), so questions of performance, embodiment, instrumentality, and locality evaporated. The tendency was to celebrate music, less as a visible-sociable process, than as an invisible force. Thus music's tangible intangibility, and its implication in the conversion of air into a dense anthropogenic space—a thoroughly tactile matter of human manipulation and control. The prestige of scores, the storage of scores, and score-based practice certainly aided and abetted the claim to music's invisibility, encouraging the worship of unseen atmospheres. But the primary point of insisting upon music's abstraction (as the freest and highest of the arts) was to attune bodies to the turmoil of the elemental media regime.

The Euro-American nineteenth century, that is, established music as a biopolitical medium. Historians of the concept of "environment," Benson among them, relate how the atmospheric system was framed as an aspect of mind, in ways redolent of very current modern-day concerns about mind-world confusion, human-induced climate change, pollution, airborne disease, and breathing.[3] "High art" implies an objectification of air, and a disaffection for air, as much as a quintessentially "expressive" or modern desire to work one's way out of air. But the fundamental media system for its sounding forms was invisible. The very category "music" is implicated in my agenda here, which is to propose a biopolitical theory for nineteenth-century music tout court. Once described as an elemental art, music might be celebrated for its systemic qualities, and for the force of its subtlety coercive or acculturative powers. Worse, it might be hailed as a "medium of culture." That idea—"culture"—implies a bounded set of unseen and yet determinative media conditions wherein humanness might be artificially reconditioned. The claim to abstraction meant that the art could be used to compare evolving value systems, moral conditions, and biomedical anthropologies. More than this, musical gestalts, since they were already "in the air," might be deployed as a means to civilize moral climates. Once accepted as a medium of culture, music became, in a sense, an art of making live or letting die.

In *Stereophonica* (2020), Gascia Ouzounian also traces the theory that sound has spatial or ecological properties back to nineteenth-century ideology, though for very different reasons. Ouzounian's project is to investigate the genealogy of such novel twentieth-century phenomena as "soundscapes," "acoustemology," or "auditory perspective." Her interest is in "spaces of sound and hearing," and the abstract idea that sound or music, from a psychoacoustic point of view, should engage three-dimensional reality. Why sound-space formulations should exist is puzzling, though the answer has much to do with the newfound plasticity of modern sound. "Spaces for sound," she explains, were "increasingly measured and rationalised, surveilled and scanned, militarised and weaponised, mapped and planned, controlled and commercialised—in short, modernized."[4] The modern project required that music be far more than "an art of pleasing by the succession and combination of agreeable sounds."[5] It required that music be made useful to the serious business of environmental government.

Call this a deformation of the truth of the medium, if such a truth exists, but that is how it happened. For critics, music was special because it portended new life worlds. Implicit in each of its structures and forms was a whole climate of values, invisible and yet subtly audible. Ideally, the art was world making, which is why the immersive experience of it became so vital to aesthetic education. In the twentieth century, Ouzounian shows, music was crucial to the acoustic design, as much of personal space, as of public environments and atmospheres. The more abstract it was, the more useful it became to projects of liberal reform. The more invisible its structures, the more it furthered the spread and influence of the most sublime forms of biopolitical and governmental reason.

The moment of music's "emancipation," then, coincided with the historical construction of a vast museum and global "library" of musical commerce, exchange, collection, and exploitation, with air as the primary material, spiritual, medical, discursive, and poetic element. Within this *sensus communis*, music was not only itself; it was legible as an invisible weather world of unseen values, spirits, ideologies, and conditions. Within this storied space, men imagined the globe in all its cultural oneness and difference, as a commons of property values, globalization, suffocation, and enclosure.

This is not to say that Europe-only purviews, as experienced from the inside of the ideological sphere, are enough. In his reflections on the sonic technologies of Blackness, Alexander G. Weheliye grapples with the necessity to explain the presence of Africa within the weather-beaten colonial media system. Weheliye quotes Tavia Nyong'o: "Africa could easily be nominated (although perhaps not without contention) as the sonic grounding not only of modern black music but of modern music as such. But such a nomination of Africa as the origin for (black) music would have to contend with the terms by which Western epistemology calls itself to order by consigning to Africa all that is 'disordered' in the sonic, aural, oral, embodied, and ecstatic excesses of music."[6] Equatorial Africa may begin and end this book, but this does not mean that it is some natural *fons et origo* for it. Weheliye writes of the need to inscribe Africa, less as a "resource" than as a constitutive locus and agent in the formation of nineteenth-century modernity.[7] The point is not merely to shift the point of attack but to interrogate the geopolitics of musical knowledge: to rethink south-north paradigms, and recognize music for what it is. Racial regimes, in the words of Cedric Robinson, are "unstable truth systems" that "may collapse under their own artifices, practices and apparatuses."[8] They may fail, equally, because of anticolonial resistance, as well as other crises or contradictions endemic to the ideological status quo.

"Stories, all the way down" is how this book configures music's elemental media system, with its tropical pianos, larynxes, hyperbaric chambers, ideas about persons with albinism, air-conditioned concert halls, humanitarians, *ngombi* harps, and yellow fever.[9] If these pages brim with strange ideas, stories, twists, subversions, and reversals, they do so for a reason. It is not only because atmospheric thinking necessarily cascades into confusion. The air involves multiplicity of course, but that precisely is the point. Any media system is a thing created rather than simply there. The modern experience of music was violently affecting because of its imbrication in the project to manipulate the infrastructure of breathing. That word "infrastructure," by the way, refers to "that which sustains or holds up or organizes the common forms of life."[10] And that elemental media system, this book argues, was never merely present in the world. It had to be made present, which is why communities were forced to struggle musically over its constitution.

Stories upon stories, then. For those writing in music studies of late, some say, storytelling has lost its raison d'être. Narrative writing stands accused of attenuating the immediacy of "real music"—for diffusing the lived experience of truth.[11] For musicologists preferring their personal possessive investments in music above historical argument, narrative exposition clouds what is inviolable about the art. Historicization, to be sure, can be an at once paranoid and weak form of explanation. What better way to destroy music than to "place it in context"? There are so many problems: the lies of narrative spinning out, the overreliance on plot archetypes, authoritative claims to objective knowledge, the colonizer's archon, the historian's aesthetic attachment to quirks.[12] The need to "put music in context" takes both music and contexts for granted, when neither have been so self-evident. Contexts, like texts, are made, not given. And there has never been, for any music, a preexisting set of conditions, global or otherwise, out there awaiting discovery.

Yet nor has the "lived experience" of "inviolable music" been so self-evident either.[13] The very term "music," though often assumed free from determining conditions, never quite manages to escape mediation. The problem is that to tell stories about one conditional reality rather than another is wholly political, as is any determination made about musical placement or music's elemental place in the world. When it comes to music and media, there is no before and after. These things come together. Elemental media systems are never prior to music, or more or less real than music, even when they are ideological. And it follows that when music is formed in abstraction, then so is its media system. The medium, because it is never pregiven, determines not only "the where" of music, but "the what" of music.

Which is to say that there is nothing more powerful than a good story. And while there is always a time to critique, there is also always a time to build. Storytellers at least offer up new positivities for alternate futures. At least they interrogate the basic a priori of knowledge. By the a priori, I mean those givens that condition disciplinary statements—the basic facticity for later polemic or argument. A standard defense of storytelling goes that the labor of writing not only encourages but demands a mind double backed against itself. It requires self-conscious reassembly. Fewer defenses of historicism say that it is the public construction materials of the archive itself—the medial stuff of history—which is at stake.[14] Struggles over history, in the latter sense, are struggles over content. Matters of fact count, perhaps even before the narrative amalgamation of things and ideas formerly unrelated, which is why this book raises the composite matter of air. The point of "atmospheric musicology" introduced in this book is to configure music as an art of air, yes. But it is also to inject air and some of the chaos of air back into an overly air-conditioned aesthetic system. The point of the struggle, Ben Okri observes, is to "change the stories we live by."[15]

Here, then, is this book's unlikely cast of characters: a harp player of mythic force who, by and through airs of his own making, supposedly held back the process of his own racialization; a French dramatic soprano whose voice depended on incubation in a hyperbaric chamber; laboring-class English choral singers who understood music as a means to cope with polluted industrial environments; officials in a city on the Amazon who speculated that while you are a creation of the air, you may control its influence by "curing" it; a tenor and master of breath control for whom art implied suspension of the need for air; a humanitarian, for whom the music of Bach provided salvation in the midst of a pathologized moral climate. These are just a few creatures of the air.

The term "creature" as per the title of this book, Alfred North Whitehead observed in the 1920s, carries a double meaning. Any creature, Whitehead noted, has two natures. At first, according to its fourteenth-century English etymology, the creature was a thing created and then latterly in history, a creating thing, endowed with a godlike capacity to create. Whitehead, in fact, coined the term "creativity" in his 1926 volume *Religion in the Making*, promulgating the modern view that creativity is irresistible, ubiquitously spread abroad, and universal. "Creativity," for him, was a "principle of process," observable everywhere.[16] According to the doctrine of "Imago Dei"—the credo that God created men and women in His own image—mankind did more than merely create with the materials at hand. "The individual fact is a creature," wrote Whitehead, "and creativity is the ultimate behind all forms, inexplicable by forms, and conditioned by its creatures."[17] To be creative was to be a powerful actant in the maelstrom of life. All creatures, for Whitehead, participated in the ceaselessly generative designs of a unified elemental order. They were both made and making.

Premodern users of the word preferred not to indulge like-minded heresies. Even the ancient Greeks were without terms corresponding to "to create" or "creator," preferring the word *poein* ("to make"), which applied as much to poetry (*poiesis*) as it did to makers or poets (*poietes*). In European intellectual history, creation, especially of the ex-nihilo sort, was the sole province of the Judeo-Christian Creator God. In the terms of this first usage, musicians—like all creatures great and small—were subject to air, in that they were formed according to it, like farm animals. If air is destiny, then creatures were "of the air" because "in Him we live and move and have our being," to quote Epimenides on the sky and thunder god of Greek antiquity, Zeus.[18] When "nurslings of the air" sang, unconsciously, they did so according to the divine law that nature sang through them first. This was the first sense of the lowly form of the "creature." Rather than a thing doing, the creature was a thing that was done to. The humble creature, classically, knew nothing of circumstance and nothing of why or how.

A stronger reading of the phrase *creatures of the air* suggests something more modern. The phrase suggests, as Herder did, that civilization is possible, and that men of property might actively create environments, altering the air through agriculture, swamp clearance, industrialism, musical practice, and so on. When creatures create, personhood may be understood to be bound up with atmospheres and things in ways that constitute persons as persons. "To achieve proper self-development—to be a person—an individual needs some control over resources in the external environment," Margaret Jane Radin sums up in view of Kant's *Philosophy of Law* and Hegel's *Philosophy of Right*. "The necessary assurances of control," she continues, "take the form of property rights."[19] To be in possession of self was not just to be in possession of property; it was to derive the capacity to "create" property. The rights ascribed to legal subjects depended on their ability to seize upon freedom amid the primitive brutality of the given. Thus, in a context of mind-world confusion, the need for "expression," which this book frames as an ex-appropriative act. For this breed of creature, "to express oneself" was to mediate, godlike, between the Real and the Ideal. It was to take leave of air and take hold of a new set of properties, by creating an atmosphere all of one's own.[20]

If music is an art of atmosphere, then those moderns convinced of their own creative agency have become, not merely perpetuators, but victims of the cosmology they have built for themselves. One of the great ironies of the great musical media construct I have described in this book is that it portends both salvage and catastrophe. Those moderns enamored of abstraction found music's freedom and drama, not merely useful, but materially constitutive of a global media environment of their own making.

The fate of the Great Globe at the center of Chapter 3 in mind, even the most ardent "creatures of the air" knew that someday they would need to take leave of this Truth. (It needs emphasis that the elemental media ecology engineered by systems of atmospheric government is a Truth.) If humanity is to survive as a species, it will need to get out of the building, or at least give up on owning the property. The problem is not that Nature needs to be saved, as most prominent nineteenth-century environmentalists thought. The problem, rather, is the cosmology itself. The Globe that modernity sanctifies in reference to universal aestheticism is no longer viable as an existential home. Appeals to universal values or musical atmosphericism, unfortunately, tend to reinforce rather than solve the problem. The entire structure needs to be rethought, because, as it stands, it is an interior within which only the most propertied few can breathe.

Acknowledgments

The places and people caught up in the pages of this book are many. It is difficult to know where to start. One place to begin is onstage in the Great Hall of the University of Witwatersrand in Johannesburg, the city I love, lifting the dampers on the concert grand just to hear the giant instrument breathe. My memories of Jozi are dear: my college friends, choir people, my political experience of that extraordinary university, and the people I have left behind. It is obvious, in retrospect, that these people are still very much bound into what and how I write. My dad taught me to question everything. Ma sat with me at our piano. My three brothers are here too.

It was in Europe (when Britain was still in Europe), paging through nineteenth-century vocal tutors, that I became aware of an energy or thermodynamic logic informing modern obsessions with atmospheric resonance and breathing. Early on, ideas in vitro, Roger Parker, still my best reader, arranged for an "early drafts discussion" at King's College London. I remember the contributions of Benjamin Walton, Gavin Williams, Kathy Fry, and Flora Willson. My trips from Waterloo Station color my recollection of the intellectual genesis of the book. Andrew and his family gave me a place to stay. They made me look forward to the clickety-clack of the South Western Railway service to Barnes. It was in London that I first imagined writing a history of music's elemental media system.

A Humanities Research Fellowship from the McEnerney Endowment in the Division of Arts and Humanities at University of California at Berkeley funded a sabbatical in 2017–18. I drafted most of the book in that year. In Paris, I met my editor-in-chief, Rebecca Dowd Geoffroy-Schwinden, waiting for the archives to open, and sometimes not. She read chapters, several times over, and worked to calm my prose. Her annotations of multiple rejected grant proposals led to the theoretical frame of the book in final form. I cannot thank her enough. Fellow Little Ray, Darren Mueller, updated me on sound studies and helped me understand the wrong kind of football. Others I met in Paris inspired: Timothée Picard, Céline Frigau Manning, Fanny Gribenski, who invited me to Berlin, Isabelle Moindrot, who taught me about the 1903 Soterkenos "aspirator" used to remove dust from the Opéra, and François Ribac, whose brilliance inspired chapter 3. Also that year, I visited New Haven, where I met the scholars who had animated elemental media studies for me: Gundula Kreuzer, John Durham Peters, and Gary Tomlinson, who gave generous and detailed feedback. Carolyn Abbate's creative input, at an early stage, supplied critical encouragement. I talked ideas through with Ellen Lockhart, Roger Moseley, and Emily I. Dolan in Berkeley, Munich, and Warsaw. Two anonymous reviewers submitted amazing reports. The ever-patient Marta Tonegutti and Kristin Rawlings at the University of Chicago Press guided the manuscript through its final phase.

At Berkeley, I have the best colleagues. My friend Nick Mathew teaches me how to be a professor. I hope, one day, to be like him. Mary Ann Smart sets the tone for us and has fought for me at every stage—thank you! I treasure Emily Zazulia's friendship, as she drove me home late, listened to my complaints, and offered solidarity. The extraordinary thinking of Delia Casadei is in these pages, as is the thoughtful scholarship of Lester Hu, who coached me through difficult days. I cherish having gotten to know former colleague Maria Sonevytsky, the energy of Jocelyne Guilbault, and others in the past and future of Morrison Hall. The love of Anna Maria Busse Berger and Karol Berger has been a blessing, as has the kindness of Martha Feldman. The brilliance of Weihong Bao and the Townsend Humanities Fellows gave me the confidence to believe I could finish.

I owe debts to the teachers I have taught. Kim Sauberlich made chapter 4 possible. Her political edge invades my thought and writing. I cannot thank her enough for the many ways she has contributed. Kirsten Paige has been invaluable in the movement for a critical atmospheric musicology, recommending books to read, and improving chapter 3. Back in 2014, a seminar with her, Danielle Simon, Edward Jacobsen, and Saraswathi Shukla sparked an interest in political ecology. Danni and Alessandra Jones got me thinking about "viral sound." I am heavily indebted to the graduates of "Sound Reproduction Ecologies," co-taught with Gavin Williams: Susan Bay, Virginia Georgallas, Anne Greenwood, and especially Parkorn Wangpaiboonkit, who made me think better about colonial approval. Melissa Scott taught me everything I know about humanitarianism reason. Others here are Desmond Sheehan, Melanie Gudesblatt, Katherine Gray, Amalya Lehmann, Edmund Mendelssohn, and Martyna Wlodarczyk, who told me more about the Reszkes. I am forgetting others but know that you are present in these pages too. The elegiac, Nietzschean tone of this book, anxious about its complicity in the inglorious status quo, is derived from Peter Humphrey and his critical genealogy of cybernetic audio and sound control systems.

David Trippett and Benjamin Walton provided expert input on an early version of chapter 5, which appeared as "Pneumotypes: Jean de Reszke's High Pianissimos and the Occult Sciences of Breathing," *Opera and Science in the Long Nineteenth Century* (Oxford: Oxford University Press, 2019). Kirsten Paige transformed chapter 3 into *"Elijah's Nature"* for the *19th-Century Music* special issue "Music and the Invention of Environment." Chapter 1 was expertly edited by Peter McMurray and Priyasha Mukhopadhyay as "Three Forms of Cosmopoiesis: Slave Sounds off the Gulf of Guinea, 1817," *Acoustics of Empire: Sound, Media and Power in the Long Nineteenth Century*, forthcoming with Oxford University Press. I thank Romain Collot of the Maison Albert Schweitzer in Gunsbach, where I spent halcyon days, the National Archives of Brazil, John Shepard of the Hargrove Music Library, and the staff of the Musée du quai Branly, where I wrote the early drafts, in a reading room overlooking the Seine.

Finally, I am grateful for Thea and Benedict, my figures of authority, who make me proud, and Sheila, to whom I dedicate this book.

Notes

Introduction

1. Eduard Pechuël-Loesche, *Tagebücher von der Loangoküste (1875–1876)*, ed. Beatrix Heintze (Frankfurt am Main: 2011), 104–5.

2. Pechuël-Loesche was born the son of a miller near Leipzig, which explains his comparison to the figure of Schubert's "Der Wanderer," in Jos. Reindl-München, "Eduard Pechuël-Loesche," *Geographische Zeitschrift* 20, no. 7 (1914): 361–67. I am quoting William Kinderman on wanderer aesthetics in "Wandering Archetypes in Schubert's Instrumental Music," *19th-Century Music* 21, no. 2 (1997): 208–22, 209. For Schubertian landscapes, see Theodor Adorno, "Schubert (1928)," trans. Jonathan Dunsby and Beate Perrey, *19th-Century Music* 29, no. 1 (2005): 3–14.

3. Pechuël-Loesche described a "mysterious and insidious ailment" afflicting "whites and blacks without distinction." He complained of "very annoying air," "heavy night sweats," the sticky smell of cat urine, and "pestilent fumes" rising from lagoons and mangrove swamps. "Foul-smelling clouds of mist covered the earth," he recorded elsewhere. Pechuël-Loesche's host at the Chiloango River, an hour's walk down the beach from the research station, was Richard Cobden Philips and "temporary wife" Nännä. Himself a practiced violinist and Bach fanatic, Philips frequently took up what Pechuël-Loesche called his "African violin" to play "Bach's sonatas, which black girls like very much." Philips was an agent for Hatton & Cookson, the same as described in chapter 6. The British trading company had converted to steam navigation three years earlier in order to capitalize on raw rubber extraction. Pechuël-Loesche, *Tagebücher*, 93. Pechuël-Loesche, "Ein Palaver in Loango," *Die Gartenlaube* 38 (1878): 627–32, 628. Richard Cobden Philips, "The Lower Congo: A Sociological Study," *Journal of the Anthropological Institute of Great Britain and Ireland* 17 (1888): 214–37.

4. Pechuël-Loesche, "Ein Palaver," 628.

5. The "batuco" was described by Joachim John Monteiro, a British-Portuguese mining engineer overseeing operations begun by Brazilian slavetrader Francisco Antonio Flores at malachite deposits near Bembe (Angola). He distinguished two kinds of "batuco" dance in 1875, one pursued by "the Ambriz blacks and those of the Congo country" involving a ring of spectators, fixed positions of the head, feet and arms, with bodies "violently twitched and convulsed"; whilst "the 'batuco' of the Bunda-speaking natives of Loanda" formed a ring around a couple engaged in more "indecent" interactions; *Angola and the River Congo*, 2 vols. (London: Macmillan, 1875), II:137–38.

6. This was the venue, according to Emily Thompson, that later gave birth to "modern sound." Emily Thompson, *The Soundscape of Modernity: Architectural Acoustics*

and the Culture of Listening, in American, 1900–1933 (Cambridge, MA: MIT Press, 2002).

7. Steven Feld, *Jazz Cosmopolitanism: Five Musical Years in Ghana* (Durham, NC: Duke University Press, 2021), 232.

8. See, for example, David R. M. Irving, "Rethinking Early Modern 'Western Music History': A Global History Manifesto," *IMS Musicological Brainfood* 3, no. 1 (2019): 6–10; and Nicholas Cook, "Western Music as World Music," in *The Cambridge History of World Music*, ed. Philip V. Bohlman (Cambridge, UK: Cambridge University Press, 2013).

9. Olivia Bloechl, "Editorial," *Eighteenth-Century Music* 17, no. 2 (2020): 173–76.

10. For an exemplary account of the need for change, see Olivia Bloechl, *Native American Song at the Frontiers of Early Modern Music* (Cambridge, UK: Cambridge University Press, 2008), 15.

11. Friedrich Nietzsche, *Jenseits von Gut und Böse: Vorspiel einer Philosophie der Zukunft*, Part 1 (Leipzig: Nauman, 1894), 183, 220.

12. Jürgen Osterhammel, *The Transformation of the World: A Global History of the Nineteenth Century*, trans. Patrick Camiller (Princeton, NJ: Princeton University Press, 2009), xvii. Roger Whitson, "The Deep Nineteenth Century," Responses to the V21 Manifesto, V21: Victorian Studies for the 21st Century, March 23, 2015, http://v21collective.org/responses-to-the-v21-manifesto-2/.

13. Gary Tomlinson, "Musicology, Anthropology, History," *Saggiatore musicale: La storia della musica: Prospettive del secolo XXI Convegno internazionale di studi, Bologna* 8, no. 1 (2001): 21–37. Reinhard Strohm, ed., *Studies for a Global History of Music: A Balzan Musicology Project* (New York: Routledge, 2018). Mark Hijleh, *Towards a Global History of Music: Intercultural Convergence, Fusion, and Transformation in the Human Musical Story* (London: Routledge, 2019).

14. For a critique of ecomusicology, see Ana María Ochoa Gautier, "Acoustic Multinaturalism, the Value of Nature, and the Nature of Music in Ecomusicology," *boundary 2* 43, no. 1 (2016): 107–41.

15. Arun Agrawal, *Environmentality: Technologies of Government and the Making of Subjects* (Durham, NC: Duke University Press, 2005).

16. Achille Mbembe, "The Universal Right to Breathe," trans. Carolyn Shread, *Critical Inquiry* 47, no. S2 (2021): S58–62. Donna Haraway, "Anthropocene, Capitalocene, Plantationocene, Chthulucene: Making Kin," *Environmental Humanities* 6, no. 1 (2015): 159–65.

17. Weihong Bao, "Hermeneutics of Doubt: Atmospheric Knowing and an Ecology of the Mind," *Representations* 157, no. 1 (2022): 142–72.

18. Bruno Latour, "Why Has Critique Run Out of Steam? From Matters of Fact to Matters of Concern," *Critical Inquiry* 30 no. 2 (2004): 225–48.

19. Cheryl I. Harris, "Whiteness as Property," *Harvard Law Review* 106, no. 8 (1993): 1709–91. Sylvia Wynter, "Unsettling the Coloniality of Being/Power/Truth/Freedom: Towards the Human, after Man, Its Overrepresentation—An Argument," *CR* 3, no. 3 (2003): 257–337.

20. Brenna Bhandar, *Colonial Lives of Property: Law, Land, and Racial Regimes of Ownership* (Durham, NC: Duke University Press, 2018), 4.

21. Klaus Kropfinger, *Wagner and Beethoven: Richard Wagner's Reception of Beethoven*, trans. Peter Palmer (Cambridge, UK: Cambridge University Press, 1991), 51–2. In 1871, Wagner defined his total work of art as the product of "höchste künstlerische

Besonnenheit" in *Über dei Bestimmung der Oper Ein akademischer Vortrag* (Leipzig: Fritzsch, 1871), 36.

22. Françoise Vergès, "Racial Capitalocene," in *Futures of Black Radicalism*, ed. Gaye Theresa Johnson and Alex Lubin (New York: Verso, 2017), 72–82. Andreas Malm, *Fossil Capital: The Rise of Steam Power and the Roots of Global Warming* (London: Verso, 2016). Kathryn Yusoff, *A Billion Black Anthropocenes or None* (Minneapolis: University of Minnesota Press, 2018). Amitav Ghosh, *The Great Derangement: Climate Change and the Unthinkable* (Chicago: University of Chicago Press, 2018).

23. Simon Gikandi, "Race and the Idea of the Aesthetic," *Michigan Quarterly Review* 40, no. 2 (2001): 318–50.

24. Frantz Fanon, *The Wretched of the Earth*, trans. Richard Philcox, commentary by Jean-Paul Sartre (New York: Grove, 2004 [1961]), 30.

25. Lydia Goehr, *The Imaginary Museum of Musical Works: An Essay in the Philosophy of Music* (Oxford: Clarendon, 1992), 153.

26. Immanuel Kant, *Critique of the Aesthetic Power of Judgement*, trans. Paul Guyer (Cambridge, UK: Cambridge University Press, 2000), 89.

27. Fanny Gribenski, *Tuning the World: The Rise of 440 Hertz in Music, Science, and Politics, 1859–1955* (Chicago: University of Chicago Press, 2023).

28. Fanny Gribenski, "Tuning Forks as Time Travel Machines: Pitch Standardisation and Historicism for 'Sonic Things,'" *Sound Studies* 6, no. 2 (2020): 153–73, 155.

29. Gary Tomlinson writes that "the Romantic music trance asserted the strong distinction of Europe from the rest of the world even as it absorbed Europe back into that world" and that "the inward gaze of Romanticism, more compellingly captured in music than anywhere else, takes on new, global significance as soon as we link it to Europe's anxious, imperious outward gaze at the world around"; in "Review: Monumental Musicology: *The Oxford History of Western Music*," *Journal of the Royal Musical Association* 132, no. 2 (2007): 349–74, 368.

30. Franz Fanon, *Black Skin, White Masks*, trans. Charles Lamm Markmann (London: Pluto, 1966), 11.

31. Gary Tomlinson, "Review: Monumental Musicology," *Journal of the Royal Musical Association* 132, no. 2 (2007): 349–74.

32. James O. Young, "The 'Great Divide' in Music," *British Journal of Aesthetics* 45 (2005): 175–84.

33. Rebecca Dowd Geoffroy-Schwinden, *From Servant to Savant: Musical Privilege, Property, and the French Revolution* (Oxford: Oxford University Press, 2022). Theodor Adorno, in Taruskin's account, ends up the greatest romantic-modern polluter of them all, injecting his baby's life-support system with the noxious gas of "the life phenomenon of the humane" (which he thought his favorite music by Beethoven conveyed); Richard Taruskin, "Is There a Baby in the Bathwater?" *Archiv für Musikwissenschaft* 63 (2006): 163–85, 309–27.

34. P. J. Crutzen and E. F. Stoermer, "The 'Anthropocene,'" *Global Change Newsletter IGBP* 41 (2000): 17–18.

35. In the "preface" added to the published score of his 1854 symphonic poem *Orpheus*, for example, Liszt described "melodies that radiate from every work of art— their suave energy, their august empire, their sonorities, so nobly soothing to the soul, their undulation sweet as the breezes of Elysium, their gradual rise like the vapors of incense, their diaphanous and airy-blue Ether enveloping the world and the whole universe as if in the atmosphere, or in a transparent cloak of ineffable and mysterious

Harmony." Franz Liszt, "Liszt on the Artist in Society," trans. Ralph R. Locke, in *Franz Liszt and His World*, ed. Christopher H. Gibbs and Dana Gooley (Princeton, NJ: Princeton University Press, 2004), 291–302.

36. Franz Liszt, "About Popular Editions of Important Works (1836)," in *The Collected Writings of Franz Liszt, Essays and Letters of a Traveling Bachelor of Music*, ed. and trans. Janita R. Hall-Swadley (Lanham, MD: Scarecrow, 2012), II, 201–18.

37. In her study of the "musical mists" conjured by such prophetic musicians as Richard Wagner, Gundula Kreuzer accounts for the ways in which the poetics and histrionics of steam offered something fugitive yet "essential to our modern sensibilities themselves." Gundula Kreuzer, *Curtain, Gong, Steam: Wagnerian Technologies of Nineteenth-Century Opera* (Oakland: University of California Press, 2018), 213. Kreuzer quotes T. J. Clarke's definition of modernity as being "about steam . . . about change and power and contingency, in other words, but also control, compression, and captivity." T. J. Clark, "Modernism, Postmodernism, and Steam," *October* 100 (2002): 154–74.

38. Simon Gikandi, "Picasso, Africa and the Schemata of Difference," in *Beautiful/Ugly: African and Diasporic Aesthetics*, ed. Sarah Nuttall (Durham, NC: Duke University Press, 2007), 30–93.

39. Achille Mbembe, *Out of the Dark Night: Essays on Decolonization* (New York: Columbia University Press, 2021), 13.

40. Karl Marx, *Capital. A Critique of Political Economy. Volume One*, trans. Ben Fowkes (London: Penguin, 1976), 873–76.

41. For border thinking, Tamara Levitz, ed. "Musicology Beyond Borders?" *Journal of the American Musicological Society* 65, no. 3 (2012), 821–61. The burgeoning literature on music, empire, and coloniality includes Olivia Bloechl & Melanie Lowe, "Introduction: Rethinking Difference," in *Rethinking Difference in Music Scholarship*, ed. Olivia Bloechl, Melanie Lowe, and Jeffrey Kallberg (Cambridge, UK: Cambridge University Press), 1–52. Ronald Radano and Tejumola Olaniyan, eds., *Audible Empire: Music, Global Politics, Critique* (Durham, NC: Duke University Press, 2016). Gavin Steingo and Jim Sykes, eds., *Remapping Sound Studies* (Durham, NC: Duke University Press, 2019).

42. Jim Sykes, "The Anthropocene and Music Studies," *Ethnomusicology Review* 22, no. 1 https://ethnomusicologyreview.ucla.edu/journal/volume/22/piece/1030. Ochoa Gautier, "Acoustic Multinaturalism." Gary Tomlinson, "Musicology, Anthropology, History," *Saggiatore musicale: La storia della musica: Prospettive del secolo XXI Convegno internazionale di studi, Bologna* 8, no. 1 (2001): 21–37.

43. Richard Taruskin, "Afterword: *Nicht blutbefleckt?*" *The Journal of Musicology* 26, no. 2 (2009): 274–84, 277.

44. Michel Foucault, *The History of Sexuality: Volume 1*, trans. Robert Hurley (New York: Pantheon, 1978), 139.

45. Michel Foucault, *The Birth of Biopolitics: Lectures at the Collège de France 1978–79*, ed. Michel Senellart (New York: Palgrave Macmillan, 2004), 260.

46. Bruno Latour, *Down to Earth: Politics in the New Climatic Regime*, trans. Catherine Porter (Cambridge, UK: Polity, 2018).

47. Peter Sloterdijk, *Globes. Spheres Volume II: Macrospherology*, trans. Wieland Hoban (Los Angeles: *Semiotext(e)*, 2014). The phrase "disappearance of the outside" appears in Bruno Latour's commentary on Sloterdijk, in "Spheres and Networks: Two Ways to Reinterpret Globalization," *Harvard Design Magazine* (2009): 138–44, 144.

48. Plato, *Timaeus and Critias*, trans. Desmond Lee (London: Penguin, 1977), 83.

49. Mark Evan Bonds, "Idealism and the Aesthetics of Instrumental Music at the Turn of the Nineteenth Century," *Journal of the American Musicological Society* 50, no. 2/3 (1997), 387–420, 391.

50. Martin Heidegger, "The Origin of the Work of Art," *Martin Heidegger: Off the Beaten Track*, trans. Julian Young and Kenneth Haynes (Cambridge, UK: Cambridge University Press, 2002), 1–56, 3.

51. Ferruccio Busoni, *Sketch of a New Esthetic of Music*, trans. Theodore Baker (New York: Schirmer, 1911), 34.

52. Quoted in Mark Evan Bonds, *Music as Thought: Listening to the Symphony in the Age of Beethoven* (Princeton, NJ: Princeton University Press, 2015), 21.

53. "If no discourse is free of ideology," Kofi Agawu asked presciently of demystification back in 1992, "if such ideology can be easily decoded from writing, then why should we continue to ritually unmask our identities instead of simply getting on with the job at hand? Is not the very process of unmasking, itself contaminated by language?" in Agawu, "Representing African Music," *Critical Inquiry* 18, no. 2 (1992): 245–66, 256.

54. Jonathan Sterne, "'What Do We Want?' 'Materiality!' 'When Do We Want It?' 'Now!'" *Media Technologies. Essays on Communication, Materiality, and Society*, ed. Tarleton Gillespie, Pablo J. Boczkowski, and Kirsten A. Foot (Cambridge, MA: MIT Press, 2014), 119–28.

55. Nina Sun Eidsheim, *Sensing Sound: Singing and Listening as Vibrational Practice* (Durham, NC: Duke University Press: 2015). J. Martin Daughtry, "Atmospheric Pressures: Voice, Environment, Precarity," MMaP Lecture Series, https://www.youtube.com/watch?v=wXtbQcnI2BQ. Gilles Deleuze and Félix Guattari, *A Thousand Plateaus: Capitalism and Schizophrenia*, trans. Brian Massumi (London: Athlone, 1988). Ben Anderson "Affective Atmospheres," *Emotion, Space and Society* 2 (2009): 77–81.

56. Fredric Jameson, "The Vanishing Mediator: Narrative Structure in Max Weber," *New German Critique* 1 (1973): 52–89.

57. Brice Parfait Ndzigou, *La lumière sacrée des noirs* (Libreville, Gabon, 2006).

58. Lyon Playfair, "Air and Airs, as Illustrated by the Magdeburg Hemispheres and Black's and Cavendish's Balances," *Free Evening Lectures: Delivered in Connection with the Special Loan Collection of Scientific Apparatus 1876* (London: Chapman and Hall, 1878), 134–54, 138.

59. Playfair, "Air and Airs," 152.

60. Will Steffen et al., "The Anthropocene: Conceptual and Historical Perspectives," *Philosophical Transactions of the Royal Society* 369, no. 1938 (2011): 843, 619.

61. Alfred Gell, "The Technology of Enchantment and the Enchantment of Technology," in *The Art of Anthropology: Essays and Diagrams*, ed. Eric Hirsch (Oxford: Berg, 2006), 159–87, 160.

62. T. J. Clark, "Modernism, Postmodernism, and Steam," *October* 100 (2002): 154–74.

63. Bruno Latour, *Facing Gaia: Eight Lectures on the New Climatic Regime*, trans. Catherine Porter (Cambridge, UK: Polity, 2017), 220.

64. Alexander Rehding, "Unsound Seeds," in *Nineteenth-Century Opera and the Scientific Imagination*, ed. David Trippett and Benjamin Walton (Cambridge, UK: Cambridge University Press, 2019), 303–34, 304, 306.

65. Rachel Mundy, "Evolutionary Categories and Musical Style from Adler to America," *Journal of the American Musicological Society* 67, no. 3 (2014): 735–68, 738.

66. Rehding, "Unsound Seeds," 304.

67. Nina Sun Eidsheim, "Sensing Voice: Materiality and the Lived Body in Singing and Listening," *Senses and Society* 6, no. 2 (2011): 133–55.

68. Gell, "The Technology of Enchantment and the Enchantment of Technology," 42.

69. Philip V. Bolhman, "Johann Gottfried Herder and the Global Moment of World-Music History," in *The Cambridge History of World Music*, ed. Philip V. Bohlman (Cambridge, UK: Cambridge University Press, 2013), 255–76.

70. Johann Gottfried Herder, "Our Earth Is Enveloped in an Atmosphere, and Is in Conflict with Several of the Celestial Bodies," in *Outlines of a Philosophy of the History of Man*, trans. T. Churchill, 2 vols. (London: J. Johnson, 1803), I:22–26, 24.

71. Herder, "Our Earth Is Enveloped in an Atmosphere," I:295.

72. Herder, "Our Earth Is Enveloped in an Atmosphere," I:316.

73. Eva Horn, "Air Conditioning: Taming the Climate as a Dream of Civilization," in *Climates: Architecture and the Planetary Imaginary*, ed. James Graham (New York: Columbia University Press, 2016), 233–41.

74. Philip V. Bohlman writes of "the remarkable rise of folk song as the paradigmatic form of world music" in "Johann Gottfried Herder and the Global Moment of World Music History," in *The Cambridge History of World Music*, ed. Philip V. Bohlman (Cambridge, UK: Cambridge University Press, 2013), 255–76. Jürgen Trabant, "Herder's Discovery of the Ear," in *Herder Today*, ed. Kurt Mueller-Vollmer (Berlin: De Gruyter, 1990), 345–66.

75. Matthew Gelbart, *The Invention of "Folk Music" and "Art Music": Emerging Categories from Ossian to Wagner* (Cambridge, UK: Cambridge University Press, 2007), 104.

76. Edward B. Tylor, *Primitive Culture: Researches into the Development of Mythology, Philosophy, Religion, Art, and Custom*, 2 vols. (London: John Murray, 1871).

77. Johann Gottfried Herder, "On Music [from *Kalligone* (1800), part II]," trans. Philip V. Bohlman, in *Song Loves the Masses: Herder on Music and Nationalism* (Oakland: University of California Press, 2017), 249–59.

78. Peter Sloterdijk, *Sphären I—III. Bd. I.: Mikrosphärologie: Blasen. Bd. II: Makrosphärologie: Globen. Bd. III: Plurale Sphärologie: Schäume* (Frankfurt: Suhrkamp, 1998–2004).

79. Peter Sloterdijk, *Terror from the Air*, trans. Amy Patton and Steve Corcoran (Cambridge, MA: Semiotext(e), 2009).

80. Kim Coleman, *A History of Chemical Warfare* (New York: Palgrave Macmillan, 2005), 7.

81. The artistic need to control air, to extract air, or deny oxygen in his apocalyptic narrative, is sinister, one where the control freaks will eventually suffocate us all. See Coleman, *A History of Chemical Warfare*, 47. The claims made in Sloterdijk's *In the World Interior of Capital* (Cambridge, UK: Polity, 2013) are thankfully more benign.

82. John Durham Peters theorizes the "elemental medium" in *The Marvelous Clouds: Toward a Philosophy of Elemental Media* (Princeton, NJ: Princeton University Press, 2015).

83. Robert Mitchell, *Experimental Life: Vitalism in Romantic Science & Literature* (Baltimore, MD: Johns Hopkins University Press, 2013).

84. Michel Foucault, *The Order of Things: An Archaeology of the Human Sciences* (London: Routledge, 2005), 175.

85. Life was most often held to be literally present in "the medium." Guillory writes of the "puzzle of nineteenth-century spiritualism" that "the most surprising common use of the word *medium* in the period, however, is . . . a person believed to be in contact with the spirits of the dead and to communicate between the living and the dead." John Guillory, "Genesis of the Media Concept," *Critical Inquiry* 36, no. 2 (2010): 321–62, 347.

86. Canguilhem, "The Living and Its Milieu," 8.

87. Robert Mitchell, *Experimental Life: Vitalism in Romantic Science & Literature* (Baltimore, MD: Johns Hopkins University Press, 2013), 145.

88. Etienne S. Benson, *Surroundings: A History of Environments and Environmentalisms* (Chicago: University of Chicago Press, 2020), 1.

89. Friedlind Riedel, "'The Atmospheres of Tones': Notions of Atmosphere in Music Scholarship Between 1840 and 1930," in *Atmosphere and Aesthetics: A Plural Perspective*, ed. Tonino Griffero and Marco Tedeschini (London: Palgrave Macmillan, 2019), 293–312.

90. Thomas H. Ford, *Wordsworth and the Poetics of Air: Atmospheric Romanticism in a Time of Climate Change* (Cambridge, UK: Cambridge University Press, 2018), 3.

91. William Wordsworth, "Tintern Abbey," in *Lyrical Ballads, with a Few Other Poems*, ed. William Wordsworth and Samuel Taylor Coleridge (London: Arch, 1798), 201–10, 207.

92. E. T. A. Hoffmann, "Beethovens Instrumentalmusik," *Zeitung für die elegante Welt* 13, no. 246–7 (1813): 1964–1967 and 1973–1975.

93. Adolf Bernhard Marx, to cite another example, described "atmospheres of tones" that transformed "the entire space of the air" into "resonant matter" (*mitklingende Materie*). In 1839, Marx described living emanations, feeling-states conjured by *Schallmasse*, harmonics and combination tones, that suffused his entire listening body as he contemplated those musical artworks that most engendered "fullness of being." Friedlind Riedel, Juha Torvinen, *Music as Atmosphere: Collective Feelings and Affective Sounds* (New York: Routledge, 2019), 2.

94. Steve Goodman, *Sonic Warfare: Sound, Affect, and the Ecology of Fear* (Cambridge, MA: MIT Press, 2010).

95. "Hardly ever have I known another man," proclaimed Albert Einstein, "in whom mercy and desire for beauty are connected that ideal as in Albert Schweitzer." *To Dr. Albert Schweitzer: A Festschrift Commemorating His 80th Birthday From a Few of His Friends*, ed. Homer A. Jack (New York: The Profile Press, 1955), 37. "The Greatest Man in the World," *Life Magazine*, January 1, 1949.

96. Pechuël-Loesche, *Kongoland: Amtliche Berichte und Denkschriften* (Jena: Hermann Costenoble, 1887), 418.

97. Dylan Richardson, *Hungry Listening: Resonant Theory for Indigenous Sound Studies* (Minneapolis: University of Minnesota Press, 2020).

98. Eduard Pechuël-Loesche, *Volkskunde von Loango* (Stuttgart: Strecker & Schröder, 1907), 112. Kubik speculates that, though Vili speakers seemed to European ears to sing the same songs in different modes every day, they used "a non-modal heptatonic system with harmony in three parts"; Gerhard Kubik, "African Tone-Systems: A Reassessment," *Yearbook for Traditional Music* 17 (1985): 31–63.

99. John Durham Peters, "The Media of Breathing," in *Atmospheres of Breathing: Respiratory Questions of Philosophy*, ed. Lenart Škof and Petri Berndtson (Albany: State University of New York Press, 2018): 179–95. Luce Irigaray, "The Age of Breath," in *Key Writings*, ed. Luce Irigaray (London: Continuum, 2004), 165–70.

Chapter 1

1. Achille Mbembe, *The Critique of Black Reason* (Durham, NC: Duke University Press, 2017), 128.

2. Scholars wrangle over terms like "Gabon" or "Mpongwe." In 1602, a Dutch trader-explorer described the estuary as the domain of "three powerful Kings . . . one King on the northern corner is named Caiombo, and the other on the southern corner named Gabom, and the other on the island named Pongo"; Pieter de Marees, *Beschryvinge ende historische verhael van het Gout Koninckrijck van Gunea* (The Hague: Martinus Nijhoff, 1912, 1602), 245. Bucher revives the venerable 1876 theory of Robert Bruce Napoleon Walker, father of Raponda-Walker, that Mpongwe speakers were not descendants of the "Pongo," but late-comers to the estuary, arriving mostly in the seventeenth and eighteenth centuries, usurping the name of their predecessors and amalgamating its remnants. Jan Vansina claims that the ancestors of Mpongwe peoples arrived with a great Bantu-speaking migration before 1000 CE. Kairn Klieman's review of archeological and linguistic evidence suggests 1500 CE. Jeremy Rich, *A Workman Is Worthy of His Meat: Food and Colonialism in the Gabon* (Lincoln: University of Nebraska Press, 2007), 4. According to one oral source (Olivier Ambaye, traditional head of Mpongwe speakers in the 1970s), the group originally passed to the Upper Bakoué River from Ethiopia and Zanzibar. In oral traditions, "pygmies" are generally "at the root of the world," the Ndiwa arrive later (Bucher says around the fifteenth century). "The Mundah and Muni rivers as well as the Como," Bucher writes," play a crucial role in Mpongwe creation stories and oral traditions." "All six of the Myènè-speaking groups begin a statement with 'Myènè' or 'I say that,' hence the origin of the name Myènè"; Henry H. Bucher, "Mpongwe Origins: Historiographical Perspectives," *History in Africa* 2 (1975): 59–89, 62, 64, 71, 74.

3. "Fleuve du Gabon, levé et dressé en 1849 par M. Ch. Ploix (Depot-General de la Marine, 1852)," British Library Maps H.F.SEC.8 (1395). The "conspicuous tree" is noted in the hydrographic map "River Gaboon, from the French Surveys to 1890 . . . under Captain W. J. L. Wharton (London: the Admiralty, 1893)," British Library Maps SEC.XI (1877); the tree is beautifully depicted in "Plan de la partie intérieure de l'Estuaire du Gabon" British Library Maps H.F.SEC.8 (3414), a map made possible by the voyage of the steamer "le Pygmée" (Dépôt des Cartes et Plans de la Marine, 1875). For depictions of the clearing and three trees, see "River Gaboon, surveyed by Mr. Ch. Floix [*sic*] with additions from Officers of H.M.S. (1849)," British Library Maps SEC.XI.1877.

4. For what it's worth, an account of ethnic and clan lineage occurs in Abbé André Raponda Walker, "Notes d'histoires du Gabon" (Brazzaville, 1960).

5. Mary Orr, "Women Peers in the Scientific Realm: Sarah Bowdich (Lee)'s Expert Collaborations with Georges Cuvier, 1825–33," *Notes and Records of the Royal Society* 69, no. 1 (2014): 37–51. "A Visit to Empoöngwa; or a Peep into Negro-Land," *Friendship's Offering: A Literary Album* (1833): 294–304. Mrs. Lee, "A Visit to Empoöngwa," *Stories of Strange Lands: And Fragments from the Notes of a Traveller* (London: Edward Moxon, 1835), 309–36. Kheshti argues that white women, under this modernity, took on the mantle of song-hunting, listening, especially to and of invented radical alterity, being constructed as a highly gendered practice; Roshanak Kheshti, *Modernity's Ear: Listening to Race and Gender in World Music* (New York: New York University Press, 2015).

6. In a January 3, 1819, letter; see *The Letters of John Keats: Volume 2, 1819–1821: 1814–1821*, ed. Hyder Edward Rollins (Cambridge, UK: Cambridge University Press, 1958), 28.

7. Mrs. R. Lee (formerly Mrs. T. Ed. Bowdich), *Memoirs of Baron Cuvier* (London: Longman, 1833). "Mrs. Lee's Memoirs of Cuvier," *Monthly Magazine* 4, no. 2 (1833): 159–78, 160.

8. Sarah Bowdich took a piano to Cape Coast Castle (modern Ghana) in 1817, at a time when abolitionists were arguing that the trade in slaves would only end once Britain took full occupation of the entire Gold Coast. The piano "contributed to the happiness" of "Adoo [Adu] Bradie, ambassador and favorite material nephew of Osei Bonsu, the Asantehene (king of the Ashanti)"; Mrs. Lee, *Stories of Strange Lands*, 177.

9. "In the quiet of his own home, Moscheles found his real element of happiness, brightened as it was by the faces of many dear and distinguished friends. More than one is still among us to remember that home where social intercourse and the cultivation of art for its own sake were so happily blended, and will recall to mind the image of Moscheles as he would alternately play, listen, or converse, or as he would sit correcting proof sheets, not only of his own works but of those of friends who frequently delegated such duties to him. Chorley, the well-known art-critic of the *Athenaeum*, who now settled in London, soon became intimate with the Moscheles [sic] and was for many years their highly-esteemed, generous, and often indispensable friend. [Also habitually there was] the respected authoress, Mrs. Bowdich Lee, whom Cuvier complimented as a first-rate naturalist"; Charlotte Moscheles, *Life of Moscheles: With Selections from His Diaries and Correspondence*, trans. A. D. Coleridge, 2 vols. (London: Hurst and Blackett, 1873), I:265–66.

10. Libreville was founded more than thirty years later when fifty-two enslaved Vili speakers freed from a Brazilian slaver in 1846 by the Anglo-French blockade were "resettled" to provide manual labor for a model township.

11. T. E. Bowdich, *A Reply to the Quarterly Review* (Paris: J. Smith, 1820), 12.

12. "To place residents in situations to mediate between the great contending kingdoms, and to originate commerce, is not only the most humane, the most prudent, and the most economical, but the only legitimate method of acquiring political influence and power." T. E. Bowdich, *The African Committee* (London: Longman, 1819), 18.

13. For a description of the mission, see "Mr. Thomas Edward Bowdich and Mrs. Sarah Bowdich," MS Archives of the Royal Literary Fund, Registered case 13/465. Paris, May 13, 1822.

14. "Les fleuves se ramifient d'une manière singulière dans l'intérieur du pays; l'esquisse que nous trace Bowdich de cette étrange ramification, se rapproche beaucoup de l'hypothèse de Reichhard, sur l'embouchure du Niger dans le golfe de Guinée," Karl Ritter, *Géographie générale comparée ou Étude de la terre* (Paris: Paulin, 1835), 390. T. Edward Bowdich, *Essay on the Superstitions, Customs, and Arts Common to the Ancient Egyptians, Abyssinians and Ashantees* (Paris: J. Smith, 1821), 390.

15. I borrow "migratory consciousness" from John Manning Cinnamon, "The Long March of the Fang: Anthropology and History in Equatorial Africa" (PhD diss., Yale University, 1998), 2. In Gray's formulation "the kinship structures [which were the main source of social and cultural identity] for these peoples knew no limits"; Christopher J. Gray, *Territoriality, Ethnicity, and Colonial Rule in Southern Gabon 1850–1960* (Bloomington: Indiana University Press, 1995).

16. On poetic cartographies, see Steven Feld, "Sound Worlds," in *Sound*, ed. Patricia Kruth and Henry Stobart (Cambridge, UK: Cambridge University Press, 2000), 173–200.

17. Jeremy Rich, "Savage Frenchmen: Masculinity and the Timber Industry in Colonial Gabon, ca. 1920–1960," *Afrique et Histoire* 7, no. 1 (2010): 235–64.

18. Charles Holtzapffel, *Turning and Mechanical Manipulation intended as a Work of General Reference and Practical Instruction* (London: Holtzapffel, 1843), I, 73.

19. Other exotic items onboard included large numbers of parrots and monkeys, as well as "the first African panther [leopard] brought alive to England," which was presented first to the Duchess of York and then to Exeter Exchange, the future site of Exeter Hall; Lee, *Stories of Strange Lands*, 348. Robert Adelson et al., eds., *The History of the Erard Piano and Harp in Letters and Documents, 1785–1959*, 2 vols. (Cambridge, UK: Cambridge University Press, 2015), I:209.

20. Iris Brémaud et al., "Effect of extractives on vibrational properties of African Padauk (*Pterocarpus soyauxii Taub*)," *Wood Science and Technology* 45, no. 3 (Berlin: Springer Verlag, 2011): 461–72. In 1876, the annual exportation of barwood from Gaboon to England, France, Germany, and the United States of America was estimated at ten thousand tons, though rival official French estimates put the export of barwood and ebony at twenty-five thousand tons; R. B. N. Walker, "The Commerce of the Gaboon and Its Future Prospects," *Journal of the Society of Arts* 24, no. 1224 (May 12, 1876): 585–97, 591. Richard King's Gaboon business enabled his rise to become mayor of Bristol in the 1840s. He took an active part, cutlass in hand, in repelling the mob during the Bristol Riots of 1831. Martin Lynn, "British Business and the African Trade: Richard & William King Ltd. of Bristol and West Africa, 1833–1918," *Business History* 34, no. 4 (1992): 20–37.

21. Bucher, *The Mpongwe of the Gabon Estuary*, 123.

22. Nicolas Metegue N'Nah, *Histoire du Gabon: Des origines à l'aube du XXIe siècle* (Paris: L'Harmattan, 2006), 83–86. Joseph Ambouroué Avaro, *Un people gabonais à l'aube de la colonization. Le Bas-Ogowè au XIXe siècle* (Paris: Karthala, 1981), 107–14.

23. Bucher suggests that compared to northern shore tradeposts, Ngango "was more intricately tied to the slave trade . . . through the Ogooué trade" and a system that reached onward into the three-hundred-year-old "Tio system" at Malebo (Stanley Pool). Henry Bucher, "The Atlantic Slave Trade and the Gabon Estuary: The Mpongwe to 1860," in *Africans in Bondage: Studies in Slavery and the Slave Trade*, ed. Paul E. Lovejoy (Madison: University of Wisconsin Press, 1986), 136–54.

24. Walker, "The Commerce of the Gaboon," 87.

25. Sarah Bowdich reveled in stories of mutual astonishment. "Several new slaves, from the interior," she wrote, "declared that I was an evil spirit, and they should die if they looked at me." Mrs. R. Lee [formerly Mrs. T. Edward Bowdich], "A Visit to Empoöngwa," *Stories of Strange Lands*, 322, 325–26.

26. Obituaries wrote that "he has fallen victim to the cause for which alone he lived," lamenting that "Mrs. Bowdich is returning to England in a state of destitution." A subscription for the support of the widow was opened by Charles Konig of the British Museum, J. G. Sowerby, John Tompkins, and Coutts and Co.; "Mr. Bowdich," *The Norfolk Chronicle and Norwich Gazette*, April 24, 1824. In an 1824 letter, Sir Benjamin Hobhouse pleaded that "Mr. Bowdich has literally died a victim to his ardour in the cause of Science," MS Archives of the Royal Literary Fund.

27. Lee, *African Wanderers*, 135.

28. Thomas Edward Bowdich, *Mission from Cape Coast Castle to Ashantee* (London: John Murray, 1819), 439.

29. For thermometric tables, see appendix 5 in T. E. Bowdich, *Mission from Cape Coast Castle*, 497–502. "Mr. Thomas Edward Bowdich, and Mrs. Sarah Bowdich, his widow (Mrs. Lee)," MS. Archives of the Royal Literary Fund, registered case no. 13/465 (1822).

30. Jan M. Vansina, *Paths in the Rainforest: Towards a History of Political Tradition in Equatorial Africa* (Madison: University of Wisconsin Press: 1990), 46.

31. Ephesians 2:2, *The Holy Bible (King James Version)* (London: Robert Barker, 1611).

32. Lee, *Friendship's Offering*, 297.

33. T. E. Bowdich, *Mission from Cape Coast Castle*, 427.

34. Bucher, *The Mpongwe of the Gabon Estuary*, 183.

35. François Ngolet, "Inventing Ethnicity and Identifies in Gabon. The case of Ongom (Bakele)," *Revue française d'histoire d'outre-mer* 85, no. 32 (1998): 5–26.

36. Lee, *The African Wanderers*, 179. "Ngango" suggests "medicine" or "remedy" in Evongwani. This was appropriate, given the purported moral hygiene of this "town of one street, wide, regular, and clean," as the Bowdiches described it; though the word might have referred just to the prevalence here of the secretive healing-divination societies of *Ombwiri/Mwiri* medicine.

37. An 1846 description of "le bouquet d'arbres séculaires qui couronne le village du roi Georges" occurs in "Nouvelles excursion dans le haut de la rivière du Gabon," 283. "Le village du George, qu'on connait aisément de loin a une touffe de grands arbres" situated on an elevated plateau; M. Pigeard, Lieutenant de Vaisseau, "Exploration du Gabon, en Août et Septembre 1846," *Revue coloniale* 9 (March 1847): 263–95, 270–1.

38. B. B. N. Walker, "The Commerce of the Gaboon: Its History and Future Prospects," *Journal for the Society of Arts* 24 (May 12, 1876): 585–97, 586.

39. Bowdich, "A Visit to Empoöngwa," 302.

40. Lee, *Friendship's Offering*, 295.

41. Wilson reported that "most of the men, perhaps four fifths, speak intelligible English. A few speak imperfect French, Portuguese and English with equal freedom. The native language, which is pleasant to the ear, is particularly acquired by most of the captains who have been long engaged in the Gaboon trade"; "American Board of Commissioners for Foreign Missions," *The Missionary Herald, Containing the Proceedings of the American Board of Commissioners for Foreign Missions* 39, no. 6 (1843): 229–40, 231.

42. Karl David Patterson, *The Mpongwe and the Orungu of the Gabon Coast, 1815–1875: The Transition to Colonial Rule* (Stanford, CA: Stanford University Press, 1971), 57.

43. Bucher, *The Mpongwe of the Gabon Estuary*, 123.

44. T. E. Bowdich, *Mission from Cape Coast Castle*, 423. When he was eight to ten years old, Richard was sent to England on the Juno but was taken by a French privateer en route. The other boy arrived in France as planned. Both returned by 1818. Both could write and read. "Affaire de jeune nègre fils du prince du Gabon, pris sur le navire anglais la Junon," Archives nationales d'outre-mer, Sénégal et côtes d'Afrique, sous-série C^6 (1588/1810), FR ANOM COL C^6 1–35 (1809), 24. Patterson *The Mpongwe and the Orungu*, 106.

45. Bucher, *The Mpongwe of the Gabon Estuary*, 197–98. "When Mr. Henderson sailed from New York to Gaboon, there was on board the Son of one of the Kings of a District on that River.... He was constantly saying how they obtained the Negroes for Slaves in his Part of the Country, and that if he should be so fortunate as to find a Vessel in that River trading for Slaves, he would become a great Man"; "Report 1: Slaves: Evidence of Mr. David Henderson," *Reports of the Lords of the Committee of Council Appointed for the Consideration of All Matters Relating to Trade and Foreign Plantations* (March 29, 1789). Edward Bowdich recorded that English slavers, in contrast to French ones, were known by the Mpongwe to promise an education in England to the sons of the *oga* and then sell them into slavery; Bowdich, *Mission*, 425n. Henry Bucher, "John Leighton Wilson and the Mpongwe: The 'Spirit of 1776' in Mid-Nineteenth Century Western Africa," *Journal of Presbyterian History* 54, no. 3 (1976): 291–315, 296.

46. Bowdich, "A Visit to Empoöngwa," 318.

47. "Plate XXXI," Michael Praetorius, *Syntagma Musicum II, De Organographia parts I and II* (Wolfenbüttel: Elias Holwein, 1619), II.

48. Henry Bucher, "Canonization by Repetition: Paul du Chaillu in Historiography," *Revue française d'histoire d'outre-mer* 242–3 (1979): 15–32, 18.

49. See Pierre Sallée's *Disoumba: Liturgie musicale des Mitsogho du Gabon central* (Le Centre national de la recherche scientifique, 1969), http://videotheque.cnrs.fr/doc=410?langue=EN. Sallée describes (inaccurately as Ngolet has shown) the "Kele" as dispersed and close to extinction in ways that attest at once to their persecution as well as to their demi-nomadic lifestyle. Sallée blames Du Chaillu for "the invention of Pygmies." Du Chaillu printed what Sallée calls "un dessin fort précis d'une harpe qu'il remarque aux mains des Kele." Pierre Sallée, "L'arc et la harpe: contribution à l'histoire de la musique du Gabon" (PhD diss., Université de Paris X, 1985), 66, 77. These words, "l'idole est un monstreuse et indecent figure de bois, du sexe féminin," actually come from a description of a "Bakele" statue, described in Paul Du Chaillu, *L'Afrique sauvage: nouvelles excursions au pays des Ashangos* (Paris, Michael Lévy, 1868), 258.

50. T. E. Bowdich, *Mission from Cape Coast Castle*, 450. Lee, *Stories of Strange Lands*, 321.

51. On an 1858–59 expedition to find the source of the Como, Jules Édouard Braouezec reported that "on me montra sur une montagne un arbre gigantesque, où, selon leur tradition, Dieu créa les hommes." See his "Notes dur les peuplades riveraines du Gabon," *Bulletin de la Société de géographie* (May/June 1861): 345–59, 352.

52. Several visitors at Ngango noted the tall trees on the elevated site or "le bouquet d'arbres séculaires qui couronne le village du roi Georges." Méquet, "Nouvelles excursion," 283. Another French officer wrote of "le village du George, qu'on connait aisément de loin a une touffe de grands arbres"; M. Pigeard, Lieutenant de Vaisseau, "Exploration du Gabon, en Août et Septembre 1846," *Revue coloniale* 9 (March 1847): 263–95, 270–71.

53. For more on Mpongwe involvement in slavery and the Bakele, who did not own slaves themselves but administered slave convoys (often along paths lined by breadfruit trees planted under sixteenth-century Portuguese influence), see François Ngolet, "Reexamining Population Decline along the Gabon Estuary: A Case Study of the Bakèlè," in *Culture, Ecology, and Politics in Gabon's Rainforest*, ed. Michael C. Reed and James F. Barnes (New York: Edwin Mellen, 2001), 137–63, 145–46.

54. T. E. Bowdich, *Mission from Cape Coast Castle*, 427.
55. Voltaire, *Des Singularités de la nature* (London, 1768), 98–99.
56. Lee, *The African Wanderers*, 144.
57. T. E. Bowdich, *Mission from Cape Coast Castle*, 451.
58. Sallée, *L'arc et l'harpe*, 6.
59. Sallée, *L'arc et l'harpe*, 361–69.
60. For the guitar, see Mrs. Lee, *Stories of Strange Lands*, 341.
61. Kofi Agawu, *The African Imagination in Music* (New York: Oxford University Press, 2016), 72–73.
62. T. E. Bowdich, *Mission from Cape Coast Castle*, 448.
63. Steven Feld, "A Rainforest Acoustemology," in *The Auditory Culture Reader*, ed. Michael Bull and Les Back (New York: Berg, 2003), 223–39.
64. James L. Mackey, "Journal of a Tour in Western Africa (1853)," *Journal of Presbyterian History* 40, no. 2 (June 1962): 113–18, 116.
65. Thanks to Gaetano Speranza, "Mbaïki," a site more than six hundred miles inland in today's Central African Republic, now features prominently in the genealogical myth of the *ngombi* harp. In his exhaustive comparative morphology of the harps of Central Africa (as pillaged for Euro-American museums), Speranza identifies a harp (played by Ngbaka-speaking peoples on the right bank of Ubangi River and the forest-dwelling Ngombe-South speakers now just across the border in the DRC's Congo River) as the closest ancestor to the classic Gabonese exemplar. His test case is a ten-string anthropomorphic harp, also named *ngombi*, which was expropriated by Jean Chevalier at Mbaïki around 1931–33 and is now owned by the Musée de la Musique in Paris. France Cloarec-Heiss, "Les harpes: ce que leur nom révèle," and Gaetano Speranza, "Les harpes," in *La parole du fleuve: harpes d'Afrique centrale*, ed. Philippe Bruguière and Gaetano Speranza (Nanterre: Cité de la musique/musée de la Musique, 1999), 35–47, 40–41, 59–94, 90; also 280, 360.
66. Sallée takes seriously Du Chaillu's claim that "it is as though [the Bakele] were all their lives vainly fleeing from the dread face of death. This, indeed, is the refrain of all their sad songs, the burden of every fear. Having little else to lose, they seem to dread, more than any other people I ever saw, the loss of life. And no wonder; for after death is to them nothing. 'Death is the end.' 'Now we live; by-and-by we shall die; then we shall be no more.' 'He is gone; we shall never see him more; we shall never shake his hand again; we shall never hear him laugh again.' This is the dolorous burden of their evening and morning songs." Du Chaillu, *Explorations*, 432. Sallée, *L'arc et la harpe*, 75.
67. Sallée, *L'arc et la harpe*, 24.
68. Kairn A. Klieman, *The Pygmies were our Compass: Bantu and Batwa in the History of West Central Africa, Early Times to c. 1900 C.E.* (Portsmouth, NH: Heinemann, 2003).
69. See, for example, James W. Fernandez and Renate L. Fernandez, "'Returning to the Path'": The Use of Iboga(ane) in an Equatorial African Ritual Context and the Binding of Time, Space, and Social Relationships," *The Alkaloids: Chemistry and Biology* 56 (2001): 235–47.
70. Julien Bonhomme, "Le Miroir et le Crâne: Le parcours rituel de la société initiatique Bwete Misoko (Gabon)" (PhD diss., Ecole des Hautes Etudes en Sciences Sociales [EHESS], 2003).
71. Kairn A. Klieman, "Of Ancestors and Earth Spirits: New Approaches for In-

terpreting Central African Politics, Religion, and Art," in *Eternal Ancestors: The Art of the Central African Reliquary*, ed. Alisa LaGamma (New York: Metropolitan Museum of Art, 2007), 33–61, 49.

72. Klieman, "Of Ancestors and Earth Spirits," 51.

73. Du Chaillu printed what Sallée calls "un dessin fort précis d'une harpe qu'il remarque aux mains des Kele" in *L'arc et la harpe*, 66. Paul B. Du Chaillu, *Explorations and Adventures in Equatorial Africa* (New York: Harper, 1861), 339. The statue stood "in the very hilly country between the Ofoubou [Ofubu] and Ovenga [Doubanga] Rivers."

74. Klieman, "Of Ancestors and Earth Spirits," 38.

75. Patterson argues, in view of available clan genealogies, that Ngango was settled by Mpongwe clans from 1700–25, in *The Mpongwe and the Orungu of the Gabon Coast*, 67.

76. Patterson claims that powerful Ndiwa traders originally settled among the Pygmy first peoples around two hundred years. One legend has it that they were "birthed from the earth" at the estuary; others report that, by 1698, the Ndiwa were decimated after a century of Dutch attacks, in *The Mpongwe and the Orungu of the Gabon Coast*, 29. Annie Merlet, *Le pays des trois estuaires, 1471–1900* (Libreville: Centre Culturel Français, 1991), 14.

77. "Gaboon: Letter from Mr. Porter, October 1, 1851," *The Missionary Herald, Containing the Proceedings of the American Board of Commissioners for Foreign Missions* 48, no. 3 (1852): 83.

78. T. E. Bowdich, *Mission from Cape Coast Castle*, 449.

79. Christopher Gray suggests that this kind of linguistic parsing can get messy, writing that this precolonial "masculine association or secret society" was known as "mwiri" among speakers of Gisir, Sango, Varama, Vungu, Punu, Lumbu, Nzabi, Ngowe and Eviya; "omwetsi," "mwetsi," or "mwetvi" among speakers of Mpongwe or Seke; "mweli" or "mwele" among speakers of Kele or Benga; "mwedi" among speakers of Nzadji; "mwee" or "va-mwei" among speakers of Tsogo; "omweli" among speakers of Apindji; and "omwiri" among speakers of Nkomi and Orungu. Associations performing similar functions were called "vasi" among Galwa speakers, "indo" or "ukuku" among the Mpongwe, and "ungala" among speakers of Kele and peoples of the upper Ogooué. "[The] coastal Mpongwe, who were exposed to and absorbed the traditions of numerous interior peoples during the Atlantic trade, had three different societies, mwetvi, ukuku and indo performing similar functions"; Gray, *Territoriality, Ethnicity, and Colonial Rule*, 164.

80. Igor Kopytoff, "The Internal African Frontier: The Making of African Political Culture," in *The African Frontier: The Reproduction of Traditional African Societies*, ed. Igor Kopytoff (Bloomington: Indiana University Press, 1987), 1–86, 53.

81. Sallée, *L'arc et la harpe*, 218.

82. Sallée, *L'arc et la harpe*, 413.

83. Sallée, *L'arc et la harpe*, 218. See also Philippe Bruguière, "La harpe du Gabon, pirogue de vie," in *La parole du fleuve: harpes d'Afrique centrale*, ed. Philippe Bruguière and Gaetano Speranza (Nanterre: Cité de la musique/musée de la Musique, 1999), 151–55.

84. Klieman, "Of Ancestors and Earth Spirits," 52.

85. E. T. A. Hoffmann, "Beethovens Instrumentalmusik," *Zeitung für die elegante Welt* 13, no. 246–7 (1813): 1964–67 and 1973–75.

86. *Letters of Felix Mendelssohn to Ignaz and Charlotte Moscheles* (Boston: Ticknor, 1888), 3.

87. C. T., "To the Editor/On the Works of Handel," *The Quarterly Musical Magazine and Review* 1 (1818): 280–84, 281.

88. Lee, *Stories of Strange Lands*, 320.

89. Andrew S. Curran, "Rethinking Race History: The Role of the Albino in the French Enlightenment Life Sciences," *History and Theory* 48 (October 2009): 151–79, 153.

90. Georges Léopold C. F. D. Cuvier, *The Animal Kingdom, with Additional Descriptions by E. Griffith and Others* (London: Whittaker, 1827), 157.

91. T. E. Bowdich, *Mission from Cape Coast Castle*, 450.

92. James Cowles Prichard, *Researches into the Physical History of Man* (London: John and Arthur Arch, 1813), 20.

93. Braouezec, "Notes dur les peuplades riveraines du Gabon," 356.

94. Judy Knight, "Relocated to the Roadside: Preliminary Observations on the Forest Peoples of Gabon, *African Study Monographs* 28 (2003): S81–S121.

95. Chris Ballard, "Strange Alliance: Pygmies in the Colonial Imaginary," *World Archaeology* 38, no. 1 (2006): 133–51. Julien Bonhomme, Magali De Ruyter, Guy-Max Moussavou, "Blurring the Lines. Ritual and Relationships between Babongo Pygmies and Their Neighbours (Gabon)," *Anthropos* 107, no. 2 (2012): 387–406.

96. Kairn A. Klieman, "Pygmy Paradigm," *"The Pygmies Were Our Compass": Bantu and Batwa in the History of West Central Africa, Early Times to c. 1900 C.E.* (Portsmouth NH: Heinemann, 2003), 3–34. Roger Blench, "Are the Africa Pygmies an Ethnographic Fiction?" *Challenging Elusiveness: Central African Hunter-Gatherers in a Multidisciplinary Perspective*, ed. Karen Biesbrouck, Stephen Elders, and Gerda Rossel (Leiden: CNWS, 1999), 41–60.

97. T. E. Bowdich, *Mission from Cape Coast Castle*, 451.

98. For more on the "catacomb of harps" or wall paintings "discovered" in the tomb of Ramesses III by Scottish explorer James Bruce, see Charles Burney, "The History of Egyptian Music," in *The General History of Music from the Earliest Ages to the Present Period* (London: Becket, 1776), I:198–232, 225. Arthur A. Moorefield, "James Bruce: Ethnomusicologist or Abyssinian Lyre?" *Journal of the American Musicological Society* 28, no. 3 (1975): 493–514.

99. Hector Berlioz, "De l'instrumentation (premier article) [la harpe]," *La Revue et gazette musicale de Paris* 8, no. 60 (November 21, 1841): 510–12. See Guillaume André Villoteau, *De l'état actuel de l'art musical en Egypte, ou relation historique et descriptive des recherches et observations faites sur la musique en ce pays*, which is volume 14 of *Description de l'Egypte ou recueil des observations et des recherches qui ont été faites en Egypte pendant l'expédition de l'armée* (Paris: Panckoucke, 1812), 260–70.

100. Graham Johnson, *Gabriel Fauré: The Songs and Their Poets, with Translations of the Song Texts* by Richard Stokes, Guildhall Research Studies 7 (London: The Guildhall School of Music and Drama and Ashgate, 2009), 252.

101. Richard Taruskin, *Oxford History of Western Music*, 6 vols. (Oxford: Oxford University Press, 2005), IV:97.

102. For example, Elijah Wald, *Escaping the Delta: Robert Johnson and the Invention of the Blues* (New York: Amistad, 2004); Samuel Charters, *The Roots of the Blues: An African Search* (Bloomington: Indiana University Press, 1981); Michael Theodore Coolen, "The Fodet: A Senegambian Origin for the Blues?" *The Black Perspective in*

Music 10, no. 1 (1982): 69–84; and Paul Oliver, *Savannah Syncopators: African Retentions in the Blues* (New York: Stein & Day, 1970).

103. Gerhard Kubik, *Africa and the Blues* (Jackson: University Press of Mississippi, 1999), 120–21.

104. A. M. Jones, "Blue Notes and Hot Rhythm," *Newsletter (African Music Society)* 1, no. 4 (June 1951): 9–12. Alfons M. Dauer, "Grunlagen und Entwicklung des Jazz," *Jazz Podium* 4 (1955): 6. Gerhard Kubik, "Spuren des Blues. Ein Bericht aus Nigerian," *Jazz Podium* 6, no. 3 (1961): 157–60. See also Hans Werner Zimmermann, "Die 'Neutrale Terz' als Symptom," *Melos* 1, no. 20 (1953): 137–40.

105. Erich Moritz von Hornbostel, "Musik," in Günter Tessmann, *Die Pangwe*, 2 vols. (Berlin: Wasmuth, 1913), II:320–57, 329, 351.

106. Von Hornbostel, "Musik," 2. Megan Vaughan, *Curing Their Ills: Colonial Power and African Illness* (Stanford, CA: Stanford University Press, 1991). Luise White, *Speaking with Vampires: Rumor and History in Colonial Africa* (Berkeley: University of California Press, 2000). Nancy Rose Hunt, *A Nervous State: Violence, Remedies, and Reverie in Colonial Congo* (Durham, NC: Duke University Press, 2016).

Chapter 2

1. François-Henri-Joseph Castil-Blaze, "Paër," *Revue de Paris* 58 (1838): 5–34, 14. "Sur la célèbre cantatrice Banti," *Revue musicale* 8/9 (July 3, 1830): 281. "Banti," *A Dictionary of Music and Musicians*, ed. George Grove, 2 vols. (London, Macmillan, 1879), I:136. For Banti's 1806 autopsy, see Jessica Peritz, "The Female Sublime: Domesticating Luigia Todi's Voice," *Journal of the American Musicological Society* 74, no. 2 (2021): 235–88.

2. Tabarié worked among the Montpellier physicians, opening a health establishment there in 1840 before finally opening another in Paris, after settling there in 1852. See "Tabarié: Matérieux pour server a la biographie d'Auguste Comte," *La Revue occidentale philosophique, sociale et politique: organe du positivism* 11, no. 107 (1895): 86–91. Tabarié innovations were detailed by his disciple at Montpellier, E. Bertin in *De L'Emploi et des effets du bain d'air comprimé* (Paris: J-B Baillière, 1855).

3. For more on Chopin and Pravaz's holistic methods, see Davies, *Romantic Anatomies of Performance* (Berkeley: University of California Press, 2014), 111.

4. Alfred François Donné, future inventor of the photoelectric microscope and recent discoverer of *Trichomonas vaginalis*, reviewed this March 18, 1839, meeting of the Academy of Sciences, where Tabarié's "pneumatic machine" was introduced under the auspices of Humboldt and Arago. Donné remarked that those who had treated Falcon had made good use of "compressed air." He also noted that the mathematician and grandson of the leader of the *Les Vingt-quatre Violons du Roi* under Louis XVI, Louis-Benjamin Francoeur, lost his voice after a bout of "catarrhe pulmonaire," which made respiration impossible. Yet, after eleven days of treatment, Francoeur could sing again. "Observe that the door [to Tabarié's chamber] has the same dimensions as those to our apartments," Donné wrote, "and that one enters it with hat on head without stooping, and that the chamber itself is no less than eight to ten feet high with a width capacious enough to contain a bed, a table, chairs, a small piano, and so on" (translation by the author). Dr. A. L. Donné, "Académie des Sciences: Séance du 18 mars," *Journal des débats* (March 20, 1839): 1–2.

5. Ralph Barnes Grindrod, *The Compressed Air Bath: A Therapeutic Agent in Affections of the Respiratory Organs* (London: Simpkin, Marshall and Co., 1860), V, 23.

6. Grindrod, *The Compressed Air Bath*, 25.

7. Théophile Gautier, "Galerie des belles actrices. Mlle Falcon," *Le Figaro* 11, no. 83 (January 5, 1838): 3. He was following a report in *Le Courrier des Théâtres* (December 4, 1836), which reported that "until around three o'clock in the afternoon, [Falcon] has full use of every means of voice, but that, from that moment on, her voice becomes an embarrassment, in ways that absolutely prohibit its use" (translation by the author).

8. "Physiologie.—Recherches sur les effets des variations dans la pression atmosphérique à la surface du corps," *Comptes rendus hebdomadaires des séances de L'Académie des Sciences* 6 (1838): 898–99. See also Tabarié's follow-up "Influence thérapeutique de la pression atmosphérique sur l'économie animale," given on June 18, 1838: PH. B., "Académie des Sciences," *Le Siècle* 3/178 (June 28, 1838): 2c.

9. Arthur de Bonnard, *Description des Néothermes, et relation des principales guérisons obtenues par l'emploi des appareils médicaux de toute nature établis dans cette maison de bains et de santé* (Paris: Pollet, 1842), 7.

10. David Cairns, *Berlioz: Servitude and Greatness, 1832–1869* (Berkeley: University of California Press, 2000), 174.

11. Arthur de Bonnard, *Description des Néothermes*.

12. Fonds 47J D'Arcet, Institut de France, Académie des sciences.

13. Alain Corbin, *The Foul and the Fragrant: Odor and the French Social Imagination* (Cambridge, MA: Harvard University Press, 1986), 123–26.

14. Joshua Cole, *The Power of Large Numbers: Population, Politics, and Gender in Nineteenth-Century France* (Ithaca, NY: Cornell University Press, 2000), 3.

15. J.-P.-J. D'Arcet, *Collection de mémoires relatifs à l'assainissement des ateliers, des édifices publics, et des habitations particulières* (Paris: L. Mathias, 1843), xvi.

16. Isabelle Moindrot, "Quelles natures sur les scènes du grand opéra français au 19e siècle?," unpublished paper, https://medias.ircam.fr/xbf4713.

17. Jean-Baptiste Fressoz, "Gaz, gazomètres, expertises et controverses Londres, Paris, 1815–1860," *Courrier de l'environnement de l'INRA* 62 (2012): 31–56.

18. As Kimberly White points out, the Opéra, in 1836, boasted a medical team of five doctors, two surgeons, and one pharmacist. She writes that these professionals were dedicated, in particular, to the "surveillance of female artists' bodies," which "led inevitably to the supervision and medicalization of their sexuality and sexual health"; "The Cantatrice and the Profession of Singing at the Paris Opéra and Opéra Comique, 1830–1848" (PhD diss., McGill, 2012), 154.

19. Louis Véron, *Mémoires d'un bourgeois de Paris*, 5 vols. (Paris: Gabrielle de Gonet, 1853–55). Louis Marie Quicherat, *Adolphe Nourrit: sa vie, son talent, son caractère, sa correspondance*, 3 vols. (Paris: L. Hachette, 1867), I:102.

20. Diana R. Hallman, "Fromental Halévy within the Paris Opéra: Composition and Control," in *Music, Theater, and Cultural Transfer: Paris, 1830–1914*, ed. Annegret Fauser and Mark Everist (Chicago: University of Chicago Press, 2009), 29–48, 34.

21. For a description of the *les baignoires*, see "Spectacles," *Le Constitutionnel* 157 (June 6, 1831): 3–4, 4a.

22. Moreau, *Courrier Français* (June 3, 1831), 4; *Le Globe* (June 5, 1831), 624.

23. *La Gazette de France* (June 4, 1831): 1–3.

24. See *L'Entr'acte* (June 2, 1831): 1–2.

25. *La Gazette de France* (June 4, 1831): 1–3.

26. Walter Benjamin, *The Arcades Project*, trans. Howard Eiland and Kevin McLaughlin (Cambridge, MA: Belknap, 1999), 48.

27. "The compressed air bath, in a way, may be regarded as the victory over our atmosphere. We possess thus the means of augmenting or diminishing at will its natural pressure, which determines the equilibrium of the fluids circulating in our bodies." Joannis Milliet, *De l'Air Comprimé comme agent Thérapeutique* (Lyon: Louis Perrin, 1854), 25.

28. In 1848, as chapter 3 observes, Marx and Engels famously wrote that "all that is solid melts into air, all that is holy is profaned, and man is at last compelled to face with sober senses his real conditions of life, and his relations with his kind." Karl Marx and Friedrich Engels, *Communist Manifesto*, ed. Gareth Stedman Jones (London: Penguin, 1987), 222.

29. Céline Frigau Manning, "Singer Machines: Describing Italian Singers, 1800–1850," *Opera Quarterly* 28 no. 3–4 (2012): 230–58.

30. Bill Brown, "Thing Theory," *Critical Inquiry* 28, no. 1 (2001): 1–22. Jonathan Lamb, *The Things Things Say* (Princeton, NJ: Princeton University Press, 2011). Jane Bennett, *Vibrant Matter: A Political Ecology of Things* (Durham, NC: Duke University Press, 2010).

31. For an account of the shift from the metaphor of the "mimetic" machine to the "transcendental" motor in the history of the body, see Anson Rabinach, "From Mimetic Machines to Digital Organisms: The Transformation of the Human Motor," in *A Cultural History of the Human Body in the Age of Empire*, ed. Michael Sappol and Stephen P. Rice (Oxford: Berg, 2014), 237–59.

32. Longet set out his pioneering theory of periodic flow in these terms: "Air possesses, in its flow, the same viscosity as any liquid, and it obeys the same laws; the flow of gases, through orifices pierced in plates, is periodically variable, and this periodicity in speed of flow determines, in the outside air, sound vibrations analogous, although less intense, to those produced by a siren." See Longet, *Traité de physiologie*, 2 vols. (Paris: Victor Masson, 1852), I:122. For perhaps the first scientific description of voice as the product of periodicity, see Cagniard de la Tour's 1840 account of the acoustic role of pressurized air at the vocal folds in "Société philomatique de Paris/ Fin de la séance de 2 février 1840," *L'Institut* 9, no. 376 (March 11, 1841): 82–83.

33. Leo Spitzer, "Milieu and Ambiance: An Essay in Historical Semantics," *Philosophy and Phenomenological Research* 3/2 (1942): 1–42.

34. Diana R. Hallman, *Opera, Liberalism, and Antisemitism in Nineteenth-Century France: The Politics of Halévy's* La Juive (Cambridge, UK: Cambridge University Press, 2007), 17.

35. Jan Goldstein, *The Post-Revolutionary Self: Politics and Psyche in France, 1750–1850* (Cambridge, MA: Harvard University Press, 2005), 154.

36. Goldstein, *The Post-Revolutionary Self*, 13.

37. Later in the century, Hippolyte Taine derided Cousin's ideology as a "nice relaxing tepid bath into which fathers dip their children as a healthful precaution." The "comfort structures" so beloved of Cousinian establishment philosophy, built under Louis-Philippe from 1830, discouraged public discontent. Goldstein, *The Post-Revolutionary Self*, 154, 160.

38. Anselm Gerhard, *The Urbanization of Opera Music Theater in Paris in the Nineteenth Century* (Chicago: University of Chicago Press, 2000), 208.
39. Gerhard, *The Urbanization of Opera Music Theater*, 168.
40. Benjamin, *The Arcades Project*. Michel Foucault, *The Birth of Biopolitics: Lectures at the Collège de France 1978-79*, ed. Michel Senellart (New York: Palgrave Macmillan, 2004).
41. "The body is an unfailing barometer," one air-obsessed commentator from the period concurred: "being a gauge of much wider and far more powerful chemical and climatological forces." Grindrod, here, is citing Pierre Foissac's *De la météorologie dans ses rapports avec la science de l'homme et principalement avec l'hygiène publique*, 2 vols. (Paris: J.-B. Baillière, 1854) in his *The Compressed Air Bath*, 26.
42. Denis Dodart, "Mémoire sur les causes de la voix de l'homme et de ses différents tons," *Académie royale des sciences* (1700): 244-93. Félix Savart, "Mémoire sur la voix humaine," *Journal de physiologie expérimentale et pathologique* 5 (1825): 367-93.
43. In London, Frank Romer summarized Despiney's position succinctly: "On examining the vocal tube, it will be found to correspond in formation to most musical wind instruments; it has the power to elongate or shorten itself by means of the trachea. It also corresponds with wind instruments in general, in the fact that its fundamental notes depend upon the length of its tube, as with the trumpet, French horn, flute, clarinet, &c.; but it differs from all other wind instruments, in its power to contract itself at the different points that I have before mentioned." See Romer, *The Physiology of the Human Voice* (London: Leader & Cock, 1845), 6-7.
44. "Chaque passion, si légère qu'en soit la nuance, affecte à sa manière l'organe vocal et en modifie la capacité, la conformation, la rigidité, en un mot, toutes les conditions physiques. L'organe alors est un moule, qui se transforme sans cesse sous l'action des passions diverses, et communique leur empreinte aux sons qu'il laisse échapper." García claimed that "admirable souplesse" made "l'organe [vocal] alors est un moule qui se transforme sans cesse sous l'action des passions diverses" in *Traité complet de l'art*, II:54.
45. "Toute modification produite dans le timbre d'un son a son origine dans une variété analogue de la disposition intérieure du tube que parcourt la voix...; puisqu'un tuyau flexible peut subir graduellement un nombre infini de modifications, il suit de là que les differences de son se multiplient à l'infini." García, "Émissions et qualité de la voix," *La France musicale* 3, no. 39 (September 27, 1840): 354.
46. I am borrowing the excellent phrase of Julianne C. Bard on *son filé* in her translation and edition of *Introduction to the Art of Singing* by Johann Friedrich Agricola (Cambridge, UK: Cambridge University Press, 1995), 84.
47. "Le chanteur doit donc conformer l'instrument," García explained, "de manière à diriger les rayons sonores contre la partie osseuse du palais et à les réfléchir dans la direction de l'axe de la bouche, ce qui accroît le son et en favorise l'émission." García, "Émissions et qualité de la voix," 354.
48. This translation, from Fournié's *Physiologie de la voix et de la parole* (Paris: Delahaye, 1866), appears in Joseph Joal, *On Respiration in Singing*, trans. R. Norris Wolfenden (London: F. J. Rebman, 1893), 103.
49. Bill Brown, "Thing Theory," *Critical Inquiry* 28, no. 1 (2001): 1-22. Emily Green, "Memoirs of a Musical Object, Supposedly Written by Itself: It-Narrative and Eighteenth-Century Marketing," *Current Musicology* 95 (2013): 193-213.

50. On it-narratives, see for example Mark Blackwell, *The Secret Life of Things: Animals, Objects, and It-narratives in Eighteenth-Century England* (Lewisburg, PA: Bucknell University Press, 2007).

51. This was "le plus merveilleux qu'un organe ait offert depuis qu'il existe des chanteurs au monde"; G. Bénedit, "Madame Damoreau," *Galerie des artistes dramatiques de Paris* (Paris: Marchant, 1841–48).

52. Cinti-Damoreau took to the boards of the Salle Le Peletier in a season wherein the Théâtre-Italien and the Opéra were governed by the same administration. "Mademoiselle Cinti appeared on both sides," wrote Castil-Blaze in 1826, this born-and-bred Parisienne finally bringing that Italianate vocal virtuosity learned from her mentor, Angelica Catalani, to the "prudes and wigmakers" of "le vieux conservatoire des cris dramatiques"; François-Joseph Fétis, *Biographie universelle des musiciens et bibliographie générale de la musique* (Brussels: Meline, Cans, 1837), III:242. At the time of Castil-Blaze's rumination on Banti's larynx, meanwhile, Cinti-Damoreau's multiform apparatus was being heard at a third theater and in a third idiom. Almost exactly a decade later, she would famously defect from the Opéra, after a protracted contractual dispute, to become the original *première chanteuse à roulades* at the Opéra comique. Her larynx thus transmogrified thrice. As Berlioz might say, this final mutation made her organ one of the "pleasant and useful commodities daily manufactured" by that episodic, bourgeois, saccharine, and "bastard genre." Berlioz opined in 1836 that Opéra comique "is a bastardized genre which tires partisans of vaudeville by its musical exuberance, while it irritates lovers of music by its musical blemishes"; Hector Berlioz, "De l'Opéra-Comique," *Revue et Gazette musicale* 3, no. 38 (September 18, 1836): 323–25, 323. Elsewhere, he lambasted the genre as "pleasant and useful commodities which are daily manufactured in the manner of meat-pies"; Hector Berlioz, *The Memoirs of Hector Berlioz*, trans. and ed. David Cairns (New York: A. A. Knopf, 2002), 513.

53. "Vous est-il arrivé de fixer vos yeux sur un diamant où viennent se réfléchir mille paillettes de mille couleurs différentes? le regard est ébloui par toutes ces formes insaisissables; il n'analyse pas, il tombe en extase, il admire sans réfléchir; mais quand l'éblouissement est passé, lorsque la vision s'est évanouie, l'âme s'échauffe, l'esprit s'exalte, et l'on se prend d'enthousiasme pour cet effet magique de la nature." Léon Escudier, *Études biographiques sur les chanteurs contemporains* (Tessier: Paris, 1840), 221–22.

54. "Là cette pluie de perles," one witness observed, "vulgairement appelée des sons, qui tombe scintillante, dorée, du gosier le plus mélodieux qu'ait formé la nature"; "Théâtre de L'Opéra comique," *Le Monde dramatique* 2 (1835): 155–57, 157.

55. Blanchard: "Mme Damoreau est, sans contredit, la plus parfaite cantatrice que la France ait vu naître."

56. G. Bénedit, "Madame Damoreau," *Galerie des artistes dramatiques de Paris* (Paris: Marchant, 1841–43): 1–4.

57. See White, "The Cantatrice and the Profession of Singing," 14. Maurice Alhoy, *Grande biographie dramatique: Ou Silhouette des acteurs, actrices, chanteurs* (Paris, 1824), 82.

58. "Le talent lui est venu comme il vient au rossignol"; Escudier, "Mme Cinti-Damoreau" *La France musicale* 3, no. 13 (March 29, 1840): 129–31, 129.

59. Mary Ann Smart, "Roles, Reputations, Shadows: Singers of Grand Opéra," in *Cambridge Companion to Grand Opera*, ed. David Charlton (Cambridge, UK: Cambridge University Press, 2003), 108–28.

60. "Elle avait fait de l'air du Serment, une telle merveille d'exécution, qu'après la chute du rideau, la salle entière le redemanda avec des cris d'enthousiasme, et qu'elle dut le répéter, ce qui ne s'était jamais vu à l'Opéra. 'C'est de la dentelle de Chantilly,' disait Auber en parlant de quelques vocalises qu'elle avait brodées dans sa dernière retraite"; A de Rovray, "Laure-Cinti Damoreau," *Le Moniteur de la mode* 2, no. 716 (1863): 213–24, 224.

61. "Le souffle de Mme Damoreau est en quelque sorte du chant," exclaimed Escudier, "tous les accens de sa voix ont une simplicité, une grâce, un charme qui traversent votre oreille comme autant de brises harmonieuses." Escudier, "Mme Cinti-Damoreau," 131.

62. Petrus Camper, *Œuvres sur l'histoire naturelle, la physiologie, et l'anatomie comparé*, 3 vols. (Paris: H. J. Jansen, 1803), 460.

63. "Charmant rossignol, gazouillant avec grâce et méthode, luttant de pair avec la flûte de Tulou wrote Pierre Hédoin, "mais coupant les mots eu deux, en trois, et n'en faisant souvent point parvenir une seule syllabe à l'oreille de ses auditeurs!" P. Hédoin, "Académie Royale de Musique/De l'abandon des anciens compositeurs," *Le monde dramatique* 2 (1835): 291–97.

64. These words, printed in *Le Rénovateur* of March 16, 1834, are translated in Hervé Lacombe, *The Keys to French Opera in the Nineteenth Century*, trans. Edward Schneider (Berkeley: University of California Press, 2001), 44.

65. "Nous attendons de l'action, et Marguerite nous chante les ruisseaux et les fêtes, les rossignols et la fauvette, dont les refrains d'amour sont répétés par les échos des montagnes." Joseph Mainzer, "Académie Royale de Musique/*Les huguenots*," *Le monde dramatique* (1835): 247–53, 250.

66. García, *Traité complet de l'art du chant*, 2 vols. (Paris, 1847), II, 21.

67. Austin Caswell, "Mme Cinti-Damoreau and the Embellishment of Italian Opera in Paris: 1820–1845," *Journal of the American Musicological Society* 28, no. 3 (1975): 459–92.

68. "Nouvelles de Paris," *Courrier des théâtres* 12, no. 3897 (August 6, 1829): 4.

69. The critics recalled that "M. Jouy, in his *Fernand Cortez*, had already presented us a voyager-princess in the character of Amazily who, in spite of her plumes and muslin dress, frequents barracks like a true canteen-keeper" and that "décidément, à l'Opéra M. Jouy aime les dévergondées." "Théâtres. Académie Royale de Musique," *Le Messager des chambres* 217 (August 5, 1829): 3–4.

70. "Que faire de ces instruments si la sensibilité, l'intelligence et l'inspiration ne les animent? . . . Elles ont la voix, le savoir musical, un larynx agile; il leur manque l'âme, le cerveau et le cœur"; Hector Berlioz, *Mémoires*, ed. Pierre Citron (Paris: Flammarion, 1991, 1870; repr.), 440.

71. "Mlle Falcon, succédant a Mme Damoreau, n'avait pas une tâche facile: la vocalization légère n'est pas ce qui lui convient mieux," apparently in the *Revue et Gazette musicale* 2, no. 50 (December 13, 1835); cited in Bouvet, *Cornélie Falcon*, 95.

72. "C'est bien Cornélie Falcon; sa beauté est sauvée," wrote Théophile Gautier in 1840, "qu'importe sa voix!" Gautier, "Académie royale de musique," 2.

73. "Sa voix est très étendue (deux octaves, de si à ré), c'est un dessus bien caractérisé, voix blanche et d'un beau métal, comme disent les Italiens; attaquant la note avec audace et justesse, la faisant vibrer avec éclat, lui donnant tour à tour un accent flatteur, pénétrant ou plein de charme et de tendresse. . . . Je n'ai pu juger encore du degré de sa force sous le rapport de l'agilité; mais n'eût-elle pas une vocalisation digne

de rivaliser avec les virtuoses à la mode, on pourrait aisément le lui pardoner," Castil-Blaze, "Album," *Revue de Paris* 41 (1832): 49–54, 53.

74. Charles Bouvet, *Cornélie Falcon* (Paris: Librairie Félix Alcan, 1927), 115. Falcon's organ produced "des sons faibles et bien dégénérés de ceux que produit ordinairement sa belle voix"; "Nouvelles," *Revue et Gazette musicale de Paris* 4, no. 11 (March 12, 1837): 91.

75. For Louis Gentil's gossip and an excellent account of Falcon, see Kimberly White, "The Cantatrice and the Profession of Singing at the Paris Opéra and Opéra Comique, 1830–1848" (PhD diss., McGill, 2012), 226.

76. "Sa voix tout net s'étrangle dans son gosier. Elle chancelle, elle tombe, comme foudroyée. On la relève, le visage ruisselant de larmes. La salle est debout, anxieuse, oppressée, dans un impressionnant et respectueux silence. [Her mentor and teacher] Nourrit en ses bras la presse, la console, fou de douleur; il couvre de baisers comme un père ferait de son enfant—le beau visage que désormais n'éclaireront plus les feux de l'apothéose. La Falcon est morte au theater." This extract, from an article originally in *L'Eclair*, was reprinted in Sergine, "Les Echoes de Paris," *Les Annales politiques et littéraires* 28 (1897): 150.

77. Vincent Giroud, "Cornélie Falcon: une interprète d'exception," in *L'art officiel dans la France musicale au XIX siècle*, ed. Alexandre Dratwicki and Agnès Terrier (2010), 18–19, http://bruzanemediabase.com/eng/Musical-scholarship-on-line/Symposia-at-the-Opera-Comique/Official-Art-in-Musical-France-in-the-19th-Century-2010.

78. Jean-Louis Tamvaco, *Les cancans de l'Opéra: chroniques de l'Académie Royale de Musique et du Théâtre, à Paris sous les deux restaurations* (Paris: CNRS Editions, 2000), I, 195. Period speculation about moral retribution as a cause for Falcon's loss of voice (particularly for her sexual agency) recalls long-standing parallels drawn between women's vocal equipment and vaginas, as Bonnie Gordon shows in *Monteverdi's Unruly Women: The Power of Song in Early Modern Italy* (Cambridge, UK: Cambridge University Press, 2004). 77–79.

79. Hector Berlioz, "Théâtre de l'Opéra: débuts de Duprez dans Les Huguenots," *Journal des débats* (May 17, 1837): 1. Escudier, "L'Alboni," *La France musicale* 35, no. 10 (August 29, 1847): 285–86.

80. "Ce sont toujours les longs yeux passionnement noirs, la chaude paleur juive le bel ovale mélancholique, les cheveau abondans et superbes, le meme ardeur inquiète et nerveuse"; Théophile Gautier, "Académie royale de musique.—Représent. de Mlle Falcon," *La Presse* 4 (March 18, 1840): 2.

81. Charles Baron de Boigne, *Petits mémoires de l'Opéra* (Paris: Librairie nouvelle: 1857), 202.

82. "La pauvre fille n'a pu surmonter l'émotion à laquelle elle était visiblement en proie, et qu'elle est tombée, sans connaissance, entre les bras de Duprez: on a dû l'emporter." "Académie royale de musique. Représentation de Mlle Falcon," *Indépendance* (March 18, 1840): 182; in *Nineteenth-Century French Singers: A Press Anthology*, compiled by Kimberley White, http://music.sas.ac.uk/sites/default/files/files/FMC/19th-Century_French_Singers_A_Press_Anthology_2012.pdf.

83. White, "Revue dramatique. Académie royale de musique," 185.

84. "Théâtres," *Le Figaro* 2, no. 110 (March 19, 1840): 2.

85. Mary Ann Smart, "Roles, Reputations, Shadows," 116.

86. Boigne, *Petits mémoires de l'Opéra*, 202.

87. Edmond Burat de Gurgy, *Biographie des acteurs de Paris* (Paris: Chez les éditeurs, 1837), 10.

88. Charles Bouvet, "Quelques souvenirs sur Cornélie Falcon," in White, *Nineteenth-Century French Singers*, 202.

89. "Le devoir dont elle est l'esclave, et l'amour qui la dévore." Consumed by youthful passion, furthermore, she cannot know of the consequences of this "terrible invasion"; Stéphen de La Madelaine, *Études pratiques de style vocal*, 2 vols. (Paris: Joseph Albanel, 1868), II:1–42, 4.

90. "l'ouvrage le mieux fait et le mieux monté que j'aie connue dans ma longue existence de critique et de musicien"; La Madelaine, *Études pratiques de style vocal*, 5, 15.

91. Smart, "Roles, Reputations, Shadows," 116.

92. "Trois accords en *pizzicato* sur les cordes graves, séparés par les soupirs et demi-soupirs soigneusement indiqués, ressemblent à des battement de coeur interrompus par l'effroi, et leur *pianissimo* donne l'idée du mystère intérieur qui s'accomplit chez la jeune fille." La Madelaine, *Études pratiques*, 5.

93. "Ce serait alors la nature, au lieu de son imitation, qui est tout l'affaire de l'art." La Madelaine, *Études pratiques*, 7.

94. La Madelaine, *Études pratiques*, 7.

95. La Madelaine, *Études pratiques*, 14.

96. La Madelaine, *Études pratiques*, 13.

97. "Mais au moment où elle arrivait à la phrase musicale: 'Et cependant il va venir,' elle s'arrêta subitement, ne pouvant plus proférer un son, et fit tristement des signes d'impuissance"; Ernest Denormandie, *Temps passé, jours présents: (Notes de famille)* (Paris: Librairie Hachette, 1900), 236.

98. Denormandie, *Temps passé, jours presents*, 236.

99. Jules Janin, "Théâtre de l'Opéra/ Première représentation de *la Juive*," *Journal des débats* (February 25, 1835): 1–2, 2.

Chapter 3

1. Henry Knight, "To the Editor of the 'Musical News,'" *Musical News* 7 (July 21, 1894), 58.

2. "Birmingham Musical Festival," *The Leeds Times* 702 (August 29, 1846): 4. The critic spoke of "a mysterious effect" produced in that brutal recitative where Elijah condemns the Baalite priests to be slaughtered, which also featured "the continuous rolling of the drums."

3. Charles Burney, "Commemoration of Handel," *An Account of the Musical Performances in Westminster Abbey* (London: Musical Fund, 1785), 8. Grove wrote of the late eighteenth-century instrument built by Drury Lane's John Asbridge, whose drum came into the possession of Thomas Paul Chipp, "the well-known kettledrummer" and was still used from 1884 at Crystal Palace. Grove reported that even larger drums were made for the Sacred Harmonic Society (47 and 43 inches in diameter), though "no tone can be got from such overgrown instruments." George Grove, "The Tower Drums," *A Dictionary of Music and Musicians*, 4 vols. (New York: Macmillan, 1889), IV:157.

4. "Distin's Monster Drum at the Handel Festival," *Illustrated London News* 866, no. 30 (June 27, 1857): 627.

5. "A mysterious effect is produced in the recitative where Elijah condemns the

Baalite priests to be slaughtered, by the continuous rolling of the drums, which suggests the notion of the prophet's edict being delivered in thunder." "Birmingham Musical Festival," *The Leeds Times* 702 (August 29, 1846): 4.

6. F. G. Edwards, "First Performances. IV. Mendelssohn's Elijah," *The Musical Times and Singing-Class Circular* 32, no. 584 (October 1, 1891): 588–92, 589.

7. "Birmingham Musical Festival," *The Standard* 6879 (August 27, 1846): 3. See also Jack Werner, *Mendelssohn's Elijah* (London: Chappell, 1965), 15.

8. Raymond Williams famously theorized "structures of feeling" in *A Preface to Film* (with Michael Orrom, 1954), further explicating the phrase in *The Long Revolution* (1961) and particularly *Marxism and Literature* (1977). Diarmid A. Finnegan, "Exeter-Hall Science and Evangelical Rhetoric in Mid-Victorian Britain," *Journal of Victorian Culture* 16 (2011): 46–64.

9. Carolyn Merchant, *Reinventing Eden: The Fate of Nature in Western Culture* (London: Routledge, 2003).

10. Kristin Asdal, "The Problematic Nature of Nature: The Post-Constructivist Challenge to Environmental History," History and Theory 42, no. 4 (2003): 60–74.

11. Lawrence Buell, "Toxic Discourse," *Critical Inquiry* 24, no. 3 (1998): 639–665, 648.

12. Buell, "Toxic Discourse," 656.

13. *Elijah* is far from the only oratorio or opera before 1900 to deal with environmental catastrophe and its management. Governing the physical world is a persistent theme in French *tragédies en musique* (Lully-Quinault's 1682 *Persée* for example), as discussed in Olivia Bloechl's *French Opera and the Political Imaginary in Old Regime France* (Chicago: Chicago University Press, 2018), 26–27.

14. Referred to as such by American public health campaigner Charles-Edward Amory Winslow in 1923. C-E. A. Winslow, *The Evolution and Significance of the Modern Public Health Campaign* (New Haven, CT: Yale University Press, 1923).

15. Bill Luckin, "Revisiting the Idea of Degeneration in Urban Britain, 1830–1900," *Urban History* 33, no. 2 (2006): 234–52, 240.

16. Will Steffen et al., "The Trajectory of the Anthropocene: The Great Acceleration," *The Anthropocene Review* 2 no. 1 (2015): 81–95. William F. Ruddiman, "The Anthropogenic Greenhouse Era Began Thousands of Years Ago," *Climatic Change* 61, no. 31 (2003): 261–93.

17. Mary Somerville, *Physical Geography* (London: John Murray, 1848), I, 1.

18. Victoria L. Cooper, *The House of Novello: Practice and Policy of a Victorian Music Publisher* (London and New York: Routledge, 2003), 81.

19. The literature on smoke and fog in Victorian Britain includes Peter Brimblecombe, "Late Victorian Air Pollution," in *Smoke and Mirrors: The Politics and Culture of Air Pollution*, ed. E. Melanie DuPuis (New York: New York University Press, 2004); Bill Luckin, "'The Heart and Home of Horror': The Great London Fogs of the Late Nineteenth Century," *Social History* 28, no. 1 (2003): 31–48; Stephen Mosley, *The Chimney of the World: A History of Smoke Pollution in Victorian and Edwardian Manchester* (London: Routledge, 2001); Stephen Mosley, "A Disaster in Slow Motion: The Smoke Menace in Urban Industrial Britain," in *Learning and Calamities: Practices, Interpretations, Patterns*, ed. Heike Egner, Marén Schorch, and Martin Voss (London: Routledge, 2014), 114–31; and Peter Thorsheim, *Inventing Pollution: Coal, Smoke and Culture in Britain since 1800* (Athens: Ohio University Press, 2006).

20. Mark Whitehead, *State, Science and the Skies: Governmentalities of the British Atmosphere* (Oxford: Wiley-Blackwell, 2009), 2.

21. Frances Rosser Hullah, *Life of John Hullah* (London: Longman & Green, 1886), 39.
22. Carlos Flick, "The Movement for Smoke Abatement in 19th-Century Britain," *Technology and Culture* 21, no. 1 (1980): 29–50.
23. S. E. Finer, *The Life and Times of Chadwick*, 293.
24. Edwin Chadwick, *Report to Her Majesty's Principal Secretary of State for the Home Department, from the Poor Law Commissioners, on an Inquiry into the Sanitary Condition of the Labouring Population of Great Britain* (London: Clowes, 1842), 369.
25. *Health of Towns Association: Report of the Sub-Committee on the Answers returned to Questions addressed to the Principal Towns of England and Wales* (London: Clowes, 1848), 3.
26. *Health of Towns Association*, 3.
27. *Health of Towns Association*, 72.
28. A study of Birmingham's health was printed by Chadwick's Health of Towns Commission in 1845, as R. A. Slaney, *Report on the State of Birmingham and Other Large Towns* (London: Clowes, 1845).
29. I have cited the translation printed in a booklet produced to celebrate the five hundredth concert of the Sacred Harmonic Society in London's Exeter Hall: *The Sacred Harmonic Society: A Thirty-Five Years' Retrospect Annual Report: With an Appendix and the Rules of the Society* (London: Sacred Harmonic Society, 1867), 11.
30. Douglass Seaton, "Preface," in Felix Mendelssohn Bartholdy, *Elias/Elijah: op. 70* (Kassel: Bärenreiter, 2009), iv–xiv, vi.
31. Quoted in Friedhelm Krummacher, "Art—History—Religion: On Mendelssohn's Oratorios *St. Paul* and *Elijah*," in *The Mendelssohn Companion*, ed. Douglass Seaton (Westport, CT: Greenwood, 2001), 299–382.
32. Cited, for example, in Leon Botstein, "The Price of Assimilation and Affirmation: Reconstructing the Career of Felix Mendelssohn," in *Mendelssohn and His World*, ed. R. Larry Todd (Princeton, NJ: Princeton University Press, 1991), 5–42, 31.
33. Richard Taruskin, "Mendelssohn and Civic Nationalism," in *The Oxford History of Western Music*, 6 vols. (Oxford: Oxford University Press, 2005), III:166–77.
34. Steven Baur, "Music, Morals, and Social Management: Mendelssohn in Post–Civil War America," *American Music* 19, no. 1 (2001): 64–130, 81.
35. J. S. Dwight, "Music as a Means of Culture," *Dwight's Journal of Music* 30, no. 14 (September 24, 1870): 313–5, 313.
36. See letters of September 25, 1829; August 25, 1829; and May 28, 1831. Mendelssohn wrote: "There is no question that that smoky nest [London] is my preferred city and will remain so. I feel quite emotional when I think of it." *Letters of Felix Mendelssohn from Italy and Switzerland*, trans. Lady Wallace (Boston: Oliver Ditson, 1863), 159.
37. Celia Applegate ponders the usefulness of such terms as "internationalism," "cultural internationalism" (Iriye) or "cosmopolitanism" (Kant) in "Mendelssohn on the Road: The Anglo-German Symbiosis," in *The Oxford Handbook of the New Cultural History of Music*, ed. Jane F. Fulcher (New York: Oxford University Press, 2011), 228–44, 231.
38. For Elijah's Christological program, see Jeffrey S. Sposato, *The Price of Assimilation: Felix Mendelssohn and the Nineteenth-Century Anti-Semitic Tradition* (Oxford: Oxford University Press, 2006), 128–46. See also Martin Staehelin, "Elijah, Johann Sebastian Bach, and the New Covenant: On the Aria 'Es ist genug' in Felix Mendelssohn-

Bartholdy's Oratorio *Elijah*," trans Susan Gillespie, *Mendelssohn and His World*, ed. R. Larry Todd (Princeton, NJ: Princeton University Press, 1991), 121–36.

39. Cited in Sinéad Dempsey-Garratt, "Mendelssohn's 'Untergang': Reconsidering the Impact of Wagner's 'Judaism in Music,'" in *Mendelssohn Perspectives*, ed. Angela Mace and Nicole Grimes (London: Routledge, 2012), 31–48, 36.

40. George Bernard Shaw, *London Music in 1888–1889 as Heard by Corno di Bassetto (Later known as Bernard Shaw) with Some Further Autobiographical Particulars* (London: Constable, 1937), 251.

41. George Grove, "Oratorio," in *A Dictionary of Music and Musicians*, ed. J. A. Fuller Maitland, 5 vols. (New York: Macmillan, 1907), III:474–510, 501.

42. G. B. Shaw, *Shaw's Music: The Complete Musical Criticism*, ed. Dan H. Laurence, 3 vols. (London: Bodley Head, 1981), I:788.

43. It would take generations for the composer's late Victorian image as the antipode of Wagner to develop. Wagner, himself attending a Sacred Harmonic Society oratorio in 1855, derided that "spirit of English Protestantism," which induced Exeter Hall listeners to clutch one-shilling scores in the same pious way churchgoers clutched prayerbooks; the composer blamed the "perpetual cold" and cited Dante: "The Inferno, indeed, became a never-to-be-forgotten reality in that London atmosphere." Richard Wagner, *My Life*, 2 vols. (New York: Dodd, Meade, 1911), II:634–35.

44. Garratt's attack is launched against Charles Rosen's neo-Wagnerian view that Mendelssohn's music peddles a "religion and piety which dispenses with the unnecessary and inconvenient trappings of dogma and ritual." "This is kitsch," argues Rosen, "insofar as it substitute for religion itself the emotional shell of religion." James Garratt, "Mendelssohn's Babel: Romanticism and the Poetics of Translation," *Music & Letters* 80, no. 1 (1999): 23–49.

45. *Fac Simile and Translation of an Inscription by . . . Prince Albert in a Book of the Words of the Oratorio, 'Elijah,' Presented to Dr. Mendelssohn . . . in April 1847* (London, 1847).

46. As quoted by Joseph F. Ropes, "Dr. Lepsius's Universal Linguistic Alphabet," *Bibliotheca Sacra and Theological Review* 13, no. 52 (1856): 681–98, 685.

47. I am paraphrasing Werner, *Mendelssohn's Elijah*, 459.

48. Matthew Teismann, "An Emerging International: The Imperial Gaze of the Monster Globe in 1851," *Fabrications* 27, no. 1 (2017): 3–21.

49. Alexander von Humboldt, *Kosmos—Entwurf einer physischen Weltbeschreibung*, 5 vols. (Stuttgart: Cotta, 1845–1860).

50. Von Humboldt, *Kosmos*, 55.

51. Alexander von Humboldt, *Cosmos: A Sketch of the Physical Description of the Universe*, trans. O. C. Otté, 5 vols. (New York: Harper, 1850), I:71.

52. For this purpose, Humboldt wrote a long letter to the president of the Royal Society, the Duke of Sussex on April 23, 1836, presenting the case for an expanded weather network; see S. R. C. Malin, "Geomagnetism at the Royal Observatory, Greenwich," *Quarterly Journal of the Royal Astronomical Society* 37 (1996): 65–74, 68.

53. John Tresch, *The Romantic Machine: Utopian Science and Technology After Napoleon* (Chicago: University of Chicago Press, 2012), 84.

54. Katharine Anderson, *Predicting the Weather: Victorians and the Science of Meteorology* (Chicago: University of Chicago Press, 2005), 38.

55. Anderson, *Predicting the Weather*, 8.

56. Anderson, *Predicting the Weather*, 38.

57. Anderson, *Predicting the Weather*, 6.
58. Anderson, *Predicting the Weather*, 4.
59. Anderson, *Predicting the Weather*, 39.
60. Charles Dickens, "Chapters 4 and 5: Hard Times," *Household Words* 211 (April 8, 1854): 165–70, 168.
61. David Horovitz dates the popularization of the term "Black Country" to Rev. William Gresley's *Colton Green: A Tale of the Black Country, or a Region of Mines and Forges in Staffordshire* (1846), in "The Black Country," *Journal of the English Place-Name Society* 43 (2011): 25–34. See also Peter M. Jones, *Industrial Enlightenment: Science, Technology and Culture in Birmingham and the West Midlands, 1700–1820* (Manchester, UK: Manchester University Press), 22. On the "Musical Hall" proposal, see Rachel Elizabeth Milestone, "'A New Impetus to the Love of Music': The Role of the Town Hall in Nineteenth-Century English Musical Culture" (PhD diss., University of Leeds, 2009), 75.
62. Peter Brimblecombe, *The Big Smoke* (London: Metheun, 1987). Stephen Mosley, *The Chimney of the World* (Cambridge, UK: White Horse Press, 2001).
63. For an intimate biography, see the account of friend William Ayrton, "Obituary—Joseph Moore," *The Gentleman's Magazine* 35 (June 1851): 670–71.
64. Joseph Moore's papers (MS 1292/8/6). MS1292, Letters and Papers of Joseph Moore (1766–1851), Engraver and Die Sinker, Relating to the Birmingham Triennial Music Festival. Birmingham Public Library.
65. Richard Brown, "Chartist Lives: Joseph Sturge," Looking at History (blog), September 3, 2007, http://richardjohnbr.blogspot.com/2007/09/chartist-lives-joseph-sturge.html.
66. "The Musical Festival," *Aris's Birmingham Gazette* 5465 (August 17, 1846): 3.
67. "The Birmingham Musical Festival," *The Musical World* 36, no. 40 (October 2, 1858): 628. "Birmingham Musical Festival," *The Leeds Times* 702 (August 29, 1846): 4. See also Gauntlett's score in the Birmingham Public Library.
68. "The Musical Festival," *Aris's Birmingham Gazette* 5465 (August 17, 1846): 3.
69. "Birmingham Musical Festival," *The Leeds Times* 702 (August 29, 1846): 4.
70. "Birmingham Musical Festival," 4.
71. Nicholas Thistlethwaite, "The Organ in Birmingham Town Hall," *The Musical Times* 125, no. 1700 (1984): 593, 595–97, 599.
72. "Birmingham Musical Festival," *Gentleman's Magazine* 2 (1834): 520.
73. Julius Benedict, *The Life and Works of the Late Felix Mendelssohn Bartholdy* (London: John Murray, 1850), 51–52.
74. Quoted in Frederick George Edwards, *The History of Mendelssohn's Oratorio "Elijah"* (London: Novello, 1896), 81.
75. Quoted in Edwards, *The History of Mendelssohn's Oratorio "Elijah"*, 87.
76. George Dawson, "Music" and "Mendelssohn and His Works," in *Shakespeare and Other Lectures*, ed. George St. Clair (London: Kegan Paul, Trench, 1888), 434–43, 434.
77. Dawson, "Music" and "Mendelssohn and His Works," 441.
78. Quoted in Eric J. Evans, *The Forging of the Modern State: Early Industrial Britain, 1783–1870* (London: Longman, 1983), 295.
79. John Meikleham, *On the History and Art of Warming and Ventilating Rooms and Buildings* (London: George Bell, 1845), 20.

80. William McDonnell, *Exeter Hall: A Theological Romance* (Boston: William White, 1873), 3.

81. Diarmid A. Finnegan, "Exeter-Hall Science and Evangelical Rhetoric in Mid-Victorian Britain," *Journal of Victorian Culture* 16 (2011): 46–64.

82. Meikleham, *On the History and Art of Warming and Ventilating*, 186.

83. John Evelyn, *Fumifugium: or, the Inconveniencie of the Aer and Smoak of London* (London: Godbid, 1661), 6.

84. *Letters of Giuseppe Verdi*, ed. Charles Osborne (New York: Holt, Rinehart and Winston, 1972), 46.

85. "Learned Societies," *The Reader* 7 (February 14, 1963): 173.

86. Cited in Lieut-Colonel Sykes, "Atmospheric Disturbances and a Remarkable Storm at Bombay on the 6th April 1848," *Report of the Eighteenth Meeting of the British Association for the Advancement of Science* (London: John Murray, 1849), 41–47, 41.

87. "Further Disturbance in Berlin," *Times*, June 19, 1848, 8.

88. Karl Marx, *Manifest der Kommunistischen Partei (Manifesto of the Communist Party)* (London: J. E. Burghard, 1848), 5.

89. Marx, *Manifest der Kommunistischen Partei*.

90. Karl Marx, "Speech at the Anniversary of the *People's Paper* (1856)," in *The Political Writings*, ed. David Fernbach (London: Verso, 2019), 633–34.

91. The full passage: "The last vial is now trembling in the angel's hand, or rather is pouring out its contents; its first sprinklings smite the earth, and at this hour the nations begin to feel its influence, and thrones to rock beneath the first of its vibrations," in John Cumming, "Lecture 23: The Church During the Effusion of the Vials," in *Apocalyptic Sketches or Lectures on the Book of Revelation . . . at Exeter Hall* (London: Hall, 1850), 442–59, 442.

92. "Editorial," *The North Devon Journal* 1280 (December 24, 1848).

93. "Editorial."

94. John Cumming, *God in Science: A Lecture . . . in Exeter Hall* (London: Reed and Pardon, 1851), 27.

95. Cumming, *God in Science*, 27.

96. George Eliot, "Evangelical Teaching: Dr. Cumming," *Westminster Review* 4 (October 1855): 436–62.

97. Eliot traveled to London on April 21 and wrote to her friend and neighbor Mary Sibree on May 10, 1847: "I heard Mendelssohn's new oratorio, 'Elijah,' when I was in London. It has been performed four times in Exeter Hall to as large an audience as the building would hold—Mendelssohn himself the conductor. It is a glorious production." See George Eliot, *George Eliot's Life, as Related in Her Letters and Journals*, ed. J. W. Cross, 4 vols. (Leipzig: Bernard Tauchnitz, 1885), I:151.

98. John Cumming, "Lecture 22: The Seventh Vial," *Apocalyptic Sketches; or Lectures on the Book of Revelation. Delivered in the Large Room, Exeter Hall* (London: Shaw, 1849), 422–41, 422.

99. John Cumming, "Lecture 33: 1848; Or; Prophecy Fulfilled," *Apocalyptic Sketches: Lectures on the Book of Revelation, Second Series* (Philadelphia: Lindsay and Blakiston, 1854), 489–511, 495. This series was delivered at his nearby Crown Court Scotch Church off Covent Garden.

100. Cumming, "Lecture 22: The Seventh Vial," 424.

101. John Cumming, *Apocalyptic Sketches: Lectures on the Book of Revelation, Second Series* (Philadelphia: Lindsay and Blakiston, 1854), 513.

102. Cumming, *Apocalyptic Sketches*, 189.

103. John Cumming, "Music in Its Relation to Religion," *Sharpe's London Journal* 11 (1850): 143–48. For the full lecture, see John Cumming, "Music in Its Relation to Religion," *Twelve Lectures Delivered Before the Young Men's Christian Association in Exeter Hall* (London: James Nisbett, 1850), 373–410, 395.

104. John Cumming, "Sacred Music," *Lectures Delivered Before the Young Men's Christian Association in Exeter Hall* (London: James Nisbet, 1859), 425–42, 433.

105. Cumming, "Music in Its Relation to Religion," 391.

106. Cumming, "Music in Its Relation to Religion," 377.

107. Charles Babbage, "On the Permanent Impression of Our Words and Actions on the World We Inhabit," *The Ninth Bridgewater Treatise, A Fragment* (London: John Murray, 1838), 108–19, 111–2.

108. Babbage, "On the Permanent Impression of Our Words," 115.

109. Babbage, "On the Permanent Impression of Our Words," 109.

110. B. Rainbow, "The Rise of Popular Music Education I," *The Land without Music: Musical Education in England, 1800–1860, and Its Continental Antecedents* (London: Novello, 1967).

111. John Hullah, *Wilhem's Method of Teaching Singing Adapted to English Use (Hullah's Manual)* (London: J. W. Parker, 1841).

112. Chester L. Alwes, "Choral Music in the Culture of the Nineteenth Century," ed. André de Quadros, *The Cambridge Companion to Choral Music* (Cambridge, UK: Cambridge University Press, 2012), 27–42, 32.

113. "Exeter Hall," *The Musical World* 24, no. 25 (June 23, 1849): 398.

114. *Henry Fothergill Chorley: Autobiography, Memoir, and Letters*, ed. Henry G. Hewlett (London: Richard Bentley), 164. Henry Chorley, "Sacred Harmonic Society," *Athenaeum* 1017 (April 24, 1847): 441. John Hullah, *The Duty and Advantage of Learning to Sing. A Lecture* (London: John Parker, 1846), 4.

115. Hullah, *The Duty and Advantage*, 21. J. S. Dwight, "Music as a Means of Culture," 329.

116. John Hullah, "The Management of the Speaking Voice," *Contemporary Review* 10 (1869): 416–29, 423.

117. "Minute respecting Vocal Music," *Minutes of the Committee of Council on Education*, 1844 (London: Clowes, 1845), 151–56.

118. "Art. V. Part Music. By John Hullah," *Monthly Review* 3 (1842): 49–59, 58.

119. John Timbs, *Curiosities of London* (London: David Bogue, 1867), 287.

120. "Exeter Hall," *The Morning Post* 23371 (November 2, 1848): 5.

121. "Sacred Harmonic Society," *The Times* 20660 (November 30, 1850): 8.

122. "Sacred Harmonic Society," *The Musical Times and Singing Class Circular* 4, no. 78 (November 1, 1850): 87.

123. "Music," *Daily News*, November 2, 1848, 4.

124. "Sacred Harmonic Society," *The Musical World* 23, no. 45 (November 4, 1848): 705–7.

125. "Exeter Hall," *The Morning Post*, November 2, 1848, 5.

126. "Music," *Daily News*, November 2, 1848, 4.

127. James Stephen, "The Clapham Sect," *Edinburgh Review* 81, no. 161 (1844): 251–305, 305.

128. Stephen, "The Clapham Sect," 305.

129. Charles Dickens, "The Niger Expedition," *The Examiner* 2116 (August 19, 1848): 531–32.

130. A plaque in the Heritage Center of the building, given by the Chartered Institution of Building Services Engineers, claims as such.

131. George Dolby, *Charles Dickens as I Knew Him: The Story of the Reading Tours* (London: T. Fisher Unwin, 1887), 14.

132. "Opening of St. George's Hall, Liverpool," *The Musical World* 32, no. 38 (1854): 625–29.

133. For a detailed description of the organ and hall, see Robert Boult, "St George's Hall," *The Liverpool Mercury* (September 19, 1854). Also, William Mackenzie, "On the Mechanical Ventilation and Warming of St George's Hall, Liverpool," *Civil Engineer and Architects Journal* 27 (1864): 136.

134. D. B. Reid, "Notes on the Revision of Architecture in Connection with the Useful Arts, with Special Illustrations of the Ventilation of St George's Hall, Liverpool," *Journal of the Arts* 3, no. 125 (April 20, 1855): 380–86, 381. Reid, *Illustrations of the Theory and Practice of Ventilation*, xiii–xiv.

135. D. B. Reid, *Ventilation: A Reply to Misstatements Made by the Times and the Athenaeum in Reference to Ship and Buildings Ventilated by the Author* (London: Madden and Malcolm, 1845), 6.

136. Critics worried about buildings erected above "a mighty furnace—a volcano in a state of unceasing activity"; B., "Reid Ventilation," *The Times*, April 9, 1846, 7; "Editorials," *The Times*, June 8, 1846, 4.

137. B., "Reid Ventilation," 7. "[Reid] threatens to deal with the air as the Puritans dealt with religion," was the complaint, "until they made it too good for ordinary mortals to live in"; B., "Letters to the Editor," *The Times*, April 13, 1846, 5.

138. D. B. Reid, *Illustrations of the Theory and Practice of Ventilation . . . with Remarks . . . on the Communication of Sound* (London: Longman, 1844), 15–16.

139. Reid, *Illustrations of the Theory*, 71.

140. Suzanne MacLeod, *Museum Architecture: A New Biography* (New York: Routledge, 2013), 42. See Jessica Moody, "The Memory of Slavery in Liverpool in Public Discourse from the Nineteenth Century to the Present Day" (PhD diss., University of York, 2014), 289–308.

141. See the database "Legacies of British Slave-ownership": https://www.ucl.ac.uk/lbs/person/view/43667.

142. "Legacies of British Slave-ownership": https://www.ucl.ac.uk/lbs/person/view/19514; https://www.ucl.ac.uk/lbs/person/view/44514; https://www.ucl.ac.uk/lbs/person/view/8821.

143. Edward J. Gillin, "Science on the Niger: Ventilation and Tropical Disease during the 1841 Niger Expedition," *Social History of Medicine* 31, no. 3 (2018): 605–26; Dustin Valen, "Imperial Atmospheres: Race and Climate Control on the Niger," *ABE Journal* 17 (2020), http://journals.openedition.org/abe/8106. "Ventilating Arrangements Adopted in the Niger Steam Ships," *Friend of Africa: Society for the Extinction of the Slave Trade and for the Civilization of Africa* 1, no. 5 (March 24, 1841): 71.

144. Cited in "The African Institution," *The Friend of Africa* 2 (January 15, 1841): 26–27.

145. See Philip D. Curtin's "The Age of Humanitarianism, 1830–1852" in the second volume of *The Image of Africa: British Ideas and Action, 1780–1850*, 2 vols. (Madison: University of Wisconsin Press, 1964).

146. Howard Temperley, *White Dreams, Black Africa: The Antislavery Expedition to the Niger* (New Haven, CT: Yale University Press, 1991).

147. Steven Connor, "Choralities," *Twentieth-Century Music* 13, no. 1 (2016): 3–23.

148. Fyodor Dostoyevsky, *Winter Notes on Summer Impressions* (London: Oneworld, 2008), 50.

149. Here I am paraphrasing Jan Golinski's excellent *British Weather: The Climate of Enlightenment* (Chicago: University of Chicago Press, 2007), 12.

150. "Almost equally effective was [the] singing of the magnificent quartet and chorus, 'Holy, holy,' [featuring soprano Henriette Sontag] during the performance of which the entire audience rose." "Gloucester Musical Festival," *The Musical World* 25, no. 37 (September 14, 1850): 589–98, 594.

151. "Mendelssohn's 'Elijah,'" *Dwight's Journal of Music* 1, no. 25 (September 25, 1852): 196–98, 197.

152. "Mendelssohn's 'Elijah,'" 197. Proof copy of *Elijah* [for 1847 Ewer edition] with numerous corrections and alterations in several hands, some by Mendelssohn and William Bartholomew. Hanna Holborn Gray Special Collections Research Center, University of Chicago Library, alc M2003.M5E4 18-b.

153. "Mendelssohn's 'Elijah,'" 197.

154. "Mendelssohn's 'Elijah,'" 198.

155. Timothy Mitchell, *Carbon Democracy: Political Power in the Age of Oil* (London: Verso, 2011), 1.

156. James Russell Lowell, "Democracy: An Address delivered before the Midland Institute, Birmingham, England," *Pall Mall Budget* 837, no. 32 (October 10, 1884): 13–15, 15.

Chapter 4

1. Heinaccius, in his discussion of slavery, observed that the air of certain countries, ipso facto, makes inhabitants of those countries slaves, quoted in Thomas Cobb, *An Inquiry into the Law of Negro Slavery in the United States of America* (Philadelphia: T. & J. W. Johnson & Co., 1858), 1, 132. Cobb cited the principle such historians of slave law as Sue Peabody dub the "freedom principle," first established under French jurisprudence in 1738, that "the air of a free state is too pure for a slave to breathe." The original *cause célèbre* involved Pampy, a twenty-four-year-old enslaved carpenter and Julienne, an eighteen-year-old "Congo" couturière. The case of their manumission established the legal precedent, declared in 1738 Paris, that "tout homme qui y habite est libre," or, as the second sentence of a 1776 legal report put it, both persons "ont appris que l'air qu'on y respire [en France] est celui de la liberté." Gabriel Pampy, *Memoir pour un Nègre et une Négresse qui réclament leur liberté contre un Juif* (Paris: P. G. Simon, 1777), 1. In their "Free Soil: The Generation and Circulation of an Atlantic Legal Principle," *Slavery & Abolition* 32 (2011): 331–39, 331, Peabody and Keila Grinberg write: "Interestingly, the terms 'free soil' and 'free air' do not appear generally before the nineteenth century." They cite Seymour Drescher, *Abolition: A History of Slavery and Antislavery* (Cambridge, UK: Cambridge University Press, 2009), and detail earlier anticipations of the "free air" principle, which may date to the Middle Ages: Sue Peabody, "Slavery, Freedom, Statehood and the Law in the Atlantic World, 1700–1888," in *Democracy and Culture in the Transatlantic World: Third Interdisciplinary Conference, October 2004* (Växjö, Sweden: Växjö University, 2005).

2. Juliana Salles Machado, "Ilha Caviana: Sobre as suas Paisagens, Tempos e Transformações," *Amazônica: Revista de Antropologia* 6, no. 2 (2014): 283–313.

3. For alleged African/slave origins, see "Yellow Fever in the Cape Verde Islands in the Year 1868," *Medical Times and Gazette* 1 (January 30, 1869): 119–20. Batby-Berquin, "Note *sur le développement de la récente épidémie de fièvre jaune* à la Guadeloupe," *Archives de médecine navale* 12 (1869): 440–53. Alexander Turnbull, "Medical Journal of HMS *Cracker*, from 1 January to 31 December 1870: Surgeon Notes Regarding the Outbreak of Yellow Fever at Rio de Janeiro in 1869–70," The British National Archives, Kew, ADM 101/289/1B. J. F. da Silva Lima describes the quarantine conditions he ordered at Salvador, Bahia in April 1869 in "A *febre amarela importada pelo vapor Guiscardo*. Transmissão da moléstia a uma pessoa nesta cidade," *Gazeta Médica da Bahia* 4, no. 75 (1869): 25–28.

4. Percy Alvin Martin, "The Influence of the United States on the Opening of the Amazon to the World's Commerce," *The Hispanic American Historical Review* 1, no. 2 (1918): 146–62.

5. Joseph Beal Steere, *Narrative of a Visit to Indian Tribes of the Purus River, Brazil* (Washington, DC: Government Printing Office, 1903), 378, 387, 393.

6. As early as 1580–1620, enslaved Africans, *vaqueiros* (cowboys), and *ribeirinhos* (river-dwellers) had been forcibly removed to this region, first by British slavetraders, to work the cattle fazendas; Flávio dos Santos Gomes and H. Sabrina Gledhill, "A 'Safe Haven': Runaway Slaves, Mocambos, and Borders in Colonial Amazonia, Brazil," *Hispanic American Historical Review* 82, no. 3 (2002): 469–98.

7. The myth of the Amazon as a "vazio africano" betrays the intensity of transatlantic projects to enforce whitening and botanicization; José Maria Bezerra Neto, "*Do vazio africano à presença negra*: historiografia, fontes e referências sobre a escravidão africana na Amazônia," ed. Luiz Carlos Laurindo Junior, Pedro Monteiro Neves, *Escravidão urbana e abolicionismo no Grão-Pará (século XIX)* (Belém: Paco Editorial, 2020).

8. Nelson Papavero, William L. Overal, Dante M. Teixeira, Janet Hinshaw, "The Travels of Joseph Beal Steere in Brazil, Peru and Ecuador (1870–1873)," *Arquivos de Zoologia* 39, no. 2 (2008): 87–269, 121.

9. Steere described the style of the dance as a *landeau*, and "Portuguese." For the best account of the genealogy of the *lundu*, see Kim Sauberlich, "'Dances of Contagion': The Lundu and the National Body in Independent Brazil," unpublished paper, Society for Ethnomusicology (November 8, 2019); and Barbara Browning, *Infectious Rhythm: Metaphors of Contagion and the Spread of African Culture* (New York: Routledge, 1998).

10. Papavero et al., "The Travels of Joseph Beal Steere," 121.

11. Papavero et al., "The Travels of Joseph Beal Steere," 121.

12. "The ladies were not treated with . . . respect and reverence." See Papavero et al., "The Travels of Joseph Beal Steere," 112, 114. At Mexiana, Wallace witnessed a lay cult with "two of the oldest negroes" conducting a religious service in front of a makeshift altar strewn with saints "painted and gilt in a most brilliant manner," chanting "part of the vesper service of the Roman Catholic Church, and all join in the responses with much fervour, though without understanding a word"; Alfred R. Wallace, *A Narrative of Travels on the Amazon and Rio Negro* (London: Reeve, 1853), 92–93.

13. A. P. Gelpi, "Saint Sebastian and the Black Death," *Vesalius* 4, no. 1 (1998), 23–30.

14. Now registered as "intangible heritage" by Brazil's Instituto do Patrimônio Histórico e Artístico Nacional in 2013, the Festividade do Glorioso São Sebastião in Cachoeira do Arari, held in Belém for the nine days before January 20, has grown to epidemic proportions, amassing ten thousand pilgrims annually, involving processions of the icon of the saint, the lifting and toppling of the saint's flag-mast to inaugurate the perilous rainy season, and *ladainhas* (Latin chant litanies) of the sort heard and recorded by Steere. Not even the Círio de Nazaré is as venerated in the Marajó wetlands.

15. Rei Sebastião is a European military ancestral spirit, as opposed to a Black or Amerindian entity, born on January 20, 1554, the real-life king of Portugal, who battled the great Lisbon plague of 1569 and went missing in action while crusading in what is now northern Morocco. Portuguese Sebastianism has long hoped for the prophetic return of this Messianic savior-figure to rescue devotees from disease and suffering.

16. Life spirits suffuse these territories: the "beasts" of Lago Guajarás or Lago Arari, the *encantados* of the shoreline of Salvaterra, the brute forces of nature, called *caruás*, inhabiting environments at Soure. Raymundo Heraldo Maués and Gisela M. Villacorta name the islands of Maiandeua (in the municipality of Maracanã) and Fortaleza (in the municipality of São João de Pirabas) in "Pajelança e encantaria amazônica," ed. Reginaldo Prandi, *Encantaria Brasileira: o livro dos mestres, caboclos e encantados* (Rio de Janeiro: Pallas, 2001), 11–58, 19.

17. Seth and Ruth Leacock, *Spirits of the Deep: A Study of an Afro-Brazilian Cult* (Garden City, NY: Anchor, 1975).

18. Legend tells that the *encantados* of Sebastian's pantheon, longing to escape the invisible world, will one day "rise to the surface of the earth and all of the humans in São Luís and its vicinity will sink into the lower depths." Leacock, *Spirits of the Deep*, 140.

19. In 1972, the "Children of King Sebastião" or so-called *filhos da lua* (children of the moon) attracted the attention of a medical research team of the World Health Organization, who classified 3 percent of residents as persons with albinism. Madian de Jesus Frazão Pereira, "'Filhos do Rei Sebastião,' 'Filhos da Lua': construções simbólicas sobre os nativos da Ilha dos Lençóis," *Cadernos de campo* 13, no. 13 (2005): 61–74.

20. Napaleão Figueiredo, "Todas as divindades se encontram nas 'encantarias' de Belém," *Ci. & Tróp.*, Recife 9, no. 7 (1981): 51–66, 58.

21. For example: https://afinsophia.org/wp-content/uploads/2020/01/WhatsApp-Video-2020-01-21-at-18.14.24.mp4?_=2.

22. Leacock, *Spirits of the Deep*, 138.

23. See, in particular, Napaleão Figueiredo, "Cidade dos encantados: pajelanças, feitiçarias e religiões afro-brasileiras na Amazônia: a constituição de um campo de estudo; 1870–1950" (PhD diss., Universidade Estadual de Campinas, 1996).

24. Friedrich Nietzsche, *On the Genealogy of Morality*, ed. Keith Ansell-Pearson, trans. Carol Diethe (Cambridge, UK: Cambridge University Press, 1994), 158.

25. Walter Mignolo has written that "the colonial wound is not limited to the subalterns or the damnés; it cuts across the social strata" in *The Darker Side of Western Modernity: Global Futures, Decolonial Options* (Durham, NC: Duke University Press, 2011), 291.

26. Kim Sauberlich, "Contagious Bodies: Sexual and Musical Transmission in

Brazilian Lundu Songs at the Dawn of Abolition," unpublished paper, Society for Ethnomusicology (October 31, 2021).

27. Gilles Deleuze, "Postscript on the Societies of Control," *October* 59 (1992): 3–7.

28. "Negro Colonization; Brazil. Proposed by Our Minister as a Field for Colonization," *New York Times*, December 28, 1862, 2.

29. Paul Christopher Johnson, ed., *Spirited Things: The Work of "Possession" in Afro-Atlantic Religions* (Chicago: University of Chicago Press, 2014).

30. On "recursive dispossession," see Robert Nichols, *Theft Is Property! Dispossession and Critical Theory* (Durham, NC: Duke University Press, 2020).

31. The justification for property ownership, Brenna Bhandar writes in her analysis of modern property law, "remain bound to a concept of the human that is thoroughly racial in its makeup"; see Brenna Bhandar, *Colonial Lives of Property: Law, Land, and Racial Regimes of Ownership* (Durham, NC: Duke University Press, 2018), 4.

32. It was in this generation that a musicology of racial profiling and biometric surveillance took root. Take, for example, the magisterial *Histoire générale de la musique depuis les temps les plus anciens jusqu'à nos jours* (1869–70) by Belgian instrument collector and music critic François-Joseph Fétis. The progress of music, he claimed in the first sentence of his six-volume global history, could only be understood through the lens of race. "L'histoire de la musique," these lines proclaimed, "est inséparable de l'appréciation des facultés spéciales des races qui l'ont cultivée." See Jann Pasler, "Theorizing Race in Nineteenth-Century France: Music as Emblem of Identity," *Musical Quarterly* 89, no. 4 (2006): 459–504.

33. Jacques Derrida, "Plato's Pharmacy," *Dissemination*, trans. Barbara Johnson (Chicago: University of Chicago Press, 1981), 63–171. Bernard Stiegler, *What Makes Life Worth Living: On Pharmacology* (Cambridge, UK: Polity, 2010).

34. Joaquim Nabuco, *Abolitionism: The Brazilian Antislavery Struggle*, ed. Robert Conrad (Urbana: University of Illinois Press, 1977), 103.

35. Nabuco, *Abolitionism*, 172.

36. "Provincial," *Anglo-Brazilian Times* 6, no. 4 (February 23, 1870): 1.

37. "It is recognized by this name ['negrohead'] by the people of Pará," according to Bruce Warren, "Notes on the Collection and Preparation of Pará Indiarubber," *Journal of the Society of Arts* (June 5, 1874): 691–92, 691. Warren was employed in the installation of the submarine Pernambuco-Pará telegraph system from Recife to Belém, a sounding system dependent on the insulating properties of rubber. He advocated for the use of Pará rubber in telegraphic thermoplastic rather than gutta percha. The plantation lands along the Guamá River to the south of Belém were regreening, as slaveholders and steam navigation companies turned their attention to the extraction of latex.

38. Oscar de la Torre, *The People of the River: Nature and Identity in Black Amazonia, 1835–1945* (Chapel Hill: University of North Carolina, 2018), 13.

39. According to leading scholar of the region Vicente Salles, this was despite the fact that the last shipment of "raw slaves" to Belém occurred as early as 1834; Vicente Salles, *O negro no Pará. Sob o regime da escravidão* (Rio de Janeiro: Fundação Getúlio Vargas, 1971), 51.

40. For example, enslaved "mulatto" Félix crewed for the Companhia Fluvial Paraense under the assumed name of Antônio for thirteen months, having fled captivity on July 23, 1871, in José Maria Bezerra Neto, "Histórias Urbanas de Liberdade: Escravos em fuga na cidade de Belém, 1860–1888," *Afro-Asia* 28 (2002): 248.

41. Oscar de la Torre, *The People of the River*, 53.

42. On the disturbance, "que há muito tempo não se via no centro desta cidade," see José Maia Bezerra Neto, "Mercado, conflitos e controle social: Aspectos da escravidão urbana em Belém (1860–1888)," *História & Perspectivas, Uberlândia* 41 (2009): 267–98, 288.

43. Peter Fryer, *Rhythms of Resistance: African Musical Heritage in Brazil* (Middletown, CT: Wesleyan University Press, 2000), 97. Mary Karasch, *Slave Life in Rio de Janeiro, 1808–1850* (Princeton, NJ: Princeton University Press, 1987), 244. Also see Gerhard Kubik's discussion of the term in "Drum Patterns in the 'Batuque' of Benedito Caxias," *Latin American Music Review / Revista de Música Latinoamericana* 11, no. 2 (1990): 115–181.

44. Leacock, *Spirits of the Deep*, 10.

45. In January 1871, for example, Luiz de Barres, resident in "demonic" Abaeté/Abaetetuba, just northeast of Belém, was cited for practicing "treatment by maraca." Extraordinarily, the newspaper appealed to the police, explicitly citing the Balaio revolt (1838–41) in Maranhão, and the model of "Manoel Francisco dos Anjos Ferreira," a.k.a. o Balaio (the wicker basket—a word applied to basket vending and uprisings of poor free workers); *Diário de Belém* 4/34 (February 22, 1871): 2. For "winds of divination," see Jonathon Grasse, "Calundu's Winds of Divination: Music and Black Religiosity in Eighteenth and Nineteenth-Century Minas Gerais, Brazil," *Yale Journal of Music & Religion* 3, no. 2 (2017): 43–63.

46. José Maia Bezerra Neto, "Mercado, conflitos e controle social," 288–89.

47. Henry Walter Bates, *The Naturalist on the River Amazon* (London: John Murray, 1873), 95.

48. Bates, *The Naturalist*, 95.

49. There "se reúnem muitos pretos a dansarem o batuque"; "Agradecimento," *Diário de Belém* 2, no. 33 (February 13, 1869): 2.

50. José Maia Bezerra Neto, "Mercado, conflitos e controle social," 289.

51. Paul Christopher Johnson, "Law, Religion and 'Public Health' in the Republic of Brazil," *Law and Social Inquiry* 26, no. 1 (2001): 9–33, 15. A similar concern for "aural hygiene" and the state in the same period affected ideas of sound, music, and noise in Madrid; see Samuel Llano, *Discordant Notes: Marginality and Social Control in Madrid, 1850–1930* (Oxford: Oxford University Press, 2018).

52. In Belém, andiroba and slave labor illuminated streetlamps until May 17, 1864, when "gas began to flow along the streets of Pará, and 755 public street-lamps were lighted." From this date, British multinational Pará Gas Company made it possible, even in this equatorial climate, to sink an urban infrastructure of coal gas distribution lines, allowing for the "flaneur to walk upon illuminated cities of air"; "Pará Gas Company, Limited," *The Journal of Gas Lighting, Water Supply, & Sanitary Improvement* 14, no. 319 (January 10, 1865): 16.

53. *O Liberal de Pará* 1, no. 27 (February 12, 1869): 2. *O Liberal de Pará* 1, no. 29 (February 14, 1869): 1–2.

54. "Carta da provincia," *Jornal do Pará* 15, no. 225 (October 4, 1877): 2. "Carta XXX," *Boletim da Sociedade de Geographia de Lisboa* 13, no. 7 (Lisbon: Imprensa Nacional, 1894): 543–54, 545–46. José Vellozo Barreto, *Mapa do rio Amazonas para servir de auxílio à navegação deste rio desde a cidade de Belém do Pará até a de Iquitos no Peru* (Lisbon, 1877), Arquivo Nacional, Brazil. R RJANRIO F4.0.MAP.494.

55. Barreto, *Mapa do rio Amazonas*.

56. "Repartiçaõ da Policia," *Jornal do Pará* 9, no. 200 (September 10, 1871): 1; and *Jornal do Pará* 9, no. 208 (September 20, 1871): 1.

57. *O Liberal do Pará* 5, no. 109 (May 15, 1873): 1.

58. "Repartiçaõ da Policia," *Jornal do Pará* 8, no. 252 (November 5, 1869): 1; *Jornal do Pará* 8, no. 9 (January 13, 1870): 1; and *Jornal do Pará* 8, no. 13 (January 18, 1870): 1.

59. "Repartiçaõ da Policia," *Jornal do Pará* 9, no. 20 (January 25, 1871): 2; and *Jornal do Pará* 6, no. 247 (October 30, 1868): 2. Conrad Malte-Brun described this "s'étoufferent en avalant leur langue" in *Annales des voyages, de la géographie, de l'histoire et de l'archéologie* (Paris: Buisson, 1809), II:368. Karasch, *Slave Life in Rio de Janeiro*, 18.

60. *Diário de Belém* 4, no. 64 (March 21, 1871): 3. *O Liberal do Pará* 3, no. 112 (May 21, 1871): 3.

61. *Diário de Belém* 9, no. 23 (January 29, 1876): 3.

62. *O Liberal do Pará* 2, no. 250 (November 3, 1870): 3.

63. "Carta XXX," *Boletim da Sociedade*, 545. "Conferencia publica," *Diário de Belém* 15, no. 78 (April 6, 1882): 1.

64. Complainants included owner of the newspaper, Frederico Carlos Rhossard, conservative journalist, advocate of emancipation, and "slave thief." Another was Martinho Izidora Pereira Guimaráes, proprietor of Amazon steamer *São Miguel*, and likely one of Vellozo's business rivals. José Maia Bezerra Neto, *Por Todos os Meios Legítimos e Legais: As Lutas contra a Escravidão e os Limites da Abolição* (Brasil, Grão-Pará: 1850–1888) (São Paulo: Pontifícia Universidade Católioca de São Paulo, 2009), 148.

65. José Maia Bezerra Neto, *Por Todos os Meios Legítimos e Legais*, 218.

66. The nine-day festival now amasses some two million believers to Belém every October. *Diário de Belém* 2, no. 235 (October 16, 1869): 2. *Diário de Belém* 2, no. 236 (October 17, 1869): 1.

67. "Boletim da festa de S. Braz," *Diário de Belém* 2, no. 256 (November 11, 1869): 3; and *Diário de Belém* 2, no. 260 (November 16, 1869): 1.

68. Antonio Maurício Dias da Costa notes that the "mestizo music" dubbed *carimbó* was authenticated "as the typical music of the Amazonian *caboclo*, associated with rural pastoralism and festive sociability in his "A Produção da 'Música Caboclo': a polifonia formadora do Carimbó nas representações de literatos, jornalistas e folcloristas no Pará (1900–1960)," *História* 34, no. 1 (2015): 241–73.

69. *Entrudi* practices, by the 1870s, were disturbing enough to be banned by police, as attempts were made to replace these practices by the elite and organizing parading societies of Carnival. Lúcia Gaspar, "Shrovetide (Entrudo). Pesquisa Escolar On-Line, Joaquim Nabuco Foundation, Recife. Available at http://basilio.fundaj.gov.br/pesquisaescolar/. Papavero et al., "The Travels of Joseph Beal Steere," 125.

70. Kim Sauberlich describes the late-century lundu-song as "an acceptable, immunized, form of embodiment that prevented Black expression from growing and activating its disruptive potential," in "'This Lundum Gives Me Life, This Lundum Will Kill Me': Scenarios of Black Peril in Afro-Brazilian Dance-Song," unpublished paper (2021). See also, Ana María Ochoa Gautier, "On Vocal Immunity," *Aurality: Listening and Knowledge in Nineteenth-Century Columbia* (Durham, NC: Duke University Press, 2014), 165–206. Roberto Esposito, "The Immunization Paradigm," *Diacritics* 36, no. 2 (2006): 23–48.

71. Luiz Ferreira de Lemos, "Observação de uma molestia que reinou, no anno passado, no alto Amazonas (Rio Maderia), sob a forma epidêmica," *Gazeta Médica*

da Bahia 2, no. 43 (April 15, 1868): 224–25. João Francisco da Silva Lima, "Contribuição para a historia de uma molestia que reina actualmente na Bahia, sob a forma epidêmica," *Gazeta Médica da Bahia* 1, no. 16 (February 25, 1867): 183–85.

72. Nina Rodrigues's "Abasia coreiforme epidêmica no norte do Brasil" (1890) is reprinted in *Revista Latinoamericana de Psicopatologia Fundamental* 6, no. 4 (2003): 145–56.

73. Filipe Pinto Monteiro, "The 'Sick Dancers': The Construction of Medical Knowledge about the 'Epidemic of Dance' in Itapagipe, Salvador, Bahia (1882–1901)," *Studies in History and Philosophy of Biological and Biomedical Sciences* 71 (2018): 32–40. Maria Elena Castore, "A antiga indústria têxtil soteropolitana: um patrimônio industrial 'invisível'" (PhD diss., Universidade Federal da Bahia, 2018).

74. "The contortions that take over the Africans during these dances already possess *choreic* characteristics," Rodrigues explained, it being well known that "these choreographic exercises were the source of the development or relapse of the disease; one should not forget, indeed, that in both Brazilian cities where the disease reached large proportions, the number of Africans and mestizos is very high." Monteiro, "The 'Sick Dancers,'" 39. R. N. Rodrigues, *O animismo fetichista dos negros baianos* (Rio de Janeiro: Fundação Biblioteca Nacional/Editora UFRJ, 2006; first published 1896).

75. By August, the fever had killed a British diplomat, several English clerks, sailors in the harbor, and many Portuguese in Belém; Papavero et al., "The Travels of Joseph Beal Steere," 147.

76. J. O. McWilliam, "Medical History of the Expedition to the Niger during the Years 1841–2, Comprising an Account of the Fever Which Led to Its Abrupt Termination," *British Foreign Medical Review* 16, no. 31 (1843): 259–64. J. O. McWilliam, "Some Account of the Yellow Fever Epidemy by Which Brazil Was Invaded in the Latter Part of the Year 1849," *The Medical Times and Gazette* 23, no. 43 (April 26, 1851): 448–453, 450. Also see, for example, the report on an 1846 outbreak in "Fevers—Various Kinds Noticed. Letter from Dr. Deas, R. N. from Rio Janeiro," *London Medical Gazette* 12 (1851): 369–70.

77. Charles Henry Knox, *The Spirit of the Polka; Being an Historical and Analytical Disquisition on the Prevailing Epidemic* (London: John Ollivier, 1845), 58. Associated with low-level suffering, irritating elements of Bohemian "trembling" dances—rotary movements, dotty fashions, breathless hopping, and foot-stamping, so scholars say—were injected with "African" *contramétrica* basslines and *tresillo* patterns, as if to acclimatize them to new racial climates. So severe was *polkamania* in Belém that, even at the "extraordinary event" of the opening of the Provincial Assembly on August 15, 1868, a local four-act version of Jacques Offenbach's *Orpheus in the Underworld* was staged to solemnize the occasion, ending with the famous *infernal galop* or high-kicking cancan, the fastest of all polkas and alleged to have originated in Algeria; *Diário de Belém* 1, no. 9 (August 13, 1868): 3.

78. Sidney Chalhoub, "The Politics of Disease Control: Yellow Fever and Race in Nineteenth Century Rio de Janeiro," *Journal of Latin American Studies* 25, no. 3 (1993): 441–63.

79. Bates, *The Naturalist on the River Amazon*, 172.

80. In June 1851, in fact, Wallace's twenty-two-year-old younger brother Herbert Edward was killed by "the worst form of yellow fever": "the fatal black vomit." An ensuing smallpox attack, by contrast, devasted "especially the Indians, Africans, and people of mixed colour, sparing the whites almost entirely, and taking off about a

twentieth part of the population in the course of the four months of its stay"; Bates, *The Naturalist on the River Amazon*, 172.

81. Bates, *The Naturalist on the River Amazon*, 385.

82. As reported by George Miller Sternberg, *Report on the Etiology and Prevention of Yellow Fever* (Washington, DC: Government Printing Office, 1890), 40.

83. For example: M.-F.-M. Audouard's "Mémoire sur l'origine et les causes de la fièvre jaune, considérée comme étant principalement le résultat de l'infection des bâtiments négriers, d'après les observations faites à Barcelone en 1821, et au Port-du-Passage, en 1823," *Revue médicale française et étrangère* 3 (1824): 360–408. "La traite des noirs considérée comme la cause de la fièvre jaune," *Journal des connaissances médico-chirurgicales* 6, no. 1 (1838–39): 49–54. "Sur la fièvre jaune qui règne en ce moment au Brésil, et sur l'origine de cette maladie" and "Fièvre jaune et traite des noirs," *Revue médicale française et étrangère* 2 (1850): 65–68 and 643–57. "L'étiologie de la fièvre jaune dans ses rapports avec la navigation en général et la traite des noirs en particulier," *Revue médicale française et étrangère* 35 (1853): 656–72.

84. Quoted in C. Creighton, "The Origin of Yellow Fever," *The North American Review* 139, no. 335 (1884): 335–47, 339.

85. Sidney Chalhoub prefaces his citation of Barbosa with the observation that, while "environmental language remained predominant among Brazilian doctors and health officials at the turn of the [twentieth] century, they were acting on the assumption that the political goal of disease control policies was to whiten the population." "In fighting yellow fever and disregarding diseases that affected black people," he explains, "[Brazilian elites] actually set out *to change the environment in order to help 'nature.'* And nature's work, aided by miscegenation and immigration, was the quiet elimination of the African heritage—that is, the heritage of the 'inferior race'—from Brazilian society." See "The Politics of Disease Control: Yellow Fever and Race in Nineteenth-Century Rio de Janeiro," *Journal of Latin American Studies* 25, no. 3 (1993): 441–63. Chalhoub cites Rui Barbosa from Regina Cele de A. Bodstein's original "Praticas sanitarias e classes populares do Rio de Janeiro," *Revista do Rio de Janeiro* 1, no. 4 (1986): 42–43.

86. "It is to breath that I want to turn now, to the necessity of breath, and breathing space, to the breathtaking spaces in the wake in which we live." See Christina Sharpe, *In the Wake: On Blackness and Being* (Durham, NC: Duke University Press, 2016), 109.

87. Kodwo Eshun, "Further Considerations on Afrofuturism," *CR: The New Centennial Review* 3, no. 2 (2003), 287–302. Mark Dery, "Black to the Future," *Flame Wars: The Discourse of Cyberculture* (Durham, NC: Duke University Press, 1994), 179–222.

88. Ashon T. Crawley, *Blackpentecostal Breath: The Aesthetics of Possibility* (New York: Fordham University Press, 2017), 3. Frantz Fanon, *Black Skin, White Masks*, trans. Charles Lam Markmann (London: Pluto, 1986), 226.

89. "Literature of the Day. Slave Songs of the United States," *J.B. Lippincott & Co's Monthly Bulletin* 2, no. 1 (1868): 341–42.

90. Quoted in Daniel Parish Kidder and James Cooley Fletcher, *Brazil and the Brazilians Portrayed in Historical and Descriptive Sketches* (Philadelphia: Childs & Peterson, 1857), 533–54.

91. Vicente Salles, *O Negro no Pará* (Rio de Janeiro: Fundação Getúlio Vargas, Universidade Federal do Pará, 1971), 187.

92. Eustachio de Azevedo, "Literatura regional amazônica: Francisco Gomes de Amorim," *Instituto Histórico e Geográfico do Pará* (1932): 111–23.

93. Beatriz Gallotti Mamigonian, "To Be a Liberated African in Brazil: Labour and Citizenship in the Nineteenth Century" (DPhil., University of Waterloo), 222. Robert Conrad, "Neither Slave nor Free: The Emancipados of Brazil, 1818–1868," *The Hispanic American Historical Review* 53, no. 1 (1973): 50–70. In 1852, the Presidential Council of Pará granted Irineu Evangelista de Souza—soon one of the richest men in the world—the privilege of establishing steam navigation in the interior of the Amazon. Two years later, the Colônia Agroindustrial Itacoatiara was founded in the town of Serpa, in line with the foreign policy strategy to safeguard the Amazon from the geopolitical onslaught of the United States. By 1857, eighty settler workers, twenty-three Chinese, twenty-one Portuguese, and thirty-four "free Africans" had arrived to work the steam machines of the sawmill, pottery, and shipyard, see https://www.franciscogomesdasilva.com.br/africanos-livres-da-colonia-itacoatiara.

94. Three hundred and thirteen of the victims made it to Salvador and, seven months later, only 145 survived. Dale Torston Graden, *From Slavery to Freedom in Brazil: Bahia, 1835–1900* (Albuquerque: University of New Mexico Press, 2006), 12–13. Yuko Miki opens her narrative of the passage of the Mary E. Smith with a meditation on *catinga*, a word for the smell allegedly characteristic of Black bodies and Middle Passage slaveholds; see "In the Trail of the Ship: Narrating the Archives of Illegal Slavery," *Social Text* 37, no. 1 (2019): 87–105.

95. The schooner was found anchored off the quarantine station at Santo Aleixo Island off Sirinhaém; "Extract from the 'Jornal do Commercio' of November 4, 1855," *British and Foreign State Papers* 46 (1855–56): 960.

96. David Boswell Reid, *Illustrations of the Theory and Practice of Ventilation* (London: Longman, 1844), 417.

97. Slaveship surgeon Thomas Trotter is quoted in *An Abstract of the Evidence Delivered before a Select Committee of the House of Commons*, 34.

98. Alexander Rattray, "On some of the More Important Physiological Changes induced in the Human Economy by the change of Climate, as from Temperate to Tropical, and the Reverse," *Proceedings of the Royal Society of London* 18, no. 122 (June 16, 1870): 513–29.

99. "Medical Reports: UK Parliamentary Papers," *Statistical, Sanitary, and Medical Reports for the Year 1861* (London: Harrison, 1863), 408. "In a country like this," proclaimed president of Pará Abel Graça to the Legislative Assembly on February 15, 1872, "where the vigor of the vegetation can be measured by the force of the heat and humidity always constant, it is necessary to believe in these deleterious emanations, resulting from the constant decomposition of organic debris." Quoted in Conceição Maria Rocha de Almeida's "Belém do Pará, uma Cidade entre as Águas: História, Natureza e Definição Territorial em Princípios do Século XIX" (PhD diss., PUC-SP, 2011).

100. Charles Barrington Brown and William Lidstone, *Fifteen Thousand Miles on the Amazon and Its Tributaries* (London: Edward Stanford, 1878), 5.

101. Charles Creighton, *The North American Review* 139, no. 335 (1884): 335–47, 337.

102. Georges Raeders, *Le comte de Gobineau au Brésil* (Paris: Nouvelle Éditions Latines, 1934), 51.

103. "Ancient notions about the relevance of geography and climate to disease," medical historian Julyan G. Peard has written, "were, in a sense, reinvigorated by discoveries in bacteriology and the rapid advances in parasitology." Until mosquito-vector theories were "proved" around 1881, there was no consensus about the relation

between disease and the southward expansion of the empire of the *Aedes aegypti* mosquito. Julyan G. Peard, *Race, Place, and Medicine: The Idea of the Tropics in Nineteenth-Century Brazil* (Durham, NC: Duke University Press, 1999), 4.

104. Raeders, *Le comte de Gobineau au Brésil*, 23.

105. Charles Pradez, *Nouvelles études sur le Brésil* (Paris: Ernest Thorin, 1872), 92.

106. Quoted in Henry Edward Krehbiel, *Afro-American Folksongs: A Study in Racial and National Music* (New York: Schirmer, 1914), 59.

107. Frantz Fanon, *Black Skin, White Masks*, trans. Charles Lam Markmann (London: Pluto, 1986), 129.

108. Michel Foucault, *Abnormal: Lectures at the College de France 1974–1975*, ed. Valerio Marchetti and Antonella Salomoni, trans. Graham Burchell (London: Verso, 2003), 48.

109. Roberto Esposito, *Immunitas: The Protection and Negation of Life*, trans. Zakiya Hanafi (Cambridge, UK: Polity, 2011).

110. Quoted in Georges Chatterton-Hill, *The Philosophy of Nietzsche: An Exposition and an Appreciation* (New York: Applegate, 1913), 243.

111. Friedrich Nietzsche, *On the Genealogy of Morality*, ed. Keith Ansell-Pearson, trans. Carol Diethe (Cambridge, UK: Cambridge University Press, 1994), 155.

112. "Certainement l'élément noir est indispensable pour développer le génie artistique dans une race, parce que nous avons vu quelle profusion de feu, de flammes, d'étincelles, d'entraînement, d'irréflexion réside dans son essence, et combien l'imagination, ce reflet de la sensualité, et toutes les appétitions vers la matière le rendent propre à subir les impressions que produisent les arts, dans un degré d'intensité tout à fait inconnu aux autres familles humaines. C'est mon point de départ, et s'il n'y avait rien à ajouter, certainement le nègre apparaîtrait comme le poëte lyrique, le musicien, le sculpteur par excellence." M. A. de Gobineau, *Essai sur l'inégalité des races humaines*, 2 vols. (Paris: Firmin Didot, 1853), II:92.

113. Caterina Y. Pierre, "'A New Formula for High Art': The Genesis and Reception of Marcello's Pythia," *Nineteenth-Century Art Worldwide* 2, no. 3 (2003), http://www.19thc-artworldwide.org/autumn03/271-qa-new-formula-for-high-artq-the-genesis-and-reception-of-marcellos-pythia.

114. "Science at the New Paris Opera," *Nature* 11 (March 4, 1875): 349.

Chapter 5

1. Walter Benjamin, "The Work of Art in the Age of Mechanical Reproduction," in *Illuminations*, ed. Hannah Arendt (New York: Schocken, 1968), 217–51.

2. "Lohengrin at the Opera. The De Reszke Brothers Make Their Final Appearance," *New York Times*, March 30, 1901, 8.

3. According to Oscar Thompson, "On Hearing Jean de Reszke Today: Like a Dream, a Faint Voice on Wax that Propounds a Problem for Science," *New York Sun*, April 23, 1938, 28.

4. Emily Thompson, *The Soundscape of Modernity: Architectural Acoustics and the Culture of Listening in America, 1900–1933* (Cambridge, MA: MIT Press, 2004), 11.

5. Patrick Feaster, "'The Following Record': Making Sense of Phonographic Performance, 1877–1908" (PhD diss., Indiana University, 2007).

6. Willa Cather's words (from *Courier* [June 10, 1899]: 3) appears as "Lohengrin and Walküre," in *The World and the Parish: Willa Cather's Articles and Re-*

views, ed. William M. Curtin, vol. 2 (Lincoln: University of Nebraska Press, 1970), 619–21, 622.

7. William Moffatt, "A Note on Lohengrin," *Looker-On* (July 1896): 31–35, 32.

8. Cather, "Lohengrin," 622.

9. Henderson, "'Lohengrin' at the Opera," 8.

10. "I confess it bores me to hear the same narrative repeated and repeated in his music dramas," said Reszke in a 1908 interview. "It is right to cut Wagner." "De Reszke on Americans: Great Tenor Tells Charles Henry Moltzor," *Los Angeles Times*, September 13, 1908, 2.

11. William James Henderson, "Among Musicians: End of the Season at the Metropolitan Opera House," *New York Times*, March 31, 1901, 20.

12. Holbrook Curtis, *Voice Building and Tone Placing, Showing a New Method of Relieving Injured Vocal Cords by Tone Exercises* (New York: D. Appleton, 1896), 63–66.

13. Walter Johnstone Douglas, Reszke's long-time accompanist and friend, reported that "to get the maximum amount of 'forward' tone to the voice, which [Reszke] deemed 'essential,' it was his plan to imagine that you were drinking in the tone, rather than pushing it out. This idea encouraged the palate to draw back and give *timbre* to the voice, while it helped the tone to find its way into the true mask." See "His Principles of Singing," *Music and Letters* 6, no. 3 (1925): 207.

14. Harry P. Mawson, "Grand Opera in French and Italian," *Harper's Weekly* 11, no. 21 (November 21, 1891): 917.

15. "Polyglot Opera," *The Spectator*, May 4, 1889, 605.

16. William James Henderson, "The Downfall of Bayreuth," *Saturday Review of Politics, Literature, Science, and Art* 78, no. 2026 (August 25, 1894): 207–8.

17. "The Lesson of Bayreuth," *Musical Standard* 47, no. 31 (August 4, 1894): 79–80.

18. For more on Reszke's internationalism, see Karen Henson's excellent chapter on Reszke in *Opera Acts: Singers and Performance in the Late Nineteenth Century* (Cambridge, UK: Cambridge University Press, 2015).

19. For more on this dream, see Joseph Horowitz, *Classical Music in America: A History of Its Rise and Fall* (New York: Norton, 2005), 145–47.

20. Henderson, "A Week's Musical Topics," *New York Times*, December 1, 1895.

21. For eiffelesco-babelesco-pyramidal grunts, see "The Opera," *Saturday Review of Politics, Literature, Science and Art* 77, no. 2017 (June 23, 1894): 661–62.

22. "Jean de Reszke Talks of Training," *Chicago Daily Tribune* 74, no. 76 (May 17, 1895): 37.

23. "Lohengrin in German," *New York Herald*, January 3, 1896, 7.

24. Henderson, "'Lohengrin' at the Opera: An Excellent Performance in German of Wagner's Lyric Drama," *New York Times*, November 28, 1896.

25. Henry Edward Krehbiel, *Chapters of Opera*, 2nd rev. ed. (New York: Henry Holt, 1908), 266.

26. The first Paris performance of *Aida* occurred on April 22, 1876. As for Édouard, although it is difficult to distinguish him from the Italian chorus on Mapleson's *Lohengrin* cylinders, he is detectable somewhere amidst the phonographic fog singing the part of King Henry.

27. Krehbiel, *Chapters of Opera*, 277. Hillary Bell, of the *New York Press*, quoted in *The Argonaut*, January 14, 1901. For Jean's fee, see Henry T. Finck, *Success in Music and How It Is Won* (New York: Charles Scribner, 1909), 12.

28. Hermann Klein, "Modern Musical Celebrities, IV," *The Century Illustrated Monthly Magazine* (July 1903): 461–71, 467.

29. Adelaide L. Samson, "Grand Opera in English," *Metropolitan Magazine* (June 1900): 593–602, 601.

30. Frank Eugene Kidder, *The Architect's and Builder's Pocket-Book* (New York: John Wiley, 1886), 471.

31. For more on Brandt, see Gundela Kreuzer, "Wagnerdampf: Steam in Der Ring des Nibelungen and Operatic Production," *The Opera Quarterly* 27, no. 2–3 (2011): 179–218.

32. This is Franklyn Fyles's phrase from the *New York Sun*, quoted in "Jean de Reszke's Latest Triumph," *The Argonaut*, January 14, 1901.

33. "Royal Opera," *The Times*, July 5, 1900. "Jean de Reszke's Voice Is Dying," *The Argonaut*, August 6, 1900, 10.

34. Henderson, "Return of Jean de Reszke," *New York Times*, January 1, 1901, 6.

35. *The Sun* extract is quoted in "Jean de Reszke's Latest Triumph," *The Argonaut*, January 14, 1901, 11. "Jean de Reszke's Return," *The Sun*, January 1, 1901, 3. "Jean de Reszke as Lohengrin," *The World*, January 1, 1901). "Last Plays of the Century in the New York Theatres," *The Morning Telegraph*, January 1, 1901, 3.

36. Franklyn Fyles quoted in "Jean de Reszke's Latest Triumph," 11.

37. Friedrich Nietzsche, *On the Genealogy of Morality*, ed. Keith Ansell-Pearson (1887; Cambridge, UK: Cambridge University Press, 1994), 77–78.

38. Friedrich Nietzsche, *Der Fall Wagner: Ein Musikanten-Problem* (Leipzig: C. G. Naumann, 1892), 13.

39. See Theodor W. Adorno's 1952 chapter "Colour," in *In Search of Wagner*, trans. Rodney Livingstone (London: Verso, 2005), 71–84. Apart from in *La traviata*, Verdi used these same high suffocating strings for the prelude and final scene of *Aida*, with Radames (another of Reszke's favored roles) buried alive in an airless Egyptian tomb. (Verdi witnessed the Italian premiere of *Lohengrin* at Bologna in 1871.) Airlessness, of course, was always conceived differently by Wagner: scarcity of breath symbolized vacuum-sealed purity, rather than asphyxiation under oppressive conditions of tubercular or Pharaonic power.

40. Franz Liszt, *Lohengrin et Tannhäuser de Richard Wagner* (Leipzig: F. A. Brockhaus, 1851), 49.

41. See Charles Baudelaire, *Selected Writings on Art and Literature* (London: Penguin, 1972), 331. These words imply a genealogy of *Lohengrin* reception extending through Baudelaire, whose account of the "light" of the prelude music was famously influenced by Liszt and probably later absorbed by Reszke. I am indebted to David Trippett for this observation.

42. W., "A Lesson with the Master," *Music and Letters* 6, no. 3 (1925): 209–13.

43. Francesco Lamperti, *Guida teorico-pratica-elementare per lo studio del canto* (Milan: Ricordi, 1864), 16.

44. William Shakespeare, "The Management of the Breath," *Werner's Magazine* 21, no. 6 (1898): 515–19, 519.

45. Reszke also recommended *la voix étouffée* for "Nun sei bedankt mein lieber Schwan," the hero's farewell to the swan in act 1; Douglas, "His Principles of Singing," 202–9.

46. W., "A Lesson with the Master," 212–13.

47. James Stark, *Bel Canto: A History of Vocal Pedagogy* (Toronto: University of Toronto Press, 1999), 53.

48. "Mr. Frederic W. Root," *The Musical Herald*, August 1, 1894, 227–30, 229.

49. For more, see Davies, "In Search of Voice," *Romantic Anatomies of Performance* (Berkeley: University of California Press, 2014), 126–29.

50. Blanche Marchesi, *The Singer's Catechism and Creed* (London: Dent, 1932), 91–98.

51. For more on Le Mont-Dore and the burgeoning number of formal interventions made by laryngologists and physicians at the Opéra and the Conservatoire, see Kimberley Francis and Sophie Lachapelle, "Medicine goes to the Opera: Vocal Health and Remedies for Professional Singers of the Belle Époque," *19th-Century Music* 44, no. 1 (2020): 19–35, 30.

52. Joal's house, on a street named after him, is still viewable in Le Mont Dore, as are the grand hotels, the old spa-town promenade for taking the air, and the glass buildings. See *Les thermes. Le Mont-Dore: une ville d'eaux en Auvergne*, ed. Jean-François Luneau (Clermont-Ferrand: Étude du Patrimoine Auvergnat, 1998).

53. Joseph Joal, "Du mécanisme de la respiration chez les chanteurs," *Revue de Laryngologie, D'Otologie et de Rhinologie* 14, no. 8 (April 15, 1892): 225–49.

54. For imaginary telephones after Nietzsche in *Lohengrin*, see Carolyn Abbate, *In Search of Opera* (Princeton, NJ: Princeton University Press, 2001), 30.

55. For a sense of Mandl's methods, look up "breathing" and "Montserrat Caballé" on YouTube, as in Claudia Elettra Tantin, "MASTER CLASS MONTSERRAT CABALLÉ 2011," YouTube video, September 11, 2022, https://www.youtube.com/watch?v=hPLNAXUr0c.

56. Thomas J. Mays, "An Experimental Inquiry into the Chest Movements of the Indian Female," *The Therapeutic Gazette*, May 16, 1887, 297–99.

57. Elizabeth A. Chamberlayne, "Correspondence," *Musical News*, October 5, 1895, 277.

58. Scott A. Carter, "Forging a Sound Citizenry: Voice Culture and the Embodiment of the Nation, 1880–1920," *The American Music Research Center Journal* 22 (January 1, 2013): 11–34.

59. "Neglect Imperils Pupils: Supt. Maxwell Says Growths in Children's Throats Lead to Depravity," *New York Times*, November 17, 1908, 6.

60. Holbrook Curtis, "The Effects of the Vocal Cords of Improper Method in Singing," *New York Medical Journal* 65 (January 20, 1894): 70–74. The quote is from an interview with Curtis published as "Why the Singer Can Sing," *Werner's Magazine* (November 1894): 389.

61. Curtis, "The Effects of the Vocal Cords," 73.

62. Curtis, *Voice Building*, 192.

63. Curtis, "The Effects of the Vocal Cords," 73.

64. Curtis, "The Effects of the Vocal Cords," 73.

65. Aida Favia-Artsay, "White Gold in the Golden Age: Recalling the Sound of the De Reszke Brothers and One Possible Reason for its Splendor," *Opera Quarterly* 8 (1991): 44–61. Curtis, *Voice Building*, 160.

66. Curtis, *Voice Building*, 160.

67. Lilli Lehmann, *How to Sing*, trans. Richard Aldrich (New York: Macmillan, 1902), 69–70.

68. Holbrook Curtis, "The Tonograph," *Scientific American* 76, no. 22 (1897): 345–46.
69. Curtis, "The Tonograph," 346.
70. Curtis, "The Tonograph," 204.
71. Emilie I. Barrington, "Voice-Figures," *Werner's Voice Magazine* 12, no. 3 (1890): 79. Curtis, *Voice Building*, 205. Gounod's words appear in "The Opera," *Saturday Review of Politics, Literature, Science, and Art* 77, no. 2017 (June 23, 1894): 661.

Chapter 6

1. "The Greatest Man in the World," *Life Magazine*, January 1, 1949.
2. Jakob von Uexküll, *Umwelt und Innenwelt der Tiere* (Berlin: J. Springer, 1909).
3. See letter to fellow lynchpin of the *Orgelbewegung* Wilibald Gurlitt, in Harald Schützeichel, "Music and Ethics: Albert Schweitzer the Musician," trans. Monique Cuany, ed. James Carleton-Paget and Michael J. Thate, *Albert Schweitzer in Thought and Action: A Life in Parts* (Syracuse, NY: Syracuse University Press, 2016), 118–29.
4. At least since 1596, Catholic missionaries working in Southeast and East Asia had built antecedent portative bamboo organs to withstand tropical or subtropical conditions. David Irving, *Colonial Counterpoint: Music in Early Modern Manila* (Oxford: Oxford University Press, 2010), 55.
5. Albert Schweitzer, *Out of My Life and Thought* (Baltimore, MD: Johns Hopkins University Press, 2009), 157.
6. Schweitzer, *Out of My Life and Thought*, 156.
7. Schweitzer, *On the Edge of the Primeval Forest*, 112.
8. Albert Schweitzer, *The Decay and the Restoration of Civilization/ The Philosophy of Civilization Part 1*, trans. C. T. Campion (London, 1923), vi.
9. Albert Schweitzer, *On the Edge of the Primeval Forest*, 6.
10. For discussion of a "tribus de race bretonne sur la côte ouest de l'Afrique," see Petrot-Gernier, "Gallois D'Europe et Galoa D'Afrique," *Mélusine: revue de mythologie, littérature populaire, traditions et usages* (1892).
11. See, for example, Henri Trilles, *Chez les Fang: ou quinze années de séjour au Congo français* (Lille: Desclée, de Brouwer, 1912), 14.
12. Albert Schweitzer, *On the Edge of the Primeval Forest: Experiences and Observations of a Doctor in Equatorial Africa*, trans. C. T. Campion (London: Adam and Charles Black, 1922), 6.
13. Robert Hamill Nassau, *Bantu Sociology* (Philadelphia: Allen, Lane & Scott, 1914), 7.
14. Sartre's maternal grandfather, Charles Schweitzer, a professor of German, was Albert's uncle.
15. The African appears in "Black Orpheus" as "flesh of the flesh of this world," and a creature "porous to all [Africa's] breaths." Creation is an enormous perpetual delivery indeed! See Sartre, "Black Orpheus," 13–52.
16. Frantz Fanon thematized "the atmosphere of violence" conjured by colonialism: the "bloodthirsty and pitiless atmosphere, the generalization of inhuman practices, and the firm impression that people have of being caught up in a veritable Apocalypse"; *The Wretched of the Earth*, preface by Jean-Paul Sartre, trans. Richard Philcox (New York: Grove, 1991), 250.

17. Donna V. Jones, *The Racial Discourses of Life Philosophy: Négritude, Vitalism, and Modernity* (New York: Columbia University Press, 2010).

18. "L'Afrique équatoriale française," *La Dépêche coloniale* 13, no. 8 (April 30, 1913): 109–24, 122.

19. "L'Afrique équatoriale française," 109.

20. Christopher Gray and François Ngolet, "Lambaréné, Okoumé and the Transformation of Labor along the Middle Ogooué (Gabon), 1870–1945," *The Journal of African History* 40, no. 1 (1999): 87–107.

21. Catherine Coquery-Vidrovitch, *Le Congo au temps des grandes compagnies concessionnaires 1898–1930* (Paris: Mouton, 1972).

22. Gray and Ngolet, "Lambaréné, Okoumé," 96. "La Colonie du Gabon," *Les Annales coloniales* 14, no. 136 (November 25, 1913): 1–4, 3.

23. The literature on the havoc of the post-1911 period in the lower Ogooué is well-established and authoritative: from Catherine Coquery-Vidrovitch's examination of the account books of concessionary firms to the work of Christopher Gray and François Ngolet to Jean Andree Eyeghe's *Colonisation et modernisation du Gabon, 1886–1960* (Paris: Connaissances et savoirs, 2017) to Florence Bernault's excellent *Colonial Transactions: Imaginaries, Bodies, and Histories in Gabon* (Durham, NC: Duke University Press, 2019), and so on.

24. Christopher Gray, *Colonial Rule and Crisis in Equatorial Africa: Southern Gabon, ca. 1850–1940* (Rochester, NY: University of Rochester Press, 2002), 150.

25. Gray and Ngolet, "Lambaréné, Okoumé," 99.

26. Walker called the "Yassi" "a great spirit; it is also a large animal of the form and color of a chameleon, inhabiting the forests." "Cte. de St. François de Lambaréné," *BCSE* 8 (1901–1902): 591.

27. In 1907, the district around Waka was occupied militarily following the death of a white sergeant named Sampic, a white trader, and a Senegalese merchant, which pushed M'Bombé west up to Setté-Cama, where he razed many villages—burning factories at Kigotsi and Mongo-Nianga as he went; Kiloumba, "Un pays très mal administré: c'est le Congo français," *La Croix* 29, no. 7884 (November 14, 1908): 5.

28. The skull belonged to Sampic. M'Bombé died mysteriously in detention later that year. Gray, *Territoriality, Ethnicity, and Colonial Rule*.

29. Bernault, *Colonial Transactions*.

30. See, for example, "L'Afrique équatoriale française," *La Dépêche coloniale* 13, no. 8 (April 30, 1913): 109–24; "La Colonie du Gabon," *Les Annales coloniales* 14, no. 136 (November 25, 1913); or "L'Evolution de l'Afrique Equatoriale Française (1908–1912)," *Les Annales coloniales* 3, no. 144 (December 31, 1912).

31. Such statements as "we are living today under the sign of the collapse of civilization," "the spiritual atmosphere has solidified into actual facts, which again react on it with disastrous results in every respect," "we have drifted out of the stream of civilization," "it is clear now to everyone that the suicide of civilization is in progress," and "man today is in danger not only through his lack of freedom, of the power of mental concentration, and of the opportunity for all-round development: he is danger of losing his humanity" appear in Albert Schweitzer, *The Decay and the Restoration of Civilization/ The Philosophy of Civilization Part 1*, trans. C. T. Campion (London, 1923), 1–23. See Schweitzer's *Civilization and Ethics*, trans. John Paul Naish (London: A. & C. Black, 1923).

32. Charles de Brosses, *Du culte des dieux fétiches ou Parallèle de l'ancienne religion de l'Egypte avec la religion actuelle de Nigritie* (Paris, 1760).

33. Jacques Rancière, *Le partage du sensible* (Paris: La Fabrique éditions, 2000).

34. W. E. B. Du Bois, *The Negro* (New York: Holt, 1915), 74.

35. Freud's position, as evinced in *Totem and Taboo* also of 1913, was that the symbolic murder and eating of the father by the sons, was also fundamental to the healthy development of affectionate human subjects. The progressive unfolding of civilization itself depended on the regular consumption of *Lebenskraft*. "Eating-up" implied continual psychic return to reenter the existential cycle of replenishment and renewal. Sigmund Freud, *Totem and Taboo: Some Points of Agreement between the Mental Lives of Savages and Neurotics*, trans. James Strachey (London and New York: Routledge, 1950).

36. Sigmund Freud, "Trauer und Melancholie," *Internationale Zeitschrift für Ärztliche Psychoanalyse* 4, no. 6 (1917): 288–301.

37. Florence Bernault, "Body, Power and Sacrifice in Equatorial Africa," *Journal of African History* 47 (2006): 207–39, 211.

38. Albert Schweitzer, "First Impressions," *Société des mission évangéliques de Paris* 88 (1913): 207.

39. Mary Henrietta Kingsley, *Travels in West Africa: Congo Français, Corisco, and Cameroons* (London: Macmillan, 1897), 129.

40. Schweitzer, *On the Edge*, 149.

41. Robert Hamill Nassau, *My Ogowe: Being a Narrative of Daily Incidents During Sixteen Years in Equatorial West Africa* (New York: Neale, 1914), 196. Many thought Nassau's degradation caused him to choose the Mpongwe-speaking female catechist Anyentyuwe as his longtime partner, although sexual relations were denied; Henry Bucher, *Two Women, Anyentyuwe and Ekâkise* (Bloomington, IN: Lulu, 2014).

42. Kingsley, *Travels in West Africa*, 130.

43. Albert Schweitzer, *On the Edge of the Primeval Forest: Experiences and Observations of a Doctor in Equatorial Africa*, trans. C. T. Campion (London: Adam and Charles Black, 1922), 23.

44. Schweitzer, *On the Edge of the Primeval Forest*, 40.

45. In a letter of 1902 back to his PEMS superiors in Paris, Robert dreamed of forming "ainsi à la gloire de Dieu, une nouvelle race qui réagira à son tour contre le paganisme environnant et surtout contre la sordide influence des blancs des factoreries"; quoted in Othon Printz, *Avant Schweitzer* (Colmar, Jérôme: Do Bentzinger, 2004), 107.

46. Printz cites an ethnographic notice at the Musée d'Ethnographie de Neuchâtel; Printz, *Avant Schweitzer*, 136.

47. Schweitzer, *On the Edge of the Primeval Forest*, 133.

48. Schweitzer, *On the Edge of the Primeval Forest*, 135.

49. The best account is Printz, *Avant Schweitzer*, 80–140.

50. Schweitzer, *On the Edge of the Primeval Forest*, 83.

51. Abraham Aaron Roback, *The Albert Schweitzer Jubilee Book* (Cambridge, MA: Sci-Art, 1945), 93.

52. Schweitzer, *On the Edge of the Primeval Forest*, 285.

53. Gray and Ngolet, "Lambaréné, Okoumé," 87–107, 90.

54. Gray and Ngolet, "Lambaréné, Okoumé," 92. Annie Merlet, "Nkombé par les

textes," *Légendes et histoire des Myéné de l'Ogooué* (Libreville: Centre Culturel Français Saint-Exupéry, 1990), 120–49.

55. In Adolinanongo's precolonial heyday, Senegalese traders were active near this burgeoning center of circumatlantic trade, Hatton & Cookson employing "Youssouf" to procure ebony and a certain "Mané" to assist at this most advanced trading post. Kerno Mahmadou-Seydiou, who had been sent to the Gabon from Senegal as a political exile by the French, operated a "grand establishment" here before 1874. Gray, *Territoriality, Ethnicity and Colonial Rule*, 203.

56. Gray and Ngolet, "Lambaréné, Okoumé and the Transformation of Labor," 92.

57. Robert Hamill Nassau, *Fetichism in West Africa: Forty Years' Observation of Native Customs and Superstitions* (New York: Scribner, 1904).

58. Schweitzer, *On the Edge of the Primeval Forest*, 79.

59. Nassau, *Fetichism*, 60.

60. Pierre Savorgnan de Brazza went so far as plant a *drapeau tricolore* at the site as he drove through here with his Okandé crew on his grand 1875 expedition for the Société de Géographie de Paris, which worked to open the water for French colonization.

61. Emane, *Docteur Schweitzer: une icône africaine*, 68.

62. See, for example, Jacques Dupont's ethnographic film *Pirogues sur l'Ogooué* (Paris: Atlantic Film, 1946), a twenty-six-minute documentary on these songs shot as part of the Mission Ogooué-Congo, a grand colonial exercise spearheaded by ethnomusicologist Gilbert Rouget on behalf of the Société des explorateurs français, Ministère des Outre-mer, Armée de l'air française, Musée de l'Homme, Conservatoire national des arts-et-metiers, and all civil and military branches of L'Afrique équatoriale française.

63. "Journal du Docteur Schweitzer, April 1913," *Société des Mission Evangeliques de Paris* 88 (1913): 206.

64. Fernand Grébert, *Au Gabon* (Paris: Société des missions évangéliques de Paris, 1922),

65. Dieter Christensen, "Erich M. von Hornbostel, Carl Stumpf, and the Institutionalization of Comparative Musicology," *Comparative Musicology and the Anthropology of Music: Essays on the History of Ethnomusicology*, ed. B. Nettl and P. V. Bohlman (Chicago: University of Chicago Press), 201–9.

66. Reproduced in *Das Berliner Phonogramm-Archiv—Sammlungen der traditionellen Musik der Welt*, ed. A. Simon (Berlin: VWB-Verlag für Wissenschaft und Bildung, 2000), 54–55. The music betrayed a level of sonic perception, apparently, analogous to the evolutionary stage of a European motet. For an exemplary account of complex connections joining early comparative musicology, musical activities in German missions of this period, and the use of comparative linguistics to test whether parallels could be drawn between non-Western and medieval European music, see Anna Maria Busse Berger, *The Search for Medieval Music in Africa and Germany, 1891–1961: Scholars, Singers, Missionaries* (Chicago: University of Chicago Press, 2020).

67. *Das Berliner Phonogramm-Archiv*, 54–55.

68. Albert Schweitzer, *From My African Notebook*, trans. C. E. B. Russell (London: George Allen, 1938), 49.

69. For a colonial account of Nkombé's purportedly meticulous and yet brutal cutting up of an enslaved person, see Alfred Marche, *Trois voyages dans L'Afrique occidentale* (Paris: Hachette, 1879), 122.

70. Schweitzer, *On the Edge of the Primeval Forest*, 32.

71. *Société des mission évangéliques de Paris* 89 (1914): 378.

72. Schweitzer, *On the Edge of the Primeval Forest*, 50.

73. After each case, Schweitzer noted the identity of the patient, diagnosis and medicine required, the patient receiving "un ronde en carton" in exchange for a government-issue five-franc metal token. This token, handed to each of his patients to hang around their necks (with Joseph acting as secretary) was often taken to be a fetish. Albert Schweitzer, "First Impressions," *Société des mission évangéliques de Paris* 88 (1913): 211.

74. Albert Schweitzer, *J. S. Bach*, trans. Ernest Newman (Leipzig, 1911), 162.

75. Wilhelm His, *Johann Sebastian Bach, Forschungen über dessen Grabstätte, Gebeine und Antlitz, Bericht an den Rath der Stadt Leipzig im Auftrage einer Commission erstattet von Prof. Wilhelm His, nebst Schluss-Urtheil der Commission* (Leipzig: Vogel, 1895). See also Martin Krause, "Die Auffindung der Gebeine Johann Sebastian Bach's," *Allgemeine Musikzeitung* 22, no. 29/30 (1895), 384–87; and "Die Auffindung des Grabstätte J. S. Bach's," *Musikalisches Wochenblatt* 26, no. 27 (1895): 339–40.

76. Albert Schweitzer, *The African Sermons*, trans. Steven E. G. Melamed (New York: Syracuse University Press, 2003), 9.

77. Schweitzer, *The African Sermons*, xxxii.

78. Ethelreda Lewis, *Trader Horn: The Ivory Coast in the Earlies* (London: Jonathan Cape, 1927), 14.

79. For another colonial reading, see Jonathan Hicks, "Should Manrico Escape? Verdi, 'Miserere . . . Ah, che la morte ognora' (Leonora, Manrico), *Il trovatore*, Act IV," *Cambridge Opera Journal* 28, no. 2 (2016): 187–90.

80. See R. L. Garner, *The Speech of Monkeys* (New York: Charles L. Webster, 1892). Jeremy Rich cites Garner's manuscript essay entitled "A Phonograph among the Savages" in view of esoteric demonstrations of this "magical" sound-recording equipment to Fang, Gisir and Nkomi groups around 1906; in *Missing Links: The African and American Worlds of R. L. Garner, Primate Collector* (Athens: University of Georgia Press).

81. Schweitzer, *From My African Notebook*, 44.

82. For reports that music was being used to attract spirits, disease, and evil, see Augustin Eman, *Docteur Schweitzer: une icône africaine* (Paris: Fayard, 2013), 68.

83. Emane, *Docteur Schweitzer: une icône africaine*: "Le *nganga* se sert de son *ngombi*," Janvier N. M. alleged, "pour attirer les maladies et les malades lorsqu'il n'y a plus personne." By contrast, Emma Haussknecht, one of his nurses, reported in 1946 that "after the day's duties he plays on the piano with organ pedals and from our room, in the silence of the night and the midst of the big forest, we enjoy the most perfect recitals. The music hours are a comfort and an inner help." Albert Schweitzer, *My Life and Thought—An Autobiography*, trans. C. T. Campion (London: George Allen, 1956), 306.

84. Fanon famously indicted medical science for being a part of the "constellation of colonialism" (*la constellation coloniale*) and one of the occupier's chief "modes of presence" in "Medicine and Colonialism," trans. Haakon Chevalier, *A Dying Colonialism* (New York: Grove Press, 1965), 121–46.

85. James W. Fernandez, "The Sound of Bells in a Christian Country: In Quest of the Historical Schweitzer," *The Massachusetts Review* 5, no. 3 (1964): 537–62, 548.

86. Cameroonian film director Bassek Ba Kobhio's 1995 *Le grand blanc de Lamba-*

réné (San Francisco: California Newsreel, 1995) dramatizes this scene to brilliant effect. Edgar Berman, *In Africa with Schweitzer* (New York: New Horizon, 1986), 146–49.

87. See the June 10, 1976, report by the Alsatian piano firm A. Prestel. "Piano droit GAVEAU No. 55.729," Musée Albert Schweitzer, Gunsbach.

88. Schweitzer, *On the Edge of the Primeval Forest*, 110.

89. As quoted in *Music in the Life of Albert Schweitzer*, ed. Charles R. Joy (London: Adam and Charles Black: 1953), 184–85.

90. Église protestante Saint-Thomas, https://www.musiqueorguequebec.ca/orgues/france/strasbourgst.html.

91. François-Xavier Mathias and Albert Schweitzer, *Internationales Regulativ für Orgelbau: Entworfen und bearbeitet von der Sektion für Orgelbau auf dem dritten Kongress der Internationalen Musikgesellschaft* (Vienna: Artaria; Leipzig: Breitkopf & Härtel, 1909); and Albert Schweitzer, *Deutsche und französische Orgelbaukunst und Orgelkunst* (Leipzig: Breitkopf & Härtel, 1906).

92. Schweitzer, *Out of My Life and Thought*, 72.

93. These were the words that began Schweitzer's *The Decay and the Restoration of Civilization*, 1.

94. Albert Schweitzer, *J.S. Bach*, trans. Ernest Newman 2 vols. (London/Leipzig: Breitkopf & Härtel, 1911), I:295.

95. Roback, *The Albert Schweitzer Jubilee Book*, 42.

96. In some versions, this was: "In Africa he saves old n———s, in Europe old organs"; Howard D. McKinney, "Albert Schweitzer—Organs and Organ Building," *The New Music Review and Church Music Review* 32, no. 381 (1933): 381–84.

97. "Registre de fabrication, 1908–1923," *Archives Gaveau, 1908–1973*, Musée de la musique, Paris. E.2009.5.181.

98. Photographic Essay by René Mir, "Les 'Gaveau'," *La vie illustrée* 15, no. 5 (February 15, 1900): 21–24. René Beaupain, *La maison Gaveau: manufacture de pianos, 1847–1971* (Paris: L'Harmatton, 2009). *Pianos Gaveau. une usine modèle à Fontenay-sous-Bois (1896–1971)* (Fontenay-sous-Bois: Archives municipales, 2012).

99. For a comprehensive summary, see Jean-Paul Sorg's typescript "Albert Schweitzer: 'musicien à Paris,'" Association Française des Amis d'Albert Schweitzer, May 17, 2013, http://www.afaas-schweitzer.org/site/albert-schweitzer-musicien.html?idArt=60.

100. Albert Schweitzer, *J.S. Bach*, trans. Ernest Newman, 2 vols. (Leipzig, 1911), II:311–12.

101. Marie Jaëll, *Der Anschlag: neues Klavierstudium auf physiologischer Grundlage*, trans. Albert Schweitzer (Leipzig: Breitkopf & Härtel, [1902]). Also see Michael Weinstein-Reima, "Printing Piano Pedagogy: Experimental Psychology and Marie Jaëll's Theory of Touch," *Nineteenth-Century Music Review* 18 (2021): 427–53. Julia Kursell, "Visualizing Piano-Playing, 1890–1930," *Grey Room* 43 (2011), 66–87.

102. Schweitzer, *Out of My Life and Thought*, 311–12.

103. Bernault, "Body, Power, and Sacrifice," 230.

104. Bernault, "Body, Power, and Sacrifice," 66.

105. Schweitzer, *J.S. Bach*, trans. Ernest Newman, II:2.

106. Schweitzer, "What Bach Is for Me," trans. Antje Bultmann Lemke, *Die Musik* (October 1906).

107. Schweitzer, *J.S. Bach*, II:25.

108. Schweitzer, "What Bach Is for Me."

109. Schweitzer, *On the Edge of Primeval Forest*, 64.

110. "For a good player perhaps the best organ part is a piano score, in which he has entered the thorough-bass figuring and the main lines upon which he will work it out. He must not forget, however, to revise the basses, or else he unconsciously plays a number of false notes in every cantata," Schweitzer, *J.S. Bach*, II:162.

111. Schweitzer, *J.S. Bach*, II:184. I am updating Newman's translation from the German edition.

112. Bettina Varwig, "Metaphors of Time and Modernity in Bach," *Journal of Musicology* 29, no. 2 (2012): 154–90. John Butt, *Bach's Dialogue with Modernity: Perspectives on the Passions* (Cambridge, UK: Cambridge University Press, 2010), 99–101.

113. Butt, *Bach's Dialogue with Modernity*, 99–101.

114. See William H. Foerge's preface to the 1998 edition of *On the Edge of the Primeval Forest* (Baltimore, MD: Johns Hopkins University Press, 1998), 7.

115. *Albert Schweitzer: Entre es lignes*, ed. Benoît Wirrmann and Jean-Paul Sorg (Strasbourg: Bibliothèque nationale et universitaire, 2015), 43.

116. A month earlier in March 1912, Isidor Philipp had organized a similar event for the benefit of the "Ogowe Medical Mission," this time at salle Erard with student performers. "Paris et départements," *Le Ménéstrel* 78, no. 12 (March 23, 1912): 95.

117. Schweitzer, *On the Edge of the Primeval Forest*, 3.

118. Albert Schweitzer, *Out of My Life and Thought* (Baltimore, MD: Johns Hopkins University Press, 2009), 155.

119. In a 1963 letter to Dr. Robert Weiss, cited in Albert Schweitzer, *The African Sermons*, xxix.

120. Albert Schweitzer, "A Declaration of Conscience," *Saturday Review* 40 (May 18, 1957): 17–20.

121. Subcommission on Quaternary Stratigraphy, "Working Group on the 'Anthropocene,'" International Commission on Stratigraphy, International Union of Geological Sciences, May 21, 2019, http://quaternary.stratigraphy.org/working-groups/anthropocene/.

Epilogue

1. Bruno Latour, "Why Has Critique Run Out of Steam? From Matters of Fact to Matters of Concern," *Critical Inquiry* 30, no. 2 (2004): 225–48.

2. Emily I. Dolan, *The Orchestral Revolution: Haydn and the Technologies of Timbre* (Cambridge, UK: Cambridge University Press, 2013).

3. Benson, *Surroundings: A History of Environments*.

4. Gascia Ouzounian, *Stereophonica: Sound and Space in Science, Technology, and the Arts* (Cambridge, MA: MIT Press, 2020). See also, https://www.ox.ac.uk/news/arts-blog/sound-and-space-science-technology-and-arts.

5. Burney, *The General History of Music*, III, v.

6. Alexander G. Weheliye, "Engendering Phonographies: Sonic Technologies of Blackness," *Small Axe* 18, no. 2 (2014): 180–99, responding to Tavia Nyong'o's "Afro-philo-sonic Fictions: Black Sound Studies after the Millennium," *Small Axe* 18, no. 2 (2014): 173–79.

7. Weheliye, "Engendering Phonographies," 187.

8. Cedric Robinson, *Forgeries of Memory and Meaning: Blacks and the Regimes of*

Race in American Theater and Film before World War II (Chapel Hill: University of North Carolina Press, 2007), xii.

9. Steven Feld, *Jazz Cosmopolitanism: Five Musical Years in Ghana* (Durham, NC: Duke University Press, 2021), 232.

10. "Reading for Infrastructure," https://uchri.org/foundry/reading-for-infrastructure/. Lauren Berlant, "The Commons: Infrastructures for Troubling Times," *Environment and Planning. D: Society & Space* 34, no. 3 (2016): 393–419.

11. For a digest of these long-standing history-versus-aesthetic debates, see the special issue "Music Histories from the Edge," ed. Martha Feldman and Nicholas Mathew, *Representations* 154 (2021): 1–155. For a critique of "context" in view of "no-music," see James R. Currie, *Music and the Politics of Negation* (Bloomington: Indiana University Press, 2012), and Rita Felski, "Context Stinks!" *New Literary History* 42, no. 4 (2011): 573–91.

12. Mary Ann Smart and Nicholas Mathew, "Elephants in the Music Room: The Future of Quirk Historicism," *Representations* 132, no. 1 (2015): 61–78. For a defense of quirk history, see Arman Schwartz, "Don't Choose the Nightingale: Timbre, Index, and Birdsong in Respighi's Pini di Roma," *The Oxford Handbook of Timbre*, ed. Emily I. Dolan and Alex Rehding (Oxford: Oxford University Press, 2018), 433–64; and Ellen Lockhart, "Lupus Tonalis," *Representations* 150, no. 1 (2020): 120–41.

13. For a diagnosis of "lived experience" as an elite condition anathema to coalition politics, see Marquis Bey, "On Lived Experience," *Black Perspectives* (2019), https://www.aaihs.org/on-lived-experience/.

14. See Delia Casadei on "knotted thinking" in "Vico Signifying Nothing," ed. Martha Feldman and Nicholas Mathew, *Representations* 154 (2021): 129–42.

15. Ben Okri, *A Way of Being Free* (London: Phoenix House, 1997), 94.

16. Alfred North Whitehead, *Religion in the Making: Lowell lectures* (New York: Macmillan, 1926), 77.

17. Alfred North Whitehead, *Process and Reality: An Essay in Cosmology* (New York: Free Press, 1929 repr. 1978), 30.

18. H. J. Lawlor, "St. Paul's Quotations from Epimenides," *The Irish Church Quarterly* 9, no. 35 (1916): 180–93, 180.

19. Margaret Jane Radin, "Property and Personhood," *Stanford Law Review* 34, no. 5 (1982): 957–1015, 957.

20. Will Steffen, Jacques Grinevald, Paul Crutzen, John McNeill, "The Anthropocene: Conceptual and Historical Perspectives," *Philosophical Transactions of the Royal Society* 369, no. 1938 (2011): 843, 619.

Index

Abbate, Carolyn, 216
abolitionism: Associação Philantrópica de Emancipação de Escravos, 131; in Belém, 129–31; Bowdich's, 23, 33–35, 227n8; at Exeter Hall, 99–100; Lowell's, 117–18; its mission, 112–13; Nabuco's, 125–26; Prichard's, 50; publicity of, 138–39; Slavery Abolition Act, 109–11. *See also* African Committee of the Company of Merchants; Buxton, Thomas Fowell; Society for the Extinction of the Slave Trade and the Civilization of Africa
Adorno, Theodor: as polluter, 221n33; on Wagner, 156, 260n39. *See also* Taruskin, Richard
aeronautics, 101; Nadar (Gaspard-Félix Tournachon), 132
aesthetics/aestheticism, 6, 16. *See also* Gell, Alfred; Gikandi, Simon
African Committee of the Company of Merchants, 23, 32–33
Agassiz, Louis: race theories of, 120; on whitening Amazonia, 124
Agawu, Kofi: on Bowdich, 41, 223n53
Albert, Prince of Saxe-Coburg and Gotha: antislavery work, 111; on *Elijah*, 90, 99, 104
albinism, 39–41, 43, 46, 209; African whiteness, 48–51; in Brazil, 122, 251n19
Alhoy, Maurice, 71
Alvary, Max, 152
Amazon Steam Navigation Company: boat noise, 141; labor songs, 137–38; slave system of, 127, 130, 257n93; Vellozo's employment, 130, 252n37. *See also* steamships and steam navigation
Anaximenes of Miletus, 14
Anderson, Katharine: on weather prophets, 93–94
Andouard, Mathieu: on "African fever," 136
Anthropocene: definitions, 9–12; as fossil fueled, 85–86, 118; as Great Acceleration, 205; targeting air, 4. *See also* Mbembe, Achille
anthropopoiesis, 28, 178
apocalypticism, 83–84, 94; Cumming's, 102–5, 246n91; Dostoyevsky's, 113–15; Fanon's, 262n16; Mendelssohn's, 84, 89–90; Schweitzer's, 179; Sloterdijk's, 224n81
Applegate, Celia: on cosmopolitanism, 89, 243n37
Arago, François: measuring climate, 93; on Tabarié's sphere, 59, 234n4
atmospheric/steam power, 4; Brandt's air-conditioning, 154, 222n37; d'Arcet's air-conditioning, 60–61; in factories, 134; Garnier's air-conditioning, 146; invented, 84–86, 93, 95; on plantations, 126; pollution, 84–87; for popcorn, 146; printing press, 8–9; Reid's air-conditioning, 108–10; train locomotion, 97, 99; on tramways, 130. *See also* steamships and steam navigation

Auber, Daniel, 71, 239n60
Azowani, Joseph, 189

Babbage, Charles: air as vast library, 106–7
Bach, Johann Sebastian, 88, 116, 219n3; Prelude and Fugue in E Minor (BWV 548), 2, 9, 27; Prelude and Fugue in E-flat Major (BWV 552), 108; Schweitzer on, 26, 170, 184, 188, 193, 197–200; skeleton of, 190–91; St. John Passion (BWV 245), 197, 200–203; St. Matthew Passion, 200
Baillarger, Jules: on *folie communiquée*, 133
Banti, Brigida: her excised larynx, 56, 63–64, 68–70, 234n1, 238n52
Barbosa, Rui: on white death, 136–37
Bartholdi, Frédéric Auguste, 178
Bates, Eliot, 171
Bates, Henry Walter: on *Mãe da peste*, 135
batuque: as *batuco* dance in Angola, 2, 127, 219n5; as etymology and Brazil outbreak, 127–31, 133, 253n43; as "religion," 122–23
batwa: as creatures of the air, 43, 46, 54
Baudelaire, Charles: on *Lohengrin*, 156, 260n41
Bavili (Vili-speakers): court of Loango, 51; at Libreville 227n10; songs of, 27, 225n98
Bazalgette, Joseph: on Great Stinks, 86
Beethoven, Ludwig van: infinite realms, 22, 49; on the Ogooué, 182; self-possession, 5
Benedict, Julius, 98
Benjamin, Walter: on arcades, 63, 67; on aura, 147
Benson, Etienne S.: on environment, 21–22, 225n88, 268n3. *See also* environmentality
Berlioz, Hector: on arias, 81, 73, 238n52, 239n70; on Falcon, 75–77; with Paganini, 59; on Theban harps, 51
Berman, James, 193
Bernard, Claude, 21. *See also* milieu
Bernault, Florence, 176, 263n23; on colonial eating, 180–81; on fetishism, 198–99
Bezerra Neto, José Maria: on "African absence," 250n7; on *batuque*, 127–30, 254n64; on fugitivity, 127, 252n40
Bhandar, Brenna: on possession, 5, 252n31. *See also* possession/dispossession
Biot, Jean-Baptiste, 59
Birmingham: Birmingham and Midland Institute, 117; birthplace of steam, 84–86; sanitation narrative, 87, 98–99; Town/Music Hall, 83, 95–96, 108–9, 116; Town/Music Hall organ, 97, 109; Triennial Musical Festival, 97. *See also* Mendelssohn, Felix
Bispham, David, 149
Bizet, Georges, 144
Black Country, 81, 96, 98, 245n61
Blaise, Saint (São Brás), 132
Bleeth, Lola, 152
Bloechl, Olivia, 242n13
Bohlman, Philip V., 18, 220n8, 224n69, 224n74, 224n77, 265n65
Boigne, Charles, Baron de, 75–76
Bouvet, Charles, 76
Bowdich, Sarah Wallis, 23, 26; ethnographer, 42, 226n5, 228n25, 228n26, 229n36, 230n45; explorer, 30–55, 68; Mendelssohn circle, 107, 227n9; pianist, 227n8
Bowdich, Thomas Edward, 32–35, 41–42
Boyle, Robert: on embottled life, 139; separating air chemically, 14, 17
Brandt, Carl, 154
Braouezec, Jules, 50, 230n51
Brazza, Pierre Savorgnan de, 175–76, 265n60
breathing: histories of, 151; infected, 142; "inferior costal respiration," 151; Middle Passage breath, 138–39; Pythic, 146; racialized breath, 140, 160–62; superhuman, 149, 156–68; typologies of, 158–67
Bret, Gustave, 197
Brito, Paulino de, 131
Brosses, Charles de, 179. *See also* fetishism

Brown, William E., 158
Browning, Barbara, 123
Bucher, Henry, 34, 226n2, 228n23
Buell, Lawrence: on the end of Nature, 83
Busoni, Ferruccio, 12
Buxton, Thomas Fowell: antislavery work, 111, 138. *See also* abolitionism
Bwiti, 14, 42–46, 176

Cabinda, 32, 126–27
Cagniard de la Tour, Charles, 65, 236n32
Calvé, Emma, 162, 165
Campanini, Italo, 162
Campbell, Benjamin: his vital capacity, 140. *See also* breathing
Camper, Petrus, 71
Canguilhem, Georges, 21, 225n86. *See also* milieu
cannibalism, myths of, 34–36, 43, 173, 178–81, 191–92, 198
carimbó: as folklore, 132, 254n68; prohibited, 129. *See also* Dias da Costa, Antonio Maurício
Caruso, Enrico, 162, 165
Castil-Blaze, François-Henri-Joseph: on Banti, 57; on Cinti-Damoreau, 70, 238n52; on Falcon, 74
Caswell, Austin B., 73
Cather, Willa: on Reszke, 149
Caviana Island, 25, 120, 132, 134
Chadwick, Edwin, 87. *See also* sanitation
Chamberlayne, Elizabeth A., 161
Chiloango River, 1–2, 8, 26, 219n3
Chipp, Thomas, 97
Chopin, Frédéric, 57, 150
Chorley, Henry: intimate of Bowdich, 31, 227n9; intimate of Mendelssohn, 107
Choron, Alexandre-Étienne, 60
Christian, Bunsen: on universal language, 90
Christol, Noël, 187
Cinti-Damoreau, Laure, 80; larynx of, 68–70, 238n52; method of, 71–73, 75–76, 239n60, 239n61
Círio de Nazaré (Festival), 132, 251n14
Clarke, T. J., 15

Clarkeson, Thomas: on slavehold breath, 138–40
climate theories: Arago's, 59; Babbage's, 116; Cuvier's, 49; Herder's, 16; Humboldt's, 92; ideas about acclimatization, 140; Montesquieu's, 17; Sartre's 174; Schweitzer's, 184
Cockerell, Charles Robert, 111
Coleridge, Samuel Taylor: on "atmosphere," 22
Coleridge-Taylor, Samuel: at Crystal Palace, 115
Comte, Auguste, 57, 21
Coquery-Vidrovitch, Catherine, 175, 263n23
Corbin, Alain, 60
cosmopoiesis, 28, 53
Costa, Michael: his conducting ideal, 108
Cousin, Victor, 66, 236n37. *See also* Goldstein, Jan
Crawley, Ashon: on Blackpentecostal Breath, 137
Crutzen, Paul J., 8, 85, 221n34, 269n20. *See also* Anthropocene
Crystal Palace: as biopolitical, 56; in London, 82, 113–15, 241n3
Cumming, John: antislavery mission, 111; at Exeter Hall, 102–6; as preacher, 84
Curtin, Philip D., 113
Curtis, H. Holbrook: advancing voice culture, 162–63; nasal method of, 159; painting breath, 163–64; tonograph of, 165–67
Cuvier, Georges, 30, 49, 68, 227n9

d'Affry, Adèle, Duchesse de Castiglione-Colonna (Marcello), 144–45. *See also* Pythia
Dalstein & Haerpfer, 195
dance, epidemics of, 133–35, 255n74; African roundelays, 169; "dances of Africans" at Belém, 132–33; dancing beriberi/polka fever, 133–35, 255n77; Steere's "*landeau*," 121, 250n9; as torture, 142. See also *batuque*; *carimbó*
Dapper, Olfert, 38, 50

d'Arcet, Jean-Pierre-Joseph: air work of, 60–64. *See also* Paris Opera
Dauer, Alfons M., 52
Daukes, Henry, 108
Dawson, George: as preacher, 98–99
de la Torre, Oscar: on Black Amazonia, 127
Despiney, Félix, 68, 237n43
Dias da Costa, Antonio Maurício, 132. *See also carimbó*
Dickens, Charles; on Coketown, 96; on Exeter Hall humanitarianism, 109
d'Indy, Vincent d,' 197
Diogenes of Apollonia, 14
Distin, Henry, 82
Dodart, Denis, 68
Dolan, Emily I., 171, 207
Dolmetsch, Arnold, 196
Dona Doca (spiritual leader), 123
d'Ortigue, Joseph, 71
Dostoyevsky, Fyodor, 113–15. *See also* Crystal Palace
Drummond Hay, James de Vismes, 131
Du Bois, W. E. B.: on fetishism, 180
Du Chaillu, Paul, 39, 43–44, 192, 230n49, 231n66
Dukas, Paul, 197
Duponchel, Henri, 64, 74
Duprez, Gilbert-Louis, 75, 240n82
Dwight, John Sullivan: Mendelssohn cult of, 88–89, on "Yet Doth" in *Elijah*, 115–17
Dyck, Ernest van, 152

Earle, William: slave activities of, 111
ecomusicology, 4, 220n14
elemental media, 2–3, 20. *See also* Peters, John Durham
Eliot, George: on Cumming's apocalypticism, 104
Emane, Augustin, 193, 266n82
entrudo, 132, 254n69
environmentality, 9–12, 21–23. *See also* Benson, Etienne S.
equatorialism, 3; as nuclear, 9, 30, 119, 179, 209. *See also* milieu
Escudier, Léon, 70–71, 75, 238n53, 239n61

Eshun, Kodwo: on Afrofuturism, 137
ethnicization: Bakele/Ongom, 34–36, 40, 42–44, 52–53, 230n49, 230n53, 231n61; Baseke, 43, 45, 232n79; Fang, 53, 173, 176–82, 187–89, 192, 198; Galwa, 169, 173, 176, 179, 185, 189, 195; Mitsogo, 40, 43–44, 176; Mpongwe, 23, 29–34, 44–48, 52, 173, 185, 226n2, 230n45, 230n53, 232n72; Ndiwa, 45, 226n2, 232n76. *See also* Bavili
Evelyne, John: *Fumifugium*, 101
Exeter Hall, London, 83, 91, 99–109; choral association, 86, 99–100; history, 228n19; hosting *Elijah*, 90; pious audiences, 100, 244n43, 246n97; sanitation narrative, 87; ventilated, 108. *See also* Sacred Harmonic Society

Falcon, Cornélie: hyperbaric enclosure, 23–24, 56–59, 234n4; as organism, 63–65; voice atmosphere, 74–80, 235n7, 239–40nn71–78
Fanon, Frantz: on atmospheres of violence, 6–7, 262n16; on breath, 137; on colonial medicine, 193, 276n84; on vitalism, 143, 174
Fauré, Gabriel, 52–53, 197
Feaster, Patrick, 149
Feld, Steven, 2, 42
Feldman, Martha, 216
Fernandez, James, 193
fetishism: Afro-Brazilian, 122, 134; *batwa*, 44, 46; bell charms, 187; commodity fetishism, 143; definitions, 179–80; fetishized music writing, 7, 9, 200–201; fetishmen, 179, 189; hospital fetishes, 266n73; reliquary boxes, 189–93; war fetishes, 176. *See also* Brosses, Charles de; Marx, Karl
flatulent hobgoblin, 110
Foucault, Michel, 7, 19; on biopolitics, 20–21, 67, 224n84, 237n40; on modern power, 10–11, 222n44, 222n45; on plague, 143, 258n108
Fournié, Edouard, 69–70
Franck, César, 196
Freire, Domingo: "black ptomaines," 141
Fressoz, Jean-Baptiste, 61

Freud, Sigmund: on cannibalism, 180–81, 264n35

García *fils*, Manuel: glottal focus of, 158–60, 163, 237n45, 237n47; larynx fetish of, 68–70, 237n44; on "Sombre forêt," 72–73
Garner, Richard Lynch, 192, 266n80
Garratt, James, 90, 244n43
Gauntlett, Henry, 97
Gauss, Carl Frederick, 92
Gautier, Théophile: on Falcon, 59, 74–75, 235n7, 239n72, 240n80
Gaveau (firm): its concert hall, 197, 201, 203; materials, 193–95; Schweitzer's pedal piano, 169, 172, 267n87; worker village, 196–97
Gelbart, Matthew, 18
Gell, Alfred: on universal aestheticism, 14–15. *See also* aesthetics/aestheticism; Gikandi, Simon
genius: Black, 144–45; for Herder, 18; Mendelssohn's, 90; as spirit, 28; Wagner's, 152; as white, 48–51. *See also* Handel, George Frideric
Geoffroy-Schwinden, Rebecca Dowd: on property, 8
Gerhard, Anselm, 67
German Society for Equatorial African Research: Loango Expedition, 1
Gikandi, Simon, 6–9, 221n23, 222n38. *See also* aesthetics/aestheticism; Gell, Alfred
Glaisher, James, 84; 1848 prophesies, 101–2
globalization/globalism, 28–30, 96, 118, 143, 205, 209. *See also* Great Globe
global music history, 3–9
Gobineau, Arthur, comte de: on Black genius, 144, 258n112; racism of, 141–42. *See also* genius
Goehr, Lydia: on imaginary museums, 6–8
Goldstein, Jan: on *juste-milieu*, 66–67. *See also* Cousin, Victor
Gounod, Charles-François, 145, 151, 168
Grau, Maurice: his opera administration, 153

Gray, Christopher, 32, 175–76, 232n79
Great Globe, 91–93, 99, 113, 213. *See also* globalization/globalism; Wyld, James
Grébert, Fernand, 187
Gresley, William, 96. *See also* Black Country
Gribenski, Fanny, 7
Guillory, John, 21
Guilmant, Alexandre, 197
Guivier, Jean Prosper, 97
Guizot, François, 66
Gurney, Joseph John, 112

Halévy, Fromental: *La Juive*, 75–80
Handel, George Frideric: "genius" of, 49–51; kettledrums of, 81–82; music of, 106; scores of, 115
Harris, Augustus: as impresario, 151–52
Harris, Cheryl I.: on whiteness, 4
Hatton & Cookson: Chiloango, 1, 219n2; Gabon Estuary, 33; Ogooué, 181–82, 184–86, 192, 265n55
Haydn, Franz Joseph, 56
Haytham, Ḥasan Ibn al-: as air scientist, 14
Hédoin, Pierre, 71
Heidegger, Martin, 12
Heineccius, Johann-Gottlieb: on air making slaves, 119, 124
Henderson, William James, 152, 155
Herder, Johann Gottfried von: *Zögling der Luft*, 16–19, 212
His, Wilhelm, 190–91
Hoffmann, E. T. A., 5; on infinite realms, 22; on Orpheus's lyre, 49
Hornbostel, Erich von, 52–54
Hugo, Victor, 67
Hullah, John Pyke, 84–85; choral mission, 107–8; friendship with Mendelssohn, 86
humanitarianism: for Brazilian abolitionists, 125, 131; "cannibal humanitarianism," 170, 178–81, 203, 211; coinage of, 96; discourses of, 5, 11, 26; at Exeter Hall, 99; Humane Society, 100; making human, 28, 34; the Niger Expedition, 111–13; slave morality, 144

Humboldt, Alexander von, 30, 84; anti-slavery, 111, 113; atmospherics, 234n4; the cosmos, 92–93, 106, 244n52

Imbeekee/Mbiki/Mbaïki, 29, 40–43, 231n65
Irigaray, Luce: age of breath, 27, 207
Irving, Edward, 94
Isouard, Nicolas, 61
Izak, Pierre, 198

Jaëll, Marie: vitalism, 198
Joal, Joseph: *pulvérisateur*, 161, 163, 261n52; thermal therapy, 159–60
Johnson, Paul Christopher: on public hygiene, 129–30
Jones, Arthur M., 52
Jones, Donna V.: on Afrovitalism, 174
Jousset, Alfred: his racial pneumometry, 139–40
Jouy, Étienne de, 73, 239n69

Karl Woermann (firm), 185
Kaulfuss, Adolfo José, 131; "A Cidade de Belém," 135
Kautschukmelodie, 27
Keats, John, 30
Kellogg, John Harvey, 161
Kingsley, Charles, 98
Kingsley, Mary: describing the Ogooué, 182–83
Klein, Hermann, 153
Klieman, Kairn A., 43–46, 48, 226n2
Kniese, Julius, 153
Kreuzer, Gundula: on steam, 222n37
Kruger, Eduard, 89
Kubik, Gerhard, 52, 225n98, 253n43

Lacerda, João Baptista de, 141
La Madelaine, Stéphen de: on Falcon, 77–80
Lamperti, Francesco, 162; *appoggio*, 157
Lamperti, Giovanni Battista, 158
Latour, Bruno, 4, 207, 268n1; Climatic Regime, 11, 222n46, 222n47; Great Enclosure, 15, 223n63
Lawrence, George Hall: his slave activities, 111

Lawson, Tom, 38–41
Leacock, Seth and Ruth: on Afro-Brazilian religion, 127; on Saint Sebastian, 122–23, 251n18. See also *batuque*
Lebrun, Louis-Sébastien, 70
Ledsam, Joseph Frederick, 96
Lehmann, Lilli: on vocal imaginary, 164–65
Lemos, Antônio José de, 131
Lewis, Ethelreda: on Trader Horn, 192
Lind, Jenny, 105; in *Elijah*, 105; in *I masnadieri*, 101
Lister, Thomas Henry, 93
Liszt, Franz, 198; on *Lohengrin*, 156, 260n41; *Orpheus*, 8; on steam-printing, 8
Loango, court of, 1, 26, 51
Lockhart, Ellen, 216
Longet, François Achille, 65, 236n32
Louemba, 176
Loughridge, Deirdre, 171
Louis-Philippe I, 66, 236n37
Lowell, James Russell: on democracy, 117–18. See also abolitionism

Mabizoro, Ekoro, 198
MacDowell, Samuel Wallace, 131
Mackay, John William, 153
Maffei, Countess (Clara), 101
Mahmadou-Seydiou, Kerno (trader), 185, 265n55
Makita, Nyonde (Mavurulu), 176
Malançon, François, 75
Mandl, Louis: on abdominal breathing, 161, 163–64, 261n55
Manns, August, 115
Mapleson, Lionel: Edison record, 148–50, 168. See also Reszke, Jean de
Marchesi, Blanche: against Reszkian breath control, 159
Martin, John, 93
Marx, Karl, 21, 63, 84; on melting into air, 63, 102, 236n28, 246n88, 246n89; on primitive accumulation, 9, 15, 143, 222n40
Maupertuis, Pierre Louis Moreau de, 41
Maury, Mathew Fontaine, 130

Mays, Thomas Jefferson: racial pneumography, 161
Mbembe, Achille, 9; cult of spirits, 28, 226n1; on great chokehold, 4, 220n16; nuclear power, 54, 222n39
M'Bombé, 176
McWilliam, James O.: as Niger River pilot, 112; on "polka fever," 134
Meikleham, Robert Stuart, 99; on London smoke, 101
Mendelssohn, Felix, 24; in Birmingham, UK, 97–99; connected to Bowdich, 31–32; *Elijah*, 81–85, 104–5, 114–17; as prophet, 49, 87–90; *St. Paul*, 89
Merchant, Carolyn: on Eden recovered, 83
Merlin, Martial Henri (General), 175
Meyerbeer, Giacomo, 67; *Les Huguenots*, 56; *Robert le diable*, 61
milieu, 21, 54–55, 65–66; as equatorial, 119; as *juste-milieu*, 66–67, 80. See also Bernard, Claude; Canguilhem, Georges; equatorialism; Spitzer, Leo
Mitchell, Robert, 21, 224n83, 225n87
Modjeska, Helena, 150
Monet, Claude, 163–64
Moore, Joseph: *Elijah*, 96–98
Moscheles, Ignaz and Charlotte: Bowdich ties, 30–33, 49, 107, 227n9; *Elijah* ties, 97
Moseley, Roger, 171
Mozart, Wolfgang Amadeus, 105, 115
Mühlmann, Adolph, 147
Mundy, Rachel, 15
Muntz, George, 87
Murray, William (Lord Mansfield): "air of England," 138–39

Nabuco, Joaquim: on servile air, 125–26
Nassau, Robert Hamill: aural insanity, 183, 264n41; on Congoé Hill, 185; on Fetish Point, 186
Nau, Maria, 75
Ndongo Nzigue, 198
Ndzigou, Brice Parfait, 14
Neukomm, Sigismund: *David*, 97, 107
nganga: at Cabinda, 1, 9; Schweitzer as, 189–93, 266n83. See also Ngango

Ngango, 29–30, 44–45, 54–55, 185, 228n23, 232n75; suggesting "medicine," 229n36; the tree at, 36–39, 43–44, 230n52. See also *nganga*
Ngolet, François, 36, 176, 230n49, 230n53, 263n23
ngombi, 5, 23; anthropomorphic, 39–42; Ongom/Kele, 42–44, 47, 52–55, 197; Schweitzer's, 193; as white mythology, 51–52
Niedermeyer, Louis, 74
Niemann, Albert, 152
Nietzsche, Friedrich: on age of disintegration, 123; on airless Wagner, 156; on modern breathlessness, vi, 3, 22; in Schweitzer, 179, 199; on "tropical man," 144
Nkombé/Nkomb'Adembaon (Sun King), 204; reported brutality, 265n69; sacred power, 185–86, 192; usurping his power, 188–89
Nordica, Lillian: as Elsa in *Lohengrin*, 149, 152–53
Nott, Josiah: on microbes, 141
Nourrit, Adolphe, 75, 240n76
N'tolé, Emane, 176
Nyong'o, Tavia: on modern music, 209
Nzame/Nzambi, 13
N'Zeng, 189

Ombwiri/Mwiri, 45–47, 176, 229n36, 232n76
Orfila, Mathieu and Anne Gabrielle, 76, 78
organs/organ manufacture: Cavaillé-Coll (Catedral Nossa Senhora de Belém, 1882), 131; Cavaillé-Coll (Saint-Sulpice and Saint-Clotilde, 1858–59), 196; Cavaillé-Coll (Salle Gaveau, 1900), 197; Dalstein-Haerpfer (Église Saint-Sauveur de Strasbourg, 1907), 195; Gray & Davison (Crystal Palace, 1857), 115; Hill (Birmingham Town Hall, 1834), 97; *Orgelbewegung*, 179, 195; Schweitzer on, 170, 194–96; Silbermann (Mühlbach, 1736), 195; Silbermann (St. Thomas's in Strasbourg, 1737),

organs/organ manufacture (*continued*) 195; St. George's Chapel Windsor, 105; Walcker (Boston Music Hall, 1863), 2; Walker (Exeter Hall, 1840), 108, 111; Willis (St. George's Hall Liverpool, 1855), 109–11

Orpheus, myths of: E. T. A. Hoffmann's, 49; Imbeekee, 54–55; Liszt's, 9, 221n35; Offenbach's, 255n77; Sartre's, 169, 173, 262n15

Osterhammel, Jürgen: European century, 3

Ouzounian, Gascia: on auditory space, 208

Paganini, Nicolò, 59. *See also* Berlioz, Hector

Pajelança, 122

Panseron, Auguste, 59

Paris Bach Society, 26, 169, 197, 201

Paris Evangelical Missionary Society, 169, 184; its journal, 172

Paris Opera: Palais Garnier, as global milieu, 144–46; Palais Garnier, as global model, 129; Salle Le Peletier, steam heating, 59–64; Salle Le Peletier, as venue, 70, 73–75, 238n52

Pasteur, Louis, 141

Patteson, Thomas, 171

Paxton, Joseph, 113. *See also* Crystal Palace

Pechuël-Loesche, Eduard, 126, 219n1, 219n2, 219n3, 219n4; his fever, 1–2, 4–5, 8, 26–27

Peters, John Durham, 20. *See also* elemental media

Petit, John Upfold, 137

Pimenta Bueno, Manuel Antônio, 137–38

Plançon, Pol, 162, 165

Plato, 11

Playfair, Lyon, 14

Pliny the Elder, 50

Porter, Rollin, 45

possession/dispossession, 5, 142; in Belém climate, 129; of the enslaved, 46; as epidemiological, 149; as "recursive dispossession," 124–25; as right to self, 212; in spirit possession discourse, 25, 121–23. *See also* Pythia

Pradez, Charles: on parasitic air, 142

Praetorius, Michael, 39

Pravaz, Charles-Gabriel, 57

Prichard, James Cowles, 50

Priestley, Joseph, 14, 17

Ptolemy, 49

pygmies, myths of, 46, 50, 232n76

Pythia (Delphic Oracle), 144–46. *See also* d'Affry, Adèle; Paris Opera

radio, 5, 20, 25; radioactive fallout, 85, 204–5

Rassondji, 23, 36–40, 44–46

Rattray, Alexander, 139–40

Rawlinson, Robert, 111

Rebordello, 119–20, 124

Rehding, Alexander, 15

Reid, David Boswell: antislavery medicator of, 112, 134, 138; buildings of, 109–10, 248n137; father of airconditioning, 84, 108

Renoké ("Blind King"): death, 188–89; territory, 182, 186, 204

Reszke, Édouard de (Edward Mieczysław), 147, 159

Reszke, Jean de (Jan Mieczysław): association with doctors, 158–64; atmosphericizing air, 168; international standard, 151–54; Lohengrin record, 147–50; sound images, 164–67; technique, 150–51, 156–58

Rhome, Romulus John, 124

Rich, Jeremy, 192, 226n2, 266n80

Richard & William King Ltd., 33

Riedel, Friedlind: on atmosphere, 22

Rigondja, 176

Robert, Maurice: Village of Love, 183–84, 264n45

Robinson, Cedric: on racial regimes, 209

Rodrigues, Nina: on "dancing" illness, 134, 255n74

Roscoe, William, 111

Rossini, Gioachino, 70; *Guillaume Tell*, 61, 72–73

Royer-Collard, Pierre Paul, 66

rubber-latex: from Belém, 126, 131, 252n37; from Cabinda, 26, 219n3; *Kautschukmelodie*, 27; from Lambaréné, 175, 186, behind Lehmann's nose, 165
Russell, John, 103
Russell, Lillian (Mrs. Canada), 191

Sacred Harmonic Society, 89, 241n3; history, 99–100; mission, 107–8; Wagner on, 244n43. *See also* Exeter Hall, London
Sallée, Pierre: on "breath of God," 47–48; on hyperpoetry, 41–42; on *ngombi* morphology, 39; on *ngombi* origins, 42, 230n49, 231n66, 232n73. See also *ngombi*
Salles, Vincent: Belém slavery past, 252n39; stevedore song, 137
Sandbach, Henry Robertson: his slave activities, 111
Sanger, Frederick W., 153
sanitation: in Belém, 125, 129–31, 135–36, 253n52, 257n99; in Birmingham, 98–99, 117–18; in Liverpool, 111; in London, 100; sanitary narrative, 86–87
Sartre, Jean-Paul: on Orpheus, 169, 173–74, 262n14, 262n15
Sauberlich, Kim, 123, 250n9
Savart, Félix, 68
Sbriglia, Giovanni: Sbriglia belt, 163
Schillinger, Johann Jakob, 195
Schlegel, August Wilhelm, 12
Schleiermacher, Friedrich: theology of feeling, 88
Schopenhauer, Arthur, 10
Schubert, Franz, 7; Symphony no. 7 (D. 729), 115; "The Wanderer" (D. 489), 1
Schubring, Julius: Mendelssohn work, 87–89
Schumann-Heink, Ernestine, 147
Schweitzer, Albert, 5, 34, 225n95; Bach, 197–203, 268n110; on elemental thinking, 171–73, 204–6; equatorial piano, 169–70, 193–97; harps, 40, 47; ingesting vitality, 178–88, 263n31;

266n73, 266n83; as *nganga*, 189–93; reverence for life, 171–73, 204–6
Sebastian, Saint: *encantados* of the pantheon, 251n18; festival of, 119–21, 124; King Sebastião, 122–23, 251n19; wounded whiteness, 124, 133, 143
Seidl, Carlos, 131
seperewa, 42
Sharpe, Christina: on Middle Passage air, 137, 256n86
Shaw, George Bernard, 89–90
ships and shipping: *Adalia*, 106; *Bristol*, 140; *Felicité*, 106; *Lord Mulgrave*, 32–34; *Vigilante*, 139; *Wilberforce*, 113
Silbermann, Andreas, 179, 195–96
sleeping sickness (and *trypanosomata*), 184–85
Sloterdijk, Peter: artificial air, 19–20, 224n81; on the Crystal Palace, 56
Smart, Mary Ann, 71, 77
Smith, Ralph F., 87
Society for the Extinction of the Slave Trade and the Civilization of Africa, 111–13. *See also* abolitionism; Buxton, Thomas Fowell
son filé, 69, 72–73, 237n46
Southcott, Joanna, 94
Southwood Smith, Thomas, 87
Spitta, Philipp, 199
Spitzer, Leo, 65–66. *See also* milieu
Spohr, Louis: *Fall of Babylon*, 93
Staudigl, Josef, 81–83
steamships and steam navigation: on the Amazon, 120, 124; as biblical, 104; on the Chiloango, 219n3; on the Ogooué, 181, 183; Reid's system, 111–12, 134; on the Remboué, 226n3; for Verdi, 101. *See also* Amazon Steam Navigation Company; atmospheric/steam power
Steere, Joseph Beal, 24, 132; as music ethnographer, 119–21, 250n9, 251n14; on "possession" discourse, 124–25. See also *entrudo*
Stephen, James, 109
Sterne, Jonathan, 13
Stumpf, Carl: Gabonese songs, 187–88
Sturge, Joseph, 96–97

Tabarié, Emile: pneumatic chamber, 57–59, 63, 65–68, 234n2, 234n4
Tarde, Gabriel: on crowd psychology, 133–34
Taruskin, Richard: on Adorno, 221n33; on Fauré, 52; on Mendelssohn, 88
Taylor, Michael Angelo, 87
Temperley, Howard, 113
Ternina, Milka, 147
Thompson, Emily: on Boston Music Hall, 219n6; on modern sound, 148
Tomlinson, Gary, 7–8, 220n13, 221n29, 221n31, 222n42
Tresch, John: on "cosmic symphenomenony," 92–93
Trilles, Henri, 173
Tudor, Frederic, 154
Tulou, Jean-Louis, 71, 239n63
Tylor, Edward Burnett: on "culture," 19

Vansina, Jan, 32–35, 41, 226n2
Vellozo Barreto, José: as Amazon merchant, 130; close to emancipationists, 131; complaints against him, 130, 138, 254n64; slave activities, 131
Verdi, Giuseppe: *Il trovatore* in Africa, 192; suffocating strings in *Aida*, 52, 260n39
Vergès, Françoise: Racial Capitalocene, 5
Vernier, Paul-Elie, 183
Véron, Louis: his opera administration, 61, 64, 73–74, 76
Viardot, Pauline: in *Elijah*, 109, 115
Victoria, Queen (Alexandrina Victoria), 91, 103–4
Villoteau, Guillaume, 51
Vismes, Jacques de, 56
vital capacity: Jousset's racial pneumometrics, 139–40; May's racial pneumometrics, 161; Reid's racial pneumometrics, 110. *See also* breathing
Vogel, Theodor, 113
Voltaire, 41

Wagner, Richard: airless aesthetic of, 154–56, 260n39; *Die Meistersinger von Nürnberg*, 154, 200; *Lohengrin*, 148–50, 152, 156–68; musical steam, 222n37; reputation, 90, 244n43; on self-possession, 5, 220n21
Walker, Robert Bruce Napoleon: travel from Ngango, 186; writings, 226n2, 228n20
Walker, William, 38
Wallace, Alfred Russel: account of music, 250n12; plagued in the Amazon, 135, 255n80; seeking evolution, 121
Walton, Benjamin, 77
Watt, James, 85, 96, 98. *See also* atmospheric/steam power
Watts-Hughes, Margaret: her "voiceprints," 166–67
Webb, J. Watson, 124
Weheliye, Alexander G., 209
Werner, Eric, 90
Wesley, Samuel Sebastian, 109
Whitehead, Alfred North: on creativity, 211
Whitehead, Mark: on atmospheric government, 86
Widor, Charles-Marie, 196–97
Wilhem, Guillaume-Louis, 107
Williams, Raymond: structures of feeling, 83, 242n8
woods (musical), 33, 228n20; barwood, 186; ebony, 175, 186, 265n55; mahogany, 169, 175, 194–95; okoumé, 175
Wyld, James, 91, 99. *See also* Great Globe

yellow fever: as "African," 119, 250n3; as dengue, 134; etymology, 136; infecting Belém harbor, 141; as mosquito-borne, 141; moving below equator, 126; Pechuël-Loesche's, 1; as spread in ships, 119; white fear of, 134–35, 255n80, 256n85
Young, James O., 8
Young Men's Christian Association, 105

Zingara Marie, 145